# Ancient Maya
## *The Rise and Fall of a Rainforest Civilization*

In this new archaeological study, Arthur Demarest brings the lost pre-Columbian civilization of Maya to life. In applying a holistic perspective to the most recent evidence from archaeology, paleoecology, and epigraphy, this theoretical interpretation emphasizes both the brilliant rainforest adaptations of the ancient Maya and the Native American spirituality that permeated all aspects of their daily life. Demarest draws on his own discoveries and the findings of colleagues to reconstruct the complex lifeways and volatile political history of the Classic Maya states of the first to eighth centuries. He provides a new explanation of the long-standing mystery of the ninth-century abandonment of most of the great rainforest cities. Finally, he draws lessons from the history of the Classic Maya cities for contemporary society and for the ongoing struggles and resurgence of the modern Maya peoples, who are now re-emerging from six centuries of oppression.

ARTHUR DEMAREST is the Ingram Professor of Anthropology at Vanderbilt University, Tennessee. For more than twenty-five years he has directed archaeological field excavations at ancient sites in the highlands, coasts, and rainforests of Central America and is considered a leading authority on the Olmec, Aztec, Inca, and, particularly, the ancient Maya civilizations.

D1236544

*Case Studies in Early Societies*

*Series Editor*
Rita P. Wright, New York University

This series aims to introduce students to early societies that have been the subject of sustained archaeological research. Each study is also designed to demonstrate a contemporary method of archaeological analysis in action, and the authors are all specialists currently engaged in field research. The books have been planned to cover many of the same fundamental issues. Tracing long-term developments, and describing and analyzing a discrete segment in the prehistory or history of a region, they represent an invaluable tool for comparative analysis. Clear, well organized, authoritative and succinct, the case studies are an important resource for students, and for scholars in related fields, such as anthropology, ethnohistory, history and political science. They also offer the general reader accessible introductions to important archaeological sites.

Other titles in the series include:

1 *Ancient Mesopotamia*
   Susan Pollock

2 *Ancient Oaxaca*
   Richard E. Blanton, Gary M. Feinman, Stephen A. Kowalewski, Linda M. Nicholas

3 *Ancient Maya*
   Arthur Demarest

4 *Ancient Jomon of Japan*
   Junko Habu

5 *Ancient Puebloan Southwest*
   John Kantner

6 *Ancient Cahokia and the Mississippians*
   Timothy R. Pauketat

# Ancient Maya

*The Rise and Fall of a Rainforest Civilization*

Arthur Demarest

CAMBRIDGE
UNIVERSITY PRESS

CAMBRIDGE UNIVERSITY PRESS
Cambridge, New York, Melbourne, Madrid, Cape Town, Singapore, São Paulo,
Delhi, Tokyo, Mexico City

Cambridge University Press
The Edinburgh Building, Cambridge, CB2 8RU, UK

Published in the United States of America by Cambridge University Press, New York

www.cambridge.org
Information on this title: www.cambridge.org/9780521533904

First published 2004
8th printing 2011

Printed in the United Kingdom at the University Press, Cambridge

*A catalogue record for this publication is available from the British Library*

ISBN 978-0-521-59224-6 Hardback
ISBN 978-0-521-53390-4 Paperback

# Contents

# List of figures

# Acknowledgments

I found it very difficult to synthesize more than thirty years of reading and research on the ancient Maya into a short, general text. I was finally able to construct this extended essay only with the help of many people. My first thanks go to virtually all of my colleagues in the field for their advice and information (much unpublished) on the Classic period of Maya civilization. To all, I apologize for the necessarily brief coverage of their discoveries and interpretations demanded by the length and format of a general overview. To those scholars working in the Postclassic period, I express my regret that their work was not more fully covered, as my text was intended to focus on the nature, prehistory, and history of the Classic Maya kingdoms. Special appreciation for reactions, suggestions, and critique on sections of this text goes to David Freidel, Don and Pru Rice, Federico Fahsen, Rita Wright, Sarah Jackson, and Ron Bishop. My own ever-shifting views on the ancient Maya were refined with the help and inspiration of these scholars, as well as Bill Fash, Bob Sharer, Will Andrews, Richard Hansen, Juan Antonio Valdés, Diane and Arlen Chase, Pat Culbert, Hector Escobedo, Takeshi Inomata, Nick Dunning, Norman Hammond, Peter Mathews, David Stuart, Mike Love, and the late Linda Schele. These and others whose works are cited in this text were generous with feedback on specific and general points and access to unpublished data, drawings, and photos.

Rita Wright, the series editor, deserves heartfelt thanks for her support, ideas, feedback, and incredible patience with my writing of this text. Special thanks are also due Simon Whitmore and Jessica Kuper at Cambridge University Press, as well as Allison Price, Matt O'Mansky, Brigitte Kovacevich, George Higginbotham, Arik Ohnstad, and Michael Callaghan, whose help was critical with all aspects of the completion of the book.

I hope that any future references will cite the full title of this book, *Ancient Maya: The Rise and Fall of a Rain Forest Civilization*, so as not to confuse this extended, interpretive essay with *The Ancient Maya* by Robert Sharer (with previous editions by Sharer, Morley, and Brainerd;

Morley and Brainerd; and Morley), which is a much longer and more comprehensive (almost encyclopedic) text. That work has been for many decades, and continues to be, an essential reference work for our sub-field.

As always, I am grateful to the late Robert Wauchope and Gordon Willey, who (through their mentorship and guidance) are partly to blame for inflicting me and my intense perspective upon the field of Maya archaeology and my Mayanist colleagues.

Finally, I thank my sons, Andrew and Matthew, and all the dogs – for the constant interruptions, distractions, and crises that have greatly interfered with the writing of this book, but that have made life much more entertaining!

# 1    The mystery and the challenge of the ancient Maya

Buried beneath the jungle vegetation lie sprawling ruined palaces of fine masonry architecture, still magnificent and beautiful despite the ravages of over a millennium. Scattered between the palaces rise great stone temples, some towering over the level of the dense jungle canopy of mahogany, cedar, and ceiba that reaches two hundred feet above the forest floor. On and between the palaces and temples lie scattered slabs of stone exquisitely carved with elaborate scenes and inscriptions (Fig. 1.1). On these eroded and broken monuments, the complex imagery that remains intact struggles against time to reveal its esoteric secrets. The scattered masonry and rubble of what were once the warm family homes of peasants and the elegant palaces of nobles are strewn for miles into the sea of jungle that stretches in all directions . . .

## Images and realities of the ancient Maya

Such is the popular image, and the physical reality, of the ruined centers of the ancient Maya. From many centuries before Christ to about AD 900, the lowland Maya civilization achieved its apogee in the Petén forest of northern Guatemala and the adjacent portions of Mexico, Belize, and western Honduras, what today we call the "Maya lowlands" (Fig. 1.2). For over 1,500 years, this region was covered by a network of kingdoms dominated by "holy lords," sacred kings who were linked by complex ties of kinship, ritual, trade, and military alliance. Their political and religious centers included great acropoli of massed palaces, temples, stone tombs, and ballcourts. These centers of power and pageantry were supported by nearby populations of thousands of farmers who practiced a complex system of rain forest agriculture – a system which only now is beginning to be understood. Maya monuments displayed remarkable achievements in astronomy, mathematics, and calendrics, as well as an elaborate cosmology and a volatile and violent political history. The accomplishments of the ancient Maya still astonish us today and the decline and disappearance

1

Figure 1.1  Fallen monuments at the Petén site of El Peru

of this society continues to challenge the imaginations of the public and the efforts of scientists.

For nearly two centuries we have been fascinated by the mystery and romance of the archaeology of the ancient Maya civilization. Nineteenth-century explorers found the Maya stone palaces, temples, ballcourts, and monuments buried beneath the dense vegetation of the jungle canopy (Fig. 1.3). The romantic popular scenario was completed by the ancient Maya's enigmatic, only partially deciphered, hieroglyphic-inscribed monuments, and by their royal tombs filled with treasures of art and precious jade. Then we have the evidence, much debated, of a sudden and unexplained collapse for this sophisticated, literate civilization. The mysteries of ancient lowland Maya civilization have inspired the many "lost jungle cities" of fiction and film, which combine Classic Maya features with an incongruous montage of stylistic elements from other cultures.

Many essays and texts on Maya archaeology begin with a debunking of these melodramatic renderings of ancient Maya civilization and its mysteries. It is true that the popular obsession with the mysterious elements of Maya archaeology has led to wild versions of the Maya past. Some have linked the ancient Maya with the lost tribes of Israel, colonists from the sunken continents of Atlantis and Mu, extraterrestrial visitors,

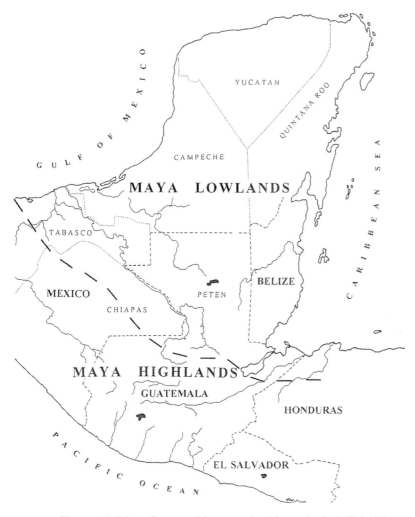

Figure 1.2 Map of eastern Mesoamerica (drawn by Luis F. Luin)

or presented millennial predictions from the Maya calendar of the future as variously heralding a "New Age" or the Apocalypse. Recent theory in the social sciences has emphasized that the ancient past is a "text" into which those in the present "read" their own meanings and reflect their own concerns (e.g. Hodder 1986). Such reflexive uses of the past are certainly characteristic of Maya archaeology and its popular representations. Lost Maya cities, jungles, secret scripts, and tombs have provided the raw material for a wide range of colorful popular interpretations that

Figure 1.3 Catherwood drawing of the ruins at Palenque, Chiapas (from Stephens 1841)

sometimes have little or nothing to do with the ancient Maya and, in some cases, have been quite condescending toward their modern oppressed descendants (Montejo 1991; Castañeda 1996; Hervik 1999).

Still, while scholars may be amused or offended by these misuses of the Maya, even careful professional studies usually portray the archaeology of the Maya as a series of challenges or problems, many of those enigmas broadly similar to those addressed by popular presentation and speculation. Perhaps beneath the public's naïve fascination with the Maya there always has been an intuitive grasp of some elements which are the genuine intellectual challenges that Maya archaeology presents to social science.

One such central challenge has been the very presence of this high civilization in a "rain forest" (technically not a true rain forest but a "humid subtropical forest"). In general, jungles have been perceived by the public as the realm of less complex peoples – "tribes" or even "savages." Theory in the social sciences has differed from this popular perception more in style than in substance, since scholars, too, have been puzzled by the presence of this complex society in a rain forest environment. Historians and archaeologists traditionally had looked to highland basins or to desert river valleys for the heartlands of civilizations. Such environments had the proper settings to apply the alleged "prime movers" for the development

of complex society; that is, settings with factors that demanded centralized management, such as irrigation, conflict over limited land or water,
control of trade routes, and so on. The rise of civilization in a rain forest
was baffling, given the few navigable rivers, no obvious need for irrigation,
and no apparent need for centralized forms of agricultural management.
The rain forest setting of the Maya continues to challenge our interpretations and an understanding of this environment is central to any accurate
view of Maya civilization and its long history.

Other major aspects of research on the ancient Maya also began with
initial impressions that were unfocused, but nonetheless insightful. The
popular appeal of Maya archaeology has always been enhanced by the
beauty and complexity of the vast corpus of ancient Maya art, including artifacts, murals, monuments, and architecture. As scholars began
to interpret Maya iconography, hieroglyphics, and art, they also were
seduced by the complexity of Maya art and the sophistication of their
calendrics, mathematics, and cosmology. As we shall see, this vast investment of ancient lowland Maya society in monuments, architecture, and
other manifestations of elite culture may reflect the distinctive political
structure of this civilization and the "cultural capital" of its elites (Bourdieu 1977). Again, beneath the romantic images lie basic truths about
the intellectual challenges presented by our "readings" of this ancient
society.

Another element in the popular fascination with the ancient Maya is
the mystery of the sudden "collapse" of their greatest cities in the southern lowland Petén rain forest. The first explorers found massive acropoli
of public architecture and extensive domestic ruins that had been long
abandoned. Other sites were only occupied by small groups of Lacandon
Maya, who offered incense and prayer before the remnants of the ancient
temples, stelae, and altars. The mystery of the abandonment of these
ancient Maya cities has spawned several generations of speculations and
theories on its causes – ranging from epidemics and earthquakes to elite
decadence, peasant revolts, and foreign invasions.

The enigma of the decline and abandonment of the Maya cities of
the Classic period (AD 300 to 900) not only fed public fantasy, but
also helped stimulate a century of serious archaeological research. The
controversy on the nature, causes, and even the existence of the so-called
"Classic Maya collapse" remains hotly debated.

Some presentations of the "Classic Maya collapse" have tended implicitly to denigrate the later achievements of the Postclassic kingdoms or
even the continuing vigorous cultural traditions, resistance, and activism
of the millions of Maya peoples living today (see Montejo 1991; D. Chase
and A. Chase 2004; Demarest and García 2003; P. Rice et al. 2004). It
is critical to circumscribe and define what exactly happened to many of

the lowland Maya cities of the Classic period, rather than to speculate vaguely on some general "collapse" of the Maya.

In this text we will review the interpretations of this complex phenomena, the evidence, and the beginnings of a consensus on some issues. In some parts of the southern lowland region of the Maya world, the decline of the Maya cities at the end of the Classic period was a relatively rapid process with a dramatic drop in the level of political complexity and drastic population decline. In other regions Maya states were more gradually transformed into a different form of society. In the past decade, approaches to understanding the mystery of the decline of the jungle cities of the Maya have moved beyond simplistic and uniform characterizations. The end of Classic period lowland Maya civilization has proven to be one of the most exciting aspects of Maya archaeology for scientific studies that touch upon universal questions about the causes of the decline of complex societies. Despite the existence of exaggerations and wild theories, scholars should concede that popular perceptions helped to propel scientific research on the collapse in directions that have revealed the central, distinctive themes of Classic Maya civilization.

## True mysteries and central themes in Maya archaeology

Three themes will be emphasized in this brief overview of the nature of ancient lowland Classic Maya civilization. One is the issue of the fundamental connection of all aspects of Maya society to its ecological and economic adaptation to the rain forest environment. Up until a few years ago, international conservation agencies had argued that such environments can only be saved by holding human populations down to a very low level. Contrary to this modern wisdom, the ancient Maya raised a remarkable, complex civilization in the Petén rain forest with populations in the millions, and they sustained it for nearly two millennia. What were the secrets of the ancient Maya adaptation to the rain forest? How did they achieve a sustainable rain forest civilization? The answers are complex, but recent studies have begun to reveal the nature of Classic Maya ecological adaptations. In turn, these new characterizations of Maya ecology and economy have implications for understanding their volatile and dynamic political structure, their vast investment in political ideology and ritual, and the inherent instability that facilitated the ninth-century decline of many of their cities in the lowland regions.

Another central feature of Maya archaeology, also reflected in public interest, is the vast and complex corpus of Maya art, monuments, and hieroglyphic inscriptions, and the elaborate ideology that it presents. The complexity of ancient Maya astronomy, astrology, calendrics, and cosmology has mesmerized modern scholars and devoted lay followers. Yet this emphasis on the detail of Maya esoterica has sometimes lacked any real grasp of the fundamental nature of the Classic Maya investment in ideology. With the decipherment of many inscriptions, more systematic study of political history, and comparative study to parallel institutions in other civilizations, we are now beginning to discern the political rationale in the mystical haze of Maya cosmology and elite culture. Later we will explore some aspects of Maya religion and political history, and how Maya elite dependence on ideology and imagery for power can be related to their unstable political dynamics.

Finally, a third theme of intellectual import, as well as popular fascination, is the long-standing mystery of the so-called "Classic Maya collapse." Later we will review the rapid decline of many Maya cities in the southern rain forest zone of the Maya civilization. Recent researches have demonstrated the great *variability* of Classic Maya civilization in art, architecture, economics, and political developments. It is not surprising, then, that we have discovered variability in the regional manifestations of the ending of this Classic Maya culture. Still, some common processes and structural features have begun to emerge in the histories of the Maya states of the different regions of the lowlands between AD 750 and 1000. These parallels will also be linked to the other two themes: the Classic Maya rain forest adaptation, and their rulers' dependence on ideology for political power.

Modern scholars, who have had the benefit of hindsight and a century of new evidence, should concede the perceptiveness of some of the early explorers and the public on these "mysteries" of the Maya civilization. Ethnocentrism, and reflexive and personal romantic readings of the ancient Maya ruins, abound both in early scholarship and even in recent popular presentations. Yet each of the popular "mysteries" did arise from the underlying problems that still challenge archaeology. The scientific exploration of these questions has highlighted the very areas where Maya archaeology can make a general contribution to social science. Two centuries of investigation of these themes has made Classic Maya civilization somewhat less mysterious. Instead, Classic Maya archaeology has become a source of potential insights into the general study in the social sciences of the nature, the rise, and the struggles of all civilizations. In our own subjective, personal readings of the story of this civilization, which was very complex and very different from our own, we as readers can also find our own reflexive philosophical meanings – speaking perhaps not so much about the ancient Maya as about ourselves.

## 2    Background: geography, chronology, and theoretical perspective

### Geographic setting

The setting of Maya civilization is the eastern portion of what archaeologists call "Mesoamerica." Geographically, Mesoamerica is simple enough to define. It covers most of what is today Mexico and the countries of Upper Central America: Guatemala, Belize, El Salvador, and western Honduras (Fig. 2.1). Anthropologists and archaeologists use this designation to refer to a "culture area," a region of similar culture traits and features. For several millennia the various societies and civilizations of most of Mexico and Central America were in constant interaction through trade, migration, conquest, and other contacts. These interactions, as well as some common linguistic and ethnic origins, resulted in a sharing of many features across this vast and geographically diverse region.

Some of the features traditionally listed as characteristic of the "Mesoamerican culture area" (e.g. Kirchoff 1943; Helms 1975) included specific features, such as forms of a game played with a rubber ball in a rectangular court and "codex" books made of sheets of bark paper or deerskin coated with stucco and folded like screens. More important common traits were beliefs and concepts shared by the societies of Mesoamerica, such as the ritual importance of blood offerings and human sacrifice. Another trait was a shared concern with astronomical knowledge, and the recording and worship of the calendric cycles of the sun, the moon, the planet Venus, and the stars. Most societies in Mesoamerica also shared a common diet dominated by maize corn, beans, squashes, and chiles. Maize was ground on stone querns (*metates*) with stone hand pestles (*manos*) and then either grilled as flat *tortillas* or steamed or roasted in the familiar thicker *tamales*. (The latter were more common in Classic Maya cuisine.)

Being defined by cultural traits and traditions, the exact boundaries of Mesoamerica as a "culture area" shifted over time with the shifting distribution of those traits, so archaeologists debate its precise limits (Helms 1975; Boone and Willey 1988; Porter-Weaver 1993). In general

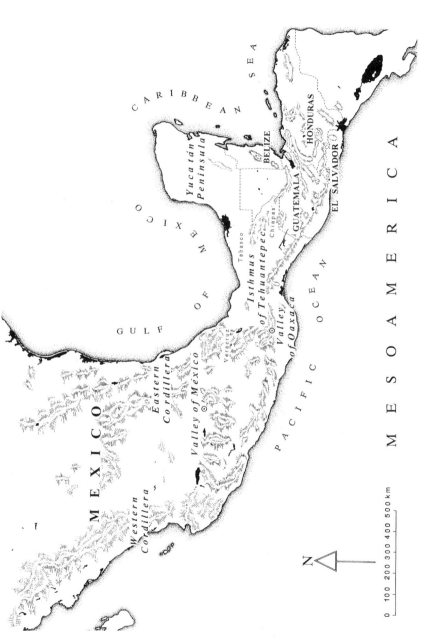

Figure 2.1 Mesoamerica, showing major geographical features (drawn by Luis F. Luin)

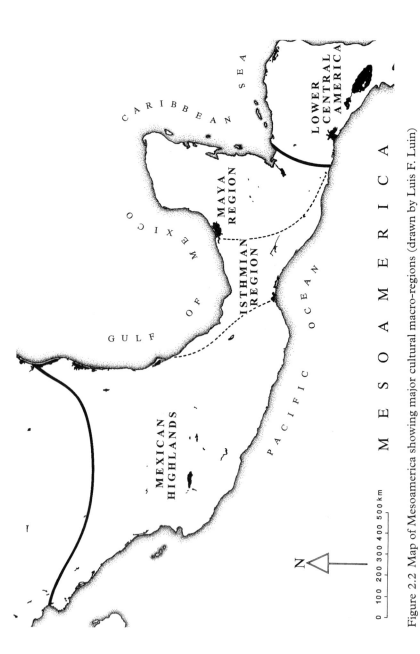

Figure 2.2 Map of Mesoamerica showing major cultural macro-regions (drawn by Luis F. Luin)

its western and northern boundary is drawn somewhere across the deserts of the northern part of the Central Plateau of Mexico. The southern boundary of Mesoamerica is traced from northwestern Costa Rica up to western Honduras, where this complex of shared features and concepts begins to become diffuse in the archaeological and ethnohistoric record (Fig. 2.2).

Defining cultural subregions *within* Mesoamerica (Fig. 2.2) is more arbitrary, since regions of greater cultural similarity, shared language, ethnicity, or political unity changed with each period. Generally, the highland cultures of modern central Mexico and the Mexican state of Oaxaca had distinctive cultural traditions with a high degree of continuity. Each of these areas had a sequence of civilizations centered on rich highland basins, most notably the Valleys of Mexico and Oaxaca. Other basins and valleys lie nestled within portions of the great western and eastern mountain ranges (*cordilleras*) that frame the natural geography of Mexico (West 1964).

To the northeast and east another broad culture area could be defined by the regions which define and border the Isthmus of Tehuantepec: the Mexican Gulf Coast states of Tabasco and Veracruz, the state of Chiapas, and the Pacific coast of southern Guatemala (Fig. 2.2). Together these formed a corridor of communication and population movement in pre-Columbian times. This "Isthmian Zone" (Lowe 1978; Parsons 1978) was a varied landscape of coasts, swamps, valleys, and hill ranges that separated the Maya world from western Mesoamerica, while also providing natural routes of contact, trade, and migration across Mesoamerica. Within this Isthmian region a variety of cultures flourished with great changes from period to period in ethnic, linguistic, and political groups.

The Maya cultures inhabited the eastern portion of Mesoamerica from the volcanic mountain ranges of southern Chiapas and Guatemala, north across the central highlands of Guatemala, and down into the lowland rain forests that extend to the north from northern Guatemala, western Honduras, and Belize, across the Yucatan peninsula to the Gulf of Mexico (Fig. 2.2). The geography of the Maya world itself in eastern Mesoamerica is generally divided ecologically and culturally into "highlands" and "lowlands" (Sanders 1973; Coe 1966). To the south the "Maya highland" zone is of particular importance to any discussion of the early stages of Maya civilization. The earliest known sedentary village societies of eastern Mesoamerica have been found on the southern Pacific coastal plain of Guatemala and Chiapas. Much of the evidence on the evolution of early Maya writing, art, high chiefdoms, and early states has come from the Pacific slopes and intermontane basins of the southern highlands.

The "Maya lowland" region (see Fig. 6.5) consists of flat to slightly rolling limestone plain and hills that cover Guatemala's Department of Petén, Belize, and the Yucatan peninsula of Mexico (Siemens 1978; Harrison and Turner 1978). This Maya lowland zone was covered by the subtropical rain forest environment that sustained Maya civilization for over two thousand years. Its complex geography and ecology, and the ancient Maya adaptations to them, are discussed in more detail in Chapter 6. Together, the varied mix of coasts, jungles, volcanic ranges, and basins in eastern Mesoamerica gave rise to the great states and centers of the Classic Maya civilization and to the indigenous Maya cultures that still flourish today.

### Chronological frameworks: an overview of Mesoamerican culture history

Definitions of historic or prehistoric periods in any field are subject to constant debate and revision since they often combine two distinct functions: the convenient lumping of blocks of time for description versus the defining and characterizing of presumed "stages" of development. Problems with chronological "stages" quickly arise as new discoveries shift the dating of cultural developments and as differing sequences are found for the rise of complex societies in different zones (Willey and Phillips 1958; Sabloff 1990). Ultimately, archaeologists and historians accept some odd mix of terms that largely serve as arbitrary units of time, but still have residual implications (accurate or not) regarding level of development.

Mesoamerica and the Maya world are no exception to this pattern, and several similar alternative chronological terminologies are common (Willey and Phillips 1958; Sanders, Parsons, and Santley 1979; Sharer 1994). All of them are flawed in that the terms used originally referred to perceived *developmental* periods, such as "Formative" or "Preclassic," "Classic," and so on. New evidence has moved back in time the perceived periods of development and florescence in the Maya area, but the chronological framework continues in use. The period designations that follow (Paleo-Indian, Archaic, Preclassic, Classic, and Postclassic) reflect this inevitably awkward mix of neutral temporal divisions and developmental designations. Overall temporal frameworks and broad characterizations are listed below and in Fig. 2.3. A more detailed discussion of these periods and the rise of Maya civilization are given in subsequent chapters, but here it should be useful to preview the chronology broadly.

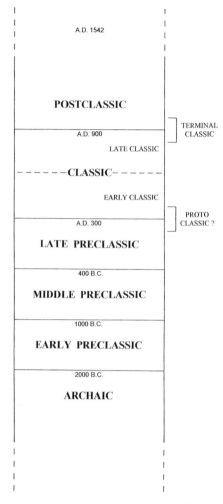

Figure 2.3 Chronological periods for eastern Mesoamerica (drawn by Luis F. Luin)

*Paleo-Indian period (before 12,000 BC to about 7000 BC)*

Most chronologies of Mesoamerica begin with a long period during which social groups were primarily small nomadic bands that subsisted on the collection of wild plants and the hunting of animals. Chronologies vary as to the beginning of this epoch, depending on the dating of the settlement of the New World by the groups that crossed the Bering Strait (Willey

1971; Fagan 1987; Lynch 1978, 1991; Dillehay and Meltzer 1991). Some would see such a crossing from Asia as early as 100,000 years ago, but all agree that by *no later than* 12,000 BC bands of hunters and gatherers had crossed into the New World and were rapidly filling up the varied environments of this hemisphere (Jennings 1978; Willey 1971; Lynch 1991).

### *Archaic period (7000 BC to 2000 BC)*

Climatic changes, corresponding shifts in ecology, and the extinction of important species of megafauna occurred between 10,000 and 7,000 BC. By the latter date, hunting and gathering groups had begun a series of gradual adaptations to a wider range of eco-niches through more varied subsistence strategies. During this period emphasis on systematic collecting of wild plants and hunting or trapping of small game, birds, and fish set the stage for the beginnings of agriculture. In some areas this transition had occurred by as early as 5000 BC. By 3000 BC in most regions, populations were larger, with sedentary or semi-sedentary villages, and increased dependence on farming. By 2000 BC there were settled farming villages in most of Mesoamerica.

### *Early Preclassic (2000 to 1000 BC)*

As in many other world regions, agriculture and sedentism were followed relatively rapidly by population increases and the development of socially and politically more complex societies. In the millennium after 2000 BC, early chiefdoms with religious and political leadership began to appear in central Mexico, the Valley of Oaxaca, the Pacific coasts of Chiapas and Guatemala, and the Gulf coast swamps and highlands of Veracruz and Tabasco. By 1500 to 1200 BC some Mesoamerican societies had public constructions, long-distance exchange systems, differential access to power and wealth, and complex information systems. The latter included the beginnings of monumental art, iconography, and the calendric and writing systems used later by the Classic Maya and other Mesoamerican societies. The events and processes of this Early Preclassic (or alternatively "Early Formative") period are still very poorly understood, particularly in the southern Maya lowlands, where there is little archaeological evidence before about 1000 BC.

### *Middle Preclassic (1000 to 400 BC)*

Between 1000 and 400 BC incipient complex societies in many regions of Mesoamerica evolved into "archaic states," with more centralized political and religious authority, public architecture, monumental art, economic complexity, and social stratification. During this period there was continued development of the pan-Mesoamerican complex of iconographic, astronomical, calendric, and writing systems. These information systems varied regionally, but shared similar structures and even many individual elements. During this period the "Olmec civilization" flourished in Veracruz and Tabasco, and there were complex societies in other regions that shared elements of Olmec art and ideology (Sharer and Grove 1989). Again, the processes are poorly understood, but interregional interaction between emerging elites was clearly central to these developments.

### Late Preclassic (400 BC to AD 300)

By 400 BC states with distinctive regional variants of Mesoamerican civilization had emerged or were emerging in central Mexico, Oaxaca, the Maya region, and elsewhere. This period saw the rise of the great urban center of Teotihuacan in the Valley of Mexico and Monte Albán in the Valley of Oaxaca. Comparable centers in both the Maya highlands and lowlands had large populations, political complexity, and monumental architecture. In the last three centuries of this period, interregional contacts and still poorly understood events led to the distinctive complex of artifactual traits and political ideologies characteristic of the "Classic period" of the Maya lowlands.

### Classic period (AD 300 to 900)

This period, along with its archaeological manifestations (especially in the southern half of the Maya lowlands), is the principal chronological and regional focus of this text. Traditionally, the Classic epoch was defined as the period of the use in the lowlands of distinctive forms of the ancient Maya writing and calendric systems in carved stone texts, as well as polychrome ceramics, corbeled vault or false vault stone architecture, the stela-altar monument complex, and a series of other specific traits (Sabloff 1985; Willey 1987). This epoch was once believed to be *the* period of cultural florescence of the ancient Maya. Now we know that most of these traits predated the "Classic" period and that there were several "florescences" of Maya civilization, evidenced by the presence of urbanism and monumental architecture on a large scale in the previous Late Preclassic period, as well as urban centers in the subsequent Postclassic era. Still, the Classic period does appear to have some degree of integrity (or, at least, utility) as a concept because all of the traits referred to above were present at a large number of centers associated with widespread, shared ceramic styles. More recently, some scholars have emphasized the dominance of the ideology of divine kingship in art, iconography, and politics throughout this Classic period – the so-called "Ajaw complex," as discussed below in Chapters 8 and 9 (e.g. Schele and Freidel 1990; Freidel 1992).

Traditionally, the Classic period has been divided into an Early Classic (*circa* AD 300 to 550) and a Late Classic (*circa* AD 600 to 900) originally with a "hiatus" or period of cultural recession between the two (Prosk-ouriakoff 1950; Willey 1974). Now, from more specific hieroglyphic deci-pherments of historical texts, we know that the "hiatus" between the Early and Late Classic was probably merely a period of defeat and decline for some important states in the central Petén, while elsewhere competing states flourished (Chase and Chase 1987; Schele and Freidel 1990; Chase 1991; Martin and Grube 1996). Nonetheless, a broad separation between Early (AD 300 to 600) and Late (AD 600 to 900) Classic is a convenient tool for synthetic summaries, and the Late Classic period does corre-spond to rapid changes in ceramic styles and an acceleration of important economic and political developmental trends in most subregions of the Maya world (Culbert 1991; Sabloff and Henderson 1993).

### *The Terminal Classic and the "Collapse" (AD 800 to 1000)*

Though seldom designated as a specific period, the last century of the "Classic period" and the first of the so-called "Postclassic" were centuries of change and transformation in the Maya lowlands. This controversial epoch of collapse, transition, and transformation is given special atten-tion in this text (Chapter 10). Intensification of interregional contacts, radical population changes, migrations, and economic and political transformations characterized the AD 750/800 to 1000/1050 period in most areas of the Maya world, although in differing ways in each zone (Culbert 1973; Sabloff and Andrews V 1986; Demarest, Rice, and Rice 2004a).

### *Postclassic period (AD 900/1000 to 1542)*

The focus of this text is on the Classic period in the lowland rain forest regions. Consequently, I will give only a brief summary of the Postclassic and the Conquest periods. As we will see, recent discoveries and interpre-tations in some regions have blurred the distinction between the Classic and the Postclassic periods (Chase and Rice 1985). In northern Yucatan

and other areas the political and economic transformation of May
after AD 800 was a process that involved foreign influence and a
experimentation. At the end of these two centuries, the Ma
Yucatan peninsula in the north and the Guatemalan highlan___
south were dominated by new forms of conquest states. While arguably
producing less spectacular art and architecture, these populous Postclassic states thrived in northern Yucatan, the central Petén lake district, and
the southern highlands. The institutions and economies of the Postclassic
states allowed them to expand into even larger competing alliances until
the sixteenth-century Spanish Conquest.

*Alternative chronologies*

There are, of course, many alternative chronological schemes. In the past,
a "Protoclassic" epoch was proposed somewhere between AD 150 and
350 as a period of coalescence of Classic Maya civilization (Gifford 1976;
Willey 1977). Recent studies have failed to demonstrate any consistent
chronological definition for such a proposed period (Pring 1977; Brady
*et al.* 1998). The presence of great centers and political complexity by
the beginning of the Late Preclassic period, several centuries earlier, also
invalidates the original Protoclassic concept.

We should also note that the beginning and the ending dates for every
period or sub-period vary between authors by a century or more. Such
inconsistencies are of little real importance in interpretations of Maya
archaeology, where we have a fairly reliable absolute chronology based
on dated hieroglyphic monuments and associated specific polychrome
ceramic styles. Often Maya archaeologists can date Classic historical
events or cultural phenomena to the century, year, or even day, regardless
of how we name these periods.

### The nested civilizations of Mesoamerica: interpretive frameworks

A more substantial disagreement exists between Mayanists and some
Mesoamerican archaeologists working in central Mexico or Oaxaca.
Some scholars (including authors in this series) have accepted an alternative chronological scheme (Price 1978; Sanders, Parsons, and Santley
1979; Blanton *et al.* 1999). Such a system is structured by the premise
that gradual developmental sequences in each region were periodically crosscut by periods of intensified pan-Mesoamerican interregional
contacts, migrations, or conquests. These so-called "horizons" are often

characterized as periods in which dominant core areas radiated influences that stimulated rapid changes in other regions (e.g. Rowe 1956, 1962; Sanders and Price 1968; cf. D. Rice 1993a).

Thus, an "Early Horizon" of influences from the precocious Olmec chiefdoms of the Gulf Coast of Mexico is believed by some to have been responsible for widespread shared motifs and ceramic modes, as well as some specific iconographic elements present across much of Mesoamerica between about 1200 and 800 BC. Similarly, this perspective posits a "Middle Horizon" beginning at about AD 350, a time of great commercial and military interactions across Mesoamerica. Architectural forms, ceramic styles, and central Mexican iconography are found at many sites in each region of Mesoamerica between about AD 300 and 500 and have been attributed to influence from the great city of Teotihuacan in the Valley of Mexico (Sanders and Santley 1983). Finally, a Late Horizon was defined based on solid historical documentation recording the fifteenth-century expansion through conquest of the Aztec Empire from its Valley of Mexico homeland.

There are great problems with such a chronological scheme and the interpretive framework that underlies it (D. Rice 1993a; Demarest and Foias 1993; Braswell 2003a, 2003b). The model implicitly envisions regional cultural sequences as somewhat isolated territorial developments episodically punctuated by stimulating periods of pan-Mesoamerican influence in the form of these "horizons" (Fig. 2.4). The horizon-interpretive framework actually reflects better the structure of contemporary academics – with regional experts conceding evidence of contact in certain periods to indicate "horizons" of pan-Mesoamerican contact connecting their zones. It tends to focus proposed periods of intensified exchange and cultural advance into narrow chronological bands.

It is more probable that communication was continuous, intense, and unbroken between most regions of Mesoamerica from the beginning of the Preclassic era to the Conquest. From the origins of the Mesoamerican civilizations, the ancient patterns of contact formed more of a lattice of ongoing exchanges of information, iconography, and scientific knowledge, moving in multiple directions between emerging elites in each region (Fig. 2.5). Such patterns of multidirectional interregional contact have been found to be characteristic of the coevolution of the distinctive civilizations of the Near East and central and south Asia, as well as other world regions (see Lamberg-Karlovsky 1975, 1989, and case studies in this series, e.g. Pollock 1999; Wright in press). Again, scholars of those world regions initially resisted notions of continuous interregional communication and the coevolution of civilizations. Now we are beginning to appreciate the degree to which regional civilizations can

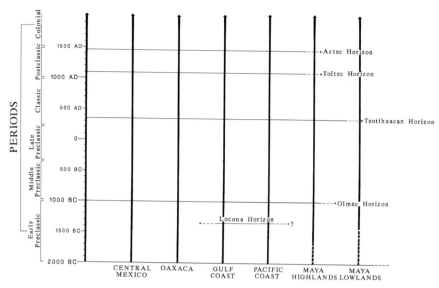

Figure 2.4 Schematic interregional chronology using the "horizons" concept (drawn by Luis F. Luin). Heavy vertical bars indicate periods in which that region was precocious in development and particularly influential on other regions

absorb or project specific concepts and traits without dramatic changes in other aspects of material culture or symbolic systems. Indeed, acceptance or rejection of "foreign" styles, symbol systems, or other cultural contacts often can be better explained by the needs of locally evolving elites, rather than by reference to conquest, migration, economic dominance, or other external factors.

In any case, one interpretive bias of this text is my view that civilizations in most world regions, including Mesoamerica, arose in a coevolving lattice of multidirectional innovation, communication, and influence. As presented in Fig. 2.5, certain zones of Mesoamerica were more precocious or influential in given periods. Yet even such asymmetrical cultural influences and exchanges were variable in their intensity and in the extent of their pan-Mesoamerican impact, and they do not correspond to the template of "horizons" of influence projected from presumed "core areas" or "nuclear zones." For the same reasons the interpretations here do not follow the more sophisticated, but similarly flawed, "world systems" theories. In practice, world systems theory often guides archaeologists to presuppose economic interdependence as a central force behind interregional contacts. Borrowed from modern

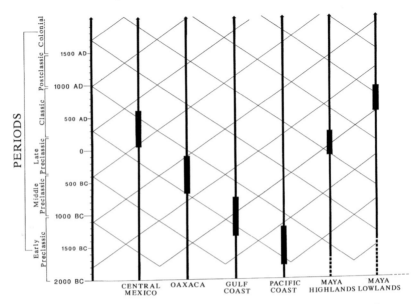

Figure 2.5 Schematic chronology based on assumption of continuous interregional interaction. Heavy vertical bars indicate periods in which that region was precocious in development and particularly influential on other regions (drawn by Luis F. Luin)

political science, world systems theory has a tendency to shape views of ancient world regions into "core areas" and "peripheries." While there were continuously interacting and coevolving cultures in Mesoamerica, there is no reason to assume *a priori* that economics was the principal force for interaction and integration, nor that "core areas" stimulated cultural advances elsewhere. Instead, here the Maya world is viewed as having been nested within a continuous lattice of mutual communication and influence between the various regional civilizations of Mesoamerica.

## Theoretical perspectives

In addition to controversies concerning chronology and frameworks for culture-historical interpretation, there are also broader theoretical issues and positions which underlie any synthetic discussion of ancient civilizations. Such theoretical perspectives are best stated explicitly, allowing open critique of our necessarily subjective interpretations.

### *The question: why civilization?*

Perhaps the greatest question addressed by anthropology, archaeology, and history is the mystery of human "cultural evolution." Why have many human societies over the past 10,000 years changed from small, simple, egalitarian hunting and gathering groups to vast, complex, hierarchically organized, urban civilizations? What are the processes, tendencies, or circumstances that have caused this transformation again and again in different parts of the globe? While these questions have long concerned philosophers and historians, modern anthropologists have systematically explored them through the study of comparative history, ethnography, ethnohistory, and, especially, archaeology. These disciplines examine "cultural change," "historical development," or "cultural evolution" by studying present and past societies – positing evolution or historical development from so-called "less complex" societies to chiefdoms, states, or empires with variously defined higher levels of complexity in economic systems, social stratification, and forms of governance. The grand theories of history and anthropology on the causes of the rise and fall of civilizations have been tested by looking at cultural change within regions as it is actually recorded in the archaeological and historical record. The theorizing, research, testing, and debates that have been involved in this process of research on "cultural evolution" have created much of modern anthropological theory. Yet much of this thinking has been challenged in recent years.

## The search for regularities and theories of cultural evolution

Theories of cultural evolution or historical development such as cultural materialism and Marxism try to address the "big questions" of what factors or processes have led, again and again, in many world regions, to the development of economically and politically complex societies. Some of these became "civilizations" or states, which had institutions that nucleated political power in the hands of a leadership group and that stratified individuals into differing levels of wealth and power. In the Near East, Egypt, Pakistan, Peru, China, the American Southwest, and many other regions including Mexico and the Maya area, most scholars see a broadly parallel sequence of development. First came the domestication of animals and the origins of farming and village life, then the rise of societies with some degree of differences in access to power and resources (e.g. ranked societies or "chiefdoms"), and, finally, the emergence of states with urbanism, monumental architecture, hereditary wealth and power, intensive systems of food production, large-scale warfare, and complex economic institutions. Another parallel between civilizations is the repeated cycle of rise, florescence, and fall – the "fall" being manifest either by conquest, transformation, or disintegration. In the case of the Classic Maya civilization, the question of the "fall," decline, or transformation has been a particularly powerful stimulus to the development of Maya archaeology and to continuing controversy and debate.

In seeking to discover the regularities and common processes in these broadly parallel sequences of civilizations, anthropologists and archaeologists have traditionally tended to emphasize broad economic or ecological regularities, trends, "processes," or even "laws" that could explain the parallels in the development of civilizations. Based on analogy to biological evolution, nineteenth-century thinkers such as Herbert Spencer, Lewis Henry Morgan, Karl Marx, and Frederick Engels struggled to create a comparable set of scientific principles and mechanisms to explain the regularities and parallels in human historical development or evolution. Racist or politically unacceptable aspects of these early "grand narrative" theories of cultural evolution led to their rejection in twentieth-century American anthropology until the 1950s.

### Evolutionism and processual archaeology

The return of evolutionism to American archaeology came with the work of Julian Steward (1955), Leslie White (1959), and others who emphasized cultural ecology and economic adaptations in their revival of theories of cultural evolution. This materialist orientation viewed human societies in an evolutionary competition in which social groups survived, reproduced, and spread through more ecologically or economically adaptive technologies, ecological strategies, or economic institutions (e.g. White 1959; Harris 1964, 1968, 1979). Such ecologically and economically oriented evolutionism was enthusiastically accepted and applied in American archaeology as a set of guiding principles for explanation of ancient culture change and for the formulation of research designs (e.g. Binford 1962, 1965; Watson, LeBlanc, and Redman 1971; Schiffer 1976).

This general acceptance of an ecologically oriented version of theories of cultural evolution reflects the realities of the nature of archaeology and its development in the 1950s, 1960s, and 1970s. During that period there were many technological and methodological breakthroughs in archaeology. Most of these related to dating and chronology or to the recovery of subsistence evidence and the reconstruction of ancient ecological systems (e.g. Brothwell and Higgs 1970; Butzer 1982). It was natural, then, that ecological and economic models captured the interest and efforts of archaeologists. In turn, archaeological research successfully applied these concepts to recover evidence of the role of economic factors in cultural evolution, including innovations in subsistence techniques or new cultigens, increasing populations, warfare over limited resources, the development of irrigation systems, and the formation of marketing networks.

Such ecological and economic approaches were particularly successful in Mesoamerica, especially in central Mexico. There interpretations were based on environmental features and constraints, ecological heterogeneity, irrigation, and demographic pressure, which were applied to explain many aspects of the archaeological record and the development of complex societies and, subsequently, of states (e.g. Sanders 1968, 1972; Sanders and Price 1968; Palerm 1973; Parsons 1974; Wolf 1976; Santley 1983). Archaeologists had convincingly identified regularities in the patterns of agriculture, population growth, further intensification of agriculture, and parallel increasing complexity in trade, craft specialization, and the power of political and economic leaders. As in other world regions, Mesoamerican archaeologists carried out systematic regional "settlement pattern" studies of the location of sites and their relation to ancient ecology. Researchers have also recovered much subsistence evidence, reconstructed ancient environments and economic networks, and related these to changes in population size, wealth differences, and political institutions. In the 1970s and 1980s, field researches often applied a scientific (or pseudoscientific?) format of testing specific hypotheses derived from broader theories – in general, theories which stressed the role of ecological adaptation, economic advances, and competition between groups in this materially guided social analogue of biological evolution.

In archaeology this systematic, scientific, and predominantly economic form of evolutionary theory came later to be designated as "processual archaeology" by some of its practitioners and most of its critics. In truth, this designation actually covers a wide range of approaches, and only a small cadre of archaeologists explicitly accepted any specific dogma of scientific, deductive, and rigid materialist theory. There did seem to be, however, a largely implicit consensus among archaeologists that ecology and economics had guided cultural evolution. There was also a sense that some factors in human behavior were too complex or too idiosyncratic to be accurately perceived and interpreted in the archaeological record. These included such elements as the role of religion, ideology, and individual action in culture change, as well as the internal complexities and subgroup struggles that do not allow human societies to be accurately modeled as ecologically adaptive collective "organisms."

*Materialist theory and the Maya problem*

The Maya area was more problematic for cultural materialist and ecolog-ically deterministic theory. The success of this high civilization in a rain forest with thin soils, fertile – but fragile – ecosystems, few navigable rivers, and no need for irrigation challenged some of the more popular causal scenarios of economically oriented archaeology. Attempts to apply conventional processual, materialist explanations to the enigmas of the rise and fall of the Classic Maya were strained and involved somewhat circular arguments. Some of these theories stretched relative terms like "environmental heterogeneity" (e.g. Sanders 1977) or "circumscription" to fit the Maya region (e.g. Carneiro 1970), while other interpretations assumed, without strong evidence, that rulers or the state had controlled early intensive agriculture or trade systems (e.g. A.P. Andrews 1980a and 1980b; Santley 1983; see critique in Demarest 1989a). Still others main-tained a culture-materialist dogma in the Maya area only by forced under-estimation of the scale, level of development, or duration of lowland Maya civilization (e.g. Meggers 1954; Sanders and Price 1968) or by attribut-ing its rise to external stimulus from the more ecologically "appropriate" civilizations of the Mexican highlands (Sanders and Michels 1969; Price 1978).

By the 1980s, Maya archaeologists had begun to point out problems in the application of a rigid materialist evolutionism to explanation of the rise and fall of Classic Maya civilization. Challenges to ecologically determin-ist interpretations were posed by the massive ancient Maya investments in ritual and religion, their weakly developed market systems, their largely decentralized economy and agriculture, and yet their surprisingly large early populations (e.g. Andrews IV 1965; W. Coe 1965a; Matheny 1987). Evidence for Mexican stimulus for Maya state development became largely discredited with new discoveries (described in Chapter 4) pushing back the rise of complex Maya centers to at least 600 to 400 BC (Freidel 1979; Matheny 1980; Hansen 1984, 1989, 1996; Demarest and Foias 1993).

Finally, archaeologists began to find increasing evidence that religion, ritual, and cosmology were themselves an actual major source of ancient Maya political power, rather than just a "legitimization" of authority based on control of agricultural systems, trade, or economic resources (Haviland 1970; Freidel 1979; Freidel and Schele 1988a; Demarest 1989a, 1992a, 1992b; Hansen 1992, 1998; McAnany 1995). Indeed, evidence was – and remains – spotty and weak for state involvement in the basic agricultural or economic infrastructure of the Classic Maya realms of the southern lowland rain forests (Demarest 1992b; Dunning *et al.* 1997). All things considered, the Maya case fit poorly with standard forms of materialist theory and processual archaeology.

### *The postprocessual identity crisis in archaeology and the quest for new approaches*

Of course, the problems of interpreting ancient Maya cultural history were but one small element in a general theoretical transformation in world archaeology. The ancient Maya – with their rain forest environment, massive investment in religious ritual, and specific political institutions – simply represented an acute version of the challenges confronting materialist theories of cultural evolution. In other world regions, as in Mesoamerica, archaeology in the 1960s and 1970s had concentrated on innovative approaches to settlement patterns. Great success was achieved through the recovery and recording of settlement distributions and paleoecological evidence and the interpretations of patterns in that data in terms of population dynamics, irrigation systems, and trade (e.g. R. McC. Adams 1965; Wright and Johnson 1975; Wolf 1976; Sanders *et al.* 1979; Spooner 1972). Yet even within those economically oriented evolutionary schools, doubts had arisen that population dynamics, subsistence systems, and ecological adaptations were sufficient as "prime movers" in the explanation of culture change and the rise of states and civilizations. Instead scholars began to realize that a complex interaction between social, political, and ecological factors was involved in the rise of state societies (e.g. R.McC. Adams 1965, 1969, 1981, 1984; Flannery 1972, 1976; Willey 1976; Blanton 1976, 1980; Cowgill 1979).

One concern was that important aspects of society and human behavior had been ignored by theories of cultural evolution and the archaeological investigations that they inspired. Ideology (beliefs, symbolic systems, cosmology, etc.) had been given little attention in the explanation of culture change or was explicitly dismissed as "epiphenomenal," i.e., derivative in its role (e.g. Harris 1968). Yet evidence from history, ethnohistory, and archaeology provided many examples in which religious beliefs, rituals, political ideologies, or cosmologies were critical factors in long- and short-term culture change (e.g. Flannery 1972; Drennan 1976; Flannery and Marcus 1976; Willey 1976; Freidel 1979, 1981; Conrad and Demarest 1984; Demarest 1987a, 1989a; Miller and Tilley 1984; Demarest and Conrad 1992). Some Marxists and structural Marxists, although themselves proponents of an economic theory of history, were also concerned about the absence of ideology from the processual models. While Marxist theory emphasizes the importance of the development of the economy and economic relations, it also explores the role of religion and ideology in "legitimating" the power and privilege of elites. Many modern Marxists also have seen ideology as a potentially dynamic force for political action (e.g. Friedman 1974, 1975; Godelier 1977, 1978a; Miller and Tilley 1984).

Another source of dissatisfaction with ecologically oriented evolutionary theory was its deterministic quality, which ignored the role of the individual and the internal dynamics of groups *within* societies. There was little consideration of the active role that individual and group decisions and actions must have played in the past, the true initial sources and agents of change (Giddens 1979; Bourdieu 1977; Hodder 1985). Instead, theories of cultural evolution broadly "explained" how whole societies adapted to their environments and competed with each other as they evolved more politically and economically complex institutions. This "processual" approach, while it successfully guided broad descriptions of cultural history and adaptation, glossed over the very dynamics of culture change itself, and the conscious or unconscious human actions within that created those adaptations and cultural history.

Thus, criticism of processual archaeology, cultural materialism, and broadly generalizing theories of cultural evolution came from a variety of different perspectives and generated a series of differing critiques and theoretical alternatives. Some scholars have referred to this range of new concerns and approaches as "postprocessual archaeology." Others refer to it as "postmodern" anthropological theory. The latter designation acknowledges the influence on archaeology during the 1980s and 1990s of "postmodern" theory from philosophy, art, literary analysis, and history. Truly postmodern approaches in archaeology today also include much broader concerns with theory of knowledge: awareness of the biases that we bring to research and the way in which the ancient past and our "scientific" studies reflect our own worldview and political agendas (e.g. Foucault 1965, 1972, 1973). Critical theory, feminist theory, radical theory, hermeneutics, and other new perspectives in the social sciences and humanities reached archaeology in the 1980s and 1990s, initiating our own "postmodern" period of soul-searching and self-critique (Preucel ed. 1991; Hodder 1986, 1987; cf. Knauft 1996). Meanwhile, within Maya archaeology itself some scholars have challenged the ways in which modern archaeology and ethnography have projected condescending or ethnocentric interpretations of the Maya (e.g. Castañeda 1996; Hervik 1999; Montejo 1991, 1999).

At their best, all of these new perspectives help us to refine our reconstructions of the past and make them more complex and realistic. We are also more conscious of the weaknesses in our interpretations regarding issues such as individual actions, subgroup ideology, women's roles in ancient society, and the belief systems that motivated past actions. At their most extreme, however, postmodern approaches attempt to wrestle with philosophical issues such as the subject/object distinction, the possibility of knowledge, the relativity of all truth, and the very existence of the past (see Preucel ed. 1991; Shanks and Tilley 1987; Bell 1987, 1991; Feyerabend 1988). In these latter manifestations, archaeological theory drifts into profound debates about the relativity of knowledge and truth that began with the dialogues between the Sophists and Socrates in the fifth century BC and have remained unresolved through the entire history of Western thought (e.g. Derrida 1976, 1981; cf. Tilley ed. 1990). It seems a bit unrealistic (if not immodest) to believe that archaeology will contribute much to these broader philosophical debates. I do not question the importance of these deeper epistemological issues – only our ability in archaeology to add much new to the dialogue.

Nonetheless, the last two decades of "postmodern" self-questioning have allowed us to sharpen our concern with inherent problems in our presentations and our understandings of the past. It has also returned archaeologists to a realistic perspective regarding the degree to which our interpretations of the ancient past are not purely "scientific" but rather are subjective and interpretive – reflecting individual and cultural concerns and biases. Such a more humble and cautious perspective can allow us to study ancient Maya archaeology with greater awareness of the highly reflexive nature of our own perspectives on ancient societies.

*Theoretical position: the Maya, ecology, ideology, and social identity*

In keeping with the nature of this series, I draw heavily in this text on my own three decades of research and theoretical writings on pre-Columbian civilization. Consequently, like myself, the theoretical perspective of this book is unrepentantly eclectic, drawing upon both the traditional processual "grand narrative" theories and recent "postprocessual" concerns. It shares with the postprocessual view an interest in the role of individual practice and group action or agency in the dynamics of power that form and maintain complex societies or "civilizations" (Bourdieu 1977; Giddens 1979; Hodder 1982, 1985; Shanks and Tilley 1987, 1988). Such ancient Maya decisions, actions, and dynamics were clearly greatly influenced by religion or the more general forms of belief referred to as "ideology" or "worldview" (Giddens 1979: 188–194; Bourdieu 1977: 183–190; Mann 1986; Hodder 1982). It is argued here that, in the Maya civilization, there was a seamless relationship between ecology, religion, and the forms and sources of power in the ancient Maya states (cf. Freidel 1981; Demarest 1992a, 1992b; McAnany 1995; Flannery and Marcus 1976; Willey 1976).

This text, nonetheless, maintains a strong ecological perspective. While cultural materialists and "processual" archaeology may have ignored too many other factors, it remains certain that ecology and ecological adaptations were central to Maya cultural history. Even those most skeptical of extreme materialist approaches agree that environment – and our adaptations to it – is critical to the history of civilizations, since "the materialist matrix . . . is where life begins, where populations are sustained, and where certain limits are set on sizes and groupings of human societies" (Willey 1976: 203). The lowland Maya civilization of the Late Preclassic and Classic periods (circa 400 BC to AD 900) had a distinctive configuration of traits that related the power of the rulers to their ecological adaptations to the rain forest. The interplay – still incompletely understood – between ancient Maya political institutions and the rain forest economy and ecology generated the form of ancient Maya states and alliances, their volatile and complex political histories, and their collapse or transformation in the ninth century.

This ecological perspective must be combined with some of the insights of recent postprocessual or postmodern anthropology: that historical events and actions, successes and failures were all created by individuals' decisions, which in turn were motivated and guided by many nonecological factors, including the cosmological and philosophical perspectives of that society, what anthropologists sometimes call their "worldview." These beliefs or ideologies, and the rituals that reinforce them, provide answers to the questions and enigmas that confront all individuals, families, and social groups. The Maya, like all peoples, wished to know: who are we? how do we create a social identity for ourselves? how do we confront death and the central enigmas of human existence? A society's worldview, ideology, and religion provide some answers to these questions of individual and collective identity and security. A society's answers to these "unanswerable" existential questions, particularly about death, form much of its culture.

In turn, worldview can define aspects of the economy of a society (Godelier 1978a; Demarest and Conrad 1983; Conrad and Demarest 1984), as well as the acceptable limits, forms, and sources of political power (Godelier 1978b; Haas 1982; Tilley 1984; Miller and Tilley 1984; Demarest 1989a). For example, the worldview and beliefs about death of the Quechua peoples of the Inka empire of South America led them to expend much of their wealth and energies in maintaining and venerating the mummies of their ancestors. Indeed, Inka political and economic institutions and the history of that civilization can only be understood through knowledge of their cult of the dead and its relationship with all aspects of that society (Conrad and Demarest 1984). For the Mexican Aztec empire of central Mexico, cosmology and cults of sacrifice were a central political force that legitimated the power of Aztec rulers while driving their armies to the victories and conquests of their expanding hegemony (Demarest and Conrad 1983). Ideological factors have also been identified as central to the economic and political structure of the Harappan civilization of early Pakistan and India (Miller 1985) and many other prehistoric societies (e.g. Miller and Tilley 1984).

In the modern world it is obvious that political systems and agendas of many non-Western nations and groups are driven by religious fervor and broader ideology. To Europeans and North Americans (other than social scientists and philosophers), it is sometimes less apparent that our own Western civilization is not a purely "rational," economically driven system. Our government and economic systems devote massive resources to the care of the poor and the aging and other ethical concerns that have their roots in predominantly Judeo-Christian ideological values. Our foreign policies, involvements, and even wars have been motivated to some degree by concerns (however misplaced) for human values or for idealized concepts of "freedom." Meanwhile, our most vigorous internal political debates revolve around unresolved religious or ethical details of our loosely shared common ideology (abortion, the death penalty, assisted suicide, same-sex marriage, etc.). Political power in America derives from ideology as much, or more than, from economic agendas. Recent sociological approaches show how in practice individuals act within cultural structures and systems of behavior in which economic, political, aesthetic, or ideological elements are all engaged. Indeed, the very distinction between economic, political, and religious behavior may not – in practice – be a meaningful one (cf. Giddens 1979; Bourdieu 1977).

As individuals today, the forces that motivate us, that inform our decisions, and that fuel our economy include the search for symbols of identity, achievement, and security. Philosophers and social scientists have argued that these motivations (and the bustling economy that they produce) are displaced from the universal search for individual and group identity and from the search for answers to (or distractions from) the existential questions of life and death. Anthropologists and archaeologists have come to recognize that such philosophical, cosmological, and ideological views are (and were) central to the rules of thought and action that guided ancient behavior, just as they influence us today. To explore ancient, non-Western civilizations, and to *learn* from those civilizations, we must examine such aspects of individual and societal worldviews, without ignoring the systematic study of ancient ecological and economic adaptations. As Clifford Geertz (1973: 30), a proponent of broadly interpretive anthropology, has observed:

To look at the symbolic dimensions of social action – art, religion, ideology, science, law, morality, common sense – is not to turn away from the existential dilemmas of life . . . ; it is to plunge into the midst of them. The essential vocation of interpretive anthropology is not to answer our deepest questions, but to make available to us answers that others . . . have given, and thus to include them in the consultable record of what man has said.

It is with this perspective, and these sensitivities, that I have tried here to explore the Classic period civilization of the ancient Maya.

The Classic Maya responded to some basic human existential questions with a complex ideology and investment in rituals, art, and architecture to express and support these beliefs. As we will see, the great Classic Maya stone temples, monuments, ballcourts, causeways, and elaborate artworks were stages, settings, and props for the spectacular state displays and the more routine daily rituals that defined for the Maya their place in the universe and their relationship to their ancestors, their gods, and the natural forces and temporal cycles of the cosmos. The political power of the rulers rested, to no small degree, on their role as "holy lords," as sacred intercessors with those entities and forces. Their power also came from their leadership in orchestrating the rituals that satisfied the Maya's need for identity, security, and for a definition of the universe and their place in it. Yet they also responded to the requirements, potentials, and limitations of their rain forest environment and their need to compete economically, and militarily, with their neighbors. These two themes of ideology and environment – the physical demands of survival and the cultural definition of identity – were the warp and weft that together wove the tapestry of ancient Maya society.

This extended essay, then, is based on archaeological and historical data on Maya cultural evolution in "scientific" and "processual" terms. Yet from a postmodern perspective it also is a reflexive interpretation of the ancient Maya record as a "text" that allows us today to speak to intellectual and personal issues. Like the ancient Maya – and with no greater wisdom – we struggle with these same, at times irreconcilable, aspects of the human condition: our material need for physical well-being, and our individual and collective need for identity. The decisions about these struggles, and the outcomes of those decisions, delineate the histories of all societies.

# 3     The exploration and archaeology of the Maya: a brief history

The history of Maya archaeology really begins with the first European contact and continues to develop unevenly into the systematic archaeology of the past century. Often popular presentations on Maya archaeology do not trace back to initial European contact but begin with a description of the famous explorations of the American writer John Lloyd Stephens and his gifted artist, Frederick Catherwood. In their expeditions from 1839 to 1842, Stephens explored the ruined sites of Yucatan and Central America, while Catherwood penned the romantic drawings (e.g. Fig. 3.1) that captivated the public's imagination. Their work defined, even until today, the popular image of the "lost jungle cities" of the Maya. Stephens's anecdotal tales of travel and lively speculations on the ruins, together with Catherwood's striking art, became bestsellers and created great interest in the ancient Maya civilization (Stephens 1841, 1843).

Yet such an astute entrepreneur and publicist as Stephens was not really carrying out risky explorations of an unknown world. Rather he was carefully following the less widely publicized reports of several centuries of investigation by Spanish and Creole priests, soldiers, bureaucrats, and scholars. Through a series of earlier publications, some of the discoveries of European and Colonial scholars had become known in England, providing Stephens, an experienced travel writer, with an itinerary for his romanticized literary journey.

## The Spanish and Colonial historians and explorers

The study of ancient Maya culture had begun four centuries before Stephens and Catherwood's expeditions. It began with the detailed recording of native history and beliefs by clerics in their vigorous efforts to conquer and convert the Colonial-period Maya to Catholicism. Meticulous recording by Colonial priests and inquisitors was a necessary step in their modification of native culture to absorb it into the Spanish empire and its Catholic regime. Despite these distinctly nonanthropological

Figure 3.1 Catherwood drawing of the site of Tulum, Quintana Roo, Mexico (from Stephens 1843)

motives, the descriptions left by those clerics were remarkable in their detail and their utility to later research.

The writings of Bishop Diego de Landa have been especially important in the history of Maya studies. Landa was a fanatical and sometimes brutal bishop and inquisitor. In fact, he wrote his *Relación de las Cosas de Yucatan* in 1566 while on trial for his abuses of power during his tenure as Bishop of Yucatan (Bernal 1977; Hammond 1983). His most infamous act was the burning of many of the Maya painted books, or codices. Yet Landa's writings were remarkable in their careful – at times, openly admiring – recording of Maya culture, including aspects of their oral history, beliefs, rituals, writing, calendar, and economy. His volume was rediscovered in a Madrid archive three centuries later. It would provide scholars of the late nineteenth and twentieth centuries with critical keys to understanding Maya civilization. Though flawed, his descriptions of the writing and the calendar systems of the Maya grasped enough correct detail to facilitate, even today, the decipherment of the ancient Maya inscribed stone monuments and their hieroglyphic texts.

Other Spanish priests and administrators visited the ruins in Yucatan and Central America, leaving their subjective, but not inaccurate, impressions in various reports and letters (Bernal 1977; Hammond 1983; Brunhouse 1973; Deuel 1967). Perhaps because they worked so closely with the native Americans, these Spanish priests and writers never doubted that the ruined cities had once been inhabited by the ancestors of the Maya. It was only later that fanciful speculations began about lost races or tribes of "mound builders" from Israel, Egypt, or from the imagined lost continents of Atlantis or Mu (Wauchope 1962, 1965). By contrast, Spanish officials such as Antonio de Ciudad Real and Diego Garcia de Palacio left remarkably accurate early descriptions of Maya sites like Uxmal and Copan. These reports set the stage for the beginning of a period of systematic investigations in the late eighteenth and nineteenth centuries by royal and later Colonial officials (Ciudad Real 1872; Bernasconi and Calderon 1946).

Early rumors about the magnificent ruins of Palenque led to the first of these expeditions in the late eighteenth century. Descriptions of the ruins found their way to the desks of the closest advisors to the King of Spain. They recommended royal expeditions that produced the reports that constituted the beginning of Maya archaeology. Some of these investigations were, at least in concept, truly "scientific." One, led by the royal Spanish architect Antonio Bernasconi (Bernasconi and Calderon 1946) had specific, explicit goals, collected materials, and recorded architectural plans at the site of Palenque, Chiapas. Captain Antonio del Rio directed another official exploration to Palenque (del Rio 1822) accompanied by his artist Ricardo Alméndariz, marking the first such pairing of explorers and artists that led to the tradition later followed by Stephens and Catherwood. A few years later, Captain Guillermo Dupaix, accompanied by his artist, Jose Castañeda, would travel across Mexico and Central America on a more extensive investigation ordered by the Spanish Crown. Yet another government expedition to Maya ruins was led by Juan Galindo, governor of the Petén province, who visited the great sites of Tikal, Copan, Yaxha, and others. The discoveries and drawings of these famous eighteenth-century royal projects (Fig. 3.2) were later published or reported in European journals or in somewhat more popular and widely distributed books like those of French traveler and self-designated archaeologist Jean-Fréderick Waldeck (Waldeck 1838). Lord Kingsborough of England published the nine-volume *Antiquities of Mexico* (Kingsborough 1831–48) with such high "production values" and lavish illustrations that it helped to drive that eccentric, but devoted, enthusiast into bankruptcy. The work and drawings of these early travelers and official expeditions eventually made their way to Stephens and Catherwood, giving them a guide for their own better financed and more widely published "explorations."

Figure 3.2 Castañeda's drawing of the palace and tower at Palenque, Chiapas, Mexico (from Kingsborough 1831–1848)

### The nineteenth-century explorers and archivists

While Stephens and Catherwood's work merely continued the tradition of the earlier reports and Spanish expeditions, there is no doubt that the publication of *Incidents of Travel in Central America, Chiapas, and Yucatan* in 1841 found a new, larger audience and gave fresh impetus to explore the ruins, art, and inscriptions of the Maya. The work became a bestseller, was reprinted many times and quickly followed by a bestselling sequel. Recall that this was also the period of the popularization of early archaeological exploration and decipherment in Egypt and Mesopotamia. The antiquarianism of the period, fueled by Stephens and Catherwood's books, led to an intensified interest in the Maya by the public and scholars alike.

Some of the writers of the period, such as Augustus le Plongeon and Désiré Charnay, were prone to imaginative digressions and drawn to wild speculations on the ancient Maya (Wauchope 1962, 1965; Brunhouse 1973; Deuel 1967). Le Plongeon, James Churchward, and many others attributed the origins and achievements of the Maya and other New World civilizations to lost tribes from the Old World or from sunken continents (Fig. 3.3). Unfortunately, such fantastic speculations are very effective in capturing public interest. Just as this epoch of popular antiquarian writings had launched modern scientific archaeology, it also seeded the development of the lunatic fringe of Maya archaeology (who even today

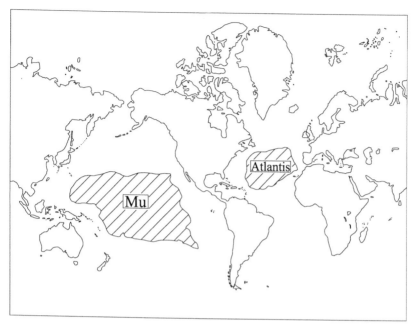

Figure 3.3 James Churchward map showing the lost continents of
Atlantis and Mu (redrafted by Matt O'Mansky after Churchward
1932)

besiege archaeologists with letters and emails on extraterrestrial influences, Atlantis, and the lost Semitic tribes!).

   Out of the nineteenth-century ferment of discovery, recording, popularization, and bizarre imaginings was born the beginnings of legitimate
scholarship and the academic tradition in archaeology. Two serious scholarly paths emerged – usually, but not always, followed by different individuals. One led to exploratory archaeology, while the other was the approach
of the archivist and textual scholar who meticulously studied the drawings of monuments and hieroglyphs, the few surviving bark paper books
or "codices" of the Maya (Fig. 3.4), and the conquest and early Colonial
accounts of clerics and conquistadors, such as Bishop Landa. This second
tradition led to the present professions of the Maya ethnohistorians who
study the Colonial documents and sixteenth-century oral traditions, the
epigraphers who decipher and interpret the ancient Maya hieroglyphic
texts and codices, and the art historians who struggle to decode the meanings of the complex and esoteric images that cover ancient Maya monuments, buildings, pottery vases, and other artifacts. These latter textual
scholars have been as critical to our reconstructions of these vanished

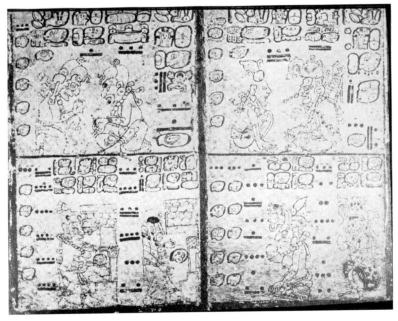

Figure 3.4 Page of the Dresden Codex (from Spinden 1924)

societies as the work of the teams of field archaeologists that unearth the ancient cities and survey their hinterlands.

An early and extraordinary figure of the archivist tradition was Abbe Brasseur de Bourbourg, a young French priest who traveled to Mexico and Central America, recorded highland Maya oral traditions, and returned to Europe, where he pored over the archives for documents and reports from the Conquest and Colonial periods (Brasseur de Bourbourg 1866). It was Brasseur who rediscovered in the archives of Madrid a copy of Bishop Landa's *Relación de las Cosas de Yucatan* and published it in 1864 (Tozzer 1941). The rediscovery of Landa's descriptions of Maya culture and folklore of the sixteenth century and his descriptions of Maya calendric and writing systems were quickly followed by breakthroughs in the interpretation of the hieroglyphs, calendric systems, and religion. These decipherments were made by a host of brilliant amateurs, such as the librarian Ernst Förstmann (1904, 1906), the newspaper proprietor Joseph Goodman (1897), Boston businessman C.P. Bowditch (1910), and others. Their natural gifts and tenacious interest led to the establishment of a basic understanding of the Maya dating system, writing, religion, legends, and oral history that structured and guided all of the subsequent field and archaeological explorations.

The British, German, and American archaeologists and explorers of the late nineteenth century followed in the footsteps of Antonio de Ciudad Real, Galindo, and Stephens. They did so, however, with a heightened understanding of what to look for and how to record what they found – a mission (today antiseptically referred to as a "research design") that was informed and invigorated by the breakthroughs of the less romantic archivists and epigraphers. With the unintended guidance of the long deceased inquisitor Landa and the insights of his nineteenth-century interpreters, the explorers returned to the field with a more sophisticated understanding of *what* they needed to discover and why. Through the fusion of the library studies and the more colorful field explorations, Maya archaeology had been born. Yet it should not be forgotten, as it often has been, that both the field and textual approaches built upon three centuries of even earlier explorations by Spanish and Latin American officials (Bernal 1977).

### The genesis of early scientific archaeology: 1880 to 1920

In the late nineteenth and early twentieth centuries these two traditions, the gentlemen explorers and the library scholars, rapidly developed in precision and purpose into the beginnings of the modern fields of Maya archaeology, ethnohistory, art history, and epigraphy. The explorers of the Maya world were consciously imitating the widely publicized breakthroughs in Old World archaeology. Artifacts and monuments from Egypt and the Near East had filled the museums of Europe, provoking intense public and scholarly interest in the ancient past. The decipherment of the Rosetta Stone opened up Egyptian history, exemplifying the importance of the careful recording or copying of inscriptions and monuments. While the publications of Stephens and Catherwood drew world attention to the Maya, it was the work of the archivists and early epigraphers, as well as the development of Old World archaeology, that set the new standards for the fieldwork of the late nineteenth and the early twentieth centuries.

The explorers Alfred Maudslay and Teobert Maler were determined to meet this new standard in their explorations in the 1880s and 1890s. They took careful field notes and precise measurements in recording their visits to the Maya sites and used casts, artwork, and, above all, pioneering photography to return with more precise images of Maya architecture, art, and inscriptions. Maudslay's publications are considered by some scholars to mark the first modern archaeology in the Maya world, although he

Figure 3.5 Maudslay in tower in Palenque palace (from Maudslay 1889, vol. 4: plate 26)

undertook little excavation beyond clearing of vegetation from temples and monuments for his photographs (Fig. 3.5).

German explorer and archaeologist Teobert Maler worked independently in the same period and even at some of the same sites as his British counterpart Maudslay. At Tikal, Seibal, Altar de Sacrificios, Coba, and other great centers Maler cleared, described, and photographed carved monuments and temples. Much of his work was published in the *Memoirs* of Harvard's Peabody Museum, one of the first of the institutional monograph series that later would form the core data sets of twentieth-century Maya archaeology (Maler 1901, 1903, 1908, 1911).

The Peabody Museum also sponsored and published the first "digging" expeditions by George Gordon in the exquisite temples and palaces of the Copan Valley of Honduras (1896; Gordon and Mason, 1925–43) and E.H. Thompson's excavations in Yucatan (1932). Thompson even used divers and dredged the famous Sacred Cenote at Chichen Itza (Fig. 3.6). From the murky depths of this deep, natural karstic sinkhole, his divers

Figure 3.6 Edward Thompson and divers at the sacred cenote of Chichen Itza

and pumps recovered ancient Maya treasures of jade, gold, wood, bone, and even rubber balls that had been hurled into the sacrificial well as offerings a thousand years earlier (Coggins and Shane 1984). Many of these treasures were smuggled out of Mexico by diplomatic pouch to Harvard's Peabody Museum, where they remain today. Obviously, neither the methodology nor the diplomacy of these scholars was of modern standards, but their efforts went beyond the survey, clearing, and recording to actual recovery of artifacts.

In the early twentieth century the decoding of the secrets of Maya calendrics, writing, and religion progressed with the help of these imperfect efforts at archaeology and, more importantly, the systematic recovery of monuments, codices, and Conquest-period records by explorers and archivists. By 1910 to 1915, scholars of the ancient Maya had come to understand many of the basic principles of the Maya numbering system, calendar, dates, deities, and religious concepts and were beginning to be able to historically relate the sites to each other through the Long Count dating system (described in Chapter 8).

As the archivists and epigraphers began to create a chronology for ancient Maya history, scholars like Raymond Merwin and Sylvanus Morley took the steps necessary to raise the quality of the

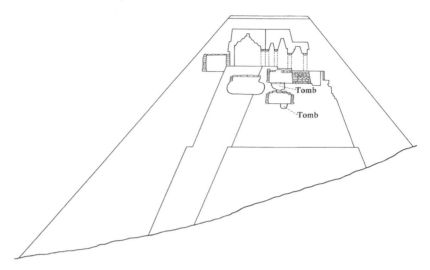

Figure 3.7 Profile of a temple at Holmul showing cache placement
and construction levels (redrawn by Luis F. Luin after Merwin and
Vaillant 1932)

explorer/recorder tradition of fieldwork to the level of true, scientific,
stratigraphic archaeology. At Holmul in Guatemala, Merwin carried out a
Peabody Museum-sponsored excavation of a buried sequence of temples,
one construction superimposed over another and each containing sealed
tombs and caches (Fig. 3.7). The innermost, earliest temples and tombs
had sealed within them early "monochrome" vessels of a single ceramic
style. The later, outer temples had tombs and caches containing more
complex and elaborate pots slipped and painted in many colors, especially black, orange, and red (Merwin and Vaillant 1932). Later such
sequences of ceramic styles, together with the monuments dated in the
Maya Long Count system, would define the periods of the Preclassic,
Early Classic, Late Classic, and Postclassic. At other sites scholars also
began to excavate, including Edgar Hewett at the site of Quirigua (1912,
1916) and others at Copan and in Belize.

Meanwhile, a young, devoted North American Mayanist, Sylvanus
G. Morley, further transformed the gentleman-explorer tradition of
Stephens and Maudslay into a relentless, systematic effort carefully to
compile photographs and drawings of every possible Maya monument
and their hieroglyphic texts in his *Inscriptions of the Petén* (Brunhouse
1971, 1973). His many published volumes provided more detailed hieroglyphic texts that would lead to better decipherments, including some of
his own (e.g. Morley 1915, 1920, 1937–38). His work also recorded for

posterity the texts of monuments that have long since been damaged or destroyed.

## Modern multidisciplinary archaeology begins

Sylvanus Morley's greatest contribution to Maya studies may have been his instigation of the first great team projects in the 1920s and 1930s (Brunhouse 1971). These large-scale projects, first sponsored by the Carnegie Institution of Washington, pulled together the tradition of the explorers, and that of the museum scholars who studied the ethnohistorical accounts and ancient Maya codices and texts. The Carnegie project teams also included experts on flora and fauna, and ethnographers. Studies by the ethnographers of the modern descendants of the Maya sought surviving beliefs, cultural practices, and lifeways that might be used to elucidate the ancient evidence.

Multidisciplinary modern archaeology had been born, and projects like the Carnegie Institution explorations to Chichen Itza, Copan, and Uaxactun combined outstanding scholars from different disciplines with artists, photographers, and workmen to survey, map, excavate, record, and interpret the ancient sites (Willey and Sabloff 1974; Sabloff 1990). They explored not only the elite temples, palaces, tombs, and monuments, but also the surrounding residences of craftspeople and farmers. The Carnegie Uaxactun Project team members, all later renowned leaders in the field, began a series of sophisticated studies and debates on ancient Maya agriculture, population sizes, and urbanism. While Maya archaeology has a reputation (generally well deserved) for an overemphasis on elite culture, monuments, tombs, and museum artifacts, it should also be noted that even these earliest Carnegie multidisciplinary projects paid great attention to counts of house mounds (e.g. Ricketson and Ricketson 1937), to commoner house forms (Wauchope 1934, 1938), and even to the ecological enigma of how the ancient Maya sustained such large populations in the fragile rain forest (Lundell 1933, 1938). Indeed the healthy disagreements between the scholars on these first early great projects covered most of the issues that still bedevil and inspire archaeological researches and debates today – including questions of Maya origins, ecology, demography, political form, and the enigma of the so-called ninth-century "collapse" of Classic Maya civilization in the southern lowlands.

Thus by the 1920s and 1930s most of the broad outlines of Maya archaeology were already in place. The nineteenth- and early twentieth-century explorations had compiled a vast corpus of hieroglyphic texts, and scholars had already deciphered the Long Count dating system and most of the other features of Maya calendrics and astronomy. Broad aspects of ancient Maya religion, mythology, and ritual also had been reconstructed by studies of the Conquest- and Colonial- period chronicles and the oral literature of the sixteenth-century Maya groups of the southern highlands and Yucatan (e.g. Thompson 1970). The different versions of the *Popol Vuh*, *Chilam Balam*, and other Maya oral histories recorded by the Colonial clerics and later scholars described the calendric and writing systems with sufficient accuracy as to facilitate later decipherments (Tozzer 1941; Roys 1949, 1965b, 1967). This ethnohistory also helped with the decipherment of dates on the monuments recorded in the photographs and drawings of Maudslay, Maler, Morley, and others. By the era of the great Carnegie projects of the 1920s and 1930s, the Maya stone monuments could give precise dates for the ancient cities. Meanwhile, also with the help of ethnohistorical and ethnographic evidence, art historians were able to begin interpreting the imagery of the exquisite sculptures, carved jades, and painted vessels that were being recovered from caches and tombs of the Maya nobles and kings (e.g. Spinden 1913).

In the 1930s, 1940s, and 1950s, large-scale Carnegie Institution projects added to the ethnohistorical and textual evidence with their extensive surveys and excavations in all corners of the Maya world. Major multidisciplinary large-scale projects were carried out during this period at Uaxactun in the heart of the Petén rain forest (Smith 1937), at Chichen Itza in northern Yucatan (Ruppert 1931, 1935, 1943), at Copan in Honduras in the far southeastern frontier of the Maya world (Stromsvik 1942, 1952; Longyear 1952), and at Kaminaljuyu, a mile above the rain forest in the cool volcanic highlands of southern Guatemala, near modern Guatemala City (Kidder, Jennings, and Shook 1946). Other large-scale projects and regional surveys were sponsored by the University of Pennsylvania and Tulane University, institutions that remain centers of Maya studies today. Maps of sites, excavations of tombs and houses, counts of house mounds, and recovery of new monuments and artifacts led to an explosion in our knowledge of the material culture and sequence of monuments, ceramic styles, and public architecture that marked the rise, florescence, and decline of the great Maya centers (Willey and Sabloff 1974; Sabloff 1990).

At sites like Uaxactun and Holmul, the basic lowland Maya ceramic sequence was established: simple Preclassic monochrome "Mamom" and "Chicanel" pottery from 1000 BC to AD 300, followed by the polychrome painted plates and vases of the AD 300 to 900 Classic period, followed by diverse Postclassic wares after the decline of many Classic Maya centers in the Petén itself. Methodological approaches were standardized for the excavation of architecture and the classification and interpretation of the thousands of potsherds and artifacts recovered. Early discussion of economic and demographic issues began, based on the regional surveys and house mound counts around centers and also on comparative studies of modern Maya agriculture.

## Traditional views of ancient Maya civilization

Together, this evidence began to allow scholars to present a synthetic vision of ancient Maya civilization. This picture, while it drew from a wide range of sources, was still flawed by the biases of the tradition of "gentlemen scholars" that had dominated the early field explorations and the archival scholarship. Such an elitist perspective was further reinforced by the seductive complexity and beauty of Maya art, iconography, and hieroglyphic inscriptions. Early scholars could not resist (as we still cannot today) an overemphasis on the elegant and exotic imagery of the Maya nobles, kings, and deities as presented on their carved stone monuments, palaces, bas-relief panels, murals, and incised jade and bone treasures. The museum sponsorship of these expeditions and the desire for exhibition pieces also led to a bias in discussion towards the high culture and ideology of the Maya kings and their courts. In a sense, this seduction of Maya scholarship is a testament to the effectiveness of ancient Maya art and public monuments, whose original function (consciously or unconsciously) was to legitimate the power of the elites and aggrandize the achievements of the rulers.

Since the first Carnegie projects at Chichen Itza, and especially after the Uaxactun project, Mayanists attempted to broaden their research and sampling to emphasize the demography, economics, and ecology of this ancient society. Yet in the textbooks and synthetic articles of the late 1940s through the 1960s, an idealized view of ancient Maya civilization came to be accepted. The picture was drawn from an incomplete view of Maya elite culture, as found in temples, palaces, and only partially deciphered monuments, combined with a stereotype of modern Maya "peasant" society and economy based on ethnography and the Colonial historic record. Some of the results of the field studies then available on ancient Maya non-elite populations already seemed to contradict aspects of this traditional perspective on ancient Maya agriculture and commoner settlements (Ricketson and Ricketson 1937; Lundell 1933, 1938). Yet such hints were ignored in favor of reconstructions based more heavily on somewhat stereotyping ("essentializing") ethnographies of the lifeways of modern Maya villagers (Redfield and Rojas 1934; cf. Castañeda 1996).

This traditional view of ancient Maya culture was best described and popularized by Sir J. Eric S. Thompson, a dominant figure in

Maya archaeology for decades. A leading archaeologist, ethnohistorian, and epigrapher, Thompson's elegantly written syntheses presented the ancient Maya as the most civilized of peoples (J.E.S. Thompson 1966, 1970). Site epicenters with their massive acropoli of concentrated temples and public buildings were believed to be ceremonial centers where priests presided over periodic rituals and where the peasantry congregated from small villages scattered across the countryside. Based on comparison to modern Maya agriculture, Thompson believed that this peasantry subsisted almost exclusively on "slash-and-burn" jungle farming (also called swidden or *rosa*) in which forest plots were cut, dried, and burned. This system allows only a few years of productive farming of maize, beans, and squash before soil exhaustion requires farmers to move to a new plot of jungle. This swidden system would explain, indeed it would require, the perceived dispersed population at ancient lowland Maya sites (J.E.S. Thompson 1971; U. Cowgill 1961). The leadership of these dispersed farming societies was believed to be purely theocratic in nature, with public life focused on ceremonial centers dedicated to the worship of great cycles of time and the astronomical bodies that marked them (J.E.S. Thompson 1966).

Such a perspective arose from the fact that the hieroglyphs of the Maya writing system that had been deciphered at that time were those glyphs dealing with Maya calendrics and astronomy. Their measurements and conceptions of time were based on the cycles of the sun, the moon, Venus, and other astronomical bodies. Only later would decipherments reveal that these lengthy texts of dates and calendric inscriptions were reference points for descriptions contained in the undeciphered portions of the texts. These detailed historical events, including the coronations, marriages, alliances, births, and deaths of kings. Similarly, the view of the Maya centers as sparsely occupied loci for periodic rituals reflected, to a large degree, the paucity of systematic excavation and survey of the suburbs and countryside beyond the great acropoli. Viewed with postmodern cynicism, we may also suggest that this view of the Maya as a peaceful, highly civilized society dominated by a priestly scientific elite may be a direct, albeit unconscious, reflection of the social milieu of early Maya studies with its gentlemen scholars and explorers sponsored by the best museums of Europe and the North American Ivy League.

In fairness, it should be noted that there was never a monolithic consensus on the nature of ancient Maya society, and there were both field studies and art historical interpretations that presented variations from Thompson's views. We should also acknowledge (after several decades of pendulum swings in positions) that there was some basis, however exaggerated, for aspects of the traditional model popularized by Thompson.

Today, hieroglyphic breakthroughs and decades of settlement pattern and ecological studies have detailed the complex nature of Classic Maya society, with its densely populated cities, extensive warfare, and rulers who were as concerned with their own earthly ambitions as with the cycles of time and the propitiation of the deities. Still, as detailed below, Maya cities *were* more dispersed than the urban formations of highland Mesoamerican cities and most other ancient states. Maya states were *not* theocracies in any sense, but many scholars now believe that these polities were, indeed, very heavily dependent on religion, ritual, and monumental propaganda as "ideological legitimation" to bolster their rulers' rather insecure hold on power. The periodic mass pageants and rituals in the temples and great plazas of the Maya sites were a major source of political authority, and the calendric cycles of time were associated with many of these empowering events.

In some ways, then, Thompson's model of the Classic Maya as a non-urban theocratic society dominated by religion had stereotyped and hyperbolized a few selected features of this ancient civilization. Yet it is certain that the theocratic ceremonial centers idealized by J.E.S. Thompson and others were also a creation of systematic gaps in the archaeological data and hieroglyphic decipherments, enhanced by the elitist worldview of the early scholars themselves.

### Revisions and breakthroughs: 1955 to 1990

The unraveling of the traditional theocratic "vacant center" model of Maya society began in the late 1950s and 1960s as the inevitable result of changes in each of the two traditions of Maya scholarship: new field strategies by the archeologists, and new insights by the students of Maya art and writing into the decipherments and content of the Classic-period texts and images.

In the textual studies of the late 1950s and early 1960s, scholars like Heinrich Berlin (1958, 1959) and Tatiana Proskouriakoff (1960, 1961, 1963, 1964) began to make breakthroughs in decipherment. These moved our understanding of the Maya hieroglyphics beyond the level of the previous century, when scholars could read only ancient Maya dates, calendrics, and astronomical information (e.g. J.E.S. Thompson 1950). These new developments proved that the ancient Maya monumental texts were not merely concerned with astronomy and religion, but rather were self-aggrandizing records by ancient kings and their descendants of their wars, marriages, alliances, and deaths (see Chapter 9).

At the same time the Russian linguist Yuri Knorozov had begun to discover that Maya hieroglyphs were not purely "picture writing" but had

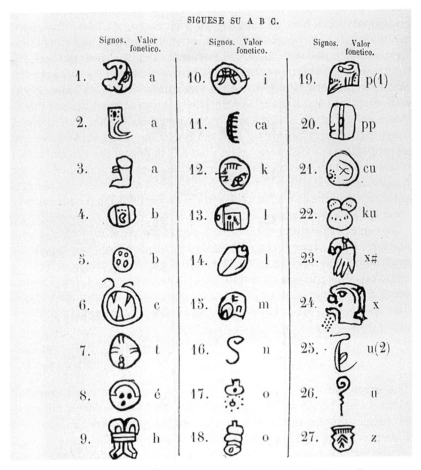

Figure 3.8 Landa's recording of a "Mayan alphabet" (actually a syllabary) (from Landa 1864)

a phonetic component. Using Landa's flawed recording of a Conquest-period Maya "alphabet" (Fig. 3.8), Knorozov (1958, 1967) decoded the ancient Maya system of combining syllabic signs to produce phonetic words [see Box 1]. Subsequently, American scholars such as David Kelley, Floyd Lounsbury, Linda Schele, and David Stuart were able to decode many such syllabic glyphs, which when combined with nonphonetic "logographic" symbols (in which a sign stands for a whole word or a concept) together formed the Maya texts (e.g. Kelley 1962, 1976; M. Coe 1992; Bricker 1986; Schele 1982; Stuart 1987). Then newly deciphered

Classic-period Maya texts on monuments, ceramic vases, and artifacts were found to record not only ancient Maya religion, astronomy, and cosmology, but also the rulers' earthly political activities, rituals, and life histories. The picture revealed was one of "holy lords" who lived in a cosmologically defined universe, but who also carried out the activities and exercised the powers of true kings (e.g. Schele and Miller 1986; Schele and Freidel 1990; Culbert 1991).

---

## Box 1

### The decipherment of calendric and numeric glyphs

At the end of the nineteenth century (e.g. Förstermann 1906; Goodman 1889, 1905; Bowditch 1901, 1910), the first glyphs deciphered were those which represented number and units of time (days, months, years, twenty-year periods, etc.) in the Maya solar, lunar, and Venus calendars, as well as their ritual 260-day year (see Chapter 8 and Figs. 8.4, 8.11, 8.12). The periodicity and patterning of these symbols facilitated their early decipherment and the dates on monuments allowed archaeologists to establish a detailed chronology for the Classic period. Their early decipherment, unfortunately, also misled scholars into the belief that all Maya inscriptions concerned only calendrics, astronomy, and ritual.

### The initial decipherment of emblem glyphs and historic texts

A major series of breakthroughs in the 1950's and early 1960's by Tatiana Proskouriakoff (1960), Heinrich Berlin (1958), and others identified glyphs that seemed to name Maya kingdoms and their rulers and that specified dates for the ruler's birth, accession to the throne, death, and so on (see Chapter 9 and Figs. 9.1, 9.2, 9.3). These elements were still *phonetically* unreadable, but nonetheless could be used to begin to reconstruct the Classic period histories of major Maya centers.

### The phonetic breakthroughs

Perhaps the most critical breakthroughs occurred in the last forty years, beginning with the work of Russian linguist Yuri Knorozov (e.g. 1958, 1967), later refined by Floyd Lounsbury (e.g. 1984, 1989), David

Kelley (e.g. 1962, 1976), Linda Schele (e.g. 1980), David Stuart (e.g. 1984, 1995), and others. Knorozov first realized that the so-called Maya alphabet recorded by Bishop Landa was in fact a flawed and partial "syllabary" with each symbol representing a syllable of the form "CV" or Consonant-Vowel. These glyphs could then be combined as CV- C(V), with the last vowel usually dropped to form phonetic stem words in the Maya language (Fig. 3.9). Using this key and studying modern and Colonial Mayan languages, scholars have gradually been able to decipher over 70 to 80 percent of the ancient Maya glyphs, allowing readings of many Classic period historical texts.

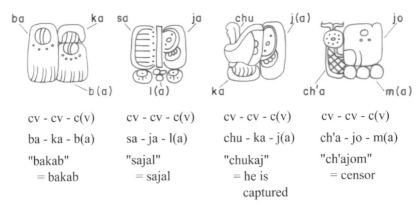

| cv - cv - c(v) | cv - cv - c(v) | cv - cv - c(v) | cv - cv - c(v) |
|---|---|---|---|
| ba - ka - b(a) | sa - ja - l(a) | chu - ka - j(a) | ch'a - jo - m(a) |
| "bakab" | "sajal" | "chukaj" | "ch'ajom" |
| = bakab | = sajal | = he is captured | = censor |

Figure 3.9 Glyphs phonetically readable in ancient Maya using CV-CV or CV-C(V) syllabic combinations (note: "bakab" and "sajal" are office titles – see Chapter 9)

Meanwhile, in archaeology a revolution in field approaches had led to an even more dramatic transformation of Maya studies and a radically different view of ancient Maya society, ecology, history, and prehistory. The introduction by Gordon R. Willey of formal regional settlement pattern studies to Maya field work in the 1950s and 1960s led inevitably to the revision of our views of ancient Maya demography, population distribution, and ecological adaptations. First developed by Willey in Peru (Willey 1953), settlement pattern archaeology begins all aspects of investigation with the survey and mapping of the sites of different sizes in a region, and then the mapping of structures, including low house mounds, within a site. Then, chronological control is established through excavation and study of sites and structures of apparently different scales or types. Next, patterns of center and residence location in a given period are plotted and compared to ecological features, soil types, defensibility, or other factors allowing a more systematic and holistic perspective on human/land relationships in a given period. Finally, changes between periods in site size, number, scale, distribution, spacing, and relation to the environment can be identified and interpreted in terms of internal events, invasions, change in economic or ecological strategies, or other social processes in the ancient past (Willey 1953; Willey *et al.* 1965; Sabloff 1990).

While the introduction of settlement pattern studies, with their implicit ecological rationale, had a great effect on archaeology in many regions, it was particularly transformative in Maya fieldwork. It forced archaeologists out of the exquisite architecture of the epicenters and obliged them to develop techniques of surveying in the dense vegetation of the rain forests that cover most of the Maya world. Mayanists have often been criticized for their field techniques by archaeologists who work in the sparsely vegetated, arid regions of Mexico or in the government-owned deserts of the US southwest where settlement survey, aerial reconnaissance, and sampling strategies are comparatively easy to apply. Willey's settlement pattern approach forced Mayanists to confront the considerably greater challenges of regional studies in the dense rain forests and swamps of Guatemala, Belize, and Yucatan.

Settlement research provided a central axis for a new generation of multidisciplinary team projects that built upon the tradition begun by Morley and the Carnegie projects several decades earlier (Sabloff 1990). In moving outside the ceremonial centers with their dated stone monuments, the archaeologists had to develop better methods of dating the low earth and stone platforms of the ancient Maya villages and smaller centers. This challenge led Maya archaeologists to systematize and standardize the classification and comparison of non-elite ceramics and artifacts using systems like the formal "type-variety" scheme and the statistical analysis of ceramic style traits and type distributions (Willey and Phillips 1958; Willey *et al.* 1967; Smith and Gifford 1965).

Initially, the multidisciplinary projects directed by Willey with his settlement pattern strategy did not seem to contradict the traditional ceremonial center model. Indeed, his Belize River Valley project and related surveys by William Bullard in the northeastern Petén concluded that dispersed populations were serviced for their religious needs by a hierarchy of large, medium, and small ceremonial centers for periodic gatherings for rituals (Bullard 1960; Willey and Bullard 1965). Still, the outcome of this settlement survey strategy in the Maya area was inevitable. Willey's subsequent Peabody Museum projects at Altar de Sacrificios and Seibal in the southwestern Petén (Willey 1973, 1975) and a large-scale Tulane University project at the sprawling site of Dzibilchaltun

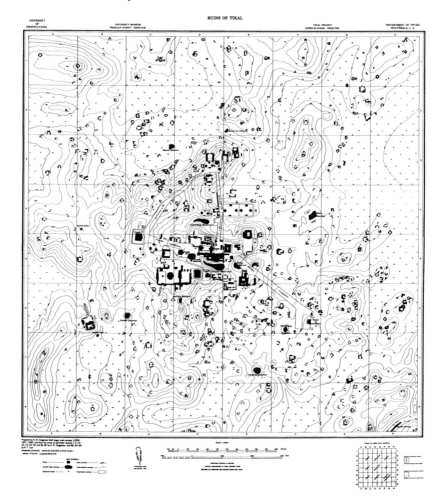

Figure 3.10 Map of settlement in greater Tikal

in far northern Yucatan (Andrews IV 1965), further refined field techniques and revealed greater densities of house platforms near centers and
evidence of the considerable complexity at these large sites.

The deathblow to the vacant ceremonial center model was delivered by
the Tikal project of the University of Pennsylvania. There Edwin Shook,
William Coe, and a virtual army of archaeologists, specialists, and workmen undertook regional survey, sampling, and major excavations of all
sections of this vast site of over sixteen square kilometers (Fig. 3.10)
(Shook *et al.* 1958; W. Coe 1962, 1965a, 1965b, 1968). Their findings

proved, once and for all, that Maya centers could, and often did, have concentrated commoner populations and a fully resident large population of elites, officials, priests, and craftspersons, organized in a political and economic system far more complex than previously believed. Furthermore, the counts of the low platforms of house mounds that supported the commoners' perishable huts were so dense around Tikal as to indicate an urban center with a population of over 50,000 – quite sizable for any preindustrial city (Haviland 1970). In turn, these demographic estimates cast serious doubt on the notion that Maya populations were primarily, if not exclusively, supported by slash-and-burn maize agriculture, which today can only sustain small and scattered Maya populations.

These various settlement survey projects then stimulated the last three decades of researches on Maya agriculture and ecology in our efforts to explain how the Maya had sustained such large populations (Harrison and Turner 1978; Puleston 1974; Sabloff 1990). As discussed in Chapter 6, these researches revealed a highly complex picture of Maya agriculture, which contradicted the simple slash-and-burn regime proposed by earlier archaeologists. The first generation of scholars who had rejected the traditional model of small, scattered populations ruled by theocracies had expected to find instead state-managed intensive agricultural systems (R.E.W. Adams 1980; Turner and Harrison 1978). Such state-controlled systems would explain the high populations of the ancient Maya cities of the Petén and would also provide a functionalist rationale for the emergence of Maya elites and state institutions. As discussed in Chapter 6, these expectations were *not* fully met, leaving us still somewhat puzzled about the economic role of the ruling class in ancient Maya society.

The new findings of the settlement surveys of the 1950s, 1960s, and 1970s also led us to look more closely at the internal organization of these cities and their trade and political relations with each other and with their adjacent highland and coastal neighbors. These issues were explored through new techniques, such as neutron activation and other compositional analyses that can suggest original clay sources of traded vessels and the volcanic sources of hard stones like obsidian (Sabloff 1975; Bishop 1980). The exploration of Maya economics also began to use technological analyses and statistical interpretations to look at local and regional manufacture and exchange of ceramics, chert, worked bone, and other artifacts (e.g. Hester and Shafer 1984; P. Rice 1984; Ball 1983, 1993b). Though still incomplete, we now have some understandings of Classic Maya economy and trade (see Chapter 7).

The settlement surveys at Tikal and other sites had challenged all of the demographic, political, economic, and ecological parameters of the previous half-century of thinking on Classic Maya society (W. Coe 1965a;

Puleston 1974; Haviland 1970). Other field projects made unexpected discoveries simply by virtue of the great increase in the size and breadth of our sample of ancient Maya civilization. New evidence was found bearing on the Preclassic beginnings of Maya civilization, foreign contacts and influences, fortifications and warfare, and the nature of the decline of many Classic Maya city-states during the ninth century. The major excavation and settlement survey projects in the 1960s, 1970s, and 1980s provided us with a broader view of the variations in time and space of ancient Maya civilization. Such investigations included projects in the far western Petén at Palenque, at the Pasión River sites of Altar de Sacrificios and Seibal, and work by many projects in the northern Yucatan at Dzibilchaltun, Mayapan, Becan, Sayil, Komchen, Cozumel, Coba, and elsewhere (Willey 1981, 1982, 1987; Sabloff 1990; Fash 1994). A host of excavation and survey projects virtually invaded Belize with major digs and regional surveys at Cuello, Lubaantun, Altun Ha, Lamanai, Nohmul, and hundreds of other sites (Hammond 1981; Adams and Hammond 1981). These and other projects revealed the great variability of ancient Maya civilization from region to region, as well as its long span of survival and change. We now know that complex states were present during the Preclassic period, long before the Classic-period Maya florescence, and that other forms of states continued into the Postclassic after the southern lowland decline. The new early sites were different in form and probable nature from what we had held to be the Classic-period "norms" of Maya centers in the lowlands.

It is now much more difficult to describe succinctly the ancient Maya civilization than it was in J. Eric S. Thompson's time (and it is even more difficult to be as elegant in our descriptions!). The great regional variability and temporal dynamism of Maya political and economic forms defy simple and concise description. Indeed, many of the disagreements in modern Maya archaeology today, touched upon in the following chapters, are really caused by archaeologists arguing from differing regional or temporal segments of Maya civilization – like the tale of the three blind men and the elephant!

# 4  Obscure beginnings and the Preclassic florescence

In the study of any civilization, a major set of issues in archaeology and social theory concerns initial development, the "rise of civilization" – or, more properly, the development of politically and economically complex society. For the ancient Maya there have been a large number of theories on and interpretations of the "causes" of the development of Maya states. The topic is of special interest because of the rain forest environment in which the Classic Maya states arose. The problem has not been a shortage of theories, but rather the scattered, incomplete, and contradictory nature of the archaeological evidence. In the past two decades, exciting finds have pushed back by six or seven centuries the dating of the rise of great Maya ceremonial centers, but we have little evidence on the developments that led to these early centers. At this moment in the history of Maya archaeology, new discoveries have toppled traditional views and overturned even more recent interpretations on the beginnings of Maya civilization. Yet, we do not have sufficient information to construct new models. Here we can only review the current state of the evidence and the prospects and possibilities for future research. Conclusions on processes or even chronology are, at this point, pure speculation.

### New World antecedents: before 12,000 to 3000 BC

Despite the many fanciful theories mentioned in Chapter 3 that traced the ancient Maya to Atlantis, Mu, or the lost tribes of Israel, archaeologists are guided by the overwhelming evidence from archaeology, linguistics, and physical anthropology indicating that the ancestors of all New World peoples, including the Maya, migrated from Asia as bands of nomadic gatherers and hunters. We debate whether those migrations across what is now the Bering Strait occurred at about 12,000 BC, 40,000 BC, or even earlier (e.g. Lanning 1970; Lynch 1990, 1991; Taylor and Meighan 1978).

In any case, the first archaeological evidences in eastern Mesoamerica are scattered spearheads (Fig. 4.1) left by bands of Paleo-Indian hunters and gatherers over 10,000 years ago (M. Coe 1960). From other

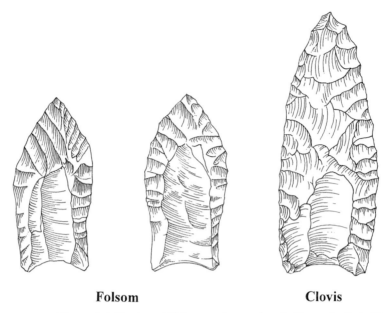

**Folsom**                    **Clovis**

Figure 4.1 Clovis and Folsom style spearheads (drawn by Luis F. Luin)

regions of the New World we know that such groups, moving in small nomadic bands, hunted bison, horse, and other megafauna with stone-tipped spears and later spear-throwers (Lynch 1978, 1990). The core subsistence of these "big game hunters," as they have been traditionally known, was, in fact, the systematic collecting of wild plants and the trapping of small game. Mastodon or bison kills leave the most dramatic remains and probably provided the best fireside stories in Paleolithic times, but the wider range of daily gathering, fishing, and trapping techniques provided most of their food (Tankersley 1998). Such broad-based subsistence methods could be modified, developed, and expanded in response to seasonal shifts, different environments, and long-term environmental change.

It was this collecting and small game hunting subsystem of the Stone Age technologies of the Paleo-Indians that was able to survive the great climatic changes of 11,000 to 7000 BC. These food-collecting strategies became the core of a new series of ecological adaptations sometimes referred to as the "Archaic." In a number of areas in Mexico (Fig. 4.2), including the Tehuacan Valley, the Valley of Oaxaca, and the northern Mexican state of Tamaulipas, drier conditions have allowed preservation of a full range of evidence on the gradual transition from the Paleo-Indian bands to the Archaic gathering societies, and, later, to the introduction of

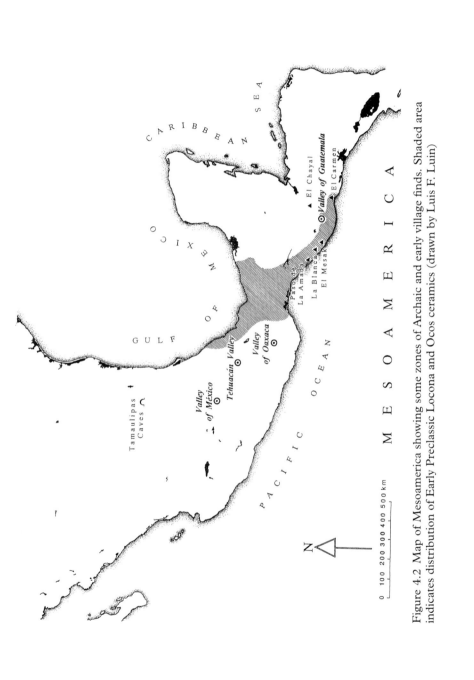

Figure 4.2 Map of Mesoamerica showing some zones of Archaic and early village finds. Shaded area indicates distribution of Early Preclassic Locona and Ocos ceramics (drawn by Luis F. Luin)

some cultigens and the beginnings of New World agriculture (MacNeish 1964; Stark 1981).

In the Maya lowland area the rain forest environment creates problems of preservation as well as difficulties for survey and discovery of the lithic scatters and small camps that would be characteristic of this period. Archaeological remains recovered from Belize and caves in Chiapas demonstrate the presence of Paleo-Indian and Archaic groups in the Maya hills, lowlands, rain forest, and coast (MacNeish, Wilkerson, and Nelken-Turner 1980). Yet the evidence is too meager to provide a clear picture of the transition from the Paleo-Indian bands to Archaic collecting and hunting societies, and, finally, to settled agricultural villages. We must rely primarily on archaeology in the Mexican highlands and the Pacific and Gulf coasts for our understanding of these earlier periods. Indeed, scholars debate whether such a full transition from hunting and gathering to settled farming villages occurred in the Maya lowland area, or if agriculture and village life spread into the lowlands from elsewhere (R.E.W. Adams 1977; Andrews V and Hammond 1990; Lowe 1977, 1978).

## The beginning of village life, ceramics, and complex societies: 3000 to 1300 BC

By 3000 to 2000 BC, settled agricultural villages growing maize, beans, squash, chiles, gourds, and other cultigens are found in several areas of Mesoamerica. In eastern Mesoamerica, bordering the Maya highlands and lowlands, the best evidence for such villages comes from the Pacific and Gulf coasts of Mexico, Guatemala, and El Salvador, where considerable research has been completed (Lowe 1978; Blake *et al.* 1995). There the evidence shows that Archaic cultures combined collecting and hunting with extensive exploitation of the fish, shellfish, and birds of the coast and estuaries. Probable house platforms have been found in association with extensive shell middens at some sites (Voorhies 1976; Stark and Voorhies 1978). The reliance on this broad spectrum of resources may have allowed some communities to become permanent or semipermanent villages even before heavy reliance on farming.

Between 2000 and 1300 BC these coastal villages and others farther inland began to rely more heavily on agriculture and also grew in size and perhaps economic complexity (Coe and Flannery 1967; Grove 1981; Lowe 1978). During this period there was also a rapid growth in population and spread of agricultural villages and related technologies across all of eastern Mesoamerica. The mechanisms and causes of this are unclear. An improvement in maize hybrids and other cultigens may have led to more reliance on agriculture, as well as greater sedentism and population increase (Stark 1981). Together with these changes there was an increase in the economic and political complexity of societies in many regions of eastern Mesoamerica, leading to the rise of chiefdoms, if not early states, in some zones of Mesoamerica possibly by as early as 1300 BC. [See Box 2 for discussion of the typologies and rationales for assessing relative political complexity.]

---

## Box 2    Traditional typologies of "level" of political complexity in human societies

Traditionally archaeologists and anthropologists sought to classify ancient or modern societies in order to facilitate comparison and discussion. The most popular traditional typologies have been those proposed by Morton Fried (1967), based on the degree of stratification, i.e. social inequality, in societies, and by Elman Service (1975), based on the degree of political and economic integration of societies.

### Service: integration typology

*Bands:* Small, loosely integrated groups of hunters and gatherers that possess a common territory in which they move nomadically. They have few differences in wealth or status and are characterized by reciprocal economic relations. Integration is through kinship and marriage.

*Tribes:* Larger societies, often with agricultural and/or pastoral economies, living in permanent (sedentary) locations. Tribes are often multi-settlement societies integrated by theoretical descent groups and voluntary association organizations (for example, warrior clubs, religious cults, fraternal organizations, etc.).

*Chiefdoms:* Often larger societies in which social integration is facilitated by the existence of prestigious leaders who direct warfare and storage or redistribution of food. Individuals often are ranked in their status according to their degree of kinship relation to the chief. Chiefdoms sometimes have ceremonial centers as the focus of religious activities, redistribution, and social integration.

*States:* Societies with highly integrated, organized, and centralized leadership with a governing body or rulers. The power of the ruler is backed by coercive force, law, and/or religious sanctions.

### Fried: stratification typology

*Egalitarian societies:* Simple societies with as many positions of status as there are people to fill them. Wealth, status, and power are acquired, not inherited. There are relatively small differences in wealth, and economic relations are reciprocal in structure.

*Ranked societies:* Societies in which there are fewer positions of status than individuals to fill them. In some cases there are a fixed number of offices, *but* the competition to fill them is not entirely hereditary.

Economic differences are somewhat restricted by expectations of redistribution by the societies' leaders.

*Stratified societies:* Societies in which positions of status are fixed and largely hereditary. A class structure and coercive force maintain these differences.

*[The state]:* A special function institution of some stratified societies that legitimizes stratification through governing bodies, laws, and police structures to maintain internal order and control class conflict.

### Current debate on evolutionary typologies

More recent discussion in archaeology has been highly critical of such universally applied typologies, since they ignore many characteristics, mask internal variability in societies, and, arguably, impose an ethnocentric, evolutionary scheme. Others argue that these designations are useful in practice, if only as loose, broad, comparative designations.

Alternative approaches include multivariate assessments of societies based on many different variables, including degree of inequality, heterogeneity, centralization, and other traits (e.g. Montmollin 1989; McGuire 1983). Many contemporary "postprocessual" theorists reject linear evolutionary typologies of any kind as stereotyping and potentially racist generalizations that pigeonhole societies into a Western materialist presumed hierarchy of development (see for example Shanks and Tilley 1987, 1989; Giddens 1981; Hodder 1986).

Unfortunately (or fortunately?), in the case of the rise of Maya civilization, such typological, terminological, and epistemological debates seldom arise; the data on the early development of lowland Maya civilization is currently so poor that it virtually defies synthesis and interpretation. The earliest Preclassic societies in the Maya lowlands are identified primarily by ceramic deposits. The first sites with public architecture (e.g. Nakbe and Cerros) were left by societies that were already at a fairly high level of complexity (however that might be designated). Here terms such as bands, chiefdoms, or states are used as only very broad, convenient descriptive terms.

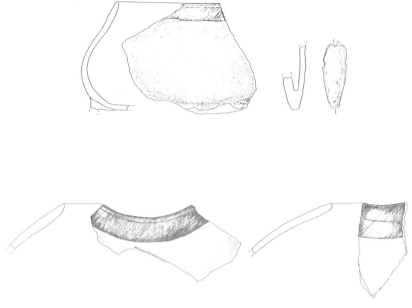

Figure 4.3 Some Locona (above) and Ocos (below) phase ceramics (drawn by Luis F. Luin)

Shortly after 2000 BC (Fig. 2.3) on the Pacific coast of Chiapas and El Salvador, one change in material technology is of particular utility to archaeologists for tracing culture change and culture contact: the development of ceramics (Fig. 4.3). The first tiny, thin-walled ceramics of the Barra period have been convincingly argued to be craft items, an artistic miniature supplement to the more practical, less fragile gourd vessels (Clark and Blake 1989, 1994). The complex forms and elaborate incised and carved designs on these ceramics of the Barra and subsequent Locona phase led to theories that the sophistication of this first pottery indicated an introduction from elsewhere, possibly South America (e.g. Lowe 1975; Lathrap 1977, 1982). It seems more likely that the sudden appearance and complexity of these earliest ceramics of eastern Mesoamerica were due to the adoption of forms and complex designs from an older tradition of carved gourd vessels (Demarest 1989b; Clark and Blake 1994).

Gradually, in the subsequent Locona and Ocos phases (*circa* 1500 to 1100 BC), these ceramic forms became larger, heavier, and more popular (Fig. 4.3) as Early Preclassic-period populations realized the advantages in size and durability of ceramics as a new means of cooking and storage.

Increased sedentism due to a heavier reliance on agriculture and the needs of farming for grain storage probably also contributed to the increased popularity and distribution of pottery – first on the coasts and later into the highland and lowland regions of eastern Mesoamerica (see Locono/Ocos distribution, Fig. 4.2).

While in itself the development and distribution of ceramic styles is not of central importance to the culture and survival of any group, it is an important diagnostic of changes in many other aspects of society – such as increased sedentism, reliance on agriculture, and storage. From an archaeological perspective, pottery provides a critical new source of direct or indirect evidence on chronology, cultural contact, trade, production, and status. We should not, however, *over* interpret ceramics. Many theories have gone too far in seeing the spread of ceramic forms and art styles as indicators of the success and physical expansion of hypothetical ethnic and linguistic populations. Such "ethnic" interpretations of ceramic or artifactual similarity ignore the many alternative mechanisms for the dissemination of styles and technologies between peoples.

In any case, between 2000 and 1000 BC settled village life, ceramics, and related technologies and styles had spread or had coevolved in all of Mesoamerica (Figs. 4.2, 4.4) (Blake *et al.* 1995; Demarest *et al.* 1988; Pye *et al.* 1999). Some Early Preclassic cultures developed into politically and economically complex societies, perhaps "chiefdoms" [see Box 2]. For example, by 1500 to 1400 BC centers like Paso de la Amada, Chiapas had large structures that some archaeologists argue were used for sponsored ritual feasts (Clark 1994; Lesure 1997; Blake and Clark 1999). These proposed early chiefdoms may also have had attached specialists in craft production and controlled exchange systems in obsidian, the natural volcanic glass that was the razor-sharp cutting tool *par excellence* of prehistoric times (Clark and Lee 1984). While other archaeologists believe that these coastal societies were somewhat less advanced, certainly by 1300 BC settled populations using eastern Mesoamerican ceramics of the Barra-Locona-Ocos tradition had evolved into complex societies in some areas. Scattered sites in the Isthmian Zone of the Pacific coasts of Guatemala, El Salvador, and Chiapas, and across Tabasco and Veracruz (Fig. 4.4), had public architecture, regional and interregional exchange systems, material goods, and art – all suggesting the development of social inequality and complexity (Lowe 1978; Demarest 1989b; Blake *et al.* 1995; Lesure 1997, 1998, 1999).

The most prominent of these evolving complex societies were the centers of the so-called "Olmec civilization" of the Gulf coast of Tabasco and Veracruz. Sites that shared *some* elements of "Olmec" material culture have been found scattered across Mesoamerica, including Chiapas,

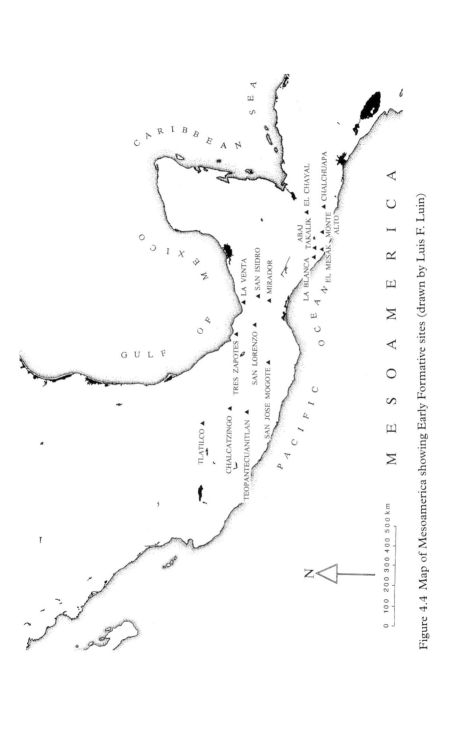

Figure 4.4 Map of Mesoamerica showing Early Formative sites (drawn by Luis F. Luin)

the Pacific coast of Central America, and even into the Maya highlands and lowlands (Lowe 1978; Demarest 1989b). Through poorly understood contacts and influences, the "Olmec period" sites of 1300 to 600 BC introduced many of the symbolic elements and concepts that were later elaborated in the Classic Maya civilization.

## The "Olmec civilization" and the "Olmec problem"

Overall, the evidence indicates that in eastern Mesoamerica after the formation of settled agricultural villages there was a rapid development of complex societies from 2000 to 1300 BC, along the coasts and in some inland zones. The record in the rain forest lowlands of the Maya area, the focus of this study, is almost silent for this entire period. A few scattered Archaic-period finds in Belize and elsewhere (MacNeish, Wilkerson, and Nelken-Turner 1980) are insufficient to give us even a sketchy view of cultural developments in the Maya lowlands during this period of the initial rise of complex societies in eastern Mesoamerica. In the surrounding zones, however, including Chiapas, the Pacific and Gulf coasts of Mexico, and the coasts and highlands of Guatemala and El Salvador, by 1300 to 900 BC centers appeared with monuments, public architecture, intricate art, and symbolic systems with some elements shared across Mesoamerica. Economies arguably had elite-controlled long-distance trade, as well as regional trade. Based on the archaeological evidence, scholars debate whether these more complex societies were high "chiefdoms" or "early states" – traditional typological distinctions [see Box 2] that are of less interest than a deeper understanding of the changes and processes under way.

Judging from public architecture and monuments, the most politically advanced of these societies, if measured in terms of control of labor (e.g. Clark 1997a), were the great centers of the Gulf coast of Mexico such as San Lorenzo, La Venta, Tres Zapotes, and other sites that are usually collectively referred to as the "Olmec civilization." The most spectacular monuments of the Olmec ceremonial centers are gigantic carved basalt heads up to 60 tons in weight (Fig. 4.5) and rectangular stone "altars" (actually thrones) with images of leaders and deities (e.g. M. Coe, 1965). Public architecture at these centers includes courts delimited by basalt columns, stone-lined ritual watercourses running through centers, and earthen temple mounds (Fig. 4.6). Within large platforms of the ceremonial centers archaeologists have uncovered buried floors with layered strata of fine sands of different colors and buried "offerings" of mosaic floors of serpentine and other fine stones, some forming enormous faces usually identified as deities. There are "caches" of portable

Figure 4.5 Colossal head from Olmec site of San Lorenzo, Veracruz, Mexico (70" × 46" × 37", 6 tons) (drawn by Luis F. Luin)

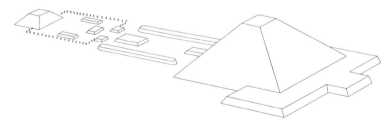

Figure 4.6 Reconstruction of a portion of La Venta, Tabasco, Mexico ceremonial center (drawn by Luis F. Luin after Coe 1994: Fig. 43)

art which include "were-jaguar" figures and carved adzes combining human and animal features. Bas-relief monuments also repeat certain themes including combined human/animal features, seated figures with headdresses emerging from caves, jaguars, "were-jaguars," and serpents

Figure 4.7 Olmec jade celt

(Fig. 4.7). Some more complex incised or carved iconography and motifs are believed to include some precursors to later Maya iconography and writing (Quirarte 1977).

Beyond the Gulf coast "heartland" of Olmec centers, other ceremonial centers with public art and architecture appear before 900 BC, if not earlier (see map, Fig. 4.4). Many of these sites also have earthen mounds, stone monuments, and portable art. In most cases artifacts are of regional styles, but some elements, motifs, and themes are shared with the Olmec "heartland" art of the Gulf coast. Centers like Chalcatzingo in Morelos, Coapexco and Tlatilco in central Mexico, Teopantecuantitlan in far western Guerrero, San José Mogote in Oaxaca, Mirador and San Isidro in Chiapas, and La Blanca, Abaj Takalik, and El Mesak on the Pacific coast of Guatemala, all display elements of cultural complexity in art, ceramics, or monuments that share features of the "Olmec" style, with its "were-jaguars" and other specific anthropomorphic, zoomorphic, and/or

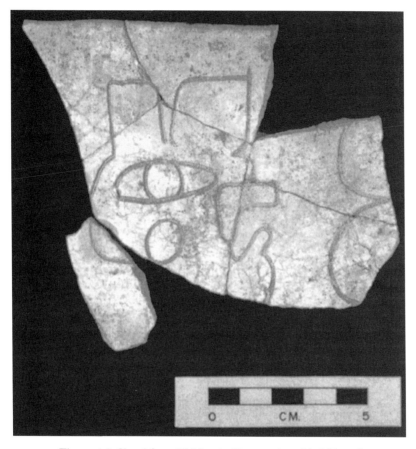

Figure 4.8 Sherd from El Mesak, Guatemala, with "Olmec" were-jaguar figure

geometric designs (Fig. 4.8). Yet many of these centers also have distinctive material culture assemblages, and some show evidence of gradual local developments with considerable time depth (e.g. San José Mogote and El Mesak). Thus, eastern Mesoamerica from 1300 to 600 BC did not have a single coherent "Olmec civilization" but rather a wide range of complex societies. Each of these had a distinctive local pattern and development, yet they shared enough elements in common to demonstrate ongoing interaction and influences.

For over three decades, debate and discussion on the archaeology of this Early to Middle Preclassic period has centered around the issue of whether the Gulf coast Olmec ceremonial centers were the "mother

culture" that developed and then spread most elements of complex society to other regions (e.g. Covarubias 1957; M. Coe 1968; Campbell and
Kaufman 1976; Clark and Blake 1989; Tolstoy 1989). This position fits
with the concept of "horizons" of pan-Mesoamerican influence critiqued
in Chapter 2. Another school of thought holds that parallel developments
occurred in each region, mutually stimulated by a "lattice of interaction between evolving chiefdoms" (Demarest 1976, 1989b; Grove 1981,
1989; Marcus 1989; Sharer 1989). The truth probably lies somewhere
between these positions. Perhaps the Olmec centers of the Gulf coast and
Chiapas were the most precocious and influential centers, contributing
considerably to parallel but locally defined developments elsewhere. In
any case, our understanding of the origins of these complex societies in
most regions (especially the "Olmec heartland") is so poor that this debate
about local developments versus interregional influences is still impossible to resolve. Ongoing intensive excavation and survey projects in the
Gulf coast region, Chiapas, and southern Guatemala should soon lead to
a better informed and more meaningful understanding of the processes
that led to the rise of these complex societies in the second millennium
BC (e.g. Arroyo 2001; Pye *et al.* 1999; Blake *et al.* 1995; Blake and Clark
1999; Lesure 1998).

Meanwhile, in the Maya lowland region we have almost no evidence
whatsoever concerning the participation of Early Preclassic societies
in the network of interactions and influences of this Olmec period.
Except for a few caches of Olmec-style jades and other sporadic finds
(Andrews V 1986; Willey 1978: 96–97; Smith 1982), our understanding of the connection between the Maya civilization and these earlier
antecedents is based, not on coeval evidence, but on the appearance
of many "Olmec" elements later in Late Preclassic- and Classic-period
Maya art, iconography, and writing (Coe 1968; Quirarte 1977). For the
past several decades archaeologists have traced the origins of later Classic
Maya art and symbol systems to the Maya highlands to the south and to
the Middle to Late Preclassic "Olmec," "Olmec related," "Olmecoid,"
or Izapan monuments and sites of the southern highlands – forming a
hypothetical indirect link with the more ancient Early Preclassic cultures.

The truth, however, is that we do not know what may have been going
on in the Maya lowlands before about 1000 BC and whether that region
had its own precocious Early Preclassic centers with their own original
local developments and direct contacts with the other evolving cultures of
this period, including those of the Gulf coast Olmec region. This possibility of yet undiscovered highly complex Early Preclassic societies in the
Maya lowlands must now be seriously researched given the new evidence
of urban or semiurban centers in the lowlands by 500 BC, if not before

(Hansen 1991b; Hansen 2001). The only alternative possibility is that the Maya lowlands were occupied (or reoccupied) *after* 1200 to 1000 BC by already complex colonizing societies moving in from the surrounding highland and coastal zones.

## The southern "corridor" of interaction

In the period from 900 to 200 BC many ceremonial centers and some truly "urban" sites appeared in the southern Maya highlands and coast. The study of these early southern Maya centers has been under way in archaeology for over a century, since some of these sites are near modern communities. Yet our overall thinking has been changed by the recent discoveries of early urban centers in the lowlands and new evidence from the south coast and highlands. The current state of the evidence on the Preclassic of the south coast and Maya highlands is a confusing profusion of diverse sites, art styles, and artifacts.

On the "boca costa" or lower piedmont of the Pacific south coast, several long-studied centers have carved stone monuments with extensive earthen temple mounds and terraces. Each of these sites had distinctive regional ceramic traditions. Among the Middle to Late Preclassic southern sites are Izapa, Chiapas; Abaj Takalik and Monte Alto on the Pacific piedmont of Guatemala; and Kaminaljuyu and Chalchuapa in the highland valleys of Guatemala and El Salvador (see map, Fig. 4.9). Many other large Middle and Late Preclassic centers have only recently been excavated, and interpretations are just beginning at such sites as La Blanca, Ujuxte, Buena Vista, and Balberta on the south coast of Guatemala. Some of these centers have a phase or component that indicates involvement in the Olmec symbolic system and art style of the period from 1300 BC to about 600 BC, as well as later components in distinctive local art styles in the later Middle to Late Preclassic period from 600 BC to AD 300 (see chronology, Fig. 2.3). While monuments at some sites have styles displaying continuity in motifs and themes from the Olmec era, art at other sites is more similar to the earliest lowland Maya bas-relief iconography of stelae and altars (Fig. 4.10). Some highland monuments share early calendric dates in the Maya cyclical and Long Count systems (discussed in Chapter 8).

These glyphs, the poses of figures, and the general style of some monuments have been used to argue for the origins of a proto-Maya art style on the coast and highlands at sites such as Kaminaljuyu, Chalchuapa, and Abaj Takalik (cf. Parsons 1981, 1986; Graham 1982; Boggs 1950; Sharer 1974). Yet carvings at other sites show complex and fluid narrative sequences with figures representing esoteric rituals or myths

Figure 4.9 Map of eastern Mesoamerica with some Preclassic sites (drawn by Luis F. Luin)

Figure 4.10 Stela 5, "Maya style" monument at Abaj Takalik, Guatemala

Figure 4.11 Stela 25 from the site of Izapa, Chiapas, Mexico (drawn by Ayax Moreno)

(Fig. 4.11). Monuments of the latter type are especially common at the site of Izapa in Chiapas and are often referred to as the "Izapan" style (Quirarte 1973). Izapan style also has been considered by some to be ancestral to elements in later Maya art, but most scholars now consider it to be part of a distinctive non-Maya subtradition (e.g. Parsons 1981, 1986).

If this coastal and piedmont mix of sculptural traditions and information systems was not confusing enough, other, presumably earlier, sites have monuments and some artifacts in typical "pure Olmec" style. Prior

Figure 4.12 "Potbellied" style monument from Santa Leticia, El Salvador, height 1.6 m. (from Demarest 1986) (drawn by LeRoy Demarest)

to its recent destruction, the Olmec-period site of La Blanca had such elements and a 25-meter-high temple mound rivaling that of La Venta in the Olmec Gulf coast heartland (Love 1991, 1999a). "Pure" Olmec-style bas-reliefs are found in reset or undateable contexts at other coastal and highland sites. Furthermore, this southern "jumble" of artistic traditions and styles also includes primitive full-round boulder sculptures, including crude jaguars, giant heads, and many nearly spherical "potbellied" monumental figures (Fig. 4.12). These cruder boulder sculptures had been proposed by some to be possibly ancestral to the monuments of the Olmec Gulf coast sites; however, they have since been dated at Santa Leticia, El Salvador, and Monte Alto, Guatemala, to between 500 BC and AD 200, proving that they were "epi-Olmec" or derivative from the earlier Olmec style (Parsons 1976, 1981; Demarest et al. 1982; Demarest 1986).

From this tangle of Olmec, "Olmecoid," Izapan, proto-Maya, epi-Olmec, and local styles, archaeologists have tried to derive various simplified schemes of evolution from the Middle Preclassic (1000 to 400 BC) styles and proto-writing to the highland and lowland Maya stela-altar complex, calendric systems, iconography, and early inscriptions (Parsons 1986). Some have gone further to try to associate particular styles and influences with specific ethnic or linguistic groups. For example, Olmec, epi-Olmec, and Izapan art styles have often been associated with hypothesized Mixe-Zoquean speaking peoples presumed to have moved into the Pacific coast and piedmont of Guatemala from the Olmec core area of the Gulf coast and Chiapas (Campbell and Kaufman 1976; Lowe 1977, 1983). Yet most sites show a mix of several styles in the monuments present with only a slight predominance of a certain style. Furthermore, recent excavations have shown that sites such as Izapa, La Blanca, Abaj Takalik, Ujuxte, and Kaminaljuyu have very different material culture assemblages, especially in domestic ceramics and even in elite artifacts (Love 1998, 1999a, 1999b; Love and Castillo 1997; Lowe 1978, 1992; Lowe et al. 1982; Hatch 1991, 1997; Hatch et al. 2001).

Scenarios for the evolution of the canons of Classic Maya art in the south are further complicated by the probable mix of ethnic and linguistic populations on the Pacific corridor throughout the prehistory and history of Mesoamerica (Bove 1989). This Pacific coastal plain and southern piedmont made a natural corridor for the movement of people and ideas (Lee and Navarrete 1978) that was at different times occupied by many ethnic and linguistic groups, including speakers of languages of the Zoque, Maya, Xinca, and, later, Nahua language families (Campbell 1976; Kaufman 1973, 1976). Preclassic trade, exchange, and cross-fertilization of cultural inventories in art, information systems, and ideology were probably built upon parallel economic, subsistence, and political alliances and exchanges – not just common ethnicity or language (Flannery 1968; Grove 1981; Hirth 1984; Demarest 1986; Demarest and Sharer 1986; Demarest 1987b; Sharer and Grove 1989; Bishop et al. 1989; Schortman and Urban 1991).

### The Late Preclassic highland Maya centers

From this rich interaction of culture groups in the Middle to Late Preclassic coast and highlands emerged the highland Maya art and ceramic styles best known from the great site of Kaminaljuyu (Fig. 4.13). This important center is covered today by the suburbs of modern Guatemala City, and its burial mounds, temple mounds, monuments, and dwellings have been systematically excavated or inadvertently discovered for a century.

The history of the exploration and interpretations of Kaminaljuyu, perhaps the largest Preclassic site in the highlands, can be viewed as an example of the general problems and the recent shifts in thinking on the

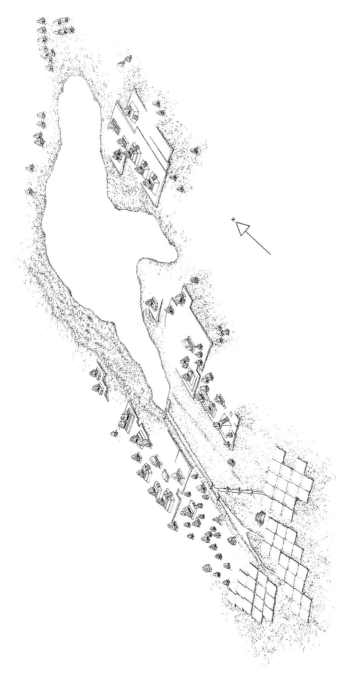

Figure 4.13  Reconstruction drawing of a portion of the site of Kaminaljuyu (drawn by Luis F. Luin)

rise of the state in the Maya highlands and lowlands. Carnegie Institution projects in the 1930s and Penn State projects in the 1960s focused on the central acropolis and adjacent elite residential zones and lithic production areas (Kidder *et al.* 1946; Sanders and Michels 1977). From these and other researches emerged a provisional cultural history of the site that viewed it as an advanced form of "chiefdom" [see Box 2].

It was assumed that this chiefdom and ceremonial center was supported by its control of nearby obsidian sources and obsidian production, together with the natural agricultural wealth of the volcanically enriched soils of the basin of the Valley of Guatemala (Michels 1979). During the Late Preclassic period of 400 BC to AD 300, Kaminaljuyu was believed to have transferred the early art styles, calendrics, and writing systems of precocious epi-Olmec coastal centers to the lowland Maya sites to the north in the Petén rain forest (then believed to be less developed). Archaeologists had hypothesized that the chiefdom of the Valley of Guatemala centered at Kaminaljuyu was, in turn, later transformed into a true state between about AD 250 and 400 through colonization, conquest, or commercial control from the great mercantile city of Teotihuacan far to the west in the Valley of Mexico [see Box 3]. Teotihuacan contact was marked by central Mexican talud-tablero style architectural façades on acropolis buildings, as well as artifacts in Teotihuacan style. Theories then posited that Kaminaljuyu and other highland sites were intermediaries for historical contacts or for the transference of Mexican influence, and that this helped in turn to stimulate state formation in the Maya lowlands to the north at sites like Tikal and Uaxactun (Santley 1981, 1983; Sanders and Price 1968; Coggins 1979).

The problem with all of these traditional interpretations is that they were based on a perspective that viewed the Maya highlands and Pacific coast as regions that merely mediated contacts between Mexico and the Maya lowlands. New discoveries of vast complex ceremonial centers in the lowlands dating to before 400 BC have rendered such interpretations obsolete. As described later in this chapter, some lowland centers were well along in their political, economic, and cultural evolution by the end of the Middle Preclassic period and may have had their own direct contacts with the centers of central Mexico and the Gulf coast (Demarest and Foias 1986; Hansen 1994, 2001; Braswell 2003a). More importantly, recent excavations at the highland and lowland Maya centers of the Middle to Late Preclassic periods have shown that local evolution had led to the formation of large populous centers with monumental architecture, complex regional economies, political institutions, and related information systems long before the hypothesized "stimulating" influences, contacts, or intrusions from central Mexico. Contacts with the

Olmec Gulf coast sites during the Middle Preclassic and with Teotihuacan at the beginning of the Classic period did communicate important ideas and in the latter case certainly involved significant historical events (see Chapter 9). However, as discussed in Chapter 2, a "lattice" of continuing, mutually stimulating contacts and cultural exchanges better models the relationship between the Preclassic and Classic societies of Mexico and the Maya highlands and lowlands. The evidence is strong in most areas of Mesoamerica, including Oaxaca, the Maya highlands, and the Maya lowlands, for coevolution of states with the rise of complex political and economic institutions. These parallel changes were brought about by a complex interplay of regional developments and international contacts.

In the case of the Maya highlands, underpublicized excavations of the past decade have quietly overturned many earlier characterizations of the Middle and Late Preclassic periods. Kaminaljuyu has been the subject of many salvage excavations supervised by the Guatemalan Institute of Anthropology and History. Salvage excavation projects in Guatemala City have received little attention, perhaps because of their publication in Spanish and their unromantic names, which translate as the "Channel 3 site" or the "Metro Centro Mall site." These conservation archaeology projects have raced before the bulldozers of the construction companies to salvage pieces of this ancient city. In fact, when taken together these excavations demonstrate that Kaminaljuyu was not merely a Maya chiefdom but a sprawling city (Fig. 4.13), and a state well before AD 300 (see Hatch 1997 and bibliographic essay at end of chapter).

While the early projects had uncovered Late Preclassic tombs of leaders with rich grave goods and sacrificed retainers (Kidder *et al.* 1946), new tombs, temple mounds, and residential areas have now been uncovered scattered beneath many parts of modern Guatemala City. Throughout the Valley of Guatemala, Late Preclassic potsherds have been found and some ceramics, including ornately incised vases and fine-paste wares, were exported to other areas of the highlands and coasts and even into the Maya lowlands to the north (Bishop *et al.* 1989). Some areas of ancient Kaminaljuyu were workshops for ceramic production. Craftpersons of Kaminaljuyu also produced obsidian cores and tools from the volcanic glass of the nearby El Chayal deposit (Michels 1979). Salvage projects also have recovered zones of specialized food production, including giant ovens and associated work areas that may have been involved in preparation of food, perhaps including roasted chocolate beans from cacao pods imported from the groves of the Pacific coast to the south (Hatch 1997). Most importantly, recent salvage projects in the western suburbs of Guatemala City have discovered a complex irrigation system (Fig. 4.14) with large clay-lined canals that fed gardens for intensive cultivation

Figure 4.14 Irrigated gardens at Preclassic Kaminaljuyu (after Hatch
1997: Fig. 91)

(Hatch 1997; Valdés 1997a; Barrientos 1997a, 1997b). These hydraulic
works could have made this highland center a breadbasket of food production and export throughout, and perhaps even beyond, the Valley of
Guatemala.

This new evidence of economic complexity in production and exchange
can now be coupled with previous and recent discoveries of carved monuments and public architecture that indicate a parallel development of
political institutions. Monuments at the site in the first centuries AD
show signs of a well-developed Maya calendric system and some of the
elements of an ideology shared with centers in the lowlands to the north.
Altar stones and stelae bear glyphs and iconography (Fig. 4.15) that some
scholars have interpreted as showing enthroned rulers (Valdés and Hatch
1996; Fahsen 2001). It is probable that an archaic state was in place at
Kaminaljuyu before the end of the Preclassic period.

This revised understanding of Kaminaljuyu is more in keeping with
evidence from other large Middle and Late Preclassic centers in the
highlands, such as Chalchuapa in El Salvador and Balberta, Abaj Takalik, Ujuxte, and other sites on the southern piedmont slopes of the
Pacific coast (Sharer 1978; Graham 1977; Bove 1989; Bove et al. 1993;

Figure 4.15 Monument 65, Seated Preclassic rulers at Kaminaljuyu (drawn by Luis F. Luin)

Orego 1998; Love and Castillo 1997; Love 1991, 1998; Schieber de Lavarreda 1998; Whitley and Beaudry 1989). These centers also display great complexity in public architecture and monuments in a variety of styles – some with elements of later Maya hieroglyphic, calendric, and iconographic systems. There is also considerable evidence of complex

Figure 4.16 Reconstruction drawing of terrace and artificial
monuments at Santa Leticia, El Salvador (from Demarest 1986:
Fig. 40) (drawn by LeRoy Demarest)

economic exchange systems in the Late Preclassic highlands. Some of
these south coast and highland trade networks may have been based on
the Pacific coastal wealth in groves of the precious cacao. Cacao beans
were the source of the chocolate that was so popular as a drink with all
Mesoamerican peoples, and they were not only traded as a commodity, but sometimes served as a medium of market exchange (primitive
"money"). Highland centers like Kaminaljuyu, Santa Leticia (Fig. 4.16),
and Chalchuapa had similar ceramics, figurines, and other artifactual
assemblages and an overlapping set of monumental art styles, including
early Maya stelae and altars, "potbellied" monuments, mushroom stones,
and pedestal sculptures (Demarest 1986; Demarest and Sharer 1986;
Parsons 1981, 1986). Compositional analyses of lithics and ceramics also
show that there were close exchange systems between these centers of
the highlands of western El Salvador and eastern and central Guatemala
(Bishop *et al.* 1989). Certainly by 500 to 400 BC this entire zone was
occupied by Maya-speaking peoples with close cultural ties.

Meanwhile, the large centers on the Pacific slopes such as Balberta,
Buena Vista, Abaj Takalik, Ujuxte, and Izapa had great variability

in settlement, architecture, ceramics, and monuments. Some of these centers have been posited to have been occupied by speakers of other language groups such as Mixe-Zoque or Xinca (e.g. Lowe 1978, 1992). Initial ceramic studies at Abaj Takalik, however, show ceramics of probable highland Maya style (Castillo 1991; Orego 1998), though this site has a wide range of monuments of every type and style, from "Olmec" to "Izapan," and "proto-Maya" to boulder sculptures (Graham 1979; Parsons 1986, 1988). Long-term projects in Esquintla at the great centers of Balberta, Alta Vista, and other sites have focused on regional economic and political development rather than the usual overemphasis of long-distance ties or ethnic affiliations (Bove 1989, 1991; Bove *et al.* 1993). The ongoing projects there and at Abaj Takalik (Orego 1998) and Ujuxte (Love and Castillo 1997; Love 1998) soon should give us a better view of the complex mosaic of regional polities on the south coast. Only then can we assess the nature of their affiliations, their cultural debt to the earlier occupations of the so-called "Olmec horizon" sites, and their influence on Kaminaljuyu and the highland centers, as well as on the emerging Maya lowland centers to the north.

### The beginnings of lowland Maya village life

In the north, on the great limestone lowlands of Yucatan, the Petén, and Belize (see map, Fig. 4.9), the nature of the archaeology and its problems contrast as dramatically with the archaeology of the highlands and coast as do their respective physical environments. In the southern highlands we have just seen that we have more information than we can accurately evaluate on the Early and Middle Preclassic from 2000 to 400 BC. By 400 BC ceremonial centers and highly complex regional societies had developed in the highland and Pacific zones, but we have yet to sort out the overlapping art styles, information systems, ceramic traditions, and external forces involved in that transformation to high chiefdoms and then states.

By contrast, in the north the Early Preclassic evidence from the rain forests of the Petén, Yucatan, and Belize is too scanty to allow credible initial interpretations. Deposits from about 1200 to 700 BC are from very small sites or from small excavation units at the very bottom of great trenches dug into the massive acropoli and temples of much later Classic-period ceremonial centers (Fig. 4.17). We have some scattered and incomplete evidence on the pre-agricultural "Archaic period," barely sufficient to demonstrate some occupation of the Maya area during the Mesoamerican Archaic transition to agriculture. Then, after about 1000 BC, we have evidence of simple agricultural villages with maize,

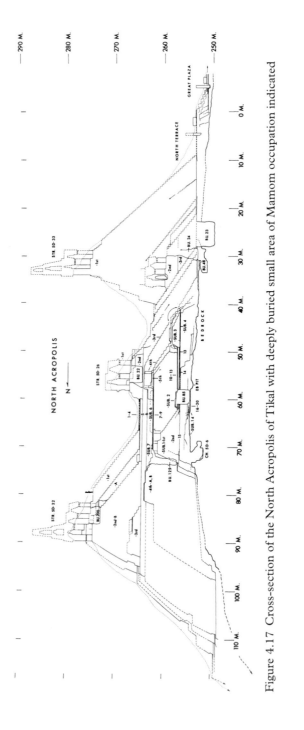

Figure 4.17 Cross-section of the North Acropolis of Tikal with deeply buried small area of Mamom occupation indicated

Figure 4.18 Mamom style ceramic vessel

beans, and squash farming and perishable huts built on low clay and cobble platforms. Occasionally, somewhat larger platforms can be argued to have more public functions (e.g. Hammond 1977). Such "Mamom" villages (or segments of them), dating back to 1000 BC, have been found buried under later architecture at many sites all across the Maya lowlands, including Uaxactun, Tikal, Seibal, and Altar de Sacrificios in Guatemala; at Cuello, Nohmul, and many other sites in northern Belize; and at Komchen, Dzibilchaltun, Loltun Cave, and elsewhere in northern Yucatan (see map, Fig. 4.9).

The characteristic artifact assemblages of the period are simple, but there is evidence for technologically excellent monochrome pottery of the style called Mamom, with thick walls, limestone temper, and colors in monochrome orange, black, and white slips on simple flat-bottomed, flaring-walled bowls, some cylindrical bowls, and jars (Fig. 4.18). The modest Middle Preclassic assemblages of most of these early lowland site components include thin-walled water jars with striated decoration, simple figurines, chert and some obsidian stone tools, and an occasional exotic artifact of shell, bone, or jade. The ceramic tradition of the Maya lowlands was in place by about 1000 BC and then evolved, with many changes but with great continuity, until the very end of lowland Maya civilization. Petén Maya ceramics were simple but clearly distinctive, and more uniform regionally in the Preclassic than the ceramics of the high-lands and coasts of Mesoamerica. The gradually developing household pottery of the lowland Maya peoples was one indicator of the cultural unity and continuing contacts between groups in this "southern lowland" or Petén region.

To the north and all across the Maya lowlands between 1000 and 400 BC villages appeared, including Middle Preclassic occupations at Becan and in far northern Yucatan at Komchen, Loltun Cave, Dzibilchal-tun, and other sites. They have a similar material culture with simple Mamom ceramics, but with distinctive northern lowland variations in pottery and artifacts. Some incipient degree of social stratification was present in slight differentials in grave goods, and some large structures that might have had public functions. At some sites there was some degree of economic specialization. For example, at Komchen, a large coastal village in far northern Yucatan, there was probably involvement in salt production and trade to farming populations farther inland, such as the sprawling Middle to Late Preclassic city of Dzibilchaltun (Andrews V et al. 1984; Andrews IV and Andrews V 1980). Despite these hints of economic complexity there is little in the archaeological record that fore-shadows the massive architecture and monumental art that appears after 600 BC at some lowland sites.

This picture of simple village life in the Early to early Middle Preclas-sic period in the Maya area is obviously very incomplete. This descrip-tion will soon be replaced, we expect, by discoveries of either substan-tial lowland Early Preclassic ceremonial centers comparable to those in Chiapas and the Gulf coast or by evidence of colonization of the Petén by already complex societies from adjacent regions – or perhaps by a combination of these two scenarios. The Middle Preclassic villages in the Maya lowlands, even those with a few public structures in the form of modest temples, were limited in scale, complexity, and architecture – in no way foreshadowing the radical transition to enormous ceremo-nial centers like Nakbe after 600 BC (see next section). In the 1980s, controversial carbon-14 analyses from the site of Cuello in Belize were believed to have pushed back the dating of early Maya village cultures to before 2000 BC (Hammond 1977). Such a chronology would have been much more compatible with the evidence that we now have on the period after 600 BC in the lowlands. After dating corrections, however, even those Belizean villages have been redated to about 1000 BC or a bit earlier (Andrews and Hammond 1990; Kosakowsky and Pring 1998), leaving us with an apparent leap in complexity at the beginning of lowland Maya cultural history. So, we still have no convincing explanation of how these simple village cultures of 1000 BC to about 600 BC could have developed into the spectacular and gigantic centers that quickly followed.

### Suddenly civilization

The site of Nakbe in the far northern Petén (see map, Fig. 4.9) is perhaps the most striking and earliest of these Petén centers to have enormous public architecture (Hansen 1991b, 1992, 2001). Evidence for the period prior to 600 BC is just now being unearthed, but some recent finds suggest even earlier evidence of political and economic complexity (Hansen 1997). At about 600 BC, the inhabitants of Nakbe constructed huge architectural platforms, some nearly twenty meters high. During the following centuries platforms and temple substructures were constructed, each with three small temples atop them and gigantic plaster masks with zoomorphic faces adorning the facades of the substructures. After 400 BC even larger structures were raised at Nakbe and similar complexes began to appear at other sites. At El Mirador, Cerros, Lamanai, Calakmul, Cuello, and Nohmul, similar complexes were constructed between 400 BC and AD 100 that have the same general pattern of massive substructures with plaster masks, topped by a triad of temples (see Hansen 2001 and the bibliographic essay at the end of this volume).

At Nakbe this new phase of construction included stepped earth and stone temple substructures with giant plaster masks with even more elaborate imagery. One temple substructure rises in terraced platforms to over forty-six meters. One plaster mask at Nakbe is over five meters high and eleven meters wide (Fig. 4.19) and portrays a deity believed by some scholars to represent the Celestial Bird of later Classic Maya art and mythology (Hansen 1991b, 1994; M. Coe 1993: 68–69). Early stone stelae at Nakbe, El Mirador, and other Late Preclassic sites (Hansen 1991a) also show the early presence of the Maya stela-altar complex with its calendric system, early versions of hieroglyphic texts, and stiff portraits of standing rulers. These monuments reveal the early development of the Maya state with the central role of ideology, ancestor veneration, and the worship of a complex pantheon of deities.

At many sites in the Petén rain forest of Guatemala and Belize, similar early variants of lowland Maya elite architecture and monuments appear after 400 BC. El Mirador is the most gigantic of these early Maya cities yet found. There hundreds of residential platforms and two great acropoli cover a 16-square-kilometer area (Dahlin 1984; Matheny 1980, 1986, 1987; Demarest et al. 1984). The eastern and western acropoli of El

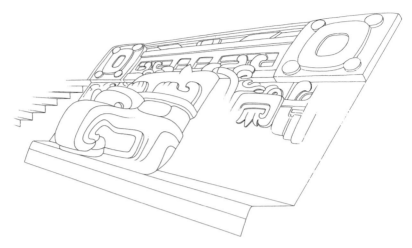

Figure 4.19 Monumental stucco mask at Nakbe (redrawn by
Luis F. Luin after Coe 1993: Fig. 33)

Mirador had massive temples (Fig. 4.20) rising up to 70 meters (Howell
and Copeland 1989). These had characteristic Late Preclassic plastered
façades over coarse masonry with a triad of temple structures above them
(Hansen 1984; Matheny 1980). The scale of construction demonstrated
the power of early rulers to mobilize mass labor (Matheny 1987; Hansen
1984; Hansen 2001) and architectural and iconographic details of the
temples show a complex ideology shared by these early lowland sites.
Other important features of these Preclassic centers were their internal complexity in urban occupation and regional interdependence. The
site of El Mirador had a dense western epicenter of temples, residential
palaces, and plazas walled as a distinct precinct, which was connected by
a kilometer-long causeway to the massive, largely ritual, eastern acropolis
complex. In the Late Preclassic period large populations and ceremonial
complexes at El Mirador were connected by long causeways running in
several directions to Nakbe and other centers (Dahlin 1984).

The details of the images, iconography, and hieroglyphics of these
great centers direct us to search for earlier external influences on the
formation of Maya lowland ideology, art, and writing. Indeed, many
specific elements of stone and plaster art, individual glyphs and symbols,
calendric elements, general formats, and even concepts of the Preclassic
lowland Maya may have been derived from the elite material culture and
monuments of the earlier "Olmec period" centers of the Gulf and Pacific
coasts. Even more specific links can be seen with Middle to Late Preclassic
centers of the southern highlands and south coast, such as Abaj Takalik,

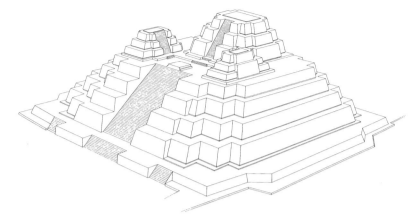

Figure 4.20 Tripartite style Preclassic temple from El Mirador,
El Tigre Group (drawn by Luis F. Luin after Hansen 1990)

Izapa, Chalchuapa, and Kaminaljuyu. As critiqued above, archaeologists
have traditionally identified outside influences on the lowland Maya as
presumably coming from the highland variants of "Olmec," "Olmecoid,"
"Izapan," or "Proto-Maya" cultures to the south and west. Yet, we should
also note that the Middle Preclassic Mamom and Late Preclassic Chicanel
ceramic assemblages and other artifacts of the Petén lowland centers
were distinct from the assemblages of the highlands, Chiapas, and the
Gulf coast, and were more closely similar between the sites of the Maya
lowlands themselves, clearly delimiting a "culture area" of more intense
interaction in the Preclassic Maya lowlands (Freidel 1979). In the rise
of Maya civilization, invasion, colonization, or dominating external influences may have been linked with internal developments or processes –
again, an interactive "lattice," rather than unidirectional flow, of influences. The large and complex ceremonial centers at Nakbe, El Mirador,
and other Petén sites suggest that by the end of the Middle Preclassic
the southern Maya lowland centers might have been active participants
in such networks of interaction between elites in different regions. The
great similarities in the public temple complexes and symbol systems of
the Preclassic sites of the Maya lowlands between 600 BC and AD 100
demonstrate that interaction between the emerging elites *within* the Maya
lowlands may have been as important as any external influences (Freidel
1979; Freidel and Schele 1988a; Matheny 1987; Hansen 1992, 2001).

In any case, the massive constructions of later periods may still cover
the evidence of the earlier Preclassic origins of complex society in
the Maya lowlands or evidence of the external factors that stimulated

the rise of Nakbe, El Mirador, and the other great lowland Preclassic centers.

## The coalescence of the Maya state in the lowlands: theories and the new evidence

By the latter part of the Late Preclassic period (*circa* 200 BC to AD 200), if not earlier, states ruled by divine kings had arisen in several regions (Matheny 1987; Hansen 1992, 2001; Freidel and Schele 1988a). By that period the iconography, images, and hieroglyphs on plaster masks, early stone stelae, and carved artifacts all show that the symbol system and specific beliefs that defined and legitimated divine kingship were in place at early city-states throughout the Maya lowlands (Freidel and Schele 1988a, 1988b; Hansen 1992). These polities also had large populations, massive public architecture, and complex site organization.

For decades archaeologists explained the development of the early state in the Maya lowland rain forest based on the limited lowland evidence, the better known sequences of other regions, and logical arguments. Initially these theories appeared to fit well with the Maya data to explain the emergence of state-level societies in the Maya lowlands, then believed to have occurred between about AD 200 and 400. Now, however, with the chronology pushed back by five or six centuries for these developments, most of these theories are invalid.

For example, some interpretations had stressed external influences or events as catalysts for the final coalescence of Maya societies into states at the end of the Late Preclassic and the beginning of the Classic epoch, including influence from the great Mexican city of Teotihuacan between AD 200 and 450 (Sanders and Michels 1977; Price 1978; Michels 1979). Now we know that while relations between the Classic Maya and that impressive Mexican city-state (see Chapter 9) were important in Early Classic Maya history, these influences occurred long after the Maya centers had already achieved great size and complexity and had the institutions of divine rulership. Another theory had linked the initiation of the Classic-period lowland florescence to a proposed AD 150 to 300 "Protoclassic Intrusion" of highland influences from movements of populations after the eruption of the Ilopango volcano in El Salvador to the south (Sheets 1979; Dahlin 1979; Gifford 1976). Again, these events are now placed centuries *after* the rise of probable state centers in the lowlands. The new chronologies show that Maya civilization at highland centers like Kaminaljuyu and at lowland Maya centers such as Nakbe,

El Mirador, Tikal, and Cerros probably coevolved through continuous contacts and mutual exchanges.

Earlier scenarios regarding *internal* factors in the lowland states have also been negated by the new chronologies and discoveries. Most of these were processualist and "functionalist" theories that explained the origin of Maya states in terms of leaders' functions in managing intensive agricultural projects, defense systems, trade, or a combination of these activities (e.g. Wittfogel 1957; Carneiro 1970; Rathje 1971; Sanders 1968; Wright and Johnson 1975; Flannery 1972). Such processualist theories have been criticized by Marxists for ignoring the often "parasitic" nature of early elites (e.g. Gilman 1981) and by postprocessualists for ignoring the role of worldview, ideology, and other non-ecological factors (e.g. Hodder 1982, 1987; Miller and Tilley 1984; Freidel 1979; Mann 1986; Conrad and Demarest 1984; Demarest and Conrad 1992; Demarest 1987a, 1989a). Now, however, they face a more direct problem: they are chronologically out of alignment with the data.

For example, several hypotheses were based on the concept that growing populations had led to pressures for centralized management of agricultural intensification (e.g. R.E.W. Adams 1977, 1980; Ball 1977; Turner and Harrison 1978; Carneiro 1970; Webster 1976, 1977). Others argued that the "environmental heterogeneity" (e.g. Sanders 1977) or the "resource deficiency" (Rathje 1971, 1977) of the Petén rain forest stimulated state management of regional or interregional trade. All of these theories of population pressure, agricultural intensification, warfare, and trade aligned well with the data from settlement surveys by major projects in the 1950s, 1960s, and 1970s that posited population growth and the rise of states at the end of the Late Preclassic period in the first few centuries AD (e.g. R.E.W. Adams 1977; Webster 1977). Sadly (as so often occurs in science), the recent discoveries have overturned these beautifully aligned theories by finding large and complex centers, probably states, by the fourth century BC or earlier.

The internal and external forces leading to the rise of the Maya states now are totally open to debate. Future interpretations will need complex scenarios that combine some weak economic pressures for internal management originating from demography and warfare, but stimulated by both external influences and the class interests of emerging shamanistic leaders. This last ideological element was clearly reflected in Late Preclassic symbolic systems, architectural features, and artifacts that were later associated with the doctrines of sacred power of the Classic-period kings. At Cerros, El Mirador, Nakbe, Lamanai, and other early centers, the images and iconography of power already display the ruler's role as the "axis mundi," the personified axis of the universe (see Freidel and Schele 1988a, 1988b and bibliographic essay). These canons defined the Maya rulers as shaman-kings who acted both as leaders in war and politics and as intermediaries in the veneration of ancestors and the worship of gods. The stucco masks, temples, early texts, and sculptures show that this Classic Maya construct of combined ideological and political power in the K'uhul Ajaw was in place by the first few centuries BC. As we shall see, this form of divine royal kingship would guide the volatile history of the lowland Maya for the next thousand years.

# 5 The splendor of the Classic Maya florescence in the lowlands

During the Classic period the Maya lowland forests of northern Guatemala, Belize, and the Yucatan Peninsula were covered with clusters of ancient Maya house groups, villages, and centers. The centers ranged in size from minor ceremonial complexes with one or two masonry residences and shrines to great sprawling cities with large populations and "epicenters" with massive acropoli of towering, superimposed temples, palaces, and public buildings with fine masonry, painted plaster façades, and stone monuments. In each region these were organized into local city-states ruled by "holy lords" who were in turn linked by diverse and complex bonds of kinship, exchange, and political alliances. This network of jungle cities and centers and their local populations generated the splendor of Classic Maya elite culture as well as its brilliant rain forest adaptations.

## The elusive essence of Classic Maya civilization

The Classic period traditionally has been viewed as the "golden age" of ancient Maya society in the lowlands. Monumental art and architecture, writing, advanced mathematics and calendrics, and other hallmarks of sophisticated civilization were believed to have first appeared in this AD 300 to 900 era. Yet we now know that most of these features actually appeared centuries earlier at some centers in the highlands and lowlands, and some of these earlier centers had huge architectural complexes and large populations. The Classic period is distinctive in prehistory, not so much for an increase in the scale of architecture or the size of sites, as for the much more extensive use of information and symbolic systems.

The Maya civilization of the Classic period was one of the few early state societies – like those of Mesopotamia and Egypt – whose interpretation is enriched by both modern multidisciplinary studies and the visions of that civilization left by its own rulers and scribes. During the Classic period the widespread use of hieroglyphic writing and calendric dates on stone monuments has left a well-preserved body of information: dates, polity names, dynastic records, and indications of elite behavior, alliances, and interactions. The elaborate and beautiful art of the Classic period, particularly the polychrome painted ceramics, provides yet more information in the form of interpretable images and brief, but revealing, texts about elite life, ritual, and religion. The prevalence of easily dateable monuments and ceramic styles allows us to correlate this information about Classic Maya leaders and elite culture with new archaeological evidence on the sustaining populations, settlements, and economic systems.

Traditional definitions of the Classic period were based on a list of specific diagnostic traits: Maya hieroglyphic writing; the recording of the Long Count and other calendric and chronological systems; mathematics using zero and a base twenty system; corbeled vault (or "false arch") stone architecture; and polychrome ceramics in orange, black, red, and white. The Classic-period ceremonial complexes have stone temples, palaces, ballcourts, and a distinctive monument complex of standing rectangular stone stelae and circular altars (Fig. 5.1), often carved with elaborate images and hieroglyphic texts. Many of these features appeared earlier, but in the Maya lowlands beginning at about AD 300 these elements were common at many ceremonial centers and cities that were linked by interaction and exchange between their ruling elites.

In defining the Classic period, archaeologists now reject the vision of Maya civilization held by some earlier scholars – that of a dispersed populace of slash-and-burn farmers only periodically united at the temples and plazas of ceremonial centers for rituals presided over by their priests. Having overturned this stereotype, it has been difficult for contemporary archaeologists to reformulate an understanding of the common characteristics of Maya sites because of differing interpretations of the evidence on Maya agriculture, economic systems, and the size and scale of states. Many of these differences reflect the actual variability of Classic-period culture between subregions of the Maya lowlands. Geological and landform diversity in the lowlands is less pronounced than in other regions of Mesoamerica, and geographical barriers between areas are fewer and less formidable. Nonetheless, geographic and cultural factors were sufficient to lead to diversity in architectural and ceramic styles and, over time, to somewhat different regional cultural formulations. Even the mix of agricultural practices and systems (e.g. swidden, terraces, raised fields, gardening) varied between regions (e.g. Harrison and Turner 1978; Dunning and Beach in press).

Archaeologists today try to look beyond the material culture trait lists to identify the distinctive configurations of cultural, economic, and political forms characteristic of Classic-period Maya civilization. In seeking common factors between Classic Maya regions, some have looked

Figure 5.1 Stela and altar at Tikal

Figure 5.2 Tikal epicenter in jungle

to a widespread political ideology that emphasized the central role of divine kings, the K'uhul Ajaw (e.g. Freidel 1992; Freidel and Schele 1988a; Schele and Freidel 1990). First developing at some sites in the Late Preclassic period (Freidel and Schele 1988b), this cult of rulership included a host of specific rituals presided over by holy lords. As discussed in Chapter 8, these rituals were a principal source of power for local elites and a basis of the networks of interaction and alliance between these rulers (Sabloff 1986; Freidel 1986b; Schele and Freidel 1990). Despite differences in many aspects of material culture and economics in the Classic period, lowland centers shared symbolic systems, religion, science, mathematics, and these common canons of rulership, warfare, and alliance. This shared ideology bound together the history and the fates of the Classic-period lowland states.

## The Classic Maya centers

The core area of each Classic Maya site, its epicenter, possessed much of the stone architecture and monuments that so impressed the early explorers and that still fascinate modern visitors. Today these epicenters consist of clusters of eroded white limestone structures separated by stretches of jungle (Fig. 5.2). Their appearance would have been quite different in the

Figure 5.3 Range structure at Uxmal

Classic period. Then, epicenters were plastered with thick stucco which formed gleaming white courtyards and towering stepped stone temples, the latter sometimes coated in red plaster with ornate stucco sculptures in red, yellow, black, and blue. Lower-range structures (Fig. 5.3) with peaked stone vaulted roofs were the receiving chambers or the homes of the elite – nobles, priests, scribes, and administrators – and their families. At first these "palace" structures were placed in simple rectangular groupings around courtyards or plazas. Over time, the stone dwellings and reception chambers of the royal families and the highest elites often agglomerated into "acropoli," irregular multilevel complexes of architecture (Fig. 5.4).

The beauty of the Maya centers was not the result of careful urban planning or highly ordered design. Rather, Maya centers had a seemingly random quality that reflected their growth and the gradual accretion of public architecture. The temples and acropoli of the older centers had numerous construction phases, usually beginning in the Late Preclassic and continuing with some gaps until the ninth-century end of the Classic period. These multiple levels of construction built up massive platforms and towering edifices, which incorporated within them the temples and palaces of previous generations of rulers. Through patient excavation with tunnels and trenches, teams of archaeologists have peeled

Figure 5.4 Reconstruction drawing by Tatiana Proskouriakoff of the Late Classic epicenter of Copan

through the construction sequence of these architectural puzzles and correlated them with the associated burials of rulers, cache offerings of artifacts, and carved stone texts (Fig. 4.17). Together these evidences often give us an accurate chronology of construction and activity in these epicenters.

The Classic-period Maya architecture of these centers had well-defined features of construction and style. The use of the "false arch," more properly known as "corbeled vault," determined both the elegant look and the structural limitations of Maya architecture. The tall narrow rooms of Maya palaces and temple chambers were the result of corbeled vault construction in which chambers were roofed by placing blocks on either side closer and closer together and then capped by a single flat stone (Fig. 5.5). The technique required massive walls to support the tall arches, which were still structurally weak. The ancient Maya turned this structural weakness into a stylistic strength – as they did with many aspects of their civilization (in politics and economics, as well as in architecture!). The tall, narrow rooms required by structural weakness were further extended to give structures an elegant appearance. In  most regional variants of Classic Maya architecture, the tall,

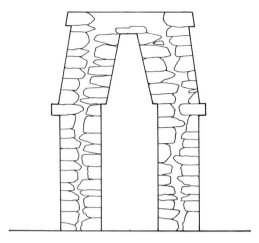

Figure 5.5 Cross-section of corbelled vault construction (drawn by Luis F. Luin)

narrow profiles of their stone structures were further exaggerated by adding elaborate "roof combs" which reached up toward the heavens. The roof combs were decorated with stone and plaster images of gods, venerated ancestors, or sacred symbols. The result was a cathedral-like elegance to the temples at many Maya sites, which still today often project above the high jungle canopy (Fig. 5.2; see also cover photo).

The construction and maintenance of these Classic Maya centers required a variety of craft skills and techniques including the production of fine plaster from limestone and the extraction, preparation, and trade of a variety of pigments, fine clays, and other raw materials. Dependent classes of full- and part-time specialists labored on painting, stone carving, the manufacture of fine ceramics and figurines, and architecture. The less skilled mass labor needed for construction projects was probably a periodic contribution by the general population of the kingdom.

The major epicenter architectural complexes were the administrative and economic cores of Maya kingdoms. Goods and produce were exchanged in their great plazas at the time of periodic gatherings and rituals, as occurs on market and ritual days of the modern highland Maya today. The royal palaces and courtyards were also administrative and social centers. Elite visitors from other states, local leaders with petitions, and leaders of subordinate polities bearing tribute would be received in formal audiences, rituals, or feasts in the palaces and plazas of the epicenters.

While the palaces and courtyard groups served as the offices and dwellings of the living kings and nobles, the temples housed the tombs of the preceding generation of rulers. They served as the foci of rituals and sacrifices to honor and propitiate the ancestors, the royal version of the general Maya practice of ancestor worship. In the tombs within the great temples, the noble dead were accompanied by beautiful polychrome ceramics, stone ornaments, carved bone and shell, and the elaborate jade jewelry and feathered headdresses of their burial attire (Fig. 5.6). Most of the treasures of Maya art found in the museums of the world were ripped destructively from these tomb chambers by looters. In contrast to the sumptuous royal tombs, average Maya families interred even their esteemed deceased patriarchs with only a pot or two beneath the floors of their homes. Many were buried with no grave goods at all. Between these extremes were many burial cysts and small tomb shrines with artifacts representative of the status of intermediate groups of administrators, craftspersons, or family leaders.

In the courtyards near the temples and tomb shrines, the Classic Maya erected great carved rectangular slabs (stelae) with circular stone altars before them (Fig. 5.1) as settings for ancestor veneration. The rituals of ancestor worship included prayer, sacrifice of animals and human captives, and, more commonly, "autosacrifice," self-laceration and the offering of blood by the pious descendants of the dead kings and their followers. Many of the stelae and altars were carved with images of the rulers and hieroglyphic texts that cite their births, accessions, wars, marriages, deaths, and the rituals over which the holy lords had presided (Fig. 5.7). The key elements in all of these texts are the inscribed dates recorded in the Maya calendric systems. Our understanding of Maya elite culture, religion, and history is structured by these texts on stone stelae, panels, and some hieroglyphic stairways. The texts, though generally brief, give us a glimpse of some Classic Maya events, political relationships, and beliefs. The inscriptions also provide secure anchor points for archaeological chronologies. They can be used to date the ceramic and artifact styles of associated caches and tombs, which in turn can be related to similar materials in the surrounding houses, middens, and burials of the general population.

Taken together, the temples, palaces, courtyards, ballcourts, and stone monuments provided a dramatic setting for the public rituals that periodically brought the populace together and reinforced the identity of the Classic Maya polities and the legitimacy of their rulers.

Figure 5.6 Excavation of a royal tomb at Dos Pilas, Petén, Guatemala

Figure 5.7 Hieroglyphic text, Copan, Honduras

## The search for patterns in Classic Maya settlement and society

Surrounding the great palaces and temples of the centers were the household groups of nobles, craftspersons, and farmers. Occupation was dispersed for many miles into the surrounding rain forest with neighboring smaller ceremonial complexes forming secondary nuclei of occupation and activity. Classic-period kingdoms included one or more major centers, satellite minor centers, and surrounding farms and residences. Populations of polities varied from a few thousand to over 50,000 inhabitants. A nested web of these major and minor centers stretches in an irregular but continuous occupation across all of the Maya lowlands.

Maya settlement patterns and site designs were also structured by the successful Maya adaptation to their rain forest environment, as described in Chapter 6. Between the residential groups, major architectural complexes, and minor centers were field systems, gardens, terraces, and reservoirs. Like architectural and artifact styles, different regions had variants of ancient Maya ecological and subsistence strategies and agricultural forms. With few exceptions all of these variants involved residential dispersion, blurring the urban-versus-rural and town-versus-farm distinctions so deeply ingrained in our own contemporary Western settlement designs and worldviews.

Many patterns of layout and activities were shared between the great stone complexes and spacious plazas of the elite and the plaza groups of huts on low platforms occupied by the most humble families in the countryside. The architecture of each of the different levels of ancient Maya society shared elements in the symbolic positioning of structures, burials, and caches, and in the nature and loci of activities. As discussed in Chapter 8, this repetition in patterning was also guided by a common ideology of ancestor worship and a shared cosmology that structured time and space for the ancient Maya.

Maya archaeology has shown unusual promise in revealing the patterning of a vanished non-Western society and the lessons that such patterns might have for contemporary social science. Repetition in architectural layouts, symbols, and activities provides one key to understanding Maya political structure and ideology. This ideological structuring of ancient material culture is more easily interpreted in the case of the ancient Maya because the ethnohistoric and modern Maya continued modified forms of these ancient traditions, beliefs, and rituals. Archaeological interpretation of patterning is now also being aided by the hieroglyphic texts found on artifacts and stone monuments, which provide information otherwise unattainable by the best archaeological research. Most such epigraphic insights concern elite culture and society, and only some features and practices can be extrapolated to the entire population. Yet, if we are careful not to naively accept and overemphasize their elite perspective, the inscriptions reveal particular aspects of Maya culture and thought, and they provide a timeline for major political events and influential trends of the Classic period.

## The broad sweep of Classic Maya culture history

The archaeology and history of the Classic period is richly detailed due to the combination of different sources on this epoch. The result is a series of complex alternative accounts of the political histories of the Maya states, dynasties, and alliances, and the ancient Maya's own perspective on their society and universe. Voluminous published interpretations of Maya history and religion are numerous, contradictory, and subject to monthly revision by scholars. The inexhaustible arcana of Maya history and religion has entranced scholars, often leading us to lose sight of the broad patterns of Maya history and the ecological and economic formations that supported ancient Maya society. To avoid this myopic perspective, it might be useful to broadly overview Classic-period archaeology and history and then turn to Maya subsistence and economics (Chapters 6 and 7).

### Chronology

In the southern Maya lowlands, the Classic period has traditionally been subdivided into Early (AD 300 to 600) and Late (600 to 900) periods based on calendric dates on monuments and specific sequences of dated ceramic styles (Fig. 2.3). Monuments dated in the Long Count system allow reconstruction of dynastic history from the late third century on, especially in the northeastern Petén region. There, sites like Tikal and Uaxactun have been extensively excavated, and our interpretations and chronology of the Early Classic period are heavily skewed toward that region. The division between Early and Late Classic periods was partly based on a gap in the sequence of construction of dated monuments at Tikal, Uaxactun, and related sites in the north central Petén between AD 534 to 593 (9.5.0.0.0 to 9.8.0.0.0 in Maya Long Count chronology – see Chapter 8). We once believed this "hiatus" to be a period of general decline in the Maya lowlands. Now, we know that Tikal and its network of allied kingdoms experienced a political crisis in the sixth century, while other centers such as Caracol and Calakmul thrived during this period.

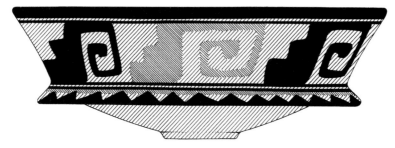

Figure 5.8 Early Classic (Tzakol style) vessel (drawn by Luis F. Luin)

In the Late Classic, stelae and other monument dedications became far more common and we have many detailed dynastic sequences. Consequently, secure chronologies anchored by Maya Long Count dates are available for many southern lowland centers and regions. In northern Yucatan, dated monuments are less common, and most of those use an abbreviated dating system called the "Short Count" calendar which lists only a portion of the date, thus creating ambiguities in interpretation (see Chapter 8). The past century of debate and confusion on many major aspects of the chronology in the northern lowlands demonstrates the great advantages that dated inscriptions have given archaeology of the southern lowland kingdoms.

Yet the extension of chronologies from the epicenters to the site peripheries and to entire regions continues to rely most heavily on the fragments of broken pottery that are found by the thousands across the surface of sites and in the middens (domestic garbage heaps) behind household groups. Most useful for dating are buried vessels or potsherds of the polychrome ceramic styles diagnostic of the Classic period. The Early Classic "Tzakol" ceramics began the widespread use of polychrome painting in red and black on orange to cream slips, with a characteristic "glossy" surface. Designs on these fine Tzakol ceramics were primarily of geometric patterns or bands or highly stylized images of animals, lords, or deities. The most diagnostic Early Classic forms were basally flanged bowls, ring based bowls, and (somewhat later) cylindrical vessels with tripod feet (Fig. 5.8).

For the Late Classic, dating is largely based on potsherds of the Tepeu ceramic style of the northeastern Petén and a variety of coeval styles in other regions. In the Late Classic, stylistic emphasis was placed on more elaborate polychrome painting rather than complexity of forms (Fig. 5.9). Perhaps the most diagnostic forms of the Late Classic were simple tall cylinder vases and open plates. The fine painted polychrome burial vases

Figure 5.9 Late Classic polychrome (Tepeu style) vase (drawn by Luis F. Luin)

of elites in the Late Classic are also an important source of information on the ideology, social practices, and politics of the highborn families of the Maya states.

There are difficulties that result from the heavy reliance on dated monuments and elite ceramics for chronology, especially at the beginning and at the very end of the Classic period. Early Classic and Terminal Classic population estimates and interpretations for residential areas may be unreliable because of the paucity, outside of site centers, of the diagnostic fine ceramics and dated monuments in those periods. Yet with each year of research, site and regional chronologies improve with more detailed study of household ceramics and the decipherment of more inscriptions. In many regions we are now able to date even nonelite household contexts to periods of less than a century.

### The problematic transition to the Early Classic

The end of the Late Preclassic was a period of rapid demographic growth and cultural florescence in both the highlands and lowlands. Incipient states had formed, as indicated by complex economies, massive public architecture, and the symbols and information systems associated with rulership. In the highlands, Kaminaljuyu had become a sprawling center of trade and intensive agricultural production. Other highland and coastal centers, such as Chalchuapa, Abaj Takalik, and Izapa, controlled exchange systems in ceramics, lithics, and other goods. The various art styles of these centers had given rise to the stela-altar complex and perhaps the hieroglyphic and chronological systems that became central features of the lowland Classic Maya society.

Meanwhile, in the lowlands, even more precocious colossal centers such as Nakbe and El Mirador dominated the northern Petén, while Dzibilchaltun, Komchen, and other sites in the northern Yucatan had large populations supported by regional economies. These sites shared symbolic systems and early forms of the cult of the K'uhul Ajaws with centers of more modest scale such as Cerros, Lamanai, Tikal, and Uaxactun. Throughout the lowlands, population levels were high, as indicated by vast quantities of Late Preclassic monochrome potsherds in these early components of many sites.

Then, at the beginning of the Early Classic between AD 250 and 450, there was an apparent dramatic reduction in population and constructional activities at many lowland centers. Nakbe, El Mirador, and other northern Petén sites have reduced occupations, and a similar decline is observed at sites as distant as Seibal on the Pasión River to the west, Komchen in northern Yucatan, and Cerros in Belize. Some archaeologists have speculated that global or regional climatic change, overpopulation and soil exhaustion, or even the explosion of the Ilopango volcano in El Salvador had disrupted the Late Preclassic florescence and caused a reduction or shift in populations. More complex theories look to changes in trade routes or political processes for the alleged cultural recession of the third and fourth centuries. Others note that regional centers, such as Calakmul north of the El Mirador Basin and Tikal to its south, continued to grow, exhibiting major architectural constructions and large populations in the Early Classic period.

The apparent Early Classic decline might be, to some extent, a methodological illusion. Commoners outside of the elite epicenters may have had little access to the Tzakol-style polychromes used to date house groups to the Classic period. Most households might have continued to use variants of Late Preclassic ceramics into the fourth or even early fifth centuries. Archaeologists could be incorrectly dating such occupations as Late Preclassic rather than Early Classic. Such an explanation is especially plausible for sites that are far from the northeastern Petén, in zones where the traditional Tzakol Early Classic ceramic diagnostics are less common (e.g. Lincoln 1985). Nonetheless, it is certain that in some zones there was a very real fourth-century population decline (Culbert and Rice 1990).

*The ascendance of the Early Classic dynasties and the
"Mexican problem"*

While other centers may have declined, the northeastern Petén center of Tikal rose to dominate Early Classic Petén regional politics in the

southern lowlands. The Tikal holy lords left a record of their achievements inscribed on architecture, monuments, and on the artifacts in the
royal tombs of that site's so-called "North Acropolis," a conglomeration
of superimposed funerary temples and tombs (Fig. 4.17).

Recently deciphered history, as discussed in Chapter 9, has shown
that at sites such as Tikal and Copan, Preclassic and initial Classic rulers were followed by new dynasties in the late fourth century
that had ties with the great distant Mexican metropolis of Teotihuacan
[see Box 3]. It remains unclear to what degree these Teotihuacan contacts
consisted of military expeditions, commercial exchanges, indirect influences through intermediary centers, marriage alliances, or the spread
of religious concepts or cults. It was most likely a combination of such
mechanisms (Braswell 2003). In some cases, local rulers and competing
princes might have relied on exotic symbols of contact with this distant
great center to enhance prestige or emphasize their own participation
in geographically wider information spheres – a universal legitimating
tool of rulers, shamans, and even modern politicians (for example, pres-
idential photo-opportunity "summits" near election time). Alternatively,
Mexican commercial or political impact may have been more forcefully
projected by Teotihuacan or its allied centers in search of exotic goods,
tribute, or religious converts. Recent epigraphic evidence (see Chapter 9)
does indicate Mexican involvement in establishing new ruling dynasties
at Tikal, Uaxactun, Copan, and other centers (Stuart 2000; Sharer 2003;
Schele 1992; Martin and Grube 2000; Fash and Fash 2000; Fahsen and
Demarest 2001). Meanwhile, ongoing excavations at the Pyramid of the
Moon at Teotihuacan have found rulers buried in tombs there dressed in
Classic Maya style, with Maya costumes and jade jewelry (Sugiyama and
Cabrera 2003).

Ongoing investigations at Teotihuacan itself will elucidate the political
and economic nature of that Mexican metropolis and the motives and
mechanisms that drove the projection of its symbols and styles to other
regions (Sugiyama 1992; Sugiyama and Cabrera 2003). What is certain
is that the founding of important dynasties at Tikal, Uaxactun, Copan,
and possibly other Early Classic states can be connected to contact
with Teotihuacan. Mexican symbols and ideas were, however, always
reworked into the canons of Maya culture and the lowland cult of divine
kingship.

*Growth, interaction, and alliance in the fifth to seventh centuries*

Perhaps bolstered by status-reinforcing support from Mexico, the late
fourth- and fifth-century Tikal dynasty exerted great influence over many
centers throughout the lowlands. Subordination, alliance, or interaction

# Box 3 Teotihuacan: colossal neighbor of the Classic Maya

By the first century AD, a huge and unique Mesoamerican city had developed at Teotihuacan in Mexico (near modern Mexico City). Dominated by its massive temple pyramids of the Sun and Moon (Fig. 5.10), this city was laid out on a gigantic grid pattern of streets and alleys (Fig. 5.11), with much of the population living in walled compounds – in contrast to the dispersed and loosely organized nature of cities in the Maya lowlands and most of Mesoamerica.

By the second to fifth centuries, Teotihuacan had become a highly organized city-state in the Valley of Mexico and a pan-Mesoamerican commercial and military power. Teotihuacan and its allies interacted with newly consolidated state-level societies in the Valley of Oaxaca, the Gulf coast region of Mexico, west Mexico, and the Maya highlands and coast. Teotihuacan-style artifacts, fine ceramics, and their trademark "talud-tablero" architectural facades (Fig. 5.12a) appear in the late fourth and fifth centuries at the highland Maya city of Kaminaljuyu, in great plastered temples housing rich burials. Some archaeologists believe that this area at Kaminaljuyu represents an intrusion of Teotihuacan warriors or merchants into the politics of the growing city, perhaps to control the nearby El Chayal obsidian source and to utilize the Valley of Guatemala to coordinate interregional exchanges (Santley 1983). Others have noted that the primarily Mayanized versions of Mexican architecture and artifacts at Kaminaljuyu may suggest a less direct exchange between the Maya highlands and central Mexico (Demarest and Foias 1993; Braswell 2003a, 2003b). Classic Maya sites such as Tikal and Copan also have elements of Teotihuacan architecture and direct historical evidence of Mexican involvement in the founding of their early Classic dynasties (see Chapter 9).

In the highlands and Pacific coast of Guatemala, the influence of Teotihuacan is visible in elite burials and caches with characteristic central Mexican-style assemblages, including thin orange ware bowls, stuccoed vases with rectangular tripod feet (Fig. 5.12b), little Teotihuacanoid pitchers, and large ornate ceramic censers with stylized Mexican symbols in clay applique. Early Classic caches and tombs sometimes contain blades of distinctive pale green volcanic glass, obsidian traceable to the Pachuca source in central Mexico. Iconography of the goggle-eyed Teotihuacan deities (Fig. 5.12c) and Mexican-style headdresses, shields, and spear-thrower weapons adorn the monuments of Maya rulers at Tikal, Uaxactun, and other sites.

It should be noted that at Teotihuacan itself, royal burials in Classic Maya style, murals with Maya glyphs and symbols, and "neighborhoods" with many Maya style potsherds and artifacts show that the Classic Maya also had a strong reciprocal influence on their great western neighbor (Sugiyama and Cabrera 2003; Taube 2003; Ball 1983).

Figure 5.10 Pyramid of the Sun, Teotihuacan, Mexico

with Tikal's rulers is manifest in Early Classic inscriptions and art styles at Uaxactun, Río Azul, Caracol, Quirigua, Copan, Tres Islas, and other sites. A mix of militarism, commercialism, and kinship ties were used by capable Tikal rulers. Some newly established Early Classic dynasties, like that of Copan, may have had links to both Tikal and to Teotihuacan or to the Teotihuacan-related elites at Kaminaljuyu in the highlands.

The nature and importance of the interregional networks of interaction between these centers in the Early Classic period is difficult to determine, since it is based largely upon elite perspectives as presented in their hieroglyphic texts, iconographic imagery, and exotic burial goods. It does appear that during the Early Classic, warfare, exchange systems in elite goods, and royal marriages and visits helped to bind together the divine kings of the lowlands and consolidate their common canons on cosmology, calendrics, writing, warfare, and political institutions (Culbert ed. 1991; Sabloff 1986; Freidel 1986a).

In most regions populations gradually increased during the fifth and early sixth centuries, and more centers began to erect monuments with carved texts proclaiming the ancestry of their holy lords and their supervision of rituals. The most common public ceremonies recorded were coronations, funerals, the sacrifice of captured nobles and kings of rival centers, and, above all, rites and temple dedications at the time of

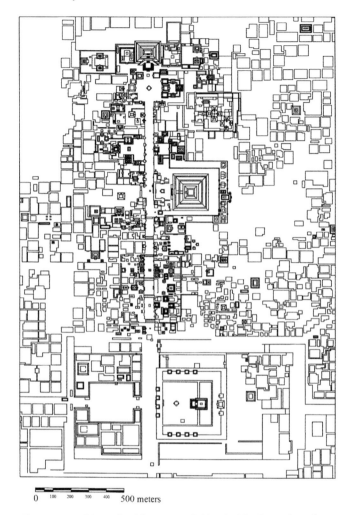

Figure 5.11 Map of grid system of Classic Mexican city of
Teotihuacan (after Millon 1993: 19, Fig. 3)

period endings in the Maya calendric cycles. At sites like Tikal, Caracol, Palenque, and Copan, repeated rebuilding of temples and expansion
of palaces began to create the great sacred hills of accumulated public
architecture that we today call epicenters or acropoli.

Trade for jade, shell, quetzal feathers, and other high-status imports or
"exotics" also intensified in these centuries to meet the growing demands
of new centers and the increased numbers of elites. Production and

Figure 5.12 Drawing of Teotihuacan diagnostics: (a) talud-tablero architectural façade (redrawn by Luis F. Luin from Kidder, Jennings, and Shook 1946); (b) slab-tripod vessels (redrawn by Luis F. Luin from Coe 1994: Fig. 76 a and b); (c) ruler with Teotihuacan style "Tlaloc" eye treatment and Mexican headdress (Stela 32, Tikal)

exchange systems had to grow to create the headdresses, ornaments, and equipment required of holy lords, priests, scribes, and others involved in ritual and bureaucracy. Contact with distant highland neighbors like Teotihuacan, Kaminaljuyu, and various Gulf and Belizean coastal Maya cities probably resulted more from the Maya rulers' own need for status goods and symbols than from highland expansionism.

By the mid-sixth century the many kingdoms of the southern lowlands had developed networks of marriage, trade, and war that linked sites across the Petén. As detailed in Chapter 9, recent breakthroughs in epigraphic decipherment indicate that some powerful kingdoms began to coordinate their efforts with other centers in military or political alliances. Scholars have identified at least two probable alliances of centers that often acted as military allies. One powerful hegemony was formed by the Petén sphere of influence of the great center of Tikal. Another was dominated by the enormous, but poorly known, city of Calakmul in southern Campeche, Mexico. Tikal and its hegemony suffered several military

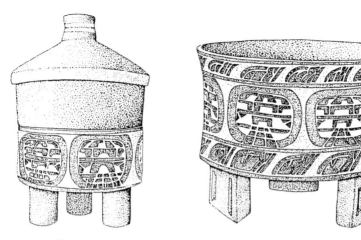

Figure 5.12b (*cont.*)

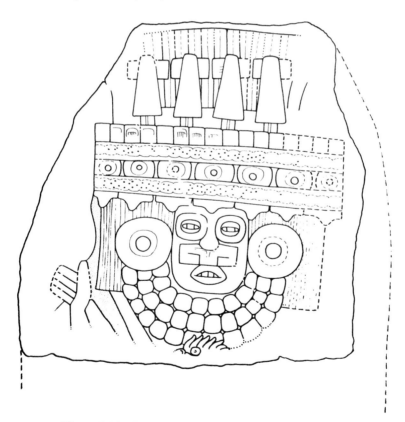

Figure 5.12c (*cont.*)

defeats from this rival alliance early in the sixth century. By the mid-sixth century, Tikal went into a period of decline for 150 years.

While the meaning of these sixth- and seventh-century political events remains unclear, they represented some type of experimentation with larger political associations, perhaps conquest states. The effect of the ultimate disintegration of these political associations may have set the stage for the intensified status rivalry and the proliferation of regional kingdoms in the Late Classic period.

### Regionalism and florescence in the Late Classic period

In the late seventh century, Tikal experienced a striking renaissance. Invoking ancient Teotihuacanoid symbols and aligning the calendric dates of their activities to the successes of the Early Classic, the revitalized Late Classic Tikal dynasty carried out a 150-year program of construction of spectacular palaces, lofty funerary temples, stone causeways, and so-called twin-temple complexes where 20-year "K'atun" endings were celebrated with royal bloodletting and other rites (see Chapter 8). Other northeast Petén centers such as Yaxha, Uaxactun, Nakum, and Xultun shared in this florescence and had similar trends in architecture, monuments, and ceramic styles.

In the seventh through mid-eighth centuries many other regions, not just the central Petén, had their own epochs of spectacular public construction, frequent monument dedications, and the establishment of many new satellite centers. Elite interaction, trade in exotic goods, investment in public and royal art, and warfare all increased dramatically along with increasing populations and areas of occupation. Status rivalry among the growing population of elites was manifest in the establishment of vigorous and internally competitive regional cultures in all parts of the Maya world. Centers throughout the lowlands developed their own regional styles in architecture, ceramics, and other aspects of material culture. Such regional styles can be defined for Belize, the Motagua valley, the Copan Valley of Honduras, the western regions of the Pasión and Usumacinta Rivers, the south central Petén, and the far western kingdoms of Palenque and its neighbors in Chiapas. In the Late Classic, especially after AD 700, more distinct architecture and ceramics flourished in Yucatan, including the northern Puuc cities, the related Río Bec and Chenes area, and the eastern Yucatec zone of the great sites of Coba and Yaxuna (see map, Fig. 9.10).

This regionalization was reflected in distinctive architectural and artifactual styles and, more importantly, in probable differences in some aspects of political and economic institutions. Nonetheless, the many Maya kingdoms – especially in the southern lowlands – were linked by networks of exchange, communication, kinship, and alliance through cultural mechanisms ranging from marriage to funerary visits and war. Chapter 9 sketches in more detail some of the cultural variability, linkages, and conflicts of these Late Classic regional cultures and some of their rapid, but very different, trajectories of florescence and decline. As we shall see, this Late Classic period of magnificence in art, science, architecture, and politics – together with the expansion of the economic infrastructure that supported it – was both the apogee of lowland Maya civilization and the foreshadowing of the ninth-century collapse of many of the southern cities.

### Collapse, transition, and transformation: the end of Classic Maya civilization

One of the greatest mysteries of Maya civilization, and perhaps the most renowned aspect of ancient Maya history to both academics and the general public alike, is the enigma of the ninth- and tenth-century "collapse" of many great lowland cities. In the late eighth and early ninth centuries, Classic Maya civilization began to unravel in many regions. A proliferation of ceremonial centers, many of them newly constructed in the eighth century, was accompanied in some regions by an increase in both warfare and ritual activities. In the early ninth century, shortly after this period of rapid expansion, Maya civilization in much of the southern lowland region of the Petén went into decline. In some areas, this was a swift and even violent process, while in others the decline was slower and more gradual. Yet in still other areas, such as Belize and northern Yucatan, many sites actually experienced a florescence in the ninth century, with population growth and new architectural styles.

Obviously, with so much variability in the evidence on the Classic Maya way of life and on the end of their Classic-period cities, there are many different explanatory theories. Much of the archaeological research of the past two decades has tried to tackle this inscrutable problem. The most recent evidences from excavations and inscriptions are described and debated in Chapter 10. It is an exciting time in Maya archaeology, as scholars are beginning to close in upon the solution of one of the long-standing questions of New World archaeology: Why, after two millennia of success, were many of the great Classic Maya cities of the southern lowlands abandoned?

*The Postclassic period and the continuing Maya tradition*

This work is primarily a study of the Classic period of Maya civilization in the lowland rain forests of Mexico and Central America. Still, it is important to note that the Maya tradition did not end, or even decline, after the tenth century. While many of the southern lowland cities were abandoned, in other regions Maya civilization transformed itself in the ninth and tenth centuries. Very different, vigorous Maya kingdoms in Yucatan, Belize, and the southern highlands continued to grow and evolve until the cataclysm of the Spanish Conquest.

Chapter 11 provides a quick glimpse of this continuing Maya tradition which survived even the Conquest, the Colonial period, and modern oppression to persist in various forms of resistance, identity, and social practice in the communities of the millions of Maya living today. The lessons of the survival, resistance, and adaptation of the Maya are even more compelling than the enigmas of the ruined jungle kingdoms of Classic-period civilization.

# 6  Settlement and subsistence: the rain forest adaptation

Central to our understanding of societies and to the comparative study of civilizations are their economic and ecological adaptations. The ancient Maya of the lowland areas of Central America and Yucatan are of special interest because of their occupation of a rain forest environment – an unusual setting for the rise of civilization. The ancient Maya occupations of the Preclassic and Classic periods were structured to survive and thrive in this rich, but fragile, environment. Interpretation of Maya society has developed through archaeology and epigraphy. Yet we have only now come close to grasping the true nature of ancient lowland Maya civilization through using new understandings from the disciplines of ecology, geography, and soil science.

### The Maya household group

The Classic Maya centers with their tombs, temples, palaces, and inscriptions long dominated scholarly discourse. Yet we now know that the basic building block of Maya society through all periods was (and remains today) the household group. It is also the basic unit for all archaeological interpretation and debate on social organization, economy, and population size.

Today, as in ancient times, Maya families live in humble, but comfortable, large huts constructed of poles and dried mud ("wattle and daub") with peaked roofs of ingeniously woven thatch (Fig. 6.1). In the lowlands, these perishable structures are often set upon low platforms, twenty to forty centimeters high, of stone and clay to raise their floors above the wet jungle soils. Other even more modest modern dwellings or storehouses are sometimes placed directly on the earth, without a platform. Modern house groups also have small sweat baths for ritual purification, shrines for periodic housing of idols or saints, corns cribs for storage, and, sometimes, small corrals for animals and small wooden huts for smoking meats. In general, the weaving of textiles on backstrap looms, ceramic production, and stone tool-making all occur within these households.

Figure 6.1  Maya thatched-roofed residence

Usually, several houses of closely related families are placed facing each other around open courtyard living areas (Fig. 6.2). In turn, several of these "plaza groups" are often placed together to form tiny hamlets of related extended families (Fig. 6.3). After a few decades of abandonment, the only remaining evidence of such plaza groups and hamlets are the very low mounds formed from their buried foundation platforms and the associated debris.

In the ancient Maya lowland sites in pre-Columbian times, such perishable dwellings and associated structures often were placed in somewhat more regular rectangular arrangements of two, three, or four platforms with huts facing each other around an open courtyard or plaza. The latter served as a living and work area for the family, as did platforms or level areas behind and near the plaza group. Kitchens, storage rooms, sleeping areas, and areas for the production of textiles, stone tools, or ceramics were sometimes separated by internal rooms or placed in separate structures. Classic Maya households show variability in construction form and details, with different household plans and forms reflecting variability in family size, status, and the craft activities present in the group – as well as regional and temporal variation. This greater variation in the archaeological fossils of Classic-period household clusters is due to the more complete and more complex social and political structure of some

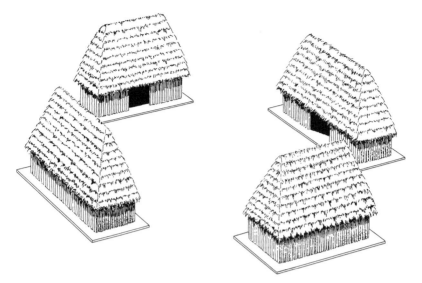

Figure 6.2  Typical Maya household courtyard group (drawn by Luis F. Luin)

Figure 6.3  Modern Maya hamlet

pre-Conquest Maya societies. Maya society had its elites reduced by disease and political and religious suppression before and during the Spanish Conquest. After the Conquest, general repression, specific resettlement policies, and indigenous responses and resistance led to a great reduction in differences in wealth and power within many communities.

Some of the social patterns of Classic Maya society were "fossilized" in architecture and artifacts in the ruins of household groups. For each household group the amount of stone masonry (versus mud and thatch) often varied with the social rank of the ancient inhabitants. Height and area of household platforms, the presence or absence of monuments, distance from the nearest epicenter, the number of courtyards, presence of plastered floors, and the types of pottery and artifacts in burials are all clues to the social and political standing of a group's ancient inhabitants. Evidence from recent settlement pattern studies shows that Classic Maya families varied almost continuously in social standing and wealth (A. Chase 1992; Palka 1995; Kovacevich 2001, 2002) – in contrast to earlier depictions of ancient Maya society as starkly divided between elites and commoners. Instead, Classic Maya households ranged from isolated huts without even a basal platform to plaza groups of noble families with fine stone masonry, plastered floors, rich tombs, and sculpture. Most household groups fell between these extremes. The Classic Maya had a complex social structure with few sharp divisions between "levels" or classes of Maya society, despite the great contrast between the poorest huts and the richest royal palaces.

The basic pattern of the simple Maya family household group was replicated at all levels of society and seems to have formed a symbolic template for Maya society and its relationship to its ecology and cosmology. Even the royal palaces of the great capitals like Tikal, Caracol, and Dos Pilas followed the template of Maya household clusters with corbeled-vaulted structures in the form of stone "huts," facing across open courtyards, where noble families lived and entertained prestigious visitors. The architecture of different levels of ancient Maya society shared many elements in the symbolic positioning of structures, burials, and caches, and in the nature and loci of activities. As in the most plebeian groups, the family dead were usually buried under floors of the house platforms or in nearby shrines (McAnany 1995). In the case of royal families, however, *some* of these shrines were enormous temple structures. As discussed in Chapter 8, the principles of ancestor worship and their vision of sacred geography and cosmology permeated all levels of Maya society as preserved in these parallel architectural patterns.

### Urban landscape and settlement patterns

To Western eyes, the ruins of Maya sites seem to have a haphazard layout, but in fact they have a settlement pattern generated by the complex structure of ancient Maya society itself. The epicenters of the sites usually had several distinct clusters of public architecture often connected by plaster-coated stone causeways for ritual processions between these temple and palace complexes. Scattered between and around these centers of public culture and elite residence were the more modest household groups of lesser nobles, craftspersons, and farmers.

Often within a few kilometers (or less) from the major architectural complexes were other minor epicenters of public architecture, shrines, and elite residences. These smaller complexes served as secondary loci for religious rituals and elite guidance, as well as residences for the local leading families, sometimes kin of the royalty in the site core. Small funerary temple shrines in these outlying elite groups were periodically enlarged and became foci for local ancestor worship. Thus, the outlying elite replicated on a small scale the great rituals of the centers and reinforced the ideological and political unity of Classic Maya culture. This settlement system helped form lines of connection between rulers and the populace through kinship, through movement to the epicenter for construction projects and rituals, and through periodic visits by the central elite to the minor centers.

While its nested and replicative urban settlement system contributed to the political and ideological linkages in Maya society, this dispersed urban settlement was even more critical for the ancient Maya ecological adaptation. At most sites, settlement became more dispersed away from the site core, with areas for fields and gardens between clusters. A variety of agricultural systems were sometimes placed between and within household clusters, as well as in site peripheries. Household waste and debris became an asset, rather than the nuisance that it is in modern cities, since it provided compost for productive Maya urban gardens (Dunning 1992, 1993). This mix of farm and residence probably made most Classic Maya cities self-sufficient in the basic elements of Maya diet – maize, beans, squash, and chiles. Regional and interregional exchange systems were only necessary for distribution of commodities such as cacao (chocolate), salt, hard stone, ceramics, crafts, and exotic goods.

Site core zones had more continuous areas of stone and plaster architecture. Yet special agricultural features have been found in the very heart of some centers. At sites like Cerros, Tamarindito, and Caracol, garden zones, terraces, and even small areas of raised fields in artificial canals

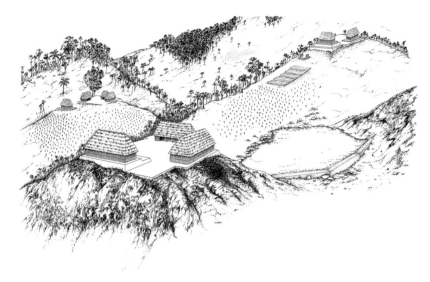

Figure 6.4 Residences, box terraces, dam, and reservoir at the Late Classic site of Tamarindito, Petén, Guatemala (drawn by Luis F. Luin)

conveniently furnished vegetables and fruits to highborn families, while *chultunes* (bell-shaped wells), sinkholes, or large clay-lined stone reservoirs assured a convenient water supply (Fig. 6.4). It is also very likely that such site core landscaping and food production areas had an important symbolic value, reaffirming through repetition the close symbiosis between house group and garden, between the Maya cities and the rain forest, between the Maya and their sacred natural landscape.

## Population sizes and distribution

Since the innovative work of the Carnegie Institution at Uaxactun in the 1930s and Gordon Willey's more systematic settlement surveys in the 1960s, archaeologists have argued over the methods of interpretation of ancient household groups. Most of the clues have been based on observation of household groups among the modern Maya and from the ethnohistorical sources such as Bishop Landa's descriptions of sixteenth-century Yucatec Mayan life. Based on these sources, some archaeologists have estimated that each residential structure was the domicile of a nuclear family of four to ten or more members. Average figures used by most archaeologists for demographic estimates range from four to seven individuals per structure. Most population estimates for sites and regions are based on counting the number of these house mounds.

Styles of potsherds from the surface and from excavations near these residences are used to date them. Then, the number of mounds for a given period is multiplied by the average estimated family size, usually about 5.6 members.

Obviously, such demographic calculations can only be taken as the most general estimates as there remain controversies about even the most basic unit of Maya society. The number of individuals per structure may have varied by region, by chronological period, and with the social standing of the family involved. In areas of lower population density or among families of higher status, the space per individual might have been higher and a single nuclear family could have occupied several structures. Recent evidence from unusually well-preserved house groups found not only such variability in residential space, but also evidence that many structures might have had special nonresidential functions (e.g. Sheets 1992; Sheets and McKee 1989; Sheets et al. 1990; Inomata 1995, 1997). Some platforms may have supported work or storage areas, or shrines for shamanistic rituals or ancestor veneration (Sheets 2000). Assumptions of uniformity in family size and structure use might be inflating many population estimates (Inomata 1995).

On the other hand, other recent archaeological excavations and ethnographic observations have raised the "invisible structure" problem: the presence of structures, including residences, that were not raised on low platforms and would be overlooked by Maya archaeologists and omitted from their calculations (D. Chase 1990; Johnston et al. 1992; Johnston 1994). The presence of such structures can lead to underestimation of population sizes. Archaeologists try to adjust for "invisible structures" by randomly testing around visible household groups and in level areas between compounds to discover such structures and try to ascertain their size, function, and frequency in a given period at a site. Then demographic estimates based on house mound groups can be adjusted by a specified factor.

Regardless of which estimates are used, Classic Maya urban populations, though dispersed, were still remarkably high for a preindustrial society. Even moving away from the site centers to intersite areas, substantial populations were still present. Rural areas between Classic-period Maya cities had estimated populations of up to 200 people per square kilometer (see Ashmore 1981; Culbert and Rice 1990). Indeed, archaeological settlement survey of transects between centers shows almost continuous occupation for some regions in the Late Classic period, and the boundaries between major sites can only be drawn arbitrarily across areas of slightly more sparse occupation. Western civilization's urban-versus-rural distinction is inapplicable to the Classic Maya world.

As centers grew in the Late Classic period, some sites became more densely populated, contradicting the generally dispersed nature of Maya urbanism. Some huge sites such as Caracol, Tikal, and Calakmul may have had populations of over 100,000 persons. In such cases, networks of road and river transport may have been used to move even basic foodstuffs to site core areas. At sites in the Petén, and especially in the drier regions of the northern and eastern Yucatan peninsula, the density of architecture and plastered plazas in epicenters allowed for collection and storage of water supplies in reservoirs and chultun wells. By the end of the Late Classic, populations in some "greater metropolitan areas" (as we would conceptualize them today) numbered in the tens of thousands at many sites. Given high occupation levels even in the intersite areas, regional populations in large zones such as the central Petén numbered in the millions (Culbert and Rice 1990). Such numbers again raise questions about the ancient Maya agricultural adaptation to the rain forest.

## The rain forest adaptations: the true secret of Maya civilization

Ancient Maya civilization in the lowlands existed in a complex environment that varied from the steamy high rain forest in the Petén region in the south to the drier, lower, and more scrubby pine and palm forest of northern Yucatan. Even in the southern lowlands where soils are often deeper, rainfall heavier, and the jungle canopy higher, the rain forest is a fragile environment and human adaptations to it must be sensitive to the details of variability in soils, surface features, and natural vegetation. As our understanding of the nature and complexity of rain forests has evolved, so has our understanding of ancient Maya economy and subsistence systems.

### Changing perspectives on the limits and potential of the rain forest

For ten thousand years Western civilization has been based upon a subsistence economy of overproduction of grains through farming in temperate zones of modest rainfall but high soil quality (Pollock 1999). Surplus grain was then used to trade for other needed products. No subsistence strategy or ecological setting could be more different from this than the complex mixed adaptation of the ancient Maya in their rain forest environment of heavy seasonal rains, thin soils, and careful local adaptations to the specific requirements of each eco-niche. Perhaps it was because their agricultural regimes and their environment were both so alien to our own economy that archaeologists and ecologists long misperceived the potential of the rain forest. Most of our own government-sponsored programs to protect rain forests in Guatemala, Mexico, and elsewhere have attempted to keep people out, based on the assumption that even modest settlement would damage, if not destroy, the forest.

It is not surprising, then, that archaeologists once insisted that Maya cities were only periodically occupied "vacant" ceremonial centers. Some prominent interpretations proposed that the collapse of many Classic Maya centers in the ninth century was the inevitable consequence of the "environmental limitations of tropical rain forests" (Meggers 1954). More intensive settlement surveys in the 1960s and 1970s led archaeologists to realize that many Maya centers had populations so large that we had to rethink our views of Maya farming methods, settlement patterns, and the rain forest itself. Now we are beginning to understand (as did the ancient Maya) that, while fragile, the rain forest is as rich in potential as it is complex in nature. If properly managed, rain forest subsistence systems can support large and complex societies.

### The rain forest and its life forms

As described in Chapter 2, the ancient and contemporary speakers of the Mayan language families occupied an area of eastern Mesoamerica that stretched across eastern Mexico, Guatemala, Belize, and western Honduras and El Salvador. The environment of this area includes: 1) the rich southern Pacific coastal plains; 2) the high fertile basins of the volcanic highlands of southern Guatemala and central Chiapas; and 3) the vast lowland rain forest region of northern Guatemala, Belize, and Yucatan (see Fig. 2.2).

It is the third zone, the lowlands of the Petén and the Yucatan peninsula, which was the heartland of Maya civilization in the Classic period and is the focus of this text. There the environment is defined by the limestone karst landscape that underlies the entire region. The lowlands generally sit at less than 100 meters above sea level, although hilly regions in Chiapas, the southern Petén, and southern Belize rise up to as many as 200 meters or more. In general, the lowlands are characterized by a flat to slightly rolling terrain with fairly thin soils above the limestone bedrock.

In the southern lowlands of the Petén and adjacent zones of Chiapas and Belize, rainfall is heavy and sharply seasonal. In the May to January rainy season, from 2 to 3 meters of rain falls on most parts of the Petén. Farther north, in the Yucatan peninsula, rainfall is significantly lower, ranging from about 180 centimeters in southern Campeche at the base of the peninsula to less than 50 centimeters in far northern Yucatan near the Gulf of Mexico (Fig. 6.5). There is, nonetheless, a dry season of

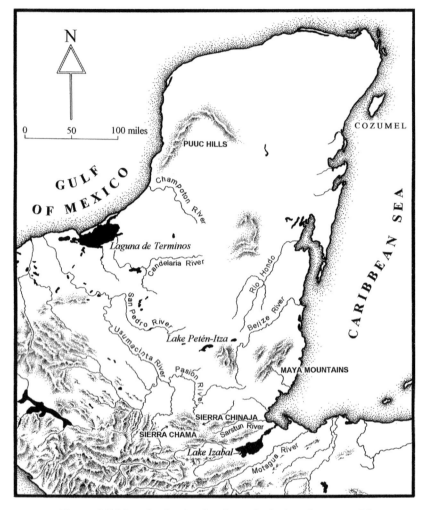

Figure 6.5 Maya lowlands, showing principal environmental features
(drawn by Luis F. Luin)

six months in the north to little over a month in the far south, at the
base of the highlands. For this reason, the Maya lowland forest is technically considered a "humid subtropical forest" rather than a true perennial
rain forest.

The nature of the jungle canopy corresponds closely to level of rainfall,
drainage patterns, and local soil conditions. In the south, in the heart
of the Petén region of Guatemala, a dense triple-canopied rain forest

Figure 6.6 Schematic view of the layers of subtropical forest canopy
(drawn by Luis F. Luin)

anchored by massive mahoganies, cedars, and ceibas rises up to 70 meters
in height (Fig. 6.6). The heavy rainfall and better surface drainage in this
southern lowland region also supports a second, slightly lower canopy of
trees including matapalo (strangler fig), cedars, and the gum-producing
sapodilla (chicle) trees. A bottom tier includes the useful rubber, ramon
(bread-nut), and avocado trees, as well as many fruit trees rising from
just above the jungle floor to about 20 meters in height. A lattice of vines,
lianas, orchids, bromeliads, and ferns laces together the trees of all levels
of the canopy into a continuous luxuriant mass (Fig. 6.7).

   A wide range of animal life flourishes within and below the rain forest
canopies of the southern lowlands. Jaguars, ocelots, deer, fox, and rabbits
inhabit the floor of the rain forest and were all utilized by the Maya
for food, pelts, and bone ornaments or tools. Agoutis (small rodents),
ant-eating tapirs of various sizes, turkeys, and herds of small wild boar
(peccaries or *havile*) also abound in the rain forest and were important in
the ancient Maya diet, as well as in their representations in ceramic art and
sculpture (Benson 1997). The canopies above are home to lively troops
of spider and howler monkeys (Fig. 6.8) and to a noisy host of exotic
birds, including the familiar toucans and parrots in many varieties (Murie

Figure 6.7 Petén rain forest vegetation

1935; L.C. Stuart 1964). Especially important in Maya ideology and imagery were the ever-present hummingbird and the stunningly beautiful giant macaws, with their long bright red or blue-green plumage (Griscom 1932). The latter, along with the quetzal from the highland slopes to the south, provided much of the plumage for the elaborate headdresses that were a critical marker of status for Maya elites, especially rulers.

The reptiles and amphibians of the rain forest are even more omnipresent in Maya ideology and art, especially the caiman (alligator), symbol of the earthly plane of existence, and many varieties of snakes, including boas, corals, rattlesnakes, pit vipers, and the most deadly *barba amarilla* (fer-de-lance) and xalpate (*bothrops numifer*) (Schmidt and Andrews 1936). Toads, frogs, and turtles are found in the forest's lakes, swamps, and rivers. The ancient Maya made effective use of these animals as well, employing the carapaces of turtles for useful tools ranging from musical instruments to hard surfaces for shields, cotton armor, and mosaics in headdresses. The lakes, rivers, and swamps also provided important elements in the Maya diet, including fish such as mojarra, catfish, and robalo, and many types of shellfish. Fish bones were utilized by the ancient Maya for needles, awls, and other tools while fragments of shell (some imported from the Caribbean or Gulf coasts) were employed for the complex mosaic imagery on Maya headdresses, shields, and

Figure 6.8 Howler monkey

ornaments, as well as in necklaces and ear spools. Even the insect life gave the Maya both symbols and useful products, including incenses and honey from wild and domesticated hives.

The density of life in the Petén rain forest remains impressive even after two centuries of misguided modern settlement and exploitation. In those zones not yet leveled by lumbering or settlement, the cacophony of rain forest life – the mingled cries, howls, calls, and buzzing of birds, monkeys, frogs, and insects – rises in the mornings and evenings to a roaring pitch. Taken together, the wildlife and vegetation of the rain forest gave the ancient Maya a nearly unlimited supply of useful products for subsistence, construction, ornament, and imagery – even without considering the agriculture that produced the bulk of their diet. The wealth of the rain forest was well understood by the ancient Maya. They stood in awe of the jungle and utilized its structure and its inhabitants as models for many aspects of their ideology (Chapter 8).

### Lowland landforms and regional variation

The landforms of the southern lowlands are primarily defined by a karst limestone geology, high rainfall, and good surface drainage which created the large rivers, streams, and lakes that were critical to ancient Maya life, subsistence, and transport. Large rivers and their tributaries defined the boundaries and the communication arteries of the Maya (Fig. 6.5). In the west, the Pasión and Usumacinta river system runs from the highlands to the Gulf of Mexico. Most major western sites and satellite centers were closely related to these rivers, their fertile levee soils, and their natural canoe portages. Similarly, in the east the Rio Hondo, the Belize River, and other streams run from the Petén to the Caribbean coast and defined the ancient trade routes in salt, shell, and other sea products, as well as transport for exotics from even farther north and south. Many of these waterways also deposited and renewed thick, rich soils along their levees and floodplains.

The salient feature of the central Petén is a series of lakes and their associated drainage basins. The largest of these, Lake Petén-Itza, was always, and remains today, a center of population due to its natural ecological potential for fishing, hunting, and especially productive farming. Nearly a dozen other lakes form smaller basins. Between these stretched the rain forest and – in the Classic period – some of the largest Maya cities and their satellite centers, hamlets, and farms. In the Petén the higher rain forest canopies, or the richer farms in cleared zones, were located on the more elevated, well-drained soils of the gently rolling landscape of this region. Lower zones include seasonally inundated *bajos*, which today are considered unusable for cultivation. We now know, however, that the ancient Maya utilized even these zones for seasonal farming and as a source of rich soils for box gardens and terraces (Dunning and Beach in press; Culbert *et al.* 1996; Kunen *et al.* 2000). The drier low-lying zones are grassy savannas with few trees and dense red clay of limited utility for cultivation (D. Rice *et al.* 1985).

In general, regardless of the local landform, soil type, and vegetation, the Classic and Preclassic Maya inhabitants skillfully utilized the local microenvironments. The limestone itself provided a malleable, easily worked building material for their masonry and when burned gave them the lime powder base for their concrete and mortar. In some areas, nodules and beds of fine, hard, cryptocrystalline chert, or flint, form in the limestone. The Maya worked these into tools for construction, wood-work, agriculture, ornament, or war. Clay deposits near lakes, rivers, and *bajos* provided the material for the Maya ceramics, including both utili-tarian and fine wares.

Moving northward from the central Petén, the environment has lower rainfall (Fig. 6.5), higher average temperatures, and generally thinner soils. The jungle canopy becomes lower and agricultural potential may have been somewhat more limited. The salient problem is a lack of surface water, since in most areas of the Yucatan peninsula the eroded karst topography has absorbed most drainages into deep subterranean passages. Water-filled sinkholes or *cenotes*, springs in caves, and artificially excavated and maintained reservoirs and wells were the principal sources of water for the ancient Maya of the northern lowlands. Note that despite this characterization, the ancient Maya also managed to utilize even the driest portions of the northern lowlands to support impressive cities with large populations (Dunning 1992). Differing adaptations in the north, as yet still imperfectly understood, have helped to shape aspects of the various northern regional forms of Classic Maya civilization.

### The rain forest agricultural strategy

While hunting and gathering activities added important sources of protein to the Maya diet and provided raw materials for their craftspeople, the bulk of the Maya diet was based, of course, on agriculture.

Rain forest farming is a very tricky business, despite the ample rainfall and favorable tropical climates of such zones. Soils in the rain forest are thin, as much of its biomass is in its multiple canopies above. As a conse-quence, most forms of clearing and farming can quickly exhaust the nutri-ents in soils and upon exposure to the intense tropical sun soils can turn into nearly rock-hard laterite surfaces. Modern agricultural exploitations that employ Western farming techniques have destroyed vast stretches of rain forests in the Petén and Yucatan.

As discussed above, the fragility of rain forest ecology and, especially, the delicate nature of its soils, were long misperceived by Western scholars as indicating that rain forests were almost incapable of supporting civilizations or even large populations. This influenced previous interpretations of the rise and the fall of Classic Maya civilization. The former was characterized as a "secondary state formation" stimulated by Teotihuacan, Kaminaljuyu, or other highland polities (whose primary state evolution had taken place in environments more acceptable to traditional ecological interpretations). The decline or collapse of southern Maya cities in the ninth century was seen as the inevitable consequence of the limitations of the rain forest (e.g. Meggers 1954).

The rain forest does present many specific challenges and problems, but the Maya were ingenious in confronting them. We have begun to understand ancient Maya agricultural strategies due to a series of recent collaborations between ecologists, geographers, and archaeologists working in the lowlands (see bibliographic essay at the end of this volume). While popular perspectives talk of the "secret" of the lost civilization of the Maya in terms of hidden treasures or hieroglyphic inscriptions, the true secret of Maya civilization was their successful, sustainable adaptation to the rain forest, a feat we have not been able to duplicate today. In broad terms, the "secret" of the Maya adaptive strategy was simply to structure their agricultural regimes to imitate the nature of the rain forest itself. As described above, the two central characteristics of the rain forest are its biodiversity and the wide dispersion of individuals of any given species over a wide area. In their gradual adaptation to the rain forest ecological regimes, the growing populations of the Maya learned to adapt their agricultural systems to mimic the *diversity* and the *dispersion* of the rain forest (Nations and Nigh 1980; Dunning and Demarest 1989; Dunning *et al.* 1992).

The Maya used a variety of farming systems, each adapted to local soils and landforms. This *diversity* in exploitation techniques parallels the structure of the forest and allowed farming systems on each parcel of land to be well suited to the drainage patterns, soil type and depth, slope, rainfall, and other microenvironmental characteristics of that particular plot. Problems of soil exhaustion, erosion, leaching of soils, and laterization were avoided by this application of a diversity of farming techniques, each sensitive to local conditions (Harrison and Turner 1978; Dunning 1996; Fedick 1996). Cultigens were also varied to suit local soils and conditions with maize-beans-squash farming alternating with stands of fruit trees, cultivation of tubers and other crops, overgrown fallow zones (*guamil*) used for hunting, and large stands of rain forest left as sources of wood and for hunting and collecting.

The second general aspect of Maya agriculture was to mimic the other major characteristic of rain forests: the *dispersion* of individual species over a wide area. The Maya farming strategy, with its varied techniques, scattered any individual form of field system over a wide area – interspersed with other forms of agriculture, fallow zones, or rain forest. Just as important to this strategy was the dispersal of the Maya population itself. We now know that Maya cities had substantial populations, but they were dispersed over a wider area than Western centers, or even than the cities of their contemporaries in the highlands of Mexico and Guatemala. Noble and non-elite household groups were more concentrated near the ceremonial architectural epicenters, but even there household gardens, reservoirs, stands of fruit trees, and even intensive farming systems were interspersed between the temples, palaces, and grand plazas, and the household groups (Fig. 6.4). Moving out from the epicenters, clusters of houses were more widely scattered between areas of gardens, farms, fallow zones, and stands of rain forest (Killion 1992; Fedick 1996).

The effect of this dispersion of populations, together with the diversity in subsistence systems, was to maximize the productive potential of the rain forest without exhausting its soils or otherwise contradicting the delicate ecological balance of any one area. This diversity and dispersion allowed ancient Maya civilization to maintain populations numbering in the millions in the Petén region alone – far beyond modern populations there, and well beyond our earlier estimations of its carrying capacity.

In recent years archaeologists and paleoecologists also have plotted the periods of overexploitation, deforestation, and resulting ecological damage from ancient Maya agricultural systems, and they have related these to periods of decline in specific regions (e.g. Abrams and Rue 1988; Santley *et al.* 1986; Culbert 1977, 1988; Dunning and Beach 2000). Such problems certainly existed in some areas, especially at the end of the Late Preclassic and Late Classic periods. Yet we should not lose sight of the generally amazing success of the ancient Maya lowland adaptations which sustained huge populations in this rain forest for two millennia.

From this description of ancient Maya subsistence systems, it should be apparent why archaeologists and even ecologists had for so long failed to grasp Maya population sizes, settlement strategy, and subsistence techniques. The ancient Maya approach to rain forest agriculture could not have been more different from Western monoculture, in which a single technique for farming one cultigen is applied to a large area. Our monoculture farming techniques are appropriate for application to vast, relatively undifferentiated areas of thick soils, such as the rich loess plains of

Kansas and Central Europe, or the thick, annually renewed floodplains of Mesopotamia. In a rain forest, however, with its thin soils and variability in rainfall, slope, drainage patterns, and soil quality, such monoculture would have been a disaster. Indeed, today, as Westernized highland Maya have settled the Petén, they have rapidly destroyed the rain forest and left large stretches of it unusable for any purpose.

A chief advantage of Western monoculture is the overproduction of a single crop, allowing sale or exchange of that product in a market economy. Again, this economic rationale works well for the well-developed market economies of Western civilization, or those of our ancestors in Mesopotamia. It would not have been suited to the ancient Maya economy which, as discussed in Chapter 7, had only weakly developed markets with local self-sufficiency in subsistence products for most communities. Perhaps it is because of this striking contrast in physical structure and economic logic that Western scholars were unable for a century to fathom the "secrets" of ancient Maya ecological strategy.

### Ancient Maya agricultural systems

Our understanding of ancient Maya farming has been guided – sometimes astray – by the contemporary agriculture practiced by millions of Maya today. Recent studies, however, have proven that important practices and strategies have changed since the Classic period due to the impact of the Spanish conquest and the incorporation of the Maya into the Colonial market economy and administrative structures. Spanish policies concentrated populations into more controllable towns and emphasized the production of staple crops, especially corn, that could be easily transported and stored. Nonetheless, some lowland groups, such as the isolated Lacandon Maya, maintained some of the Classic Maya techniques and strategies in their rain forest subsistence systems (e.g. Nations and Nigh 1980; Netting 1977). These clues, together with the recent archaeological and paleoecological researches, are now beginning to give us a view of the much wider range of Classic- and Preclassic-period approaches to agricultural production in the lowlands.

#### Swidden farming

Today the most common form of Maya rain forest agriculture is "slash-and-burn" or "swidden" farming. An extensive, rather than intensive, system, swidden begins with the cutting of trees and other vegetation in the chosen plot or *milpa*. After months in the tropical sun of the dry season in late March, April, and May, the dried vegetation is burned, leaving a

Figure 6.9  Clearing and burning of forest *milpa*

rich deposit of carbon and ash (Fig. 6.9). With a simple wooden digging stick, seeds of corn, beans, and squashes are placed into this newly created soil. The heavy rains of June and July germinate these crops and begin the cycle of care, weeding, and harvest. While initially productive, swidden *milpa* soils become exhausted after several years of this cyclical burning and reseeding of growth. Then the field must be left fallow for a number of years – depending on local soils and the number of seasons it had been cultivated. As a consequence, only a portion of potential rain forest land can be used at any given time, reducing carrying capacity and population density. Early studies of Maya civilization assumed that all agriculture was of the swidden type practiced by many Maya today (Cook 1921; Meggers 1954). We now know Maya agriculture was more multifaceted, more productive, and less destructive (e.g. Fedick 1996; Harrison and Turner 1978; Dunning *et al.* 1998, 2000).

### Sustainable swidden systems

The archaeological evidence led ethnographers and ethnohistorians also to re-examine their assumptions about Maya *milpa* or swidden farming itself (Nations and Nigh 1980; Helmuth 1977). Lacandon and early Colonial *milpa* was often practiced in a less destructive manner. In such *milpa* systems, some large trees were left standing, facilitating more rapid recovery in fallow periods. Some plot areas also may have been smaller. Cultigens were more varied, including tubers, greater reliance on fruit trees, and hunting and gathering in fallow zones and adjacent rain forest. Plots could be more intensively and continuously exploited because of the use of "night soils" (human waste) as fertilizer. Also, more continuous use may have been possible because of the less cleared, less eroded form of such plots and their alternation with other systems.

Pre-Columbian *milpa* farming was more sustainable for longer periods of time because it developed gradually over the centuries of initial farming occupations in the Petén and was more carefully adapted to the needs and limitations of jungle soils. It is also true that the highly destructive "clear-cut" forest clearing used in *milpa* agriculture today (e.g. Fig. 6.9) would be difficult and costly without modern steel axes and chainsaws. Leaving some areas in rain forest, clearing more irregular plots with stone axes and adzes, and avoiding cutting the massive ceiba and mahogany trees may have been both the least demanding and the most productive approach to rain forest clearing utilized by the ancient Maya. In any case, the resulting form of swidden was more productive for a longer period and could more quickly recover from fallow periods.

### Household gardening

The ancient Maya used small, intensive garden plots placed behind and around house platforms, as observed by Landa during the Conquest period (Tozzer 1941). The potential importance of such "infield" gardening systems only became apparent after the application of phosphate isotope studies to wide areas of some sites (Dunning 1992, 1993, 1994, 1996; Killion 1992). These studies discovered that at sites like Sayil, in the northern lowlands, and Tamarindito, in the Pasión region, even areas within the very epicenters had remnant phosphates in the soils, with isotope profiles indicating heavy agricultural usage with frequent fertilization with night soils, and, sometimes, with swamp muck brought in from nearby. These intensive, fertilized gardens around and between residences could have been very productive, with a major impact on Maya diet and population carrying capacity. Gardens, cultivated and harvested year round, also took pressure off of the swidden system, allowing application of more sustainable, but less productive, forms of swidden.

### Terracing

Another important technique practiced extensively in the lowlands in the Classic period, but not as common today, was the use of various types of terrace walls to retain soil, retard erosion, and conserve moisture. The term "terracing" covers a huge spectrum of activities involving construction of retaining walls (Dunning and Beach 1994, in press). Many pre-Columbian terraces that had a critical impact on farming productivity were simple rows of unworked rock (Fig. 6.10) piled by a family to reduce erosion on a slightly steep slope (Beach and Dunning 1995). Other terrace systems were extensive, possibly state-controlled, and involved remodeling the contours of the ancient landscape (Fig. 6.11) for kilometers around major centers such as Caracol (Chase and Chase 1987) and even throughout some entire *regions*, like the Río Bec zone in Campeche (R.E.W. Adams 1975, 1981). Some careful studies have, however, found that vast areas of contour terracing – such as that found in the Upper Belize River Valley – probably were not centrally planned or controlled (Fedick 1994).

This variability in the extent of intensive agricultural systems – as well as variability in state involvement – has caused much confusion and debate about the "true nature" of Maya agricultural systems. In fact, subsistence strategies (like economic and political systems) varied greatly from region to region, especially during the Late Classic apogee of Maya civilization in the lowlands. As we shall see, the sixth through ninth centuries witnessed rapid population growth in many regions, accompanied by experimentation with various economic and political forms. Extensive state-planned or -managed agricultural systems (especially terraces) may have been part of such experimentation in Belize, Campeche, and a few other zones (Dunning and Beach 1994; Dunning *et al.* 1998). In general, terracing at Maya sites was less formal, locally constructed, and controlled by farming families (Fedick 1994; Neff *et al.* 1995; Beach and Dunning 1995; Dunning and Beach 1994). Nonetheless, even such simple localized terraces greatly increase productivity and protect the thin lowland soils from erosion.

*Raised fields*

The ancient Maya also modified landscapes to farm in low-lying terrain considered unusable today. Some seasonally inundated swamps or *bajos* were transformed into productive fields by excavating drainage channels and piling up soils between them. This created artificial ridges or islands that could be continuously refertilized from the water and organic muck of channels and the surrounding swamp (Fig. 6.12). Year-round intensive cultivation and continuous harvests were possible from such plots. Channels and lagoons around the raised fields were used for intensive fishing, as well as the collection of mollusks and other swamp life. These

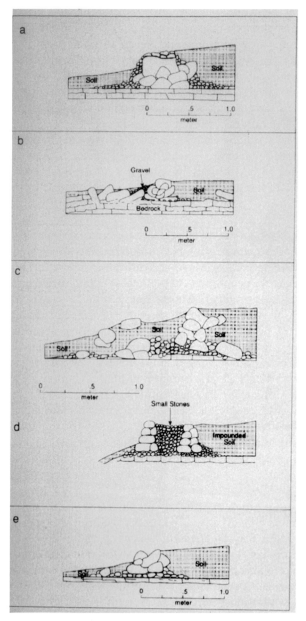

Figure 6.10 Cross-section of simple terrace forms (from Beach and Dunning 1995: Fig. 4)

terraces not mapped

Figure 6.11 Possible agricultural terraces near the site of Caracol,
Belize (from Chase and Chase 1998)

raised fields (or *chinampas*, as the Aztecs called them) were virtual
food factories that could disproportionately contribute to the subsistence
support of centers and populations nearby.

Extensive raised-field systems have been investigated in Belize at Pulltrouser Swamp (Turner 1978, 1983; Turner and Harrison, 1983), the
southeastern corner of the Yucatan peninsula in the state of Quintana
Roo, Mexico, and in northern Belize (Harrison 1981, 1990; Harrison
and Turner 1978). In the 1970s and 1980s, after the discovery of
such systems, archaeologists and paleoarchaeologists overreacted. Some
enthusiastically hypothesized that state-controlled raised-field agriculture
in *bajos* and lakes may have been the primary agricultural system and

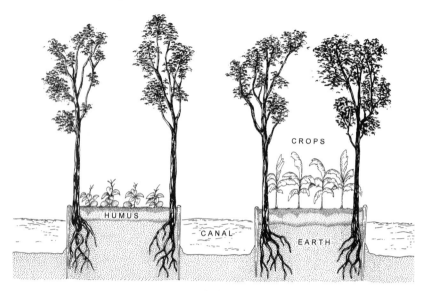

Chinampa lake-bed agriculture

Figure 6.12 Cross-section of raised field agricultural systems (drawn by Luis F. Luin)

the key to understanding the Maya ability to sustain large populations in the rain forest (e.g. Turner 1978, 1983; Harrison 1977; Hammond 1978). Aerial surveys, including satellite imagery and side-angle radar, were then used to identify vast stretches of raised fields and canal systems in the southern lowlands (e.g. Adams *et al.* 1981; R.E.W. Adams 1980). Subsequent ground survey has demonstrated that most of these proposed systems were illusions created by "bugs" in the aerial techniques or statistical data processing which misidentified natural geological patterns for field constructions.

Re-evaluation of landforms and hydrology in the Petén now indicates that raised-field systems can only be successful in areas with restricted annual fluctuation in water levels (Pope and Dahlin 1989; Dunning 1996; Dunning, Beach, and Rue 1997). Such a restriction would imply that most areas of the major river systems had little potential for annual raised-field agriculture. Instead, it is now believed that ancient Maya subsistence strategies did not rely on one or two intensive technologies, but on a complex mosaic of different types of field and subsistence systems (Fedick 1996; Dunning, Beach, and Rue 1997; Dunning *et al.* 1998). The Maya subsistence strategy was such a "managed mosaic" of many different plots with various cultigens that together provided a more secure subsistence than heavy reliance on a single method. Thus, raised fields – and their high productivity – were an important element in many local farming systems, but most areas of such fields were relatively few, small, and localized.

### Seasonal bajo agriculture

A less dramatic, but probably more common, use of *bajos* and swamp areas was their exploitation for seasonal agriculture. While these areas are inundated every rainy season, many *bajos* stay dry for a sufficient period of the year to potentially allow for a single dry season crop of maize, tubers, or other cultigens. *Bajos* also are rich areas for collecting wild plants and for hunting game in the dry season. Paleoecologists have known for some time of the potential of *bajo* zones for seasonal use, including farming (Dunning, Beach, and Rue 1995).

Recent excavations and paleoecological studies (Culbert *et al.* 1996; Kunen *et al.* 2000) have demonstrated that the Maya did, indeed, utilize this potential with agriculture and even some occupation *within* the *bajos* near some major Classic Maya centers. Dense occupations along the edges of *bajos* near the great center of Tikal were critical to its support of large populations. The fact that *bajo* use is very limited today misled archaeologists to assume that such areas are "unusable." With the high population densities of the Classic period, however, and with over a millennium of close adaptation to all of the rain forest microenvironments, the ancient Maya knew how to effectively utilize the *bajos*.

Again, regional variability must be central to any characterization of Classic Maya culture and subsistence regimes. In some areas, population densities were not so high as to require utilization of *bajos*. In other zones the specific soils or hydrology of *bajos* rendered them difficult to use even on a seasonal basis (Dunning 1996). Other areas, such as the central Petén zone of Tikal and Uaxactun, had regional ecological conditions and settlement density that led to heavy utilization of the *bajos*, not for raised fields, but for seasonal swidden farming (Culbert *et al.* 1996; Kunen *et al.* 2000). Finally, as discussed above, in those areas with controllable or stable water levels, *bajos* and lakes were used for intensive raised-field gardens.

### Other localized intensive agricultural systems

Ancient Maya adaptations were tailored in some zones to very specific landforms and soils – some of which are considered unusable today. For example, paleoecologists have identified a form of ancient Maya agriculture in sunken zones, also called *rejolladas*, where subterranean erosion and collapse of the karst limestone bedrock has left small humid depressions or sinkholes on the surface (Kepecs and Boucher 1996; Dunning, Beach, and Rue 1997). The thick soils that form in the bottom of such depressions can be highly productive for intensive gardens or fruit or cacao trees, if properly cultivated with occasional use of contour terracing to limit erosion or leeching of soils. Similarly, the Maya used "check" dams to block erosion and create alluvial fans of rich soils for farming in gullies or arroyos which would otherwise have eroded surrounding soils (Turner 1985; Dunning and Beach 1994).

In some zones, steep natural drop-offs or escarpments on the limestone ridges or the edge of plateaus were terraced with multiple low walls that stopped erosion, retained rich soils, and, sometimes, also divided up areas of responsibility for farming and control of the product (Killion et al. 1991; Dunning and Beach 1994; Dunning, Beach, and Rue 1997). In some steep areas near major centers, small stone box terraces were used as nurseries for seeding cacao trees or as vegetable gardens for palaces (Fig. 6.4). In areas of more gradual hilly slopes, thinner soils, and lower rainfall (like the Campeche-Río Bec zone of the southern Yucatan peninsula, see Fig. 9.10, page 227), larger, wider terraces were constructed to facilitate annual farming and the need for long fallow periods (e.g. Eaton 1975). Some regions, such as the El Mirador Basin of the northern Petén, have extensive *bajo* zones separating ridges or islands of higher, well-drained soils. Recent excavations and paleoecological studies in these areas have discovered possible huge gardens on the higher ridges where soils and muck were brought in from the *bajos* and re-deposited for upland gardening (Hansen 1989). Such a highly productive form of ancient landscaping might help to explain the subsistence regime of the earliest Maya cities, such as Nakbe and El Mirador (Hansen 1991b, 2001).

Much later, at the very end of the Classic period, redeposited *bajo* soils and stone box gardens appear to have been used on a smaller scale near some site epicenters. In these cases, the purpose may have been to provide for elite populations. Such stone box gardens, refertilized with human waste and redeposited soils and vegetation, could also have been a *defensible* source of food near epicenters during periods of intensified warfare. At Punta de Chimino in the Petexbatun region of the western Petén (Beach 1996; Demarest 1996a; Quezada et al. 1996) such stone box gardens were constructed *within* a moat and wall system, assuring a food supply for the besieged population in the late eighth century (Fig. 6.13).

In many cases, ecological regimes and population density were well adapted to the local rain forest soils and conditions. Population density determined the degree to which intensive agricultural systems would be

Figure 6.13 Stone box gardens at the site of Punta de Chimino, Petexbatun, Guatemala (drawn by Luis F. Luin)

used to extend farming into areas underutilized, poorly utilized, or unutilized today. In most zones, *diversity* in subsistence practices, *dispersion* in farming systems and urban occupations, and *sensitivity* to microenvironmental variation led to the success of ancient Maya rain forest adaptation.

We should not, however, idealize the success of Maya lowland adaptations. In different specific periods and locales, political pressures and miscalculations led to overuse or misuse of soils and local resources. Serious erosion due to over-clearing has been documented, especially at the end of the Late Preclassic period and, in some subregions, at the end of the Classic era. In the Copan Valley (Freter 1994; Paine and Freter 1996), the southern kingdom of Cancuen (Demarest and Barrientos 1999, 2000), and elsewhere, epicenter and sustaining populations expanded residential areas to cover – and thus remove from production – some of the most fertile farmland. Such mistakes and overexploitation contributed to some regional episodes of political crisis or decline (e.g. Abrams and Rue 1988). Nonetheless, in general the ancient Maya were well adapted to the rain forest environment in which their cities grew and evolved for over 1,500 years. As we shall see (Chapter 10), deficiencies in Maya adaptive strategies were more rooted in political, rather than subsistence, failures.

**Minor and major hydraulic systems and the Maya state**

Traditional theories on the rise of early states emphasize their alleged role in construction and management of irrigation systems or other major hydraulic projects. As we have seen, such scenarios don't work for the Maya area, where rainfall is heavy, though seasonal in most subregions, and many sites are on or near rivers, lakes, and other water sources. There are, however, small reservoirs, aqueducts, and pools at sites to allow for more conveniently located water sources, in some cases for dry season water, and as loci for water ritual (Scarborough 1996, 1998; Ohnstad *et al.* 2003; B. Fash in press). In general, the construction of Maya lowland reservoirs or modification of water holes and seasonal lakes (*aguadas*) would not have been necessary, at least not in the southern lowlands, until population levels were fairly high and concentrated; that is, these extensions of water reserves would not have been necessary until long after the rise of the Preclassic lowland rulership.

Nonetheless, some Mayanists have not been able to resist the appealing simplicity of "hydraulic functionalism" and try to explain the rise, and even the fall, of Classic Maya states based on rulers' control of water sources and systems (e.g., Lucero 2002, 2003). As noted above, such theories don't apply to the vast majority of sites and regions in the Maya world during the initial Preclassic rise of lowland states. Furthermore, most reservoir systems would simply be another aspect of the "managed mosaic" of farming and subsistence systems (Fedick 1996) that were created and controlled at the extended family or community level. For those reasons, it is a more convincing argument that in general, water reservoirs in the southern lowlands were most important at the community level as foci for ritual, local identity, and community integration (e.g. Ohnstad *et al.* 2003; Scarborough 1998; Lucero 2003; B. Fash in press; Vogt 1976, 1981, 1983). Claims of supernatural influence over rainfall, seasonality, and water-related ritual were undoubtedly always important to the power of Maya shamans, priests, and rulers. "Real" (in Western terms) control of hydraulic systems or reservoirs was more likely a later and auxiliary addition to rulers' authority at some major centers and in the driest regions (e.g. Dunning 1992; Scarborough 1996, 1998).

Yet, as with all aspects of ancient Maya civilizations, there were significant regional exceptions to this picture of small scale hydraulic projects. Water control and storage for the regionally variable dry season was a major challenge for the ancient Maya, especially in the drier northern lowlands. The Maya responded to the need for dry-season water for drinking, cooking, and gardening in a variety of ways. Most major Maya centers were located near rivers, lakes, or lagoons. The Maya solved the problem of transporting and storing household water by producing and using ceramic water jars with striated surfaces (Fig. 6.14). These textured surfaces both cooled the contents and provided a better grip. At some

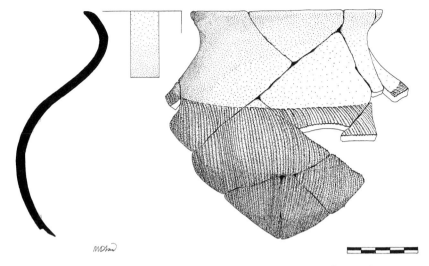

Figure 6.14 Fragments of typical Late Classic striated water jars
(drawn by David Lord)

Petén centers farther from rivers or lakes, such as Tikal and El Mirador, *bajos* were lined with clay or even stone pavements to convert them into reservoirs in the center of the cities. Farther north, in the northern half of the Yucatan peninsula, the water problem was more acute due to lower rainfall and lack of surface water. In these areas, large bottle-shaped stone wells, or *chultunes*, were carved into the soft limestone bedrock and lined with clay for water storage.

Large-scale hydraulic works near some centers remain to be fully explored and understood. A canal system around the Late Preclassic center of Cerros delimited its sacred epicenter, provided water control for a small raised-field system, and may have facilitated the defensibility of the site's palaces and temples (Freidel *et al.* 1982). Such multiple functions have also been posited for a much more massive water system at the northern Maya center of Edzna in Campeche (Fig. 6.15). There, enormous canals radiate out from its Late Preclassic- and Classic-period center, providing water storage, a transport system, water for fields, a defensive system, or even possibly artificial lagoons for fishing or fish farming (Matheny *et al.* 1983; Matheny 1976). Encircling the great center of Calakmul, Campeche, is an enigmatic canal system, possibly also a defensive perimeter (Fig. 6.16). Whatever the actual function (or functions) of water systems like those of Edzna or Calakmul, it is certain that their construction and control would have required central management

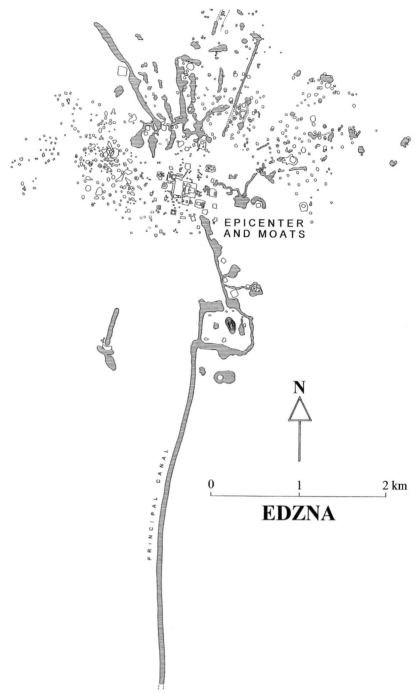

EPICENTER
AND MOATS

PRINCIPAL CANAL

N

0    1    2 km

EDZNA

Figure 6.15 Water control systems at the site of Edzna, Campeche, Mexico (drawn by Luis F. Luin after Matheny *et al.* 1983: Fig. 2)

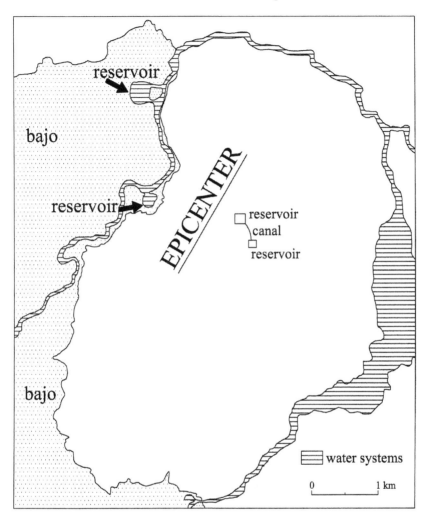

Figure 6.16 Canal systems around the site of Calakmul, Campeche, Mexico (redrafted by Matt O'Mansky after Folan *et al.* 1995)

by the state or elites (Matheny 1987). Again, such major hydraulic works were not widespread in the lowlands and do not form a general pattern in the ancient Maya world comparable to the irrigation systems of Babylonia or the raised fields of Aztec central Mexico. Rather, these are further evidence of the regional variability and the local ecological sensitivity of Maya rain forest subsistence systems.

## Arboriculture and timber exploitation

The ancient Maya exploited every other aspect of the bounty of the rain forest. Probably due to ancient arboriculture, today fruit trees of many species are most common near the great Maya centers. Wild and cultivated papaya, zapote, maguey, avocados, and other fruits provided important vitamins to the Maya daily diet, as well as serving as a source of potent fermented fruit beverages for ancient feasts and rituals (Dahlin and Litzinger 1986).

Cacao trees, the source of chocolate beans, were a central component of Maya economies. They were cultivated in scattered patches between *milpas* as well as intensively farmed in well-watered terraces and gardens, including sunken *rejolladas* gardens (Dahlin 1979; Dunning and Beach in press; Helmuth 1977). Ground chocolate beans from cacao arboriculture were a part of daily subsistence for Maya elites and commoners. Among the Maya the daily routine began (and often still begins) with a drink of thick, bitter hot chocolate. Chocolate sauces of all kinds were – and still are – popular. Chocolate was considered essential to the diet of Mesoamerican peoples. Cacao beans were a major medium of exchange, "archaic money," in pre-Columbian markets, and were also a common element in Maya art and imagery.

The trees of the rain forest provided many other foods, spices, and materials for crafts and construction. Vanilla and allspice were used for flavoring. Other trees furnished saps and resins used for binding everything from shell mosaic artwork to stone dart heads for deadly weapons. Other trees, like the copal, were the sources for incenses that were a necessary part of every ritual. Barks and seeds provided a variety of products ranging from natural insect repellents to the source of the potent *balche* ale that intoxicated Maya priests and elites at feasts and rituals. Above all, the trees provided construction materials, including the frames for Maya houses, lintels for palaces and temples, and the thatch for their roofs. The naturally cooled thatch roof, sealed by spider and insect nests, is the most comfortable form of shelter (a fact rediscovered in modern archaeological camps and luxury "ecotouristic" inns). The hardest woods of the rain forest, especially the rock-hard sapodilla wood and beautiful mahogany and cedars, were used for carved works of art that are sometimes still preserved in tombs or other buried contexts. Elaborately carved sapodilla lintels with long hieroglyphic texts have been found in outstanding condition in the doorways of temples, giving us histories of and insights into Maya temple rituals and concepts.

The lumber of the rain forest also was the source of fuels for all purposes. Wood from bushes and smaller trees was used for the treatment of stone for artifacts, heating on the cold rain forest evenings, and for fires in homes as a means to drive away the endless cloud of tropical insects. In addition, lime concrete mortar used in all Maya construction required burning of limestone in high-temperature fires. Indeed, some scholars have posited that some Late Classic Maya deforestation problems may have come as much from the production of lime plaster as from clearing land for farming (Abrams and Rue 1988).

## Animal husbandry, hunting, and fishing

Faunal remains testify to an exploitation of the forest animal life that was as broad and varied as other ancient Maya adaptations. Domesticated turkeys were raised in pens and in household gardens. Turtles and fish were constantly being netted from lakes, rivers, swamps, and the artificial reservoirs and canals. They were not only a critical source of protein, but their shells and bones were the raw material for tools, musical instruments, armor, headdresses, shields, scepters, and bloodletters that were the symbols of royal and ritual power (Emery 1997, in press). In some areas, such as the Candelaria River system of lower Campeche, fish and other aquatic life may have been pond raised (Thompson 1974). In all areas, the Maya landscaping of natural terrain and creation of canals and lagoons increased the bounty of aquatic life for consumption and crafts.

Apiculture (beekeeping) was an aspect of Maya subsistence that was much celebrated in ritual (Tozzer 1941). Honey was an important supplement to the Maya diet and a flavoring for many dishes. It was most prized, however, as a key ingredient of the alcoholic beverage *balche*. This potent drink, made from a fermented mixture of honey and *balche* tree bark, was consumed and offered to supernaturals in rituals and feasts. Hollowed logs and wooden hives were used to house the productive, stingless bees of the lowlands. As an easily stored, transportable resource, honey may have been exchanged more widely in the lowlands than most subsistence goods.

Deer were hunted, sometimes so systematically that the practice approached domestication. Fallow zones and patches of rain forest were left throughout even the most densely populated areas to assure a nearby deer population for hunting and trapping. Recent multidisciplinary studies of diet, including the consumption of deer meat (White and Schwartz 1989; Emery, Wright, and Schwartz 2000; Emery 1997; Wright in press; Wright and White 1996) and the use of deer bone for tools (Emery 1997, in press), have demonstrated the intimate relationship of the Maya with these rain forest cohabitants. By the Late Classic period, the percent of deer consumption in the diet (indicated by strontium isotope levels) was almost as reliable a measure of social status as jade or quetzal feathers (D. Chase *et al.* 1998; Wright in press). Deer bone was a major source of artifacts and tools for daily use, as well as ornaments. The deer, meanwhile, thrived on feeding in the fallow zones and fields of the Classic Maya and maize became a major component of deer diet. The human–deer symbiotic relationship was so close that the diet of the deer themselves (as revealed by studies of their bones) is one of the tools for reconstructing the extent and nature of ancient Maya field systems (e.g. Emery, Wright, and Schwartz 2000).

Hunting and trapping included, of course, many other rain forest species. Wild boar (*havile*), agoutis, tapirs, lizards, and many avian species found their way into the Maya diet. The frogs and toads that cover the rain forest trails and stream banks were supplemental food, as well as a source of specialized products, including hallucinogens. The deadly vipers and the majestic constrictors of the forest were a feared and sacred source of imagery and concepts for Maya ideology.

### Subsistence and the Classic Maya state

Traditional theories of the rise of complex society and the formation of states explain the development of elites as managers of critical aspects of the economy. Functionalist thinking dictates that if institutions of inequality in wealth and centralization of power exist, they must have arisen for a "practical" reason. Thus, early chiefs and archaic states are assumed to have been involved in aspects of the economy which required centralized management, such as construction and maintenance of hydraulic systems, management of trade in subsistence goods, and corporate organization of intensive agricultural systems. Yet, as we have seen, in the Maya lowlands one of the secrets of their rain forest adaptation was that it was decentralized – allowing local adaptations to microenvironmental conditions for each patch of ground. Farming families, drawing upon generations of knowledge of their soils, gradients, and vegetation, were able to apply any of a variety of intensive or extensive gardening or field systems to suit those local conditions. Indeed, areas most successful in avoiding erosion with sustainable agricultural systems, such as the Pasión and Petexbatun regions, were successful precisely *because* they were decentralized and locally controlled (Dunning, Beach, and Rue 1997; Dunning and Beach in press; see also Fedick 1996; Neff *et al.* 1995).

As with every aspect of Maya society, debate and disagreement about the role of the state in agricultural systems arises because of the extreme variability of lowland Maya civilization in time and space (Demarest 1996b). Some sites, such as El Mirador and Edzna in the Late Preclassic period, and Calakmul and Caracol in the Late Classic, had hydraulic or intensive agricultural systems that may have required state management. We should note, however, that these were exceptional sites in many other ways – in population size, area, and degree of economic integration. Tikal, Calakmul, and Caracol were the centers of large conquest states that represented a period of experimentation in the Maya world with larger political formations (see Chapter 9). These experiments failed (rather dramatically), accelerating intersite status rivalry and warfare, and, ulti-mately, the decline or collapse of many Classic Maya states in the south-ern lowlands (Chapter 10). The more centralized economies, grand scale, and infrastructural involvement of those states might be more the excep-tion than the rule for Classic Maya realms.

Small intensive terrace, garden, or raised-field systems controlled by the elite are found in some cases near site epicenters and palaces (e.g. Freidel *et al.* 1982; Dunning, Beach, and Rue 1997). These would provide convenient gardens to feed palace populations and might also have served to symbolically associate the elite with the agricultural system and the Maya rain forest adaptation. In ancient Egypt, the pharaoh was credited with the annual flooding of the Nile, and he was represented symbolically opening sluice gates or raising shadufs (e.g. Butzer 1976; Hoffman 1979). Water systems around the mandala-shaped architectural complexes of the Negara systems of Southeast Asia associated the state with irrigation systems that were actually locally controlled (Geertz 1980). In the same way, such epicenter field systems and water and fertility rituals of the Maya theater-states may have helped create and maintain a myth of a more direct and critical role for rulers and elites in subsistence and economic systems.

# 7    Classic Maya economics

The nature of ancient Maya economics, crafts, and market systems is another topic of much debate and disagreement among archaeologists. Thompson's view of the Classic Maya as a theocratic society of peasants ruled by priests from ceremonial centers allowed for little consideration of economic issues. During the revolution in Maya studies after the great settlement pattern projects of the 1960s and 1970s, archaeologists began more serious consideration of Maya long-distance trade, local exchange systems, and craft production. At that time, initial enthusiastic studies posited a central role for long-distance markets in the rise and decline of Classic Maya civilization (Rathje 1971, 1973). The rise of great centers such as Tikal and El Mirador was attributed to their role in east–west trade between Mexico and the Caribbean and possible state-monitored or controlled marketplaces were archaeologically identified (Jones 1979; W. Coe 1965b). In some models, the great mercantile central Mexican city of Teotihuacan was posited as a central force in trade networks that stimulated the rise of the Maya cities (Webb 1975; Santley 1983). Later, the fall of Teotihuacan and its trade system was seen as a central factor in the ninth-century decline of the centers of the southern Maya lowlands (e.g. Webb 1973; Cowgill 1979; Diehl and Berlo 1989).

Recent studies of long-distance trade in the Maya world have been aided by neutron-activation and x-ray diffraction sourcing of obsidian used to make stone tools and the clays in traded ceramics (e.g. Sidrys 1976; Bishop 1980). The results of such research have cast considerable doubt on the view that long-distance trade in obsidian, ceramics, or foodstuffs was important to subsistence or to the basic economy of lowland Maya populations (e.g. Marcus 1983a; Clark 1986). Instead, recent studies of highland–lowland exchange have emphasized the importance of traded goods such as jade, fine ceramic vessels, and quetzal feathers for status-reinforcement, for patronage networks, and to maintain the status and power of rulers and nobles (e.g. Blanton and Feinman 1984; Demarest and Foias 1993; Sabloff 1986).

148

Still, other scholars have continued to point out evidence that trade in some more basic goods such as obsidian, highland igneous rock, salt, and perhaps cacao could have been important in the formation and nature of economic institutions in the Classic and Preclassic periods – as they were in the Postclassic Maya kingdoms encountered by the Spanish in the sixteenth century (A. Andrews 1980a, 1980b, 1983, 1984; Aoyama 1999; Voorhies 1989). Population sizes at some great centers in the Late Classic, such as Tikal, have been cited to argue that there must have been regional exchange of even some basic foodstuffs (e.g. Culbert 1988: 92–95). Other centers, such as Dos Pilas, seem to have relied on regional tribute for such basic subsistence support (O'Mansky and Dunning 2004; Dunning *et al.* 1997; Dunning and Beach in press).

As debate continues on the nature of Classic Maya economic systems, studies have tended to focus on more specific aspects of trade at the local, regional, and interregional levels. Recent researchers have also examined the degree of specialization, standardization, and centralized control in the production of trade goods. Such studies are revealing complex and regionally variable economic systems for the Maya cities of the Preclassic and Classic periods.

### Local products and raw materials

Studies have demonstrated the environmental complexity and variability of the Maya lowlands (Sanders 1973, 1977). Nonetheless, basic economic and subsistence needs usually could be met within a distance of about twenty-five kilometers of any major Maya center. Through collecting or hunting, the Maya obtained critical elements in their diet such as fruits, meat, and fish, and raw materials for crafts and construction including timber, thatch, resins, incense, shell, bone, bird feathers, and pigments, as well as clays and tempers for making pottery. The ubiquitous reeds of swamps, lakes, and *bajos* were woven into basketry of all kinds and mats for seating and sleeping. The various forms of Maya field systems, gardens, and orchards provided most of their remaining needs for basic dietary staples, wood, fruits, cacao, and condiments. Cotton fields gave the fiber for daily clothing, fine textiles, and padded armor. The limestone bedrock below all of the rain forests was mined near site epicenters for stone for temples and palaces and the carving of stelae and altars. Ground and burned, the limestone also produced powder for mortar and plaster for coatings, murals, and sculpted architectural façades and roof combs. Most items for tools and weapons could also be obtained within any small region. Chert (or flint), which was used for tools, weapons, and elaborate ceremonial stone objects (called "eccentrics"), forms in nodules within limestone, and good chert sources can be found near most centers. Animal bone and wood were the raw materials for most other production of tools, weapons, and ornaments.

With such a bounty of food and resources near each major center, the need for long-distance trade and its economic importance was reduced, especially as compared to areas of dramatic environmental variability and irregular resource distribution such as the highlands of Mexico and Guatemala or the Andes. Instead, most food and other products were probably distributed through informal exchange among extended families or neighbors and small local markets. The greater needs of rulers, their families, and courts probably were met through tribute or "tithing" of goods and labor from the surrounding populations. As observed at the time of the Spanish conquest, certain products, such as exotic bird feathers, jaguar pelts, and many imported goods, were reserved for the elite through sumptuary customs and laws.

### Local and regional markets and exchange systems

Despite the natural bounty and diversity of the rain forest and the Maya subsistence systems, some basic products had to be obtained by families at local or regional markets. Ruling families and members of the royal court, including priests, scribes, craftspeople, servants and their families, would all be supported through the agricultural labor and collecting efforts of the population. Tax and tribute in produce and goods for the elite would be supplemented by trade or barter in local markets. Other craft specialists not attached to the palace would need to obtain their food through trade or barter. Even full-time farming families, the vast majority of the population, relied upon exchange to provide some pottery, salt, chocolate beans, stone tools, and variety in their diet.

Then, as now, periodic markets in the plazas of major and minor ceremonial centers were probably the major mechanism of exchange. Before and after religious rituals and on established saints' days or market days, the modern Maya in the highlands of Guatemala and Chiapas fill the plazas before the churches with temporary stalls or piles of produce, textiles, stone, firewood, and artworks for barter and sale (Fig. 7.1). The degree of management or state involvement in such markets is (and probably always was) minimal. In the Classic period local rulers may have taxed these periodic markets in some form. The state or elite families might have controlled certain specialized products, such as salt, obsidian and hard stones from the highlands, and fine textiles. It is virtually impossible to verify such assumptions or the analogies to ethnohistoric or present markets, since such periodic events leave little or no archaeological

Figure 7.1 Modern highland Maya market at Santiago Atitlan, Guatemala

evidence and the Classic-period hieroglyphic texts make little mention of economic matters except for a few references to tribute.

For the largest centers markets or state-managed redistributive systems may have integrated economies, including basic subsistence, beyond the local level. For example, the center of Tikal may have had a population of between 60,000 and 120,000 in its "greater metropolitan area" in the Late Classic period (Culbert *et al.* 1990), requiring the movement of foodstuffs from as far as 100 kilometers away (Culbert 1988). This possibility of more regional economies is great for Maya centers with large estimated Late Classic populations, such as Caracol in Belize (Chase and Chase 1996b), Calakmul in the southern base of the Yucatan peninsula (Folan 1992), and Coba in the far northeastern lowlands of Yucatan (Folan *et al.* 1983). It is notable that all of these Classic centers, as well as the Late Preclassic-period center of El Mirador, had radiating systems of causeways connecting them to satellite centers. These causeway systems may have facilitated both the market and state-controlled movements of goods and foods (Chase and Chase 1996b).

Still, studies of kingdoms of the Conquest period, based on far more detailed historical sources, have demonstrated the difficulties of moving foods and other basic subsistence goods over long distances by foot transport and without the benefits of beasts of burden, vehicles, or modern preservation techniques. Even the complex, carefully administered full market economy of the sixteenth-century Aztec empire relied for its basic food supplies on the area of central Mexico near its capital cities (Sanders and Santley 1983). More distant provinces provided tribute or market goods in luxuries, textiles, or other nonperishable goods. Transport of corn or other staples from only twenty-five kilometers away would require consumption of 16 percent of the caloric value of the load for its bearer and transport from a hundred kilometers would have cost a third of the load in expended caloric energy (Culbert 1988; Drennan 1984; Sanders and Santley 1983). Such high transport costs might have been maintained by a few Maya cities at their peak, but more generally Maya subsistence economies and markets were probably based on an area of about twenty to thirty kilometers, a day of travel, from the major center and its periodic markets. More frequent market exchanges near minor centers and daily informal barter completed the loose structure of the Maya economy in food and basic necessities.

## Commodities trade: salt, chocolate, textiles, and hard stone

Some commodities would have been imported from greater distances. These include raw materials that could be transported long distances and were of importance to local economies.

### Salt

The most important of these commodities was salt, a critical element in diets, preservation of foods, and trade in the sixteenth century in the Post-classic kingdoms of northern Yucatan, Belize, and most of Mesoamerica (A. Andrews 1980a, 1980b, 1983). Salt production involved drying seawater in flat, shallow lagoons or artificial drying beds. Seawater could also be boiled to leave salt deposits in specialized vessels. There is ample evidence that these techniques were in use from Preclassic times. The development of regional economies in Belize, Yucatan, and on the south coasts of Guatemala and Chiapas was probably stimulated by inland–coastal exchange systems in salt, as well as dried fish, shell, and other maritime resources. Some Preclassic- and Classic-period coastal communities may have specialized in such products, relying on exchange for most basic agricultural staples raised farther inland (e.g. Stark and Voorhies eds., 1978; A. Andrews 1983; Andrews V *et al.* 1984; Demarest *et al.* 1988; Ringle and Andrews 1990; Pye and Demarest 1991; Pye 1995; Pye *et al.* 1999).

What remains controversial is the extent, importance, and nature of the salt trade in the Classic and Preclassic periods. Some have argued that, since salt was absent in most of the Maya lowlands, management of long-distance trade for salt and hard stone was critical in the rise of state leadership there (Rathje 1973, 1975). In fact, many regions of the Maya lowlands are not far from the saline lagoons of the Gulf coast or Caribbean (Andrews and Mock 2002). In areas further inland, salt deposits could be mined (e.g. Dillon 1977) and salt could be produced by burning vegetation (Reina and Hill 1980). Furthermore, the importance of, rather than preference for, salt in diets and trade remains an open question. The use of salt as a medium of exchange ("archaic money") in the Postclassic and Contact periods relates to the complex market system and the critical role of maritime trade in those centuries. While salt was a commodity that required more distant exchange networks, it was probably not as important a resource for Classic-period kingdoms as it became later, in the Postclassic period (cf. Marcus 1983b; A. Andrews 1984; Andrews and Mock 2002).

## Chocolate

Another highly valued commodity was the bean of the cacao tree which, when processed, became the chocolate so heavily used in Maya sauces as well as daily drinks. Cacao beans can be roasted, then easily stored and transported. For that reason, like salt, cacao became a medium of exchange in the great market economies of the Postclassic and Contact periods (Berdan 1975). Cacao was so prized in the Aztec period as an object of trade and tribute that cacao-producing regions were targets of imperial conquest (Conrad and Demarest 1984: Ch. 2; Hassig 1988; Voorhies 1989). Similarly, some scholars have posited that control of cacao production and its trade might have been a factor in the rise of elites among the Classic Maya (e.g. Dahlin 1979).

While certain areas may have specialized in chocolate production, cacao trees can be grown in most areas of the Maya lowlands. In the Classic period, field systems within the farmlands of most Maya realms probably included cacao scattered around houses and gardens and in groves in specialized fields, such as the sunken *rejolladas* gardens (Dunning, Beach, and Rue 1997; Dunning and Beach in press). Given its storable, mobile form, cacao may have been more extensively traded than other foodstuffs, but neither long-distance trade, nor state control, would have been needed for its production and distribution. Still, particularly favorable areas for cacao groves may have overproduced for commodity trade and for tribute (e.g. McAnany *et al.* 2002).

*Textiles*

Cotton for the weaving of simple cloth and for more elaborate textiles could be grown in any part of the lowlands (Mahler 1965), and cotton fields were undoubtedly scattered among the mosaic of different types of field systems, house gardens, terraces, orchards, rain forest, and reservoirs that surrounded every major center. As with cacao, regions with especially favorable soils and conditions for cotton farming may have produced large quantities for textile production and trade, as was the case in Postclassic times. Again, however, commodity trade over long distances appears to be a less central element of Classic Maya economies than it became later.

In the Classic and Postclassic periods, as today, cotton was spun into threads on spindles weighted on one end with a clay spindle whorl. These clay disks, often decorated, are found in the ruins of Maya house groups, testifying to the household nature of most textile production (Fig. 7.2). The women of each household wove the clothing of family members (as they do today) and perhaps some finer cloth for special occasions, tribute to the rulers, or trade. Representations in codices (Anawalt 1981) and Conquest-period descriptions show that then, as now, women wove fabrics on backstrap looms within their homes. Today, the complex geometric designs and brilliant colors of Maya fabrics are filled with symbolic patterns, and each community has an identifiable set of cloth patterns and colors. Similarly, Classic Maya sculptures and ceramic art show elites dressed in costumes with extremely elaborate woven patterns (see Figs. 8.8, 8.9, 8.10).

As cloth is less perishable than food products and easily transported, it is probable that it was exchanged more widely in markets and as tribute to rulers. In later Aztec times in Central Mexico, fine cloth was demanded as tribute from subject groups. Innovative studies of textile patterns and clothing styles represented in Aztec art and codices have been used to study tribute systems, identify ethnic groups, and plot networks of interaction and trade (e.g. Anawalt 1981). In the Maya area, fine fabrics probably served these same functions – community identification, status marking, tax, tribute, and trade – although it is challenging to explore these issues in the absence of preserved fabrics.

*Hard stone*

Similarly, longer distance exchange of hard stone was needed to supplement the lithic resources of the lowlands that are dominated by a karst topography with generally soft limestone bedrock. Again, however, the role of trade in highland igneous and metamorphic rock may be overstated in theories that see such trade as a critical factor in the rise and

Figure 7.2 Maya use of a spindle whirl to prepare thread (from
Charnay 1887: 89)

maintenance of elite power (e.g. Rathje 1973, 1975; Santley 1983;
Michels 1977). As we have seen, the Maya lowlands were far more ecologically diverse than scholars once believed, and that diversity includes
its geology. Harder limestone deposits are available in almost all areas
of the lowlands, providing stone for adzes, mortars, and pestles for
daily use. Though variable in quality, chert for spears and dart heads,
weapons, axe heads, adzes, hoes, knives, and other tools can be found

Figure 7.3 Grinding chili with a stone *metate* and *mano*

in deposits in most lowland regions. Especially fine chert for weapons, ritual scepters ("eccentrics"), and bloodletters was mined in large quantities from sources in northern Belize and elsewhere *within* the lowlands for the purpose of trade with other Maya centers (e.g. Hester and Shafer 1984; Hester *et al.* 1983).

Hard metamorphic rock for stone-working, and hard *manos* (pestles) and *metates* (mortars) for corn, tuber, and pigment processing (Fig. 7.3), could also be obtained within the lowland Maya world from the Maya Mountains of southern Belize and the southeastern Petén, as well as from the far southern Petén, which borders on the highlands. Recent excavations at Cancuen on the far southern border of the Maya lowlands have revealed the great variety of sedimentary, igneous, and metamorphic rock available in that region in cobbles in its river systems (Demarest and Barrientos eds. 1999). Such hard stone from the borders of the lowlands could be easily traded farther inland along these same rivers.

*Obsidian*

Obsidian (fine volcanic glass) was valued in the pre-Columbian world as the sharpest, finest edge for cutting tools of any kind, including knives and dart points, and for edges for wooden swords and other weapons. Because of its fine cryptocrystalline structure, obsidian could be chipped into

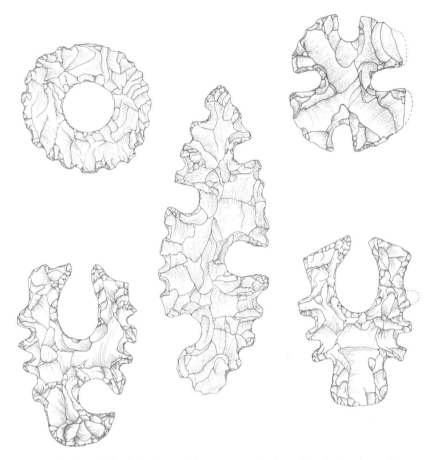

Figure 7.4 Obsidian and chert eccentrics from Dos Pilas (drawn by Luis F. Luin)

complex forms – "eccentrics" for decorative or ceremonial use (Fig. 7.4). Some eccentrics were hafted and used as weapons, scepters, or bloodletters for autosacrifice.

The fact that obsidian can be easily traced to its source has led to its frequent use, arguably its overuse, to reconstruct ancient long-distance trade systems. Unlike chert and other commodities, there were relatively few source areas for this igneous rock, all of them volcanic outcrops in the highlands. Obsidian in the Maya lowlands has most often been traced to the El Chayal outcrop near the highland center of Kaminaljuyu or to the Ixtepeque source in the Motagua Valley on the edge of the southeastern corner of the lowlands. Some obsidian came from other sources, such as the San Martín Jilotepeque source farther to the west in the southern highlands (Braswell 2002). Small quantities of prized Pachuca green obsidian derived from the distant Valley of Mexico appear in the Maya area in caches, burials, or other contexts, sometimes indicative of contact with the central Mexican state of Teotihuacan.

Through the sourcing of the obsidian used in lowland tools, archaeologists are able to trace patterns of trade (Fig. 7.5). Elites of some major centers may have redistributed obsidian through patronage networks (Rathje 1977; Hammond 1972, 1973; Aoyama 1996, 1999, 2001; Santley 1983, 1984; Sidrys 1976). Certainly, obsidian from specific sources is found in great quantities at some sites, such as Tikal, whose elites may have had special political and/or commercial ties with highland centers (Coggins 1975; W. Coe 1965b; Santley 1983; Moholy-Nagy et al. 1984). At Tikal, Dos Pilas, Copan, and other Classic centers, the quantity and diversity of obsidian artifacts in household groups was associated with other markers of status and wealth, such as fine masonry architecture, the quantity of polychrome ceramics, and the presence of other imported exotic goods (Palka 1995, 1997; Haviland and Moholy-Nagy 1992; Haviland 1982; Aoyama 1999, 2001). Indeed at Tikal, Dos Pilas, Tamarindito, and other centers ruled by the Tikal Late Classic dynastic lineage, royal tombs were coated with a clay that was filled with flakes, chips, and nodules of obsidian – a dramatic display of conspicuous consumption and royal wealth (Haviland 1992; Demarest, Escobedo et al. 1991; Valdés 1997b).

At other centers, obsidian may not be as clearly associated with status, and it appears to have been more widely distributed toward the end of the Classic period (P. Rice 1987a; P. Rice et al. 1985; A. Chase 1992). The evidence for elite control of obsidian is circumstantial at best. The concept that royal or elite control of obsidian was critical to political authority and foreign alliances (e.g. Rathje 1975; Santley 1983) exaggerates the importance of this useful resource and the ability of a few centers to control its distribution. Recall that chert, available throughout the lowlands, can also be worked into fine-edged tools – better for most purposes than obsidian tools because chert edges are less brittle and do not leave glass bits in processed foods! Indeed, obsidian would have been most clearly superior for weapons and for bloodletting rituals, which were an important aspect of Maya religious life at all levels. The fine, razor-sharp edge of obsidian blades would be effective in the cutting of genitals, ears, cheeks, and other tender flesh that was subjected to autosacrifice. If, as many scholars believe, autosacrifice was practiced at all levels of Maya society, this may have been one of its major functions.

SITES WITH OBSIDIAN
ANALYSIS UTILISED

OBSIDIAN SOURCES

Figure 7.5 Some major trade routes of the Petén (drawn by Luis F. Luin)

Access to obsidian would have been difficult for the elite to control (e.g. Clark 1986; Braswell 2002). There were several different sources in the southern highlands of Guatemala alone and one of these, Ixtepeque, was near the southeastern corner of the lowland Maya region (see Fig. 7.5). As hundreds of blades can be struck from a single core or nodule of obsidian, the mass of transported material would be small and would not necessarily require state planning or any great investment (Clark 1986). Rulers, other elites, and merchants of the emerging Maya "middle classes" (Chase 1992) could have carried out direct or indirect transport of obsidian and other goods from the highlands. State control of obsidian trade has been assumed rather than demonstrated. The only systematic and convincing effort to prove control of obsidian by the rulers (Aoyama 1995, 1999, 2001) was applied to the Copan Valley, an area which can be considered exceptional given its close proximity to a major source (cf. Braswell 2002).

We can conclude that while elite control and redistribution of some obsidian is likely – at least for the Preclassic and initial Classic – it is by no means certain. This issue is but one aspect of the greater problem of the uncertain role of elites in the general Maya economy (e.g. Masson and Freidel 1992).

## Long-distance trade in high-status goods

One aspect of the economy that certainly *was* controlled by rulers and elites was the exchange of exotic status-reinforcing goods. Given the nature of political authority and power among the Maya, such goods were critical resources for rulers, their families, and their administrators. Though lacking in "practical" functions from a Western perspective, these goods were needed by elites for the maintenance of their power. Such high-status exotic goods included jade, pyrite, fine polychrome ceramics, imported ceramics or artifacts from central Mexico or the highlands, feathers of the quetzal or other tropical birds, finely chipped chert or obsidian scepters and eccentrics, and even occasional metal objects from Mexico or Lower Central America.

All of these materials were part of the costuming and regalia of the kings, nobles, and priests, without which they could not carry out the public rituals that were their principal duties in the eyes of their followers. Jaguar pelts, fine textiles, feathers, and other elements of regalia were probably exchanged over long distances within the lowlands to meet the demands of the growing elites. Coastal products such as shell and coral for mosaics and jewelry were traded inland in all periods (Freidel *et al.* 2002). Stingray spines, shark teeth, and spondylus shells from both the Pacific and Caribbean coasts were required equipment as genital bloodletters for high royal rituals. Fragments of shell, coral, and pyrite were formed into beautiful mosaic headdresses, shields, scepters, mirrors, and other elite regalia that appear in representations in Classic-period art. Rulers and nobles were also often buried with their flint and obsidian weapons, scepters, and bloodletters.

It was observed at the time of the Spanish Conquest in central Mexico that most such luxury goods and status-reinforcing symbols were limited by custom and formal sumptuary laws to the rulers and nobles, and to those who served them well as priests, warriors, or administrators. Similarly, Maya rulers in the Classic period would have controlled the acquisition and distribution of symbols of authority such as quetzal feathers, precious stones, and jaguar pelts (Freidel *et al.* 2002). These items were probably exchanged between elites both regionally and at long distances as dowry, bride-price or gifts at royal marriages, coronations, pilgrimages, funerals, and major religious rituals (Schele and Mathews 1991). Exotic goods and fine polychrome ceramics were also probably regularly given as tribute to rulers by subordinate conquered centers and vassals (Stuart 1995; Miller 1993).

These high-status goods were one important element in the "peer-polity" interaction that held together the lowland Maya world and unified elite patterns of behavior in ritual, religion, science, and warfare (Sabloff 1986; Freidel 1986a). From Preclassic times on, long-distance trade was probably far more focused on such exotic goods and artworks than on subsistence goods, tools, or other basic resources (Blanton and Feinman 1984). Even at early centers such as Nakbe and El Mirador, not only jade and highland ceramics but also large quantities of shell from the Caribbean were imported for the production of adornments, mosaics, and other accoutrements of religious and political power (Hansen 2001; Freidel *et al.* 2002). These long-distance exchange systems were surely accompanied by exchanges of information, including astronomical knowledge, early writing and iconographic systems, cosmology, and, most importantly, models of more hierarchical and more stratified political formations (Freidel 1979, 1981; Freidel *et al.* 2002; M. Coe 1981; Clark *et al.* n.d.; Marcus 1983b).

Thus, regional and long-distance exchange formed a second trading system that was largely controlled by the elite and based upon reciprocal exchange, gift giving, and tribute in exotic goods and works of art. These luxury goods served as elements of costumes and paraphernalia for the rites and ceremonies of the theater-state, ranging from the great gatherings and sacrifices over which the elite presided, to their marriages, wars, and, eventually, their burial with this gear. As discussed below, this elite economy in sumptuary goods also involved control of production of fine ceramics and crafts by specialized artisans and scribes attached to royal and elite households, some of whom were even members of the royal families (Stuart 1989; Schele and Miller 1986; Miller 1993).

It should be noted that the model of a two-tiered economy – local and regional markets and barter in subsistence goods and commodities, and long-distance elite-controlled exchange in exotic goods and symbols of power and wealth – is a *caricature* rather than an accurate *characterization* of evolving Maya economic systems. As Maya societies developed from the early lowland states of the Late Preclassic period, the economic and social systems became far more complex, as well as regionally variable. Considerable social mobility was available through achievements in war, crafts, and mercantile activities. Furthermore, elite polygamy and the expansion of elite families would naturally lead to a blurring of social boundaries between nobles and elites and a proliferation of other full- or part-time occupations. By the Late Classic period, if not earlier, the Maya had a complex range of intermediate classes in functions, power, and wealth. This Late Classic social reality is reflected in a wider distribution of polychrome ceramics, exotic goods, and commodities such as fine chert and obsidian (e.g. A. Chase 1992; McAnany 1993; Chase and Chase 1992; P. Rice 1987a). Indeed, by the eighth century, such elite goods, while still associated with status and relationship to the ruler, were distributed across a gradual, unbroken curve of social levels in Maya society (Palka 1995, 1997).

### Routes of trade and exchange

Routes of trade between inland and coastal areas, and especially between the highlands and lowlands, seem to have been important in most periods for the location and success of major centers. Many sites are strategically placed along natural trade routes on navigable rivers or in central positions between river routes (Sharer 1994: 452–62). Such positions were advantageous for both local and regional market exchange and for elite access to highland and coastal exotic goods. The circumstantial evidence of site positions on natural east–west (e.g. Tikal, El Mirador) or north–south (e.g. Cancuen, Seibal, Yaxchilan) routes has been tested by trace-element analyses of artifacts, especially obsidian.

Obsidian has been most useful in positing trade routes because its sources are easily identifiable. There are only a few major outcrops of this volcanic glass in the highlands of Guatemala or Mexico. Neutron-activation or X-ray fluorescence of obsidian can identify trace elements that are characteristic of each of these source zones. Archaeologists can examine patterns of distribution of obsidian from each source and propose probable trade routes from sources to the lowland sites (Fig. 7.5). We speculate that such routes would have been used not only for obsidian, but also for important perishables and less easily traced highland and coastal products such as plumes of the quetzal and other exotic birds, jade, volcanic ash for tempering ceramics, pyrite, fine ceramics, salt, hard igneous and metamorphic highland rocks for stone working, pigments, shells and stingray spines from the coasts, salt, and fine cherts from sources in Belize.

One suggested major trade route would have come from the Ixtepeque obsidian source on the edge of the Motagua River to the Caribbean, allowing canoe trade up the coast of Belize to Yucatan (Hammond 1972, 1973). A second major route would have led from the highlands of the Verapaz region of Guatemala via the upper Pasión River and the Maya trading port of Cancuen at the head of navigation (Fig. 7.5). From Cancuen, obsidian nodules or macroblades were transported up the Pasión River into the northern and central Petén, up the Machaquilá River to the southeastern Petén and Belize, and up the Usumacinta to major Maya centers such as Seibal, Altar de Sacrificios, Yaxchilan, Palenque in Chiapas, and even out to the Gulf of Mexico and the western coast of the Yucatan Peninsula (Demarest and Barrientos 1999, 2000, 2001, 2002). The circumstantial evidence of the natural geographic corridors and the sourcing of obsidian found at some Maya sites argue that these centers were located on major long-distance trade routes for highland–lowland exchange and that one of the functions of these major centers was to act as nodes of exchange – and, in a few cases, as centers for processing and production of such goods. Other highland or Motagua Valley products would follow these same routes as demonstrated by the jade, pyrite, and obsidian production areas found at the port center of Cancuen, where the western river route begins (Kovacevich *et al.* 2001, 2002).

## Craft production and specialization

Another fundamental set of economic parameters in any society concerns the degree of specialization in craft production, the definition of the groups involved in such production, and the control and distribution of the product – what Marx called the means of production and the relations of production. For the Classic Maya, we have seen that farming and the subsistence economy was very complex, yet decentralized, with a few notable exceptions. The situation with tool and craft production involved several different levels of specialization in the production and distribution of finished products. These ranged from purely household-level manufacture and use of many tools, to state control of the production and exchange of some important luxury goods.

Our knowledge of Classic craft production is aided by analogy to Maya production of textiles, ceramics, and woodwork as observed in the centuries since Western contact to the present. The artifacts of the Classic period and representations of textiles in Classic-period sculptures and painted ceramics show that techniques in most crafts have changed little. Archaeological finds of workshops, production debris, and stored products – though rare – are a more direct source of evidence. Detailed study, measurement, and statistical analyses of thousands of stone tools, bone artifacts, and ceramic vessels provide important insights into the degree of standardization, the steps in production, and the probable degree of specialization (e.g. Clark 1997b; Clark and Bryant 1997; P. Rice 1981, 1987a, 1987b, 1990, 1991; Foias and Bishop 1997; Sheets 1975; Hester and Shafer 1984; Hester and Hammond eds. 1976; Shafer 1979, 1982, 1983; Shafer and Hester 1983, 1986; Kovacevich et al. 2001, 2002). Finally, much of the best information on ceramic and lithic production and exchange systems comes from trace-element analyses such as neutron activation or X-ray fluorescence. These techniques identify trace elements in clay used for ceramic production or in the stone used for lithic tools. With comparative samples and statistical analyses, the source of these raw materials can be identified and hypotheses can be generated about the acquisition of raw materials, loci of production, the number of workshops, and trade and distribution of finished stone tools or pottery vessels (e.g. Bishop 1980; Bishop et al. 1986; Rands and Bishop 1980; Fry 1979, 1980; Sidrys 1976, 1979; Sidrys and Kimberlain 1979; Hammond 1976).

A new and unexpected source of information on craft production and specialization has come from recent discoveries and excavation of rapidly abandoned sites (Inomata and Webb 2003). At Joya de Ceren, El Salvador, Payson Sheets and his team (Sheets 1992, 1994, 2000) have uncovered a village community rapidly buried by a volcanic eruption with in situ evidences of household and community behavior, including craft production. Meanwhile, at Aguateca, Guatemala, the Vanderbilt Petexbatun Project has discovered an elite epicenter quickly overrun and burned by invading enemies (Inomata 1997, 2001). In both cases evidence revealed that Classic Maya craft activities probably were generally low volume and part-time, with only some production under elite patronage. As study of this new evidence continues (Sheets 2000; Inomata 2001), it should elucidate further the complex nature of Classic Maya craft specialization.

*General household production*

As among the Maya today, most utilitarian tools and items for daily use were produced at the level of the family or extended family. Cooperative labor of the men of these Maya household groups, which were generally patrilocal, was used to construct the low mud and stone house platforms, raise the wood and mud hut walls, and construct the thatch roofs. Simple utilitarian ceramics, the family's clothing and textiles, and simple wooden and stone tools all may have been produced in the plaza groups formed by the women and men of families or extended families. If modern ethnography and Colonial ethnohistory can be hypothesized to reflect ancient patterns, textile production and food processing were principally carried out by women, construction, hunting, and woodwork by men, and the fashioning of pottery, farming, and gardening were carried out by all adult and adolescent family members. Together, these activities filled the days of Maya families – a daily round interrupted by participation in periodic rituals in the center, occasional tribute to the elite as architectural laborers, or roles as warriors in inter-center conflicts.

*Family and hamlet specialization*

Such a pattern of household self-sufficiency probably changed for most households by the end of the Preclassic period. As a natural aspect of the evolution of social complexity, some households would begin to overproduce certain products or crafts and then trade these goods through gift exchange, barter, or local markets (e.g. P. Rice 1981, 1987a, 1987b, 1991; Brumfiel and Earle eds. 1987; Costin 1991; Arnold 1978, 1985; Sheets 2000). Individuals gifted in specific skills often begin family traditions of part-time specialization in particular crafts. In other cases, families or hamlets near particular resources such as fine clays or chert deposits might have become involved in part-time extraction and processing of such resources. Family groups, hamlets, or whole communities may have taken up part-time specialization in craft production because their local soils were poor and they need to supplement their subsistence through production, barter, and/or trade (e.g. Sullivan 2002). In the Maya case, as epicenters developed with growing elites, the possibilities for craft production increased to meet greater demands of the elite for artifacts, textiles, and specialized products.

Through this wide variety of mechanisms, family and extended family part-time specialization was well developed by the Classic period – probably even centuries earlier. Archaeologists working in all parts of the Maya lowlands have uncovered household groups involved in production of certain ceramic types, stone or bone tools, woodworking, textiles, or masonry (Abrams 1987; Aldenderfer 1991; Aldenderfer *et al.* 1989; Andrews IV *et al.* 1975; Aoyama 1994, 1996, 2001; Becker 1973a, 1973b; Haviland 1974; Mallory 1984; Moholy-Nagy 1997). Redundant storage of pottery or artifacts of a single type, the presence of special processing tools, debris or waste from lithic or ceramic production, microwear analysis of stone tools, and other archaeological clues identify such part-time craft groups (e.g. Aoyama 1996, 1999, 2001; Benco 1988; Moholy-Nagy 1990; P. Rice 1991; Brumfiel and Earle eds. 1987; Sheets 2000; Inomata 2001; Wood and Titmus 1996). By the Classic period many Maya families may have supplemented their subsistence base through trade in such crafts, or they may have provided these products as tribute to local elites (who in turn may have paid tribute to the kingdom's rulers).

Archaeologically invisible part-time specialization was probably also under way in the subsistence economy. Specialization in overproduction and trade of certain foodstuffs might have been undertaken by families with access to specific soil types, to cooperatively constructed terraces or gardens, or to nearby *bajos* for raised fields or dry season agriculture. Specialized agricultural goods such as cacao and cotton were probably normally produced through part-time specialization at the family or hamlet level. Families near good fishing holes, lagoons, or rivers, or near rich hunting grounds in the rain forest, could take up part-time specialization in fishing or hunting, as occurs today. Some of these families then also might have processed hides or made bone tools and ornaments (e.g. Emery 1997, in press).

### Community specialization

Some entire communities near valuable resources, such as chert, salt, or coastal lagoons and reefs rich in shell or coral, specialized in the trade and partial processing of those raw materials from Preclassic times on. The site of Colha in Belize was located near extremely fine flint or chert deposits. That community quarried and worked the source, trading Colha chert throughout the lowlands (e.g. Hester ed. 1979; Hester *et al.* eds. 1980, 1981; Hester and Hammond 1976; Hester and Shafer 1984; Shafer and Hester 1983, 1986). In northern Yucatan, the coastal Preclassic center of Komchen specialized in trade in salt to inland centers. Despite an agriculturally impoverished environment, Komchen managed to support a large population through such exchange systems (Andrews V *et al.* 1984; Ringle and Andrews 1988, 1990).

Other communities probably shifted more gradually to part-time specialization as Maya society evolved (e.g. Sullivan 2002). Statistical studies of vessel form, decoration, and pastes in the regions of Tikal, Seibal, and the Petexbatun have indicated that communities may have specialized in the production of certain vessel types which were exchanged within local and regional markets (Fry 1979, 1980; Fry and Cox 1974; Foias *et al.* 1996). Note that as community specialization develops, it would encourage part-time specialization by other communities and family hamlets desiring the superior crafts produced by specialists and, thus, needing themselves to overproduce crafts or subsistence goods for exchange.

### *"Attached" specialists*

A large sector of the economy was dedicated to meeting the demands of rulers, their families, and courts for elaborate artifacts, fine textiles, painted ceramic vessels, stone and wood carving, and fine masonry architecture – as well as their demand for a superior diet (Wright 1997). Much of this demand was met by tribute in food, products, or labor by surrounding populations and subordinate centers. But some of this elite demand was for artifacts, artwork, and sculptures that could only be produced by highly trained full-time specialists. Archaeologists have excavated architectural complexes in, or near, epicenters that were the residences and production centers of specialists (Fig. 7.6) including artists, shell and bone carvers, sculptors, and scribes (Inomata 1995, 1997; Webster 1989). The high status of such specialists was reflected in their residences, artifacts, diet, and even some signed works of art (Stuart 1989; Schele and Miller 1986: Ch. 6). These and other evidences show that some scribes, sculptors, and artists were even themselves relatives of the ruler, if not members of the royal family (Stuart 1989). These scribes and artists were sometimes portrayed in the polychrome vases of the Late Classic period (e.g. M. Coe 1973; Kerr 1989, 1990, 1992; Kerr and Kerr 1988; Reents-Budet 1994).

Recent studies of *in situ* evidence from rapidly abandoned households (Sheets 2000; Inomata and Triadan 2000; Inomata 2001) indicate that even artisans of elite goods may have been only part-time specialists. They also might have produced goods for their own use and for exchange or trade with others. That is, they may not have been *exclusively* "attached" to their ruler or noble patrons. As with other aspects of Classic Maya economics, production and exchange systems were less sharply defined than in some of the later full market economies of Central Mexico and the Postclassic Maya centers (e.g. Brumfiel 1987, 1998; Berdan 1980, 1986, 1993). Furthermore, more sophisticated perspectives on art, style, and crafting (e.g. Bourdieu 1977, 1984) have begun to be applied in Maya

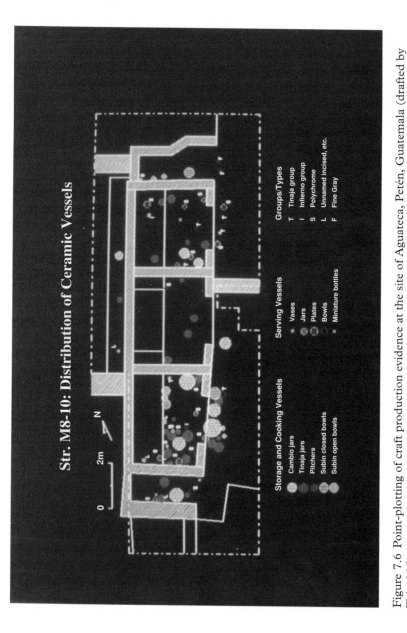

Figure 7.6 Point-plotting of craft production evidence at the site of Aguateca, Petén, Guatemala (drafted by Takeshi Inomata)

archaeology to elucidate the more complex nature of the sophisticated implications of crafting, aesthetics, and possession of objects, art, and status. The knowledge involved in crafting high-status objects (some of which bore glyphic texts) was itself a status-enhancing form of "cultural capital" which allowed artisans a variable degree of autonomy and control over their products and an elevated social position in Classic-period society (e.g. Inomata 2001; Bourdieu 1977; Reents-Budet 1998).

The complexity of Maya economics and the "negotiated" position of specialists has also been demonstrated by recent studies of jade, pyrite, and obsidian workshops at the trade and manufacturing center of Cancuen (Demarest and Barrientos 1999, 2000, 2001, 2002). There royal power was largely based upon control of exotic highland raw materials and production of items for elite and royal use, including jade plaques, earspools, and other jewelry, and pyrite mirrors. Yet even though jade production appears to have been tightly state controlled, even non-elite part-time jade workers used their position to produce other crafts and utilize byproducts of jade production (Kovacevich *et al.* 2001, 2002). Thus, the notions of attached and independent part-time specialization overlapped in complex ways, reflecting the mix of market, redistributive, and elite exchange systems in Classic Maya society.

Another group of specialists was involved in the palace-controlled economy in fine painted polychrome ceramics. These vases were a major element in inter-center contacts and exchanges and functioned as gifts, tribute, and burial offerings given to other rulers. Fine polychrome ceramics were also the serving vessels at feasts and ritual meals held by rulers (Fig. 7.7). Such events helped form and maintain alliances between different rulers and the patronage networks between these rulers and their local subordinates. The production and exchange of fine polychromes – and probably other less easily traced luxury goods – constituted a separate component of the Maya economy. Studies of paste and the production of fine polychromes have identified palace-controlled workshops at Maya sites (Ball 1993; Bishop 1980, 1994; Reents-Budet 1985, 1987, 1998; Reents-Budet and Bishop 1985, 1987; Reents-Budet *et al.* 1994). These artisans produced particular styles of serving vessels and vases identifiable as the gifts or tribute of that particular center by their distinctive pastes, slips, painting colors, and designs. Trace-element analyses of these vessels (e.g. Bishop 1980, 1994) allow us to plot the interactions and exchanges between elites of distant centers. The painted scenes on the vessels and the hieroglyphic inscriptions that accompany them are a major source of information on the lives of the ruling classes, their courts, alliances, and patronage networks (e.g. Schele and Mathews 1991; Schele and Miller 1986: Ch. 6; Stuart 1989, 1995:

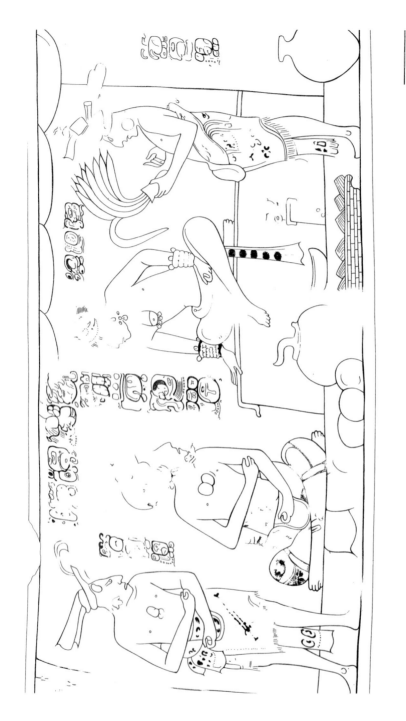

Figure 7.7 Scene from Late Classic polychrome vase showing elites with serving vessels (drawn by Luis F. Luin)

Ch. 6; Kerr 1989, 1990, 1992; Kerr and Kerr 1988; Reents-Budet and Bishop 1985). They are also a major source of information on Maya myths, religion, and cosmology (e.g. Schele and Miller 1986: Ch. 7; Reents-Budet 1994; M. Coe 1973, 1977, 1978, 1982). Such fine painted ceramics and other art were also a common element of tribute and often are found in the tombs and caches of dominant victorious centers (e.g. Miller 1993; Reents-Budet and Bishop 1985; Stuart 1995: Ch. 6; Demarest, Escobedo *et al.* 1991).

*Changing patterns of specialization and standardization*

From the Preclassic to the end of the Classic period, Maya economies underwent considerable change. There may have been increasing special- ization at the family and community level and a notable increase in attached specialists working for the growing number of elites. Such changes led to more regionally distinctive styles in most types of arti- facts by the Late Classic period (P. Rice 1981, 1987a, 1991; Ball 1993; Bishop 1994; McAnany and Issac eds. 1989; McAnany 1993; A. Chase 1992). Specialization also results in an increased standardization of prod- ucts from any given workshop and such distinctive diagnostic regional characteristics are observed in the ceramics and lithics from Late Classic contexts (Foias and Bishop 1997).

In turn, specialization of families and of communities – and especially partially or fully "attached" specialists working for rulers or for lesser elites – affected wealth differences, social mobility, and class structure. The success and wealth of specialized families and the high status of attached (or "partially attached") specialists in the Classic period began to blur distinctions between the elites and commoners (McAnany 1993; A. Chase 1992). As social mobility and specialization created "middle classes" from below, elite polygamy and the proliferation of the ruling classes also created them from above: relatives of the ruler, excluded from key rulership positions, would increasingly take up occupations as scribes and artisans. All of these processes are observed in the archaeolog- ical record of the Late Classic. Status-marking artifacts, architecture, and sculpture were distributed across multiple levels with a gradual, unbroken curve of measurable levels of status and wealth from the semi-divine ruler to his relatives, more distant relatives, attached specialists, wealthy fami- lies, merchants, and so on, down to the humblest families (A. Chase 1992; Chase and Chase 1992; McAnany 1993; Palka 1995, 1997; Kovacevich *et al.* 2001, 2002).

### Warfare and tribute

Another changing aspect of the Maya economy regards tribute from subordinate centers conquered in warfare or affiliated to major centers by alliance or voluntary association. At the elite level, we are able to identify such tribute in fine ceramics, exotic goods, and artifacts with the help of hieroglyphic inscriptions, as well as style and compositional sourcing of artifacts (e.g. Miller 1993; Reents-Budet and Bishop 1985; Demarest, Escobedo *et al.* 1991). Yet there are some indications in Classic Maya inscriptions (Stuart 1995: Ch. 8) that warfare tribute was more extensive, involving textiles, perishable artifacts, and possibly those commodities that could be easily shipped, such as woodwork, cacao beans, salt, and pelts. As warfare increased in frequency and intensity during the Classic period (see Chapter 9), the role of such tribute would have gained importance in regional and interregional economies (e.g. McAnany *et al.* 2002).

At the local level, Maya farmers, craftspeople, and local leaders paid tribute to the ruling elites in subsistence support, corvee labor, crafts, and raw materials to their ruler's extended families, courts, and attached specialists. These courts monopolized (via sumptuary laws) various products and benefited from a higher portion of meat and protein in their diets (e.g. Wright 1994). Indeed, through strontium analyses of bone, archaeologists have been able to identify specific "palace diets" characteristic of the members of the court and their attached specialists and retainers (D. Chase *et al.* 1998; A. Chase and D. Chase 2001).

Archaeologists are still unable to specify in most cases what the non-elites obtained in return for such tribute. In some cases warfare and coercion may have been the motive for tithing, but this appears to have been a secondary consideration at best. The question of elite reciprocal contribution to the general population for tribute and labor leads us to the broader, more difficult question of the role of rulers and elites in the Maya economy.

### Maya economics and the state

As with subsistence, the question of the role of the state in trade and economic systems is a very controversial issue. Scholars disagree about the "true" nature of Maya economic systems precisely because those systems were complex and varied regionally and over time. As we have seen, arguments that the Maya rulers and elites emerged due to their role as "middle men" in long-distance or regional trade are not convincing, given the nature of resources and products involved in such exchange systems. There is also little direct evidence of state involvement in most such exchanges.

As with subsistence systems, however, there are notable exceptions, particularly in the Late Classic period. The rise of some enormous centers with interregional hegemonies, such as Calakmul and Tikal, may have necessitated centralized management of regional economics. These efforts seem to have failed, however, as these larger, more unitary political and economic formations disintegrated during Late Classic times (for further debate of these issues see Fox *et al.* 1996; A. Chase and D. Chase 1996b; Demarest 1996b; Sanders and Webster 1988; D. Chase *et al.* 1990). Further evidence of Classic Maya economic variability, local complexity, and nonelite control of some aspects of production has been seen in workshop and household findings from unusual centers, such as Colha, Belize, near the finest chert sources (Hester and Shafer 1994; Shafer and Hester 1983) and Cancuen, Guatemala, which controlled highland–lowland exchange on the Pasión River trade route (Demarest and Barrientos 2000, 2002; Kovacevich *et al.* 2001, 2002).

There is no doubt, however, that Maya rulers and their courts controlled long-distance and regional exchange of many luxury goods. We should not underestimate the importance of elite control of production and distribution of items such as fine ceramics, jade, shell, quetzal feathers, and the like. Such items were powerful symbols of authority and were critical to the central role of rulers in the great ceremonies of the Classic Maya theater-states. Perhaps it was for this reason that many royal centers arose along long-distance trade routes and, as we shall see, rulers in the Late Classic period battled each other in warfare over access to such exotic goods through trade and tribute.

Despite the speculative conclusions presented here in Chapters 6 and 7, we must admit that we still cannot describe with confidence the economic roles of rulers in the ancient Maya state. In anthropological terms, we cannot specify the relationship between the institutional *structure* and the economic and subsistence *infrastructure* of Maya states. Were Maya kings substantially involved as managers of their complex rain forest subsistence systems? Were they part-time middlemen in trade and exchange? Were they principally warlords obtaining tribute resources for themselves and their polities? Or were they simply, in Marxist terms, a "parasitic elite" whose rituals, wars, and great constructions served only to legitimate their own needs?

The honest answer to these questions is that we simply do not know. At present it would appear that most Maya kings were only weakly involved in core economic activities (with some notable exceptions). It is clear that Maya kings were centrally involved in Maya ritual, religion, and warfare (see Chapters 8 and 9). Still, we cannot yet with any degree of certainty answer the basic question of the other economic or managerial activities of Maya rulers.

This embarrassing situation for Mayanists as social scientists arises for a number of reasons. The elaborate and beautiful nature of Maya art, architecture, writing, religion, and cosmology has seduced scholars for the past two centuries, leading to the neglect of some basic questions until the last thirty years (Sabloff 1990). In their art and inscriptions, the ancient Maya emphasized the role of rulers in religion, ritual, and dynastic politics – the roles of the K'uhul Ajaw or "holy lords" that they themselves may have considered most crucial for their claims to power. The great multidisciplinary archaeological projects of the last few decades have begun to correct the economic lacunae in our understandings of Classic Maya society. We have a better grasp of the complexities of ancient Maya economy and subsistence, and, hopefully, soon we will be better able to link those systems to the elite and to the role of rulers.

# 8 Religion and ideology: beliefs and rituals of the theater-states

The religions, politics, and worldviews of other cultures are difficult for historians and anthropologists to analyze either in terms of their nature or their role in relation to other institutions. That is because they move us away from the common ground of humanity in the areas of biological needs and into the realm of thought, cultural values, and philosophy. The latter respond to psychological and emotional needs which are still poorly understood for even our own Western culture. In many cases, archaeologists' responses to the data on pre-Columbian ideology tell us more about the scholars themselves and their own cultural values than about the ancient societies under study.

In the case of the Maya, we have seen extreme positions on issues of high culture. Cultural materialist scholars and ecologically oriented archaeologists have criticized Maya studies for its obsession with religion, kings, tombs, and art, and its insufficient treatment of basic questions of economics, ecology, and infrastructure (Marcus 1983a; Webster 1993; Sabloff 1990; Marcus 1995; Sanders and Webster 1988; Fowler 1997). These criticisms are largely justified, even after efforts at remediation of these problems in the last three decades (e.g. Sabloff 1990). As discussed in Chapter 3, mid-nineteenth-century to early twentieth-century archaeology was carried out by gentleman scholars from England and the North American Ivy League. Their "readings" of the pre-Columbian past projected their perspectives (albeit unconsciously), seeing the Maya priest-kings as a scholarly elite, and the Classic Maya themselves as superior to their "less literate" neighbors in Mexico and Central America (e.g. Thompson 1966). Such problems are not unique to the Maya field, but are part of the more general subjectivity that is inevitable in the process of interpreting the partial remains of an ancient and very different culture (cf. Hodder 1985, 1986; Shanks and Tilley 1987, 1988).

While recent breakthroughs in hieroglyphic decipherments have led to some new insights on Maya politics, and even some on economics, they have also led archaeologists back to the Mayanist obsession with elite culture, religion, and history. Disproportionate study is again being devoted to the elite aspects of culture. Remarkably, for the ancient Maya we can now be more certain about aspects of their religion and world-view, as expressed through ritual, than about their economic activities and structure, the reverse of the state of knowledge on most truly prehistoric societies.

It is with an awareness of these issues that this chapter explores ancient Maya worldview, religion, and ritual. We cannot dismiss as "epiphenom-enal" or irrelevant the vast Maya expenditure of resources and energy on their rites, temples, and tombs. At the same time, we should not allow ourselves to be entranced by the spectacle of ancient Maya elite culture and forget the fundamental question of the relationship between Classic Maya art and ideology and the economic and political systems with which they were integrated.

## Ancestor worship

At the core of Maya religion was a general worldview that stressed ances-tor worship, the veneration of deceased ancestors and the propitiation of them as mediators between the forces of the supernatural and their living descendants. Many aspects of Maya high ceremonialism, such as the cults of deified former rulers, were aggrandized forms of this more general ancestor worship. Archaeologists have only recently begun to emphasize the cults of the ancestors at the level of the common Maya families of the Classic and Preclassic periods (McAnany 1995). As Maya family groups were probably patrilineal and often patrilocal, the veneration of a prominent deceased male was often emphasized, sometimes with a small shrine within the household plaza group (Fig. 8.1). Yet all ancestors were nearby, generally buried beneath the floors of the family houses with a few offerings reflecting the status and wealth of the group (Fig. 8.2). Rituals, prayers, and blood from self-laceration or "autosacrifice" were offered up to these ancestors by heads of households in their plaza group shrines (Tozzer 1941: 113–121; Schele and Freidel 1990; Freidel *et al.* 1993: 204–207, 445–447).

In many ways, the great stone temples of the Maya centers with splen-did royal tombs within them were merely aggrandized versions of the household shrines. The great pageants of the ceremonial centers venerat-ing the dead kings were simply ancestor worship writ large, the celebration of the dead kings as ancestors of the ruling lineage and as a collec-tive ancestor of the entire community. Presiding over these great cere-monies was the king of that dynasty, just as family patriarchs directed the humble rites at the small shrines and simple burials of household groups (McAnany 1995). Similarly, the rituals of royal bloodletting atop the

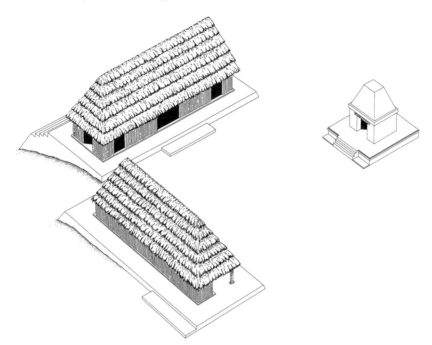

Figure 8.1 "Plaza Plan 2" residential group from Punta de Chimino with east side household shrine (drawn by Luis F. Luin)

great temples of the Maya acropoli were like the household bloodlettings offered by shamans and the patriarchs of Maya families. The difference in scale and investment between family and royal ancestor worship was very great, but with an essential unity of beliefs and rituals at all levels of Maya society (Demarest 1992b; McAnany 1995; Freidel *et al.* 1993).

## Gods and the cosmos

In addition to the ever-present ancestors, the ancient Maya world was defined by a great number of supernatural deities, entities, and sacred forces. Indeed, the Maya concept of the sacred was so all-encompassing that it is somewhat misleading to describe distinct deities with specific referents and functions. The Maya deified numbers, periods in the various calendars, geographical features, their deceased ancestors, and rulers, in addition to the specific "deities" identified by the Spanish chroniclers. The Maya sacralized their universe, which they conceptualized in specific structural terms tied to the calendar, astronomy, and physical models of

Figure 8.2 Burial with modest grave goods, from Cancuen

the cosmos. The gods were nodes in this cosmic map, and their character, associations, malevolence or benevolence, changed according to the days in the Maya calendar or the positions of the sun, moon, Venus, and the stars in the heavens. For this very reason, the shaman, priest, and early priest-ruler, using their codices and their astrological knowledge, guided the people through the tricky cosmic and calendric map. They advised on which supernaturals to propitiate, how, and when.

Gods had multiple aspects associated with the four different color-directions (red/east, black/west, white/north, and yellow/south). They also had dualistic natures associating them with day or night, life or death. The conceptual cosmogram determined the nature and aspect of the deity and only through careful study of their astronomical knowledge and calendrics could priests and rulers direct the appropriate rites needed to insure the well-being of the crops and the health and future of individuals, families, the collective communities and the city-state. This manifold and shifting nature of deities and supernaturals was common in the religions of most pre-Columbian civilizations, most of which also sacralized, anthro-pomorphized, and deified segments of a dynamic cosmogram and the astral cycle (Leon-Portilla 1963, 1968; Marcus 1978, 1989; Nicholson 1971). Yet to Westerners, such as the sixteenth-century Spanish clerics, this religious system was utterly confusing and frequently misinterpreted. At that time Greco-Roman "paganism" was their only direct model for polytheistic, non-Christian religion in a high civilization. Only in the past few decades have scholars come to understand the manifold nature of Pre-Columbian deities and the inseparability of these gods from sacred time, calendrics, and astronomy – the parameters of their cosmology (see especially Demarest 1981; Leon-Portilla 1973).

The Maya cosmogram was highly structured, with thirteen levels of the heavens and nine of the underworld, each personified in a deity and each forming a plane (Fig. 8.3). Between the upperworlds of the heavens and the underworlds of the night and death was the earthly plane of our own existence, sometimes conceptualized as a two-headed caiman or turtle lying in a great lake. Each plane in turn had its four color-directions: again, red/east, black/west, white/north, and yellow/south. Many of the major deities such as Itzamnaaj, their greatest god, and the Chaaks, the rain deities, had distinct aspects, each associated with one of the color-directions. Each deity, such as the red Chaak of the east, had its particular associations and portents according to days in the various calendars and the positions of the celestial bodies (J.E.S. Thompson 1970; Taube 1992). The great Itzamnaaj was simultaneously a creator deity, a sun god, and an embodiment of the Maya cosmogram itself. One of his aspects was

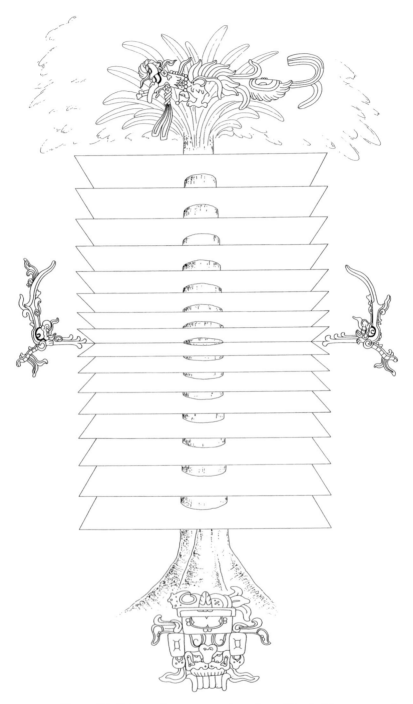

Figure 8.3 Schematic representation of one Classic Maya conception of the cosmos, showing world tree (*axis mundi*) (drawn by Luis F. Luin)

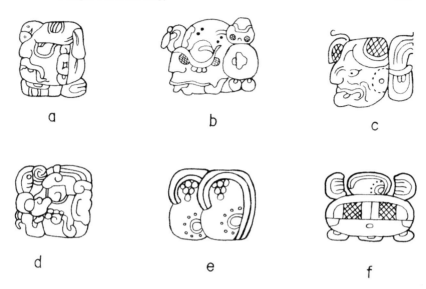

Figure 8.4 Some glyphs for Maya deities and sacralized units of time (drawn by Luis F. Luin and Sarah Jackson):
a) K'inich Ajaw, "sun-faced lord"
b) Night Jaguar, sun of the night
c) a Pawahtun
d) a Chaak
e) Bak'tun
f) K'atun

K'inich Ajaw, the sun of the day (Fig. 8.4a). Maya rulers, in their role as shaman-kings, often associated themselves with K'inich Ajaw in their iconography. In his underworld form, Itzamnaaj became the Night Jaguar, the sun as it traveled below through the night (Fig. 4b). In general, the movement of the sun across the sky and its shifting course in relation to the earth over the year appear to have been critical factors in defining the Maya structural concepts of the universe (e.g. Freidel and Schele 1988a, 1988b; Schele and Freidel 1990: 64–95).

The importance of the daily, seasonal, and annual movements of the sun, moon, and Venus was incorporated into many Maya myths, as well as in the calendar and rituals. The Popol Vuh, the most widespread of Maya creation tales, tells of the struggle of two hero twins, Hunahpu and Xbalanque, against the Lords of Night and the power of the underworld (D. Tedlock 1985). The twins descend into the underworld, perish, and are miraculously reborn. Like the Gilgamesh epic of Mesopotamia and the Persephone and Orpheus tales of the ancient Greeks, the Popol Vuh highlights the central human concern with death and mortality and also

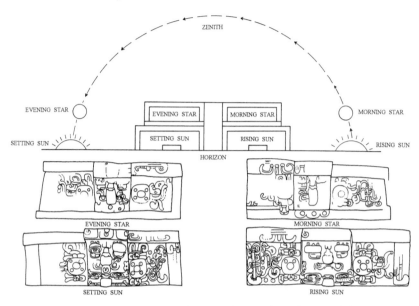

Figure 8.5 Cosmogram of Preclassic temple at Cerros, Belize
(redrawn by Luis F. Luin from Freidel and Schele 1986: Fig. II.1, 108)

provides a metaphor for the agricultural cycle and the annual rebirth of
the crops. Yet in the case of the Popol Vuh, the Hero Twins also clearly
represent the sun and Venus, who daily appear in the sky, disappear in the
full night, and reappear in the morning. The mythical journey through
the underworld, the battle with the forces of death and darkness, and the
eventual rebirth of the twins parallels the daily journey of the sun and
Venus (as the evening star) through the underworld and their rebirth the
following day as the morning sun and the morning star (Fig. 8.5). It is
notable that, in addition to the more powerful astronomical and astrological associations, the Maya origin myth also uses blood symbolism and
human sacrifice as the mechanisms for both death and rebirth.

Other Maya deities had their positions in the cosmogram, including
the moon goddess in the heavens, Ix-Chel, and the Nine Lords of the
Night on each plane of the underworld, Xibalba. The Pawahtuns, in
their four aspects (e.g. Fig. 8.4c), supported the four corners of our
earthly plane of existence. The Bakabs, who supported the heavens, each
ruling over segments of the 260-day sacred cycle (see below), had four
major forms associated with each color-direction, as well as dozens of
other poorly understood manifestations. Similarly, the very important
deities, the Chaaks (Fig. 8.4d), had four major forms associated with the

directions and also had other manifestations. These gods, dating back to at least Olmec times, controlled lightning, thunder, and the rains – the latter, of course, of paramount importance to the average Maya farmer. Periods of time such as the (approximately) 20-year K'atuns were sacralized (Fig. 8.4f), as were the numbers of the calendar from one to thirteen, the months, and other calendric markers such as the periods of the Long Count (Fig. 8.4e). Special referent deities also included the maize god, Yum Kaax, the death god, Yum Cimil, gods of creation and bloodletting such as the "Paddler Gods," and supernaturals associated with myths of creation, the north star, Orion, and the Milky Way (Taube 1992; Freidel *et al.* 1993: 59–116).

The position of the elites and the rulers in this cosmic panorama was central (Fig. 8.5), as manifest in architecture, iconography, and hieroglyphs from the earliest periods on (Clark *et al.* n.d.; Freidel 1981; Freidel and Schele 1988a; M. Coe 1981). The dazzling beauty of Maya ideology and the architecture, monuments, and pageants that accompanied it were centered on the cult of the K'uhul Ajaw, the holy lords of the Maya kingdoms (Freidel 1992). The rulers and rulership were associated with a series of deities, including aspects of gods labeled "God K" and "God L" by iconographers and epigraphers. Even the earliest iconography and architecture of the Maya ceremonial complexes placed the ruler in the central role as the axis of the universe, the connection between the earthly plane and the celestial levels and deities, as well as the underworld, its patrons, and the ancestors (Freidel and Schele 1988a, 1988b). Through public rituals of autosacrifice or genital bloodletting, other forms of sacrifices, and visions, the ruler was simultaneously made the intercessor for the people with the supernatural forces and an embodiment of the gods themselves (e.g. Schele and Miller 1986: 175–196, 301–312; Freidel 1992). In this role the ruler was essentially a religious specialist, or "shaman," drawing upon ancient principles and rites. Indeed, the ruler's shamanistic role is so clearly indicated in early iconography that many scholars believe that rulership itself developed from shamanism in the Maya world (e.g. Freidel *et al.* 1993; Lucero 2003; cf. Demarest 2002).

## Shamanism

From the Preclassic period on, and back to the period of the Olmec societies and earlier, there is ample evidence of shamanism in Mesoamerican cultures (Blake 1991; Clark 1994; Clark and Blake 1989; Demarest 2001, 2002). Shamans are religious specialists believed to have special powers and knowledge to help other members of the community deal with supernatural forces. Shamans help others communicate with deities or ancestors, heal illnesses, and predict future events through divination. Shamans exist in most cultures, although as social complexity develops to the level of statehood, they are often replaced by more formal religious institutions with dogma, priests, and hierarchical structures that parallel (and often reinforce) state institutions. One fascinating aspect of Maya civilization is that, as with ancestor worship, many of the characteristics of shamanistic practice were retained in the ideology and rituals of the advanced states of the Classic period. Indeed, many of these practices have continued since the Spanish Conquest and have evolved along with Maya culture and resistance into the practices of shamans today throughout Mexico and Guatemala.

Aspects of ancient Maya shamanism have been revealed by the inscriptions, iconography, and art of the ancient Maya interpreted with the aid of Conquest-period and Colonial ethnohistory and the study of contemporary Maya shamans (see bibliographic essay). As shamans, Maya rulers and the priests under their authority were associated with especially powerful animal alter egos or *way*, a coessence that would allow rulers or priests insights into the animal and supernatural worlds (Houston and Stuart 1989). Representations in Classic Maya monumental art often display this alter ego, sometimes a jaguar, in association with the ruler (Fig. 8.6).

Also, like modern shamans, rulers would use trance states – induced by fasting, ritual bleeding, and, sometimes, alcohol or hallucinogens – to communicate with the supernatural for divination and prophecy (see bibliographic essay). Representations in ceramic art show rulers and priests in their shamanistic role in trance states dancing, smoking powerful tobacco mixtures, having visions, or communicating with gods or ancestors.

**Royal bloodletting**

A more central and public role of rulers as shamans-in-chief was represented in monumental sculpture and architectural façades. There, rulers are portrayed during genital bloodlettings dripping their royal blood into bowls (Fig. 8.7). The paper soaked in their sacred royal blood was then burned, and in the smoke a "vision serpent" would sometimes appear to the entranced king, queen, or priests (Schele and Miller 1986: Ch. 4; Stuart 1984, 1988). Ancestors and deities associated with divination and ancestor worship would sometimes appear in the shamanistic vision of the celebrant (Fig. 8.8), presumably communicating sacred knowledge, especially about future events and portents (Stuart 1988; Schele 1985, 1987; Freidel and Schele 1988a, 1988b; Freidel et al. 1993).

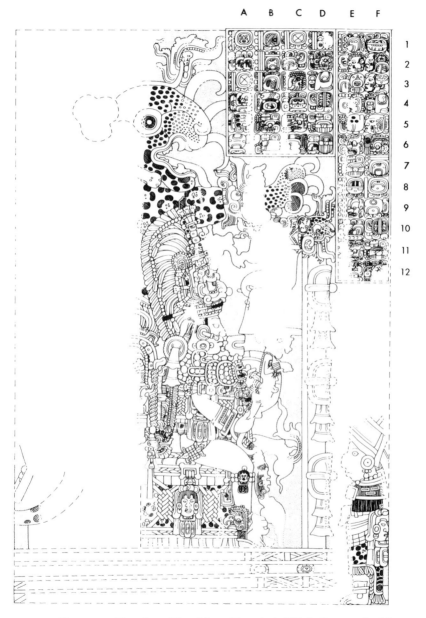

Figure 8.6 Drawing of lintel from Temple 1, Tikal, Guatemala. Note great protector jaguar *way* above seated ruler

Figure 8.7 Ruler making a blood offering (Lintel 2 from La Pasadita)
(from Freidel and Schele 1986: Plate 76, 196, drawing by Linda
Schele)

Figure 8.8 Maya queen experiencing a vision (Lintel 25 from
Yaxchilan, Chiapas, Mexico)

From a Western perspective, such shamanistic rituals of genital blood-letting and visions may seem bizarre, especially as a central role for their kings. Yet, in the pre-Columbian world, indeed worldwide, such rites fit into a pattern frequently observed by anthropologists: the creation of structurally parallel behaviors between the sexes (Bettelheim 1962). For example, in the *couvade* observed in many societies, expectant fathers suffer extreme pain and sickness paralleling their wives' real labor and childbirth. In a structurally similar form of "womb envy," geni-tal bloodletting rituals are found in many cultures among males, espe-cially shamans. Maya queens gave birth to the princes, the future of the dynasty, and queens figured prominently in Classic-period art and inscribed parentage statements (e.g. Stuart 1995: Ch. 6). In concep-tual womb envy and sexual parallelism, the Maya lords also "gave birth" through genital bleeding, pain, and hallucinations. In the case of the kings, the genital bleeding was from self-laceration, and the birth was not in the form of flesh-and-blood princes but in the form of visions of ancestors, gods, and the future through divination (Stuart 1984, 1988; Schele and Miller 1986: Ch. 4). Indeed, to further complete the parallel, Maya kings in some cases even dressed in female garments for such rites of royal genital bloodletting (Fig. 8.9). Queens also figured prominently in repre-sentations of bloodletting, assisting the kings, letting blood themselves from cheeks and tongues, or having their own visions of prophesizing deities or ancestors (Figs. 8.10, 8.8). These details confirm the sexual parallelism of royal genital bloodletting, which was considered by the ancient Maya to be among the king's most sacred duties.

The importance of bloodletting is confirmed by archaeological evidence, as well as iconographic representations and carved texts. Perhaps the principal instruments and symbols of royal power were not the crown, sword, and scepter, as with European kings, but various types of genital bloodletters. Stiletto-like, jade "penis perforators," spiny pink spondylus shells, sting-ray spines, and other tools for this purpose were represented in artwork as the key instruments of the kings and are found buried with their users in the royal tombs. Bowls for the burning of bark paper, obsidian blades for laceration, and identified settings in temples all confirm the evidence of Classic-period art and texts describing this central shamanistic rite of the ancient Maya kings and queens (e.g. Schele and Miller 1986: Ch. 4; Freidel and Schele 1988a, 1988b; Schele and Freidel 1990: Ch. 2, 3).

### Sacrifice

Shamanistic rituals, bloodletting, and visions were widespread in ancient Maya society. Royal bloodlettings were celebrated by pronouncements

Figure 8.9 Ruler Wataklajuun Ub'aah K'awiil (sometimes referred to as "18 Rabbit") after a blood autosacrifice (Stela H from Copan)

before thousands in the great plazas and were memorialized in stone sculptures. Yet shamans and family elders also practiced bloodletting at modest family shrines, houses, and in caves (McAnany 1995). Long obsidian blades, spines, and worked shells used for that purpose are found in household caches, on floors, and in caverns. Meanwhile, members of elite families offered up their own blood and prayers before the stelae and altars that celebrated their noble or royal ancestors. Major temples and small palace shrines were also settings for autosacrifice and ancestor worship by noble families.

Figure 8.10 Maya queen making an autosacrificial blood offering
(Lintel 24 from Yaxchilan)

Autosacrifice was not the only source of blood offered to the ancestors and deities. Turkeys, macaws, and bats were offered up in rituals. While mass human sacrifice on the scale of the sixteenth-century Aztecs was not practiced, the Classic Maya did carry out regular rituals with human offerings (Schele 1984). Human sacrifice, most often of war captives, took many different forms. These were celebrated in carved stone monuments, ceramic art, and in graffiti in temples and caves. Burials of sacrificed captives and caches of decapitated heads confirm the practice of such rituals from Preclassic times, yet such larger-scale sacrifice was not common among the Classic Maya (e.g. Johnston *et al.* 1989; Demarest 1984a; Schele 1984). Captives, especially royalty, were stripped, bound, and displayed in a humiliated state. Decapitation with large stone axes was a common fate for captured kings.

Yet, on a far more regular basis, autosacrifice, incense, and prayers were a part of daily life and personal ritual in the Classic period. Many offerings were directed toward family ancestors who were close by, buried beneath house floors and in shrines in household compounds. The blood offered up was conceived of as a "holy essence," *ch'ulel*, the sacred glue that bound together the universe, connecting humankind to the ancestors and deities (Stuart 1984, 1988, 1995). The various sacrificial rites and bloodletting released this sacred substance, creating portals for communication to the supernaturals, to the past, and to the future (e.g. Freidel *et al.* 1993: 201–224). The role of the family leaders, shamans, priests, and rulers was to guide these rituals of communication with the deities and ancestors – usually offering their own blood, but sometimes utilizing the sacred essence of sacrificed captives.

### Divination

Much of Maya state art (Figs. 8.7 to 8.10) celebrates the autosacrifice of the elites and their subsequent trances and visions. Archaeological evidence and ethnographic descriptions (e.g. McAnany 1995; Tozzer 1941: 115–121) indicate that similar rituals at the household level allowed families to propitiate, venerate, and even communicate with their own ancestors (Freidel *et al.* 1993). One major function of such rituals was that of prophecy or divination. Given the ancient Maya cyclical concept of time, insights into the past and predictions of the future were virtually synonymous.

Maya priests and shamans, and rulers in their priestly role, sought to communicate with the supernatural world to seek the causes of illnesses or natural disasters and to predict the future. Many aspects of ancient Maya science, ritual, and religion – from bloodletting visions to meticulous astronomy – were forms of divination. Shamans today use trance states induced by fasting, chanting, and alcohol for divination.

Ancient shamans, priests, and rulers induced their visions with the aid of massive blood loss which naturally releases opiates in the brain. They also smoked powerful tobacco mixtures or drew upon the rain forest's natural bounty of psychotropic substances. Hallucinogens made from mushrooms were used, and perhaps extracts from morning-glories, water lilies, or the glands of reptiles (Furst 1976a, 1976b, Furst and Coe 1977). Conquest-period descriptions of sixteenth-century Maya divination describe their use of the powerful mead fermented from honey and the bark of the *balche* tree. The rain forest fruit trees provided another source of alcoholic beverages for such rituals (Dahlin and Litzinger 1986).

### Astronomy and astrology

From a Western perspective, it may be difficult to relate such shamanistic rites to the patient, meticulous observation and recording by Maya scribes of astronomical data. But Maya celestial science also was a form of divination – recording the movements of astral bodies to predict the future, or in other words, astrology. Maya mathematics and astronomy carefully recorded and documented units of cyclical time as measured against the redundant and periodic movements of the sun, the moon, Venus, and the stars. The Maya sciences of calendrics and astronomy did not grow from an abstract desire to understand the cosmos nor, as has sometimes been proposed, to study the seasons in order to plan crops. Rather, like astrology everywhere, it developed as another tool of the shamans to predict future events. The ancient Maya cyclical vision of time necessarily implied that to understand the repeating cycles of time was to know the future, as well as the past. To this end, shamans recorded the periodic appearances, movements, and eclipses of the moon, the sun, Venus, and the stars, refining timetables and calendars for all their movements. These calendars could then be used to record the past in terms of datings in the cycles of each celestial body. Such dated events would also predict the future, since they would be expected to repeat, symbolically and literally, when the same set of dates in various Maya calendric cycles reoccurred years, decades, or centuries later. For this reason Maya astronomy, calendrics, and mathematics must be viewed in terms of their role in divination and prophecy.

In the sixteenth century, the Colonial priests and administrators observed Maya shamans and priests using their folding books or codices to make predictions based on the calendric cycles. While the Inquisition burned most of the Maya books and persecuted their users, three did survive amongst the booty sent back to Europe. Centuries later archivists, epigraphers, and archaeologists were able to decipher the calendric hiero-glyphic inscriptions in the codices and carved stone monuments, revealing to us the complex and fascinating ancient Maya vision of time. The cyclicity of time provided a close connection to the ancestors as it struc-turally linked the present, past, and future. This cyclical structure also facilitated decipherment, and as we saw in Chapter 3, Maya calendrics, dates, and astronomy were among the first aspects of the inscriptions read by scholars.

As with all peoples, the cosmic clocks that were used to measure and record time were the appearances of the astral bodies in relation to the earth. Maya recording and calculations of time used a modified form of the base twenty (vigesimal) mathematical system with place notation and the use of zero. Their meticulous observations of the movements of the sun, moon, and stars – combined with their sophisticated mathematical concepts – produced calendars, eclipse tables, and a level of astronomical knowledge beyond that of their contemporaries in Europe. All of these calculations, however, were made based on the periodicity of the appear-ance of the astral bodies without any Western "scientific" concepts of the structure of space, the planets, or the solar system. Nonetheless, the night sky over the jungle, the shifting of the sun over the year, the phases of the moon, the changing positions of the stars, and the frightening experience of eclipses awed the Maya (as they have all peoples). The ever-changing, yet predictable, movements of these sky gods became the domain of the shamans, priests, and rulers, generating an impressive esoteric knowledge and source of power through the understanding of time and beliefs about prophecy.

### The 365-day "*Haab*" and 260-day ritual cycle

Most of the annual round of rituals, celebrations, and sacrifices that filled the days of the ancient Maya were based on two annual calendars. One was the *Haab* or "vague solar year" of eighteen months (Winals) of twenty days (K'ins) and a special, prophetically perilous closing month of five days (Wayeb). This solar year of 365 ($18 \times 20 + 5$) days varied, of course, from the true solar year of 365.2422 days. We compensate for this in our calendar by having a 366-day "leap year" every four years. The Maya, however, had a variety of other calendric systems to give them more accurate astronomical calculations. The *Haab* functioned to set dates for ceremonies, make predictions for the populace, and guide the divinatory rites of the shamans, priests, and rulers.

The *Haab* worked in combination with a ritual calendar of 260 days. This sacred round was the most important religious calendar in the daily life of the Maya. It continued in use, guided by the shamans, through the Colonial period. In some areas of the highlands of Guatemala, the sacred count is still used today (B. Tedlock 1992). This "almanac" was defined by a continuous sequence of 260 days, named by assigning a succession of numbers from one to thirteen to a second cycle of twenty named days. The first numbered day was 8 Ahau, the second 9 Imix, and so on (see left wheels in Fig. 8.11). Thirteen, a sacred prime number, has no common factor with twenty. Thus the sequence of numbers and days would not repeat the same combination for 260 (13 × 20) days, returning only then to 8 Ahau. Each of the days had specific spiritual significance for types of divination. Shamans used the almanac to name each child after its birth date, a name that would be laden with positive and negative portents interpretable by the shaman or the priest. Mystical meanings, myths, tales of the deities, and alleged past events gave each of the 260 days its prophetic power. When the same day repeated, the Maya vision of cyclical time gave that numbered and named day historical and mythic portents.

The 260-day sacred almanac can be traced to the Preclassic period. No astronomical phenomenon can be associated with this calendar; rather, some have speculated that it might have been an approximation of the human gestation period. Rulers, nobles, and commoners alike consulted with the shamans and priests who calculated the day in the sacred round and then advised on its portent and the appropriate rituals needed to propitiate deities and ancestors. Many of the Maya codices burned by Bishop Landa and other inquisitors were divinatory guides based on astronomical knowledge and calendars and the recorded portents of the 260-day calendar or the 365-day *Haab* – all condemned by the inquisitors as "superstitions and falsehoods of the devil" (Hammond 1983: 6).

### The Calendar Round

An important fifty-two-year cycle, known to scholars as the Calendar Round, was formed by the reoccurrence only once every fifty-two years of the same combination of a date in the 260-day ritual cycle with a specific date in the 365-day *Haab* or vague solar year. Thus a date such as "12 Ik 4 Wayeb" or "4 Manik 4 Pop" would only reoccur after the passing of fifty-two of the 365-day *Haab* years. As described above (and Fig. 8.11), the 260-day count and 365-day *Haab* were also generated by their own meshed cycles of days. In Fig. 8.11 the Calendar Round date would be "8 Ahau 13 Ceh," and this paired date would only reoccur each

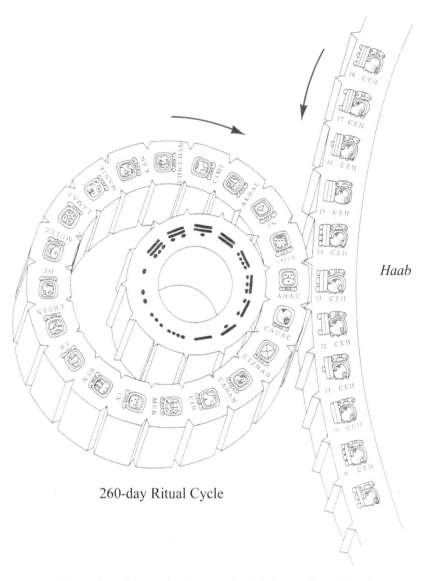

*Haab*

260-day Ritual Cycle

Figure 8.11 Schematic of the meshed "Calendar Round" cycles of the 260-day ritual almanac, or *Tzolkin*, and the 365-day "vague solar year" or *Haab* (drawn by Luis F. Luin, after Sharer 1994: Fig. 12.6). The day is "8 Ahau" in the 260-day ritual cycle (left wheels) and "13 Ceh" in the 365-day *Haab* or "vague solar year" (right wheel). Thus the Calendar Round date would be "8 Ahau 13 Ceh," a date which would repeat only every 52 years fifty-two years. Such a shortened cyclical count might be compared to "Friday October 13" without specification of the year or century. These Calendar Round dates were sometimes used as a shorthand dating in monuments without specifying longer time cycles, sometimes leaving great ambiguity in their interpretation.

Note that the Maya cyclical system of dating is no more exotic or complex than our own calendar, which combines a rotating cycle of seven days (most named for Norse gods) with twelve months (most named for Roman gods and emperors) of twenty-eight to thirty-one days, which we follow with a base ten "long count" (see below) of the years since a date agreed upon by religious councils as the birthday of Jesus Christ.

### The great cycles of time

Like our own calendars, Maya temporal cycles combined these various cyclical counts of numbered and named days, months, and years. Also like our own dates, the Maya marked time more deeply by recording a continuous count of days from a fixed starting point. In the European Gregorian calendar, this date is the official birth date of Jesus Christ. For the Classic Maya, the date for the beginning of the present creation corresponds to the 13th of August 3114 BC in the Gregorian calendar. From that date, the Maya counted forward in units based on a modified vigesimal (base 20) system and recorded their "Long Count" using their advanced mathematical devices of place notation and the zero. This absolute dating system was based on a count of days (Kins) within a count of months (Winals) of twenty days each. A count of eighteen Winals constituted the Tun of 360 days ($18 \times 20 = 360$).

Twenty Tuns formed a K'atun ($360 \times 20 = 7200$ days, or 19.7 of our years), one of the most significant units of time in terms of prophecy. K'atun endings were the most important events in stelae erection, temple refacing, and celebration of elaborate divinatory rituals and public ceremonies. At Tikal and other Central Petén sites, twin-temple complexes were erected to celebrate and commemorate K'atun endings (Jones 1969; Coggins 1979). At many Maya centers the impressive scale of monumental architecture was largely due to the accumulation over time of temples, temple renovations, and expansion and monument erection at the end of each K'atun.

Finally, the Bak'tun period counted cycles of 20 K'atuns (40 Tuns, i.e. $20 \times 20 \times 360 = 144,000$ Kins or days, or 394.5 of our years) from the start of the present era (again, this mythical date would be 13 August 3114 BC in the Gregorian calendar). Together, these units and their name/deities were carved on monuments beneath the Long Count Initial

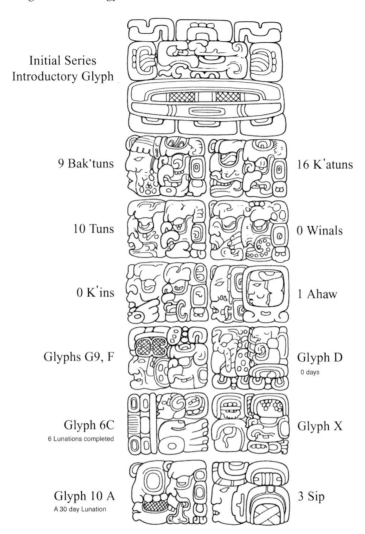

Initial Series
Introductory Glyph

9 Bak'tuns

16 K'atuns

10 Tuns

0 Winals

0 K'ins

1 Ahaw

Glyphs G9, F

Glyph D
0 days

Glyph 6C
6 Lunations completed

Glyph X

Glyph 10 A
A 30 day Lunation

3 Sip

Figure 8.12 Long Count date from Quirigua, Stela F (9 Bak'tuns, 16 K'atuns, 10 Tuns, 0 Winals, 0 K'ins, in Long Count system 9.16.10.0.0, i.e., Friday, March 17, AD 761 in our Gregorian calendar) (redrawn by Luis F. Luin from Maudslay 1889, Vol. II: Plate 40)

Series Glyph, which identifies the text as a date (Fig. 8.12). The Bak'tun units of time were the largest unit commonly used in Maya calendrics, although the Classic Maya conceptualized even greater cycles. Most of Classic Maya history fell in the eighth and ninth Bak'tun periods (AD 41–830) with the tenth of these cycles of the Long Count falling in the period near the end of the Classic era of Maya civilization (beginning at AD 830). Indeed, one set of theories holds that the disintegration of some kingdoms in the southern lowlands may have been accelerated by anxiety or despair heightened by the psychological impact of the ending of the ninth great Bak'tun (Puleston 1979).

Most Classic Maya pageants, rituals, bloodlettings, sacrifices, feasts, and new monument and temple construction celebrated the initiation and/or ending of the important periods in the Maya calendric cycles. The endings and initiations of the twenty-Tun K'atun periods were perhaps the most celebrated. Rituals of prophecy and monument dedication were also celebrated in the Late Classic at many sites to celebrate half-K'atun Lahuuntun periods (10 Tuns × 360 = 3600 Kins or days; 9.8 of our years) and quarter K'atun Hotun periods (5 Tuns × 360 = 1800 days; 4.9 years). Common rituals at each of these period endings were pageants centered around royal bloodletting or captive sacrifice. In some rites, rulers ascended the great temples and, assisted by kin and priests, lacerated their genitals and dripped their blood onto bark paper, which was then burned. Visions seen in this smoke were used for royal divinations (Fig. 8.8). These periodic events were carefully orchestrated to include participation of hundreds, if not thousands, of priests, assistants, musicians, dancers, fan bearers, and noble visitors from other centers. Such grand, theatrical rituals served to bind together the kingdom, cement associations with other centers, and reinforce the ideological basis of the king's power – his shamanistic role as the axis of communication between his people and the supernatural world, the forces of time, and the ancestors. His "sacred essence," *ch'ulel*, the blood shed through autosacrifice, was the physical bond between all elements in this elaborate system of royal ritual, power, and prophecy.

### Other sacred cycles and astronomical knowledge

The Maya recorded and celebrated many different and intersecting cycles of time in addition to the Long Count. One calendric cycle, a count of K'atuns known as the *May* (pronounced like "my"), was a cycle of thirteen numbered K'atuns. Combining thirteen and twenty, two of the most sacred numbers to the ancient Maya, this thirteen-K'atun cycle of approximately 256 years (13 × 20 × 360 days) was believed to record a repetition

## Box 4   The Short Count

The "Short Count" calendric system was often used for dating at the end of the Classic period and into the Postclassic, particularly in the northern lowlands of the Yucatan peninsula. This dating system recorded only the name of the day in the Calendar Round that a particular Long Count K'atun ended. Thus, a K'atun that ended on the day numbered "13 Ahau" in the 260-day ritual calendar and "8 Xul" in the 365-day *Haab* would be referred to as "K'atun 13 Ahau 8 Xul." Later in the Postclassic period, this reference was shortened even further to name the K'atun simply by its ending date in the ritual 260-day calendar. Thus, the above K'atun would be referred to as "K'atun 13 Ahau." Unfortunately, such a shortened dating system leads to greater ambiguity, as a K'atun with the same ending date in the 260-day ritual almanac would repeat approximately every 256 years (i.e., every thirteen K'atuns). Thus, K'atun 12 Ahau could refer to the K'atun ending on that day at 10.4.0.0.0 in the Long Count (AD 909) or to one ending at 10.17.0.0.0 (AD 1165) or to one ending at 11.10.10.0.0 (AD 1421) and so on.

This abbreviated dating system is in some ways comparable to our shortened dates, such as "8/16/52" for "August 16, 1952" and shares some of the same problems. As our change of century and millennium demonstrated at the end of AD 2000, such dates are highly ambiguous, ours repeating every century, the Maya Short Count repeating every 256 years. Many of the chronological problems and controversies of the Terminal Classic and Postclassic in the northern lowlands can be attributed to the prevalence of Short Count dates in the north.

of events in each cycle. These K'atun cycles were of particular importance to the Maya vision of cyclical time, history, and divination – and possibly even to politics. This count of K'atuns was used in conjunction with the Calendar Round to produce another dating system, the so-called "Short Count," commonly used in Yucatan in the Late Classic and Postclassic periods [see Box 4].

Sacred Maya oral and written traditions that were recorded by sixteenth-century chroniclers included the various Chilam B'alam K'atun prophecies (Roys 1949, 1965b, 1967; Edmonson 1982) that relied heavily on the *May* cycle or "K'atun count." These holy histories described propitious and catastrophic historical events that had occurred in specific previous K'atun periods, as recorded in a count of K'atuns or the "Short Count" [see Box 4]. Given the Maya cyclical concept of time, such histories were also predictions of future events. These Postclassic epics of cyclical prophecy provided tantalizing and important fragments of Maya history going back to the Classic period. Yet they have tended to confuse, as much as enlighten, modern scholars because of their cyclical logic and religious, rather than historical, intent. Nonetheless, with skeptical analysis, scholars have been able to extract important details regarding events, ethnic groups, and migrations in the centuries between the end of the Classic period kingdoms and the Spanish conquest of the highlands and Yucatan and even to make speculative references to the Classic period itself (e.g. Schele *et al.* 1995; Schele and Mathews 1998; Rice *et al.* 1993).

The ends and midpoints of the 256-year *May* cycles were celebrated with major architectural constructions and monuments (P. Rice in press). One theory proposes that the *May* cycle was critical to ancient Maya political organization (P. Rice in press). In this interpretation the critical K'atun-endings at ends and midpoints of the *May* cycle actually marked dramatic programmatic shifts in terms of which center was the dominant ritual and political capital for that period. Epigraphic and circumstantial evidence for this proposal is especially strong for the Central Petén region in the Late and Terminal Classic periods (P. Rice in press; P. Rice and D. Rice 2004).

The calendrics of Venus also were important to Maya astronomy and astrology (e.g. Aveni 1979). The position of Venus relative to the earth moves through a complex cycle, reappearing in exactly the same position on the horizon every 583.92 days. The Dresden Codex (see Fig. 3.4) shows the sophistication of Maya astronomy and mathematics, using three linked calendars of Venus and correction tables to calculate precisely its positioning and reappearances as the morning and evening star. Of course, the purpose of such knowledge was prophecy, and the codices were tools of shamans, priests, and rulers.

Lunar observations and dates were also a major aspect of Maya calendrics, inscriptions, and divination. The Dresden Codex and inscriptions on Classic period monuments reveal the skill of Maya mathematicians and astronomers at interdigitating complex cycles of time. The lunar month of 29.530 of our days required combinations of temporal cycles to align lunar and solar calendars. Most dated Classic Maya inscriptions include several glyphs specifying the date in the lunar calendar with corrections to bring the lunar dating system into correlation with the solar calendar. The pages of the lunar calculations in the Dresden Codex would also allow the accurate prediction of the moon's eclipses of the sun. This ability to predict solar eclipses, a knowledge probably dating back to the

Preclassic period, would have been a tremendous source of ideological power to shamans, priests, and rulers. The prediction of this most impressive of celestial phenomena would have verified the sacred ruler's other divinatory powers, visions, and communication with the ancestors.

We have still not fully penetrated the degree of ancient Maya astronomical knowledge. Epigraphers have found evidence of Maya predictions and accurate placement of the celestial movements of various constellations, stars, and Jupiter (e.g. Freidel *et al.* 1993: 59–107; Aveni 1992; Milbrath 1988). Conjunctions, eclipses, and the periodic cycles of these astral bodies sometimes determined the specific timing of ceremonies, architectural dedications, sacrifices, and even wars.

## Architecture, astronomy, and sacred geography

The epicenters of Maya sites were constructed as great stages for the production of the religious spectacles that bound together their polities under the K'uhul Ajaw. The temples, palaces, and ballcourts of these centers were carefully placed to draw upon the sacred knowledge of the sky (as formalized in Maya astronomy) and the earth (as embodied in their concepts of sacred geography).

Many Maya temples and buildings are aligned with heavenly bodies, including Venus and various constellations. Some buildings and even building complexes functioned as observatories with monuments, doorways, or structures aligned to observe solstices and equinoxes of the sun or Venus (e.g. Aveni 1979, 1980; Aveni and Hartung 1986). The circular observatory temple at Chichen Itza is a famous example (Fig. 8.13), but more important (and more common) were the "E-group" temples, with three small structures placed in relation to a fourth structure or a monument so as to mark the solar equinoxes and solstices (Fig. 8.14). E-group structures are found dating to the earliest ceremonial centers of the Preclassic period, demonstrating the importance of astronomy and administration in the very origins of ceremonial centers. These ideological and astrological functions for the first ceremonial centers are also verified by the specifics of iconography and architectural façades (see Fig. 8.5). These representations associate the temple and the early shaman/rulers with the sun, Venus, and the divinatory power of the Maya calendars and astronomy (e.g. Carlson 1981; Schele and Freidel 1990: 64–129; Clark *et al.* n.d.; Freidel and Schele 1988a, 1988b). The role of architecture as a stage for calendric rituals continued into the Classic period, with temples, stelae, and altar monuments erected to celebrate key points in the calendric cycles, especially K'atun endings. Symbolism

Figure 8.13 Circular Caracol temple/observatory at Chichen Itza, Yucatan, Mexico

in architectural detail and orientations, as well as carved monuments, commemorated the bloodlettings and divinatory rituals held at period endings.

As settings for ritual and religious pageantry, the ceremonial centers and their architecture drew on more than just astronomical associations. Many details reflected careful use of the natural geography and physical features to evoke sacred associations for the rulers and their rituals (e.g. Ashmore 1991; Schele and Freidel 1990: 64–98; Carlson 1981; Demarest *et al.* 2003). The temples themselves were named and conceived as sacred mountains (*witz*) and were labeled as such in glyphs and iconography. Mountains, especially those with caves and springs in them, remain today the most sacred element of the Maya landscape (e.g. Vogt 1969, 1981, 1983). Hills were considered to be the abode of the ancestors and other supernaturals, and the caves that are common in them were believed to be the entrances to Xibalba, the underworld. The temple entrances atop Maya pyramids and the rulers' tombs within them were structurally parallel to the caves within the mountains, portals of communication with the underworld and the ancestors (Schele and Freidel 1990: 71–73; M. Coe 1988; Vogt 1981; Freidel *et al.* 1993: 125–170).

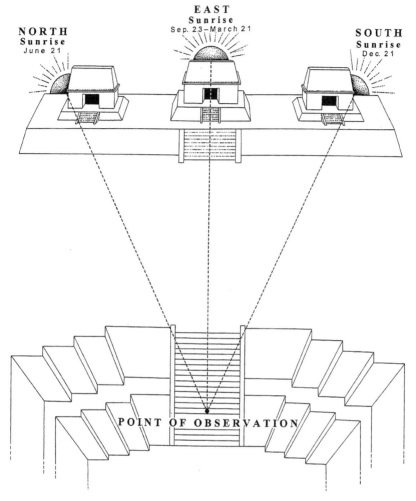

Figure 8.14 Drawing of "E-group temple" showing solar alignments at solstices and equinoxes (redrawn by Luis F. Luin after Morley and Brainerd 1956)

Recent research has demonstrated the importance of mountain and cave symbolism to Maya architecture and ceremonial centers. Exploration and mapping of cave systems in the lowlands and highlands have shown that epicenter and temple placement, as well as architectural alignment, was sometimes determined by the presence and orientation of cave systems beneath them (Brady 1991, 1997; Brady and Rodas 1992). In

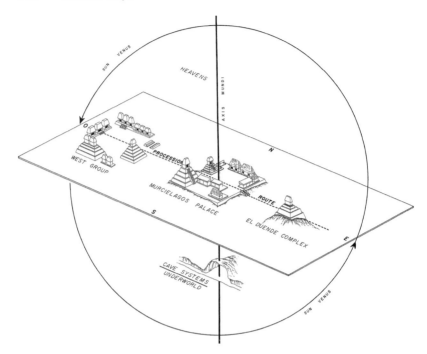

Figure 8.15 Cosmogram at Dos Pilas, showing central position of the
Murcielagos royal palace (drawn by Luis F. Luin)

fact, at sites lacking caverns in the highlands, the Maya excavated artificial
caves beneath epicenters to have these requisite features (Brady 1991b;
Brady and Veni 1992). In the Petexbatun region of the western Petén,
settlement pattern studies simultaneously mapped surface sites and architecture (O'Mansky and Demarest 1995; O'Mansky and Wheat 1997;
O'Mansky and Dunning 2004), while a second team mapped subterranean cavern systems, springs, and offerings (Brady 1990; Brady *et al.*
1990, 1991, 1997). Site and epicenter locations, temple positioning, and
architectural orientations all proved to be aligned to the extensive cavern
systems beneath the centers (Fig. 8.15). Even the details of royal palaces
at Dos Pilas and their smaller shrine structures were determined by alignment to the site's east–west caverns with temples placed above entrances
(Demarest *et al.* 2003; Demarest in press a). Meanwhile, further south
in the Upper Pasión river region near Cancuen, natural karst towers with
caves within them replaced the artificial *witz* of temples as the foci of ritual
and worship (Demarest and Barrientos 1999, 2000, 2001; Demarest in
press a; Woodfill *et al.* 2002, 2003).

## Ceremonial centers as sacred stages

This conception of the temples as mountains rising into the sacred sky defined them as the interface between the underworld, ancestors, sky deities, and people. The iconography of some temples reinforced this model by surrounding temple entrances with cave symbolism and also features of the sun, the Chaaks, and other deities, sometimes with their mouths forming the temple doorways.

Iconographic and epigraphic studies at sites such as Copan and Palenque have shown that some buildings were literally named by architectural sculpture as to their ritual function or functions (e.g. Schele *et al.* 1989; B. Fash *et al.* 1992; see bibliographic essay). The identifications confirm the role of the temples, great courtyards, and ballcourts of Maya centers as stages for the rituals and pageants of sacrifice and divination presided over by the kings and their priests. Even details of royal palace placement drew carefully on multiple alignments and sacred geography to fashion ritual stages. For example, the Murcielagos palace at Dos Pilas had every structure placed atop a sacred mountain and aligned with the east–west axis of the complex (Fig. 8.15). These orientations paralleled the stream-filled caverns that run beneath it. Ceremonial east–west procession paths for calendric rites of sacrifice passed through the palace; again, paralleling the path of the subterranean chambers below (Demarest *et al.* 2003). Indeed, one oratory temple had within it a formal "entombing" with vessel offerings and slabs sealing an entrance into the large cave network below the site (Demarest, Rodas, and Morgan 1995). At Dos Pilas and other sites, the east–west daily path of the sun through the sky, and its west–east return through the underworld at night, were incorporated into the places of sacred power in architectural complexes and the causeways between them (Demarest *et al.* 2003).

Many palaces were also designed as stages for ritual performance by the elite on a smaller scale than the great plazas and temples. The rituals in palace compounds were performed for a smaller elite audience of the royal family, visiting rulers and nobility, elite petitioners, and administrators of the kingdoms. On this more intimate scale, such palaces had sacred orientations and functions for divination, sacrifice, and the propitiation of ancestors and deities. Throne rooms and open presentation palaces were intended for review of processions and receptions and feasting with visiting elites – activities often presented in the scenes painted on Late Classic polychrome vases. Significantly, even in these structures excavations have discovered the tools of the king's ritual power – long, fine bloodletting blades, ornate effigy censers, and bowls for collecting the sacred blood (Demarest *et al.* 2003; Agurcia and Fash 1991).

### Ideology and the Maya theater-states

Many Classic Maya rulers may have had a limited role in the management of the infrastructure of their states. With important exceptions,
most Maya states were decentralized in their agricultural systems and in
networks of local and regional trade. As discussed in Chapter 7, rulers'
economic control may have been primarily in the long-distance exchange
of exotic and status-reinforcing goods. These items functioned in the religious and political systems, rather than as elements of the local market
economies. Similarly, within regions, Maya rulers controlled the production and distribution of fine painted polychrome ceramics and ornately
crafted items of carved shell, bone, or jade. Again, these products were
exchanged between the elites of different centers as gifts or tribute, marking patronage and alliance.

In contrast to the restricted role of rulers in the general subsistence and
economic systems, we have seen that architecture, iconography, artifacts,
and inscriptions define a central role for the ruler in major religious ceremonies and rituals and in the very concepts of the cosmos and the place
of humans in it. Indeed, from the earliest monuments, the rulers appear
in a shamanistic role associated with rites of communication with ancestors, deities, and sacred forces, and with the prediction of the temporal
cycles.

The cultural materialist theoretical perspective of most archaeologists
of the past several decades has prevented many from accepting the obvious fact that a major source of rulers' power and authority might be drawn
from ideology itself. Such a role appears to have been in place in the earliest ceremonial centers (Freidel 1981; Hansen 1992; Freidel and Schele
1988a, 1988b; Clark et al. n.d.). We may speculate that the position of
K'uhul Ajaw, holy lord or ruler, had developed from that of community
shaman, acquiring additional secular functions and political power as a
consequence of the initial religious power and authority of that leader.

A set of states in the tropical rain forests of Southeast Asia provides
many parallels to the Classic Maya. These better-known historical states
have been cited by Maya scholars as an ample source of comparative
analogues and insights due to similarities in their nature and structure (M.
Coe 1981; Demarest 1984b, 1992b; Sharer 1994: 510–512). Like Classic
Maya kingdoms, these "theater-states" of Southeast Asia were tenuously
held together through the power of religion, ritual, and state pageantry
more than economic integration (Bentley 1985; Geertz 1980; Tambiah
1976, 1982, 1984). Also like Maya rulers, kings of the theater-states,
or Negara, of Southeast Asia directed warfare and the redistribution of
foreign luxury goods. Such gifts, and the feasts or events on which they

were given, helped gain the support of subordinates and the good will of allies. The pageantry of the state, expressed in periodically held rituals, was a principal source of authority and power over the populace. While in traditional Marxist terms such ideological sources of power are generally regarded as "legitimation" or propagandistic reinforcement of power, in the case of the theater-states of Southeast Asia, ideology itself may have been a principal *source* of authority, rather than a justification of economic power (Geertz 1980).

A number of scholars have come to the conclusion that ideology, rite, and ritual were also a, though not *the*, major source of power for Maya kings and may have been the central element in the origins of Maya kingship (e.g. M. Coe 1981; Clark *et al.* n.d.; Demarest 1984b, 1992; Freidel 1981, 1992; Hansen 1992; Freidel and Schele 1988a, 1988b; Schele and Freidel 1990). While Maya rulers had economic roles (e.g. Aoyama 2001; Demarest and Barrientos 2001, 2002; Kovacevich *et al.* 2002), there can be little doubt that ideology was a major source of state power. The dazzling corpus of Classic Maya art, iconography, monuments, and architecture was largely devoted to the cult of the K'uhul Ajaw, to the aggrandizement of the ruler, his divine ancestry, and his sacred duties (Freidel 1992; Freidel and Schele 1988a; Schele and Miller 1986; Miller 1996). Classic-period energies and resources were lavishly expended on this monumental display and architecture. Art, artifacts, and monuments provided the stages for the ideological spectacles directed by these holy lords.

These events and rites were repeated according to the ancient Maya canons of time, movement, and ritual re-enactment, the physical tracing of the Maya cosmogram (Carlson 1981; Freidel and Schele 1988a, 1988b; Vogt 1981). This grammar of ritual movement and the definition of the sacred center through such movements has even deeper circumpacific roots in shared Asian shamanistic concepts and their later ecclesiastical elaboration (Eliade 1954, 1961). The motion of all such pageants, processions, and rituals – and the cosmic pattern that they emulated – all rotated around the "sacred center." In Maya political, cosmological, and ritual performance, as in the Negara of Southeast Asia, the ruler appropriated for himself that position in the sacred center, embodying and becoming the axis of the universe (e.g. Freidel 1992; Freidel and Schele 1988a, 1988b; Schele 1981; Schele and Freidel 1990; Schele and Miller 1986).

# 9    Classic Maya politics and history: the dynamics of the theater-states

This chapter first broadly characterizes the nature and dynamics of Classic Maya polities and traces how they developed from the Early to Late Classic periods. The forms and the evidence on Maya polities give us a general perspective on these political formations, which were very different from those of our own Western civilization. Then a more detailed discussion highlights the great regional and temporal variability in forms of Maya polities, giving a glimpse of the true complexity of their nature.

## Maya history and the forms of the Classic Maya state

While the historical record of the Classic Maya sadly is mute on most economic issues, it is remarkably rich in description of the nature and structure of political and religious power. Maya state forms flourished over a huge geographical area and a temporal span of at least two millennia. While variability was great, it is possible to identify some basic characteristics of Maya polities in the Classic period. Then we can examine the many regional and chronological variations and try to explain the dynamics behind this variability.

### Historical titles and events

Maya history and political organization have partly been reconstructed from the evidence of settlement surveys, excavations, and ethnohistorical accounts of Maya kingdoms at the time of the Spanish Conquest. Yet the evidence from archaeology speaks only indirectly to political boundaries, influences, and alliances. Conquest-period ethnohistory is helpful in hypothesizing about some details and possible political formations. However, Maya political structure, political ideology, and polity extent and scale may have changed drastically by the time of the Conquest. Significant changes in political formation occurred during the Terminal

Classic and Early Postclassic epochs, some involving the introduction of new concepts and institutions from other regions of Mesoamerica. For all of these reasons, scholars are increasingly relying upon the evidence of the ancient Maya texts left on monuments and artifacts. The interpretation of the inscriptions does, nonetheless, rely heavily on both the ethnohistoric record and analogies to preindustrial states elsewhere in the world.

Central to our ability to reconstruct the Classic-period political landscape and historical record are the "emblem glyphs" first discovered by Heinrich Berlin in 1958 (Berlin 1958). Berlin proposed that these glyphs identified Maya centers or states. Such glyphs are now known actually to represent the titles of the rulers of states. As such, they identify the basic discrete political units of the Maya world.

Emblem glyphs consist of a main sign referring to the polity or place and a series of affixes read as "K'uhul Ajaw" meaning "divine lord" or "holy lord" (Figs. 9.1, 9.2c). Thus, together the glyph cluster identifies "the holy lord of," with the main sign specifying the center (Mathews 1991). Some of these main signs, as well as other glyphs, have been identified as "toponyms," place names that refer to geographical locations or features that were associated with a particular site or its epicenter (Stuart and Houston 1994). Other toponyms merely name specific places or particular geographical features. Since emblem glyphs were the titles of kings, they have allowed us to identify the discrete states of the Maya world and plot their histories and sometimes their territories (see bibliographic essay). Studies based on emblem glyphs and the distances between centers have estimated that most Maya kingdoms in the Classic period may have been fairly small city-states, averaging about 2,000 square kilometers in area (Mathews and Willey 1991; Mathews 1985, 1988, 1997; Hammond 1993: 26–29).

Yet evidence from recent decipherments indicates that there were some much larger kingdoms or alliances (Martin and Grube 1994, 1995, 2000; cf. Marcus 1976). Certain glyphs indicate that some actions were taken by local Ajaws (Fig. 9.2a) under the orders or direction of more powerful overlords of larger centers (Martin and Grube 1995a, 2000; Stuart 1995: 256–261). One form of the Ajaw emblematic title had a prefix read "y" in Maya, which makes ajaw into yajaw or "the lord of ___" (Fig. 9.2d), indicating vassalage of the local ruler to a specified king. Other indications of vassalage and alliance can be identified by monumental inscriptions that describe an overlord's patronage at events or sponsorship of accessions to the throne at subordinate centers. Another set of glyphs was used to identify a "sajal" or lieutenant of the king (Fig. 9.2b), or in other

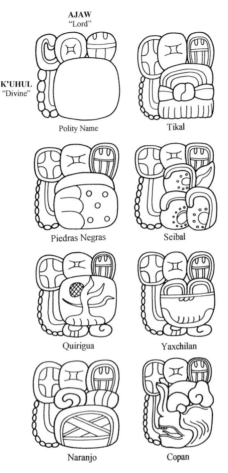

Figure 9.1 Emblem glyphs of some Classic Maya centers (drawn by Luis F. Luin)

contexts to identify one local ruler as the subordinate – "the sajal of" – another king (*u-sajal*) (Fig. 9.2e). Some larger centers, such as Tikal, had special titles for overlords (Martin and Grube 1996; 2000: 17–21). The hegemonic highest kings of that center took kaloomte' in their title (Fig. 9.2f), while subordinate kings were the basic K'uhul Ajaw or holy lords (Fig. 9.2c), and below these were leaders with Yajaw titles indicating vassalage (Fig. 9.2d). Scholars have been able to speculate about larger alliances or "super states" by using these and other epigraphic clues and comparing them to the archaeological record of site sizes, areas, and the

a.
Ajaw

b.
Sajal

c.
K'uhul Ajaw

d.
Yajaw

e.
Usajal

f.
Kaloomte'

Figure 9.2 Some glyphs for political titles of lords, vassals, and overlords (drawn by Luis F. Luin)

gifts in tombs and caches from other centers (Martin and Grube 1995). Of course, such interpretations are still tentative given the ambiguity of the archaeological record and the propagandistic nature of the monumental inscriptions of the Classic period.

More secure than characterizations of the broad political landscape, the glyphs identify many different kinds of historical events or actions of these kings. Glyphs for birth, accession to the throne, death, war, capture of others, captive sacrifice, and royal rituals of auto-sacrifice give us a detailed view of the life history and achievements of the Maya holy lords (Fig. 9.3). Inscriptions describing parentage, marriage, and spiritual concepts can also yield insights into the nature of the general society beyond the elite. Texts on painted and carved Maya vases provide a more intimate view of daily life in the royal courts – portraying the meetings, rites, and events directed by the kings, their administrators, and their priests (Fig. 9.4; see also Fig. 5.9). The perspective of all these sources was, of course, limited to the elite, and the monumental texts were clearly intended to aggrandize their kings. Still, if cautiously interpreted, the inscriptions and art of the Classic period help to extend and to interpret the archaeological evidence, and they also give us a glimpse of the Maya view of their own world.

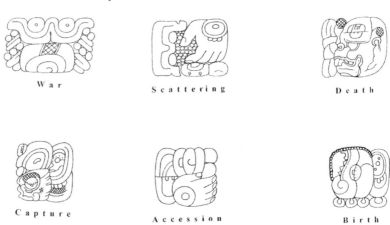

Figure 9.3 Glyphs for major events in rulers' life histories (drawn by Luis F. Luin). "Scattering" refers to a bloodletting ritual which included the ruler scattering his own blood from his hand into receptacles, as visualized in this logographic form of the glyph (see also Fig. 8.7)

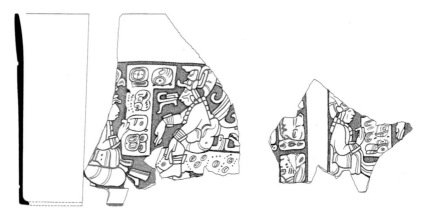

Figure 9.4 Royal court scene on Late Classic Maya vase (drawn by Luis F. Luin)

### The role of Maya leadership

The first fundamental issue concerns the nature of Classic Maya states and the role of Maya elites and rulers. In general, the relationship of elites to the populations under their control has proven to be a more subtle and complex one than envisioned by early researchers or by most comparisons to other early civilizations. As discussed in Chapters 6 and 7, traditional theories that defined elites as economic "managers" of one type or other have not worked well in applications to the Maya area. Most lowland Maya areas were largely self-sufficient in foodstuffs and basic resources. Regional trade in basic raw materials and utilitarian artifacts generally may not have been mediated by rulers (see Chapter 7). Similarly, many terraces and other intensive farming systems appear to have been constructed and managed by local groups, probably extended families, or at times through village cooperation (see Chapter 6).

In many cases the rulers apparently *did* control production and exchange of fine polychrome pottery, jade, and shell ornaments, and other status-reinforcing goods in a parallel "palace" economy (see bibliographic essay). Much long-distance exchange of exotic goods, such as Caribbean shell, jade, magnetite, and the feathers of exotic birds, was also probably elite-controlled (see Chapter 7). Many Maya kingdoms also had small, state-controlled, intensive field or terrace farming systems near palaces in the site epicenters (e.g. Dunning, Beach, and Rue 1997). In general, however, such systems were limited in extent, serving the direct needs of the palaces. With important exceptions, state economic involvement, then, in most Classic Maya polities in most regions and periods may have been limited. The power of the K'uhul Ajaw resided more in his roles in ritual and warfare, as the central actor in the theater-state. As discussed in Chapter 8, this dependence of the state on ideology for much of its power might help to explain the great emphasis on ceremony and legitimating art and architecture in Maya epicenters, as well as some aspects of the unstable dynamics of Maya states.

Having made this broad generalization about most Maya polities, it must be acknowledged that regional and historical variation was extremely great, even concerning the basic role of elites in economic infrastructure. As sketched in the brief review of Maya regional history that follows, hydraulic systems at Edzna, water storage at other northern sites, and extensive terrace systems in the Río Bec sites and at Caracol (Fig. 9.5) all may have been important infrastructural features produced by state-directed corporate labor. Furthermore, site systems connected by causeways or canals to vast epicenters at Calakmul and Caracol suggest more centralized and integrated economies. We can conclude that some kingdoms in the Classic period may have developed into larger, more regional states with a more direct managerial role for the rulers. In the case of Calakmul, its regional polity declined after AD 695, but the regional state at Caracol had a notable second florescence in the early ninth century.

Archaeologists should not see these episodes of more centralized states as a contradiction of the more general pattern of small kingdoms among the Maya. The rise and decline of more centralized regional states were part of city-state dynamics in early Mesopotamia and Classical Greece. Such regional and historical variability was a central aspect of the volatile dynamics of Classic Maya civilization.

*The size and extent of polities*

There have been many methods applied by scholars to estimate the territorial size and populations of Maya states. For many decades we have relied upon indirect measures based on archaeological data about the distance between sites, the volume of construction in sites, or the number of monuments, plazas, or structures (e.g. Adams and Jones 1981; Hammond 1974, 1975). More recently we have been able to shift to the historical record of the stone monuments and their inscriptions identifying the ruling dynasties of the K'uhul Ajaw and their political alliances, rituals, and wars (e.g. Marcus 1976; Culbert 1991). Critical to such interpretations are the emblem-glyphs and titles described earlier. A few texts even mention tribute payments by vassal polities (Stuart 1995). With such detailed data, it is possible to be more specific about which centers were dominant powers in particular periods and to plot their political relationships (e.g. Martin and Grube 2000). This epigraphic record portrays a very complex inter-elite political landscape throughout the Classic period.

As a minimal building block of Maya polities, the individual small polity, defined by a dynastic "holy lord" title or emblem-glyph, has been estimated by some scholars as being one or two days' walking distance in diameter (e.g. Hammond 1991; Mathews 1985, 1988). Probable dynastic seats or "capitals" of such minimal polities were often about ten to thirty kilometers apart. We might speculate that this size for the realm of the average holy lord befits a "theater-state" in which the K'uhul Ajaw's personal presence and celebration of rites were central to the maintenance of his authority. For a time, epigraphers and archaeologists believed that the lowland Maya world in the Classic period consisted of only such small city-states interacting in a "peer polity" system (e.g. Houston 1992; Mathews 1985, 1988; cf. Renfrew and Cherry 1986). Now, with more detailed information, we can study the tremendous variability in Maya polities and the historical development of structurally distinct regional states and pan-lowland, but short-lived, alliances.

In the Late Classic, polities had populations varying from several thousand at most major cities to several hundred thousand around some great regional capitals such as Calakmul, Tikal, and Caracol (e.g. Culbert and Rice eds. 1990; Hammond 1991; Sharer 1994: 467–473). All such demographic estimates for sites, polities, or regions are highly speculative calculations based on house mound counts, ceramic dating of mounds, ethnographic models for the number of persons per structure, and, usually, a calculation factor for "invisible" houses that lacked clearly visible substructure mounds or platforms. Combined with the epigraphic evidence on specific political formations, the speculative demography and settlement evidence allow broad, very tentative characterizations of Classic Maya political history (e.g. Culbert 1991).

### The dynamics of the Classic Maya galactic polities

Evidence from the past thirty years of research shows that larger Maya states and regional alliances had many, very different and complex trajectories of rise, florescence, and decline. For example, the great Preclassic state of El Mirador grew in population to tens of thousands of inhabitants by the Late Preclassic period and extended its hegemony over networks of other centers, only to decline at the beginning of the Classic era (Demarest 1984b; Hansen 1992, 1994; Matheny 1986a, 1987). Tikal expanded in size and influence across the lowlands in the fifth century, but its hegemony suffered defeats and declined in the late sixth. It re-emerged in the late seventh and eighth centuries as a booming, but more regionally focused, central Petén state. Meanwhile, Calakmul surged from the ranks of so-called "peer-polities" in the sixth and seventh centuries to become a gargantuan regional state with a population of over 100,000 (Braswell *et al.* 2004) that led a far-flung interregional alliance of other city-states. Other regional polities, such as Copan, had somewhat less variable histories, while yet others had very idiosyncratic trajectories. For example, the Petexbatun regional state of Dos Pilas began in the seventh century and experienced a meteoric expansion through conquest and alliance across the Pasión River Valley, only to disintegrate suddenly in the mid-eighth century (see Chapter 10).

Scholars have noted these complex dynamics and are now beginning to seek models not to define *the* Maya state, but to begin to understand the grammar of the constant change and instability of these polities and hegemonies (e.g. Marcus 1993; Hammond 1991; Demarest 1984b, 1992b, 1996b; Sharer 1991). Some have argued that our models for state dynamics should come from the ethnohistorical record of sixteenth-century Postclassic Maya polities (e.g. Marcus 1983a, 1993). Important patterns in Classic Maya politics have been identified by drawing on the detailed sixteenth-century descriptions of the Postclassic states of Yucatan and the Guatemalan highlands (e.g. Schele *et al.* 1995). These include insights into the dynamics of alliance formation (e.g. Marcus 1993) and the recognition of periodic calendrically determined ritual shifting of capitals according to the *May* cycle of thirteen K'atuns (P. Rice in press). Conquest-period states, however, were also different from those of the Classic period in important aspects. Therefore, using the rich epigraphic and archaeological record of the Classic period, we should also apply comparative interpretations from a variety of sources and test them for "best fit" to the Classic cultural-historical record.

In Chapter 8, the ideological foundations of Classic Maya "theater-states" were briefly described. Such polities, well known in Southeast Asia, have centers and rulers who model a cosmological order of belief of their subjects. The Negara theater-states of Southeast Asia were much like most Maya polities in key characteristics:

1) the dependence of rulers for power on personal performance in ritual and in warfare;
2) the loose structure and unbounded nature of political territories which were "center-oriented" networks of personal, political, and religious authority that radiated from the ruler himself;
3) the generally weak direct control or involvement of the state in local subsistence or economic infrastructure;
4) the redundancy in structure and functions between the capital center and minor subordinate centers;
5) the organization of hegemonies into capital centers loosely controlling a network or "galaxy" of subordinate sites (Tambiah 1976, 1977; Geertz 1980; Demarest 1984b, 1992, 1997).

All of these traits were present in the many polities and hegemonies, large and small, of the Classic period, a list of common traits that transcend the varying population size and territorial extent of lowland polities.

The formulations of scholars working on Southeast Asia theater-states may also help model the unstable dynamics of the Classic period and the protean manifestations of the Maya state. Tambiah (1976, 1977, 1984) has explained how such theater-states could expand into regional powers or loosely linked hegemonies in specific periods. In Southeast Asia, highly unstable ideologically based theater-states could rapidly expand as "galactic polities" through warfare or a variety of other mechanisms, which allowed the divine rulers to attract the allegiance and tribute of a growing number of "satellite" subordinate states or centers. Status-reinforcing foreign influence could strengthen the charismatic power of particular states, as could their control of imports or their foreign, "exotic" associations. In cases such as the Teotihuacan-associated Tikal hegemony, the ruler's participation in a broader, distant information sphere constituted a form of "otherworldly knowledge" structurally equivalent to spiritual or divine knowledge (cf. Helms 1979; cf. Tambiah 1982, 1984). Successes in warfare, marriage alliances, and rituals and pageants could also launch a ruler, his dynasty, and his capital center into several generations of hegemonic expansionism. Ultimately, these episodes of larger political formations were abortive and the galactic polities disintegrated into their constituent states or reformed into a different configuration of polity or alliance (Tambiah 1976: 127; Demarest 1992: 154–157). In all cases, the primarily ideological and political – rather than infrastructural – basis of power facilitated the rapid expansion of spheres of dominance, but also predisposed these systems to swift decline or disintegration.

This interpretive framework applies well to the myriad political formations seen in the Classic period in the southern Maya lowlands. As described below, the regional, more centralized state of Caracol, the expanding and contracting hegemonies of states like Calakmul and Tikal, and the more stable but limited polities of most other Maya states, can be seen as variations on the spectrum of expanding and contracting theater-states. Over two millennia of such unstable political dynamics have been described for the theater-states and galactic polities of Southeast Asia (e.g. Bentley 1986; Geertz 1980; Tambiah 1976; Gesick 1983). The segmentary structure of such polities, with redundant major and minor centers, was also like that of Classic Maya states, and carries the same problems of instability due to the ease of usurpation or succession from alliance by subordinate centers.

Such galactic theater-state formations have great difficulty unifying into pan-regional centralized states, like those found in central Mexico or Egypt at parallel levels of development. Instead the historical inscriptions of the Classic period record centuries of wars, alliances, and the formation of larger, but unstable, hegemonies. Here a brief glimpse of these Classic-period dynastic histories should illustrate the baffling complexity and variability that I have simplified in the above generalizations.

### Regional histories of the Maya states

By the Classic period, the epigraphy, iconography, and archaeology of the Maya civilization allow the reconstruction of regional cultural histories, including dated events, dynastic histories, and victories (or defeats) of individual key rulers. Here I provide only a brief summary of a few events at some of the great Maya centers. These descriptions provide a glimpse of some of the political patterns discussed above – and perhaps a sense of the "flavor" of Classic Maya history. (See the bibliographic essay at the end of this volume for recent, more detailed historical summaries.)

*The Early Classic dynasties in the Maya lowlands*

States with "holy lords" and the full political and economic rationale of Maya civilization were surely in place by the Late Preclassic period. Yet it is not until the full Classic period in the fourth and fifth centuries AD that the epigraphic record of carved monuments is sufficiently detailed to characterize accurately the history of major dynasties.

We know little more than the names of the kings of some major centers prior to the fourth and fifth centuries AD. Then, at the great centers of Tikal and Copan (Fig. 9.5), rulers took the throne claiming affiliations with the cultures of Mexico, perhaps even with the distant Mexican city of Teotihuacan itself (see Box 3, Chapter 5). The exact nature of events at this time remains unclear, but recent decipherments and interpretations indicate that a Maya war leader or agent, perhaps with Mexican affiliations, named Siyaj K'ak (formerly referred to as "Smoking Frog") was involved in wars and dynastic upheaval at the great city of Tikal and the nearby center of Uaxactun (Stuart 2000; Martin and Grube 2000: 28–36). At this same time (AD 378), a new ruler, Yax Nuun Ayiin ("First Crocodile"), took the throne of Tikal. This new king and later his son Siyaj Chan K'awiil (called "Stormy Sky" before phonetic decipherment) both claimed descent from a lord with Mexican pictographic symbols for his name glyph (a spear-thrower and an owl). This royal ancestor might have been a ruler of Teotihuacan itself (Stuart 2000), or he may have been a lord from Kaminaljuyu (Coggins 1975) or from elsewhere with Mexican affiliations or claims to such affiliation (see various interpretations in Braswell 2003c).

The new king, his son Siyaj Chan K'awiil, and all of their later descendants celebrated their claims of Mexican affiliation in art and iconography and with various Mexican-derived cults and rituals (e.g. Coggins 1979; Schele 1986). They also ushered in an epoch of greatness at Tikal, which extended its influence through alliances, sponsorship of new dynasties elsewhere, and conquests throughout the southern lowlands. In the fifth century, Uaxactun, Río Azul, Holmul, and even distant Quirigua in the southeast (Fig. 9.5) were allied with or dominated by Tikal's new dynasty (Ashmore 1980; Mathews and Willey 1985; Adams 1990).

Far to the southeast at Copan in distant Honduras another new dynasty was founded in AD 426 by a king named K'inich Yax K'uk'Mo', who again appears to have "arrived" from the west. His Early Classic dynasty at Copan, like that at Tikal, celebrated its claims of Mexican affiliation in monuments and artifacts. Recent discoveries at Copan (e.g. Fash 1991, 2000; Sharer *et al.* 1999; Sharer 2003) have revealed the magnificent

Figure 9.5  Some major Classic Maya centers (drawn by Luis F. Luin)

palaces and temples of the Early Classic rulers who followed this new founder.

Meanwhile at Kaminaljuyu in the southern highlands, strong Teotihuacan influence appeared in architecture, censers, and ceramics. Most notable are structures in the talud-tablero style characteristic of this period in central Mexico. Indeed, scholars had thought for some time that Kaminaljuyu and the southern highlands might have served as an intermediary passing Mexican influences and contacts to the Petén (e.g. Coggins 1979; Santley 1983). While the directionality of the flow of influences remains unclear, it does appear that highland–lowland interaction was important in the Early Classic and that foreign involvement was a factor. Many of these cultural exchanges may have passed between specific Maya kingdoms and central Mexico or via culture areas in Veracruz, Oaxaca, or other zones that indirectly transferred influences to and from Central Mexico (Marcus 2003; Braswell 2003b).

At the direct "gateway" between highlands and lowlands in the Cancuen kingdom of the far southern Petén (Fig. 9.5), three monuments with Teotihuacan-style figures were found at Tres Islas that date to this period of Mexican influence or affiliation. The imagery on these stelae includes Mexican elements such as Teotihuacan-style armor and spearthrowers, as at Tikal and Uaxactun (Fig. 9.6). The Cancuen kingdom was strategically placed astride the Pasión River at precisely the point where it becomes navigable after its descent from the highlands to the south. It appears that highland–lowland contacts and movements in this period of Tikal expansionism might have come through this corridor (Fahsen and Demarest 2001).

The meaning and historical specifics of these contacts remain unclear. The Teotihuacan elements and interventions might have been induced by Maya lords themselves seeking prestigious affiliations to bolster their competitive dynastic claims (Braswell 2003a). Clearly, we can no longer posit (as was once thought) that Teotihuacan influence stimulated the rise of state-level society in the Maya world, since states, cities, and kings already existed at Tikal and Kaminaljuyu, and probably at Nakbe and El Mirador, centuries earlier (Demarest and Foias 1993; Marcus 2003). Nonetheless, it is clear that Mexican contacts and affiliations were very important, at least to the Maya themselves, in the founding and legitimation of their Early Classic dynasties (Braswell 2003a).

Meanwhile, on the Yucatan Peninsula to the north, Early Classic states developed with distinctive styles and an emphasis on inland–coastal trade and salt production. Major sites like Komchen had developed in the Preclassic period, specializing in such trade with larger inland cities like Dzibilchaltun (Andrews V 1981; Ringle and Andrews V 1988, 1990).

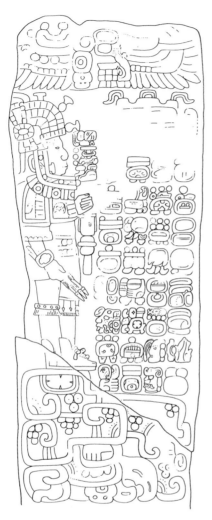

Figure 9.6 Stela 1, Tres Islas, Guatemala (redrawn by Luis F. Luin from unpublished drawing by Ian Graham)

The lower, drier, northern rain forest, even thinner soils, and more limited surface water required different adaptations, with a greater emphasis on coastal trade and various types of water catchment systems, including the development of a massive, apparently centrally controlled hydraulic system at the center of Edzna (Matheny *et al.* 1983).

In the third and fourth centuries these very different northern polities also participated in pan-Mesoamerican exchanges of styles and concepts. Architecture in talud-tablero style and stuccoed façades reflect such influences (Varela Torrecilla 1998). At Becan in Campeche near the interface of the northern and southern lowlands, fortifications and evidence of a possible siege might relate to foreign contacts (Webster 1976). A major fortification system was built there at the end of the Preclassic era, with ramparts five meters high and a six-meter-deep moat surrounding the site epicenter. The Becan population declined in the Early Classic, and caches in the site center included Teotihuacan-style "slab-tripod" vases and figurines. As at many northern sites, however, the paucity of carved monuments makes impossible more specific historical reconstruction.

While new dynasties were being founded and foreign exchanges were felt throughout the lowlands, a great center was developing in southern Campeche at the site of Calakmul. By the sixth century this giant center was ready to confront the panregional hegemony of Tikal in the south, a confrontation that came to involve many of the Maya kingdoms of the lowlands.

*Interregional alliances, wars, and "mega-states" of the sixth and seventh centuries*

The interpretation of interregional alliances in the Classic Maya world has been a difficult and controversial endeavor. As described earlier in this chapter, recent decipherments have identified terms for higher overlords, vassal lords, and subordinate nobles. Yet scholars argue as to whether these terms specify true direct political dominance and macro-states, or weaker elite alliances, or even just short-term strategic coordination of some wars (cf. Hammond 1991; Demarest 1992; Demarest and Fahsen 2003; Fahsen *et al.* 2003; Martin and Grube 1994, 1995, 2000; Houston 1992, 1994; Stuart 1995). Some point out that it is not clear whether the supervision of accessions to the throne, rites, or wars by one of the overlord kings of the great centers implied a dominance over other aspects of political life. The relative self-sufficiency of local and regional economies would argue against pressures to form meaningful macro-state economies, and tribute would probably most often have been in the form of specific commodities and elite prestige items (see Chapter 7). If such were the case, these greater alliances generally may have had a limited impact on life in the "vassal" centers.

Still, there is growing evidence that in certain periods such widespread alliances were, in fact, important, especially in warfare. Some of these coordinated wars appear to have resulted in the sacking of centers, destroying the physical core of the theater-states and with it the prestige that drew followers to a center (e.g. Freidel *et al.* 1993: 295–336; Martin and Grube 2000; Freidel in press; Fahsen *et al.* 2003).

The most notable of such interregional wars occurred in the sixth and seventh centuries between the powerful large cities of Calakmul and Tikal and their respective network of allied and vassal centers. Early in the sixth century, Tikal, arguably the greatest and most prestigious Maya center, entered a time of troubles. Internal struggles for succession and military defeats appear to have led to a destructive attack on the Tikal center itself in AD 562 (Martin and Grube 1995, 2000; Schele and Freidel 1990: 171–177). These events led to the so-called "hiatus" period, dated by some scholars from AD 562 to 692. Once believed to be a general decline of Maya centers (recently erroneously attributed to drought [Gill 2000; Adams *et al.* 2003]), we now know that the "hiatus" was only a political decline in the fortunes of Tikal and some of the centers most closely allied to it.

This same period witnessed a florescence of the great rival center of Calakmul in the north, which grew in size and extended its network of alliances during the epoch of Tikal's decline. At Caracol to the east in Belize, another political rival of Tikal (formerly its vassal) grew in wealth, power, and prestige after several sixth-century defeats of Tikal and its allies (Chase, Grube, and Chase 1991; Grube 1994a; Martin and Grube 1994, 1995, 2000: 89–95). It is not surprising that victorious centers like Caracol and Calakmul grew rapidly in size, influence, and wealth after such victories, given the nature of the Maya theater-states and the great dependence on prestige and tribute labor for their expansion.

Bolstered by such prestige-enhancing victories, as well as booty and tribute from vassal centers, Caracol and Calakmul both grew into gigantic and wealthy centers during these centuries. By the seventh century, Calakmul in Campeche covered an area of 20 square kilometers encircled by a system of canals, modified rivers, and lakes (Folan 1988, 1992; Folan *et al.* 1995). Its more than 6,000 structures housed a population of well over 100,000, an enormous size for any preindustrial city (Dominguez Carrasco *et al.* 1996; Braswell *et al.* 2003). Meanwhile in Belize, Caracol also grew into a megapolis with a regional population also estimated to have been over a hundred thousand (A. Chase and D. Chase 1996a, 1996b). The wide distribution of tombs with fine polychromes has been interpreted as a consequence of the economic and political prestige of Caracol, the flow of tribute, and the consequent development there of a more complex economy with rising "middle classes" (A. Chase and D. Chase 1987, 1996a). Nearby satellite centers and smaller communities were connected to the city by a network of causeways. Local community specialization, extensive terracing, and such communication systems

Figure 9.7  Caana temple at Caracol

argue for a more unified regional economy at Caracol, an argument that could also be made for Calakmul, and probably Tikal (A. Chase and D. Chase 1996b). As discussed earlier, such mega-states may have involved a qualitative shift in the nature of their economies in response to their quantitative scale (Demarest 1996b). Regional exchange of foodstuffs and more central economic administration may have expanded the infrastructural role of the K'uhul Ajaws of such kingdoms. Perhaps reflecting these more complex royal functions, some of the major structures of Calakmul and Caracol, such as the Caana of the latter site, combined the features and functions of temples, palaces, and administrative offices (Fig. 9.7).

During the sixth- and seventh-century epoch of its ascendancy, Calakmul reached out to establish alliances, instigate wars against Tikal, and meddle in the dynastic affairs of centers throughout the southern lowlands (Martin and Grube 1994, 1995, 2000). This meddling extended to Dos Pilas in the western Petén, where in AD 632 Tikal established a new military outpost with a young Tikal prince to block the expansion of Calakmul and its allies in the west. Carved hieroglyphic stairs discovered in 2001 have revealed that this military center was conquered by Calakmul within a few decades after its founding (Fahsen et al. 2003; Demarest and Fahsen 2003). From that time Dos Pilas became a western base for Calakmul's military conflict with Tikal. Under

Figure 9.8 Dos Pilas Hieroglyphic Stairway 4, discovered in 1990

the auspices of the Calakmul ruler, Dos Pilas made war on its relatives at Tikal, defeating them in one war in AD 679 (Houston and Mathews 1985). Recently discovered monuments, including stairways (Fig. 9.8), record this victory over Tikal and Calakmul's sponsorship of these wars (Fahsen *et al.* 2003; Demarest and Fahsen 2003; Demarest 1993, 1997; Martin and Grube 1994, 1995, 2000: 52–67; Symonds *et al.* 1990). Even later monuments record Calakmul's continuing relationship with the Petexbatun region and sponsorship of major royal rituals (see Fig. 9.9).

Calakmul also reached out to conquer or to establish dominant alliances with many other centers. With its Dos Pilas vassal, Calakmul conquered centers across the west (Demarest and Fahsen 2003). Following the route of the Mexican-affiliated Tikal dynasties centuries earlier, Calakmul established authority over the Cancuen kingdom in the far southwestern Petén which controlled the critical head of navigation of the Pasión River system, a major trade artery of the Maya world and the gateway to the highlands (Demarest and Fahsen 2003). Calakmul even placed new kings on Cancuen's throne in 656 and 677 (Martin and Grube 1994, 1996, 2000). Similar alliances were established with other western centers, such as El Perú, and in the east to Naranjo, Caracol, and other polities (Martin and Grube 1995, 2000).

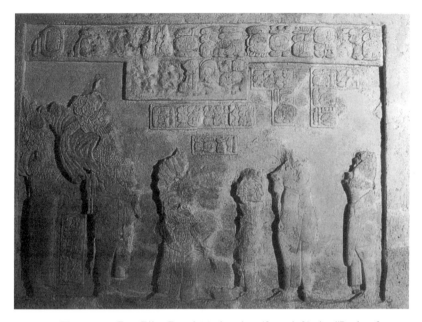

Figure 9.9 Dos Pilas Panel 19 showing (from left) the "Lady of Cancuen," Ruler 3 of Dos Pilas, attending priest, the young Dos Pilas prince bloodletting, and a visiting patron from Calakmul

*Regionalism and status rivalry in the seventh and eighth centuries*

The period of ascendancy and greatest florescence at Calakmul and Caracol ended as it had begun – with wars. Defeat of Calakmul's king in AD 695 by Tikal and a defeat of Caracol in AD 680 led to periods of decline in influence and construction activity at these two giant centers. Tikal began an era of great revitalization at this time. Yet, the period of meaningful regional alliances may have ended by the late seventh century. Instead, perhaps stimulated by interregional wars and intensifying status rivalry, powerful dynasties in each regional zone of the Maya lowlands (Fig. 9.10) raised distinctive forms of Maya civilization in the late seventh and the eighth centuries. Differences in ceramics, architecture styles, and other aspects of material culture mark these variously defined archaeological zones. The growing polygamous elite class, and especially the competing K'uhul Ajaws, invested ever more labor and resources in their distinctive regional forms of ceramics and artifacts, as well as aggrandizing art, monuments, and architecture. Out of the shadow of overarching alliances, the major centers of each zone flourished, elaborating their own

Figure 9.10 Late Classic subregions and sites of the Maya lowlands (drawn by Luis F. Luin). Numbers in each subzone indicate the approximate chronological order of the Terminal Classic changes (collapses, declines, transitions, or transformations)

regional hierarchies of centers and pursuing war and status rivalries with less distant neighbors.

Tikal itself, after its triumphs over Calakmul and other rivals, experienced a florescence in the very late seventh and the eighth centuries.

Under perhaps its greatest overlord, Jasaw Chan K'awiil, and his successors, Tikal embarked on a construction program that included its great temples I, II, IV, and VI, and its great central acropolis palace (see Fig. 5.2). Renovations and new structures were completed in its north acropolis, actually a necropolis or royal tomb complex. The cults of royal ancestor worship achieved their apogee in the Late Classic architectural constructions of the Tikal epicenter and the spectacular public rituals staged there. Other splendid palaces and temples were scattered in other epicenters at Tikal and at vassal centers in the Central Petén such as Ixlu and Yaxha. Each twenty-year period (K'atun), twin-temple complexes were constructed to worship the ancestors in a sacred, astronomically significant, artificial landscape. At many major centers in the Central Petén, such as Naranjo, Late Classic rival dynasties of Tikal generated their own magnificent architecture and monuments, celebrating the achievements of the regional K'uhul Ajaw.

### Late Classic western Petén kingdoms

In the western Petén, key portage sites along the Pasión-Usumacinta river system became the seats of competing regional kingdoms in the eighth century without controlling external powers (Fig. 9.10). Early in the Classic period important kingdoms had been established at strategic points in the river system. At the "head of navigation" in the Upper Pasión, the Cancuen-Tres Islas kingdom controlled access to the highland routes and so to sources of precious high-status goods, such as pyrite, jade, and quetzal feathers. It also became an intermediary in trade for more utilitarian hard stone commodities from the volcanic highlands, such as igneous and metamorphic rock for tools, weapons, and ritual bloodletters (Demarest and Barrientos 1999, 2000, 2001, 2002).

The ruling dynasty of Cancuen took full advantage of its strategic position at the first portage of the Pasión. The royal palace of Cancuen was surrounded by workshops that fashioned tools and works of art from the highland stones. Workshops in obsidian, chert, and chalcedony fashioned blades, spearheads, and macroblades for trade (Kovacevich et al. 2001, 2002). At others artisans fashioned mirrors from pyrite flakes and sliced plaques from imported great boulders of jade. Thousands of jade fragments and jade debris were heaped in middens and on floors in one of these workshops, together with jade boulders, jade-working tools, and half-finished ornaments (Kovacevich et al. 2002). The relationship between palace structures and nearby workshops and the nature of the materials used suggest that at Cancuen the ruler may have controlled the production of these sumptuary goods. The precious finished objects and perhaps also raw materials were used as gifts in exchange with – or as tribute to – rulers of other centers.

The Cancuen kingdom was yet another exception to generalizations about the nature of political and economic power. Recent decipherments and ongoing excavations (Fahsen and Demarest 2001; Fahsen and Jackson 2002; Demarest and Barrientos 1999, 2000, 2001, 2002) have shown that the rulers here relied upon a clever strategy of alliance formation to remain affiliated in each period with a major military power to the north – first Tikal, then Calakmul, then Dos Pilas, and later Machaquilá. With the defeat of an ally-protector, the rulers of Cancuen rapidly changed allegiance to a new successful power. Undoubtedly, these Machiavellian political strategies and alliance formations were greatly aided by Cancuen's control in the west of the exchange of precious highland goods. The marriage and military alliances recorded in the inscriptions of Cancuen and its allies were also facilitated by the ruler's awe-inspiring, sprawling royal palace, one of the largest in the Maya world (Fig. 9.11). Currently being unearthed (Demarest and Barrientos 2001, 2002), the palace had over 200 masonry, corbeled-vaulted rooms rising in three stories around a series of internal courtyards. This provided a perfect setting for the feasts, rituals, and other activities that were critical to alliance formation and status rivalry in the Late Classic period.

Farther downriver (north) on the Pasión-Usumacinta river systems at strategic portages, great kingdoms at Seibal, Altar de Sacrificios, Yaxchilan, and Piedras Negras established their own distinctive versions of Classic Maya polities. One of the most magnificent of these, Yaxchilan, had numerous enormous temple pyramids with elaborate stuccoed roof combs and exquisitely carved monuments (Mathews 1988, Schele 1991; Tate 1992). The carvings illustrated the bloodletting rituals of the rulers and extolled their royal descent and achievements in war, ritual, and alliance (see Figs. 8.8, 8.10). These Yaxchilan monuments are more explicit than at many other centers, sometimes showing the participation of queens in rituals and portraying the spiritual alter egos or animal coessences of the rulers, their *way*, which often took the form of jaguars or serpents (Houston and Stuart 1989).

Western Petén monumental texts also provide much political information, including some specific titles for subordinate rulers, such as sajals, and detailed descriptions of shifting hierarchies of power and alliance (Stuart 1993, 1995: 256–261). Texts in the western Petén, and at some eastern centers such as Naranjo, also make explicit reference to tribute gained by dominant centers from such wars and from other asymmetrical forms of alliance (Schele 1991; Stuart 1995: 354–370). Despite their explicit nature, careful historiographic studies have shown that some of

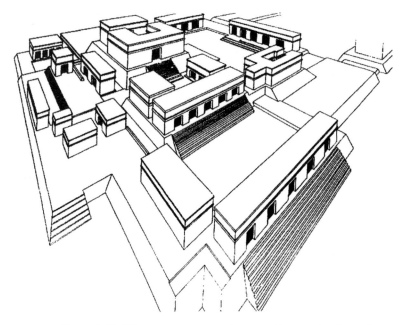

Figure 9.11 Western entrance to the sprawling royal palace of
Cancuen, Petén, Guatemala (drawn by Luis F. Luin)

the genealogy and claims on the Yaxchilan monuments may have been
conscious distortions for propagandistic ends (Miller 1991; Martin and
Grube 2000: 122–124). In the Late Classic, Yaxchilan was involved in
many wars, often with another great kingdom downriver at Piedras
Negras (Schele 1991; Schele and Mathews 1991; Stuart 1995). The
competition between Piedras Negras and Yaxchilan, as well as with other
rivals and subordinate centers, exemplifies the type of intensifying status
rivalry of the Late Classic Maya kingdoms. The murals of Bonampak,
a minor center under the sway of Yaxchilan, beautifully illustrate this
process (Fig. 9.12). Interaction among centers took the form of feasting, visits and rituals, marriage alliances, and frequently warfare. As the
number of elites and centers proliferated in the Late Classic, the intensity,
cost, and material evidence of these status rivalries increased. In the western Petén, warfare between centers would eventually disrupt other activities and contribute to the abandonment of many western centers – first
Dos Pilas in the Petexbatun region and then Aguateca, Piedras Negras,
Yaxchilan, and Cancuen (see Chapter 10).

Even farther west at Palenque in Chiapas, a regional western frontier
kingdom of the Maya produced some of the most splendid architecture,

Figure 9.12 Battle scene from the Bonampak murals (reconstruction painting by Heather Hurst and Leonard Ashby)

art, and inscriptions of the Late Classic period. In contrast to Tikal and central Petén sites, the temples and palaces of Palenque were wide, elegant structures with mansard roofs topped by a stone and stucco latticework of roof combs (Fig. 9.13). Carved stelae and altars were supplanted here by elaborate stone panels. These presented a detailed and unusual genealogy justifying the accession to power of the Late Classic kings through matrilineal descent. Art and texts associated the kings with the myths of the origins of the present universe (Schele and Mathews 1974; Schele 1991a, 1994). The beautiful cosmological imagery and texts of Palenque were an aesthetically extraordinary example of the unified religious and political ideology of the K'uhul Ajaw of the Classic Maya theater-states.

### The Late Classic of the southeast lowlands and Belize

On the opposite frontier of the Maya world, the Maya kingdom of Copan also expressed its claims to sacred power in explicit imagery and texts (Fash 1991). Here carved stelae, altars, and architectural sculptures were the medium of choice. Like Palenque in the northwest, Copan in the southeast utilized its position to be a bridge of interaction with non-Classic Maya peoples. The distinctive ceramics of Copan, such as the

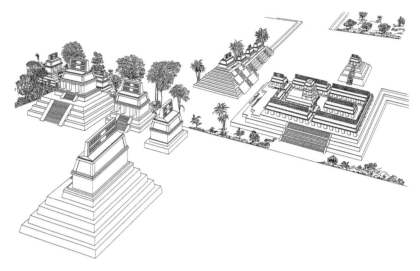

Figure 9.13 Part of the Late Classic epicenter of Palenque, Chiapas, Mexico (drawn by Luis F. Luin)

famous Copador polychrome bowls, combine aspects of Maya imagery with pseudoglyphs and wares and slips characteristic of the chiefdoms to the south and east of the Classic Maya world (Willey *et al.* 1994). The Copan Maya distributed Copador-style ceramics throughout the southeastern borderlands of El Salvador and western Honduras (Bishop *et al.* 1986).

At Copan itself, a magnificent epicenter epitomized the ritual stages of the Maya theater-state (Fig. 9.14; see also Fig. 5.4). Perhaps precisely because of their frontier positions, both Copan and Palenque used these especially explicit and detailed presentations of Maya elite ideology and cosmology in their monuments and architecture. At Copan, easy access to a soft stone trachyte, a form of volcanic tuff, allowed Classic Maya sculptors to fashion full, round, three-dimensional sculptures in stelae and in architectural sculptures. These elaborate, almost baroque stelae and building façades clearly and beautifully portrayed the rulers and other nobles in their roles in rituals of bloodletting or in detailed settings of dynastic descent. Architectural sculptures identify the builders, the cosmological significance, and the functions of many of its buildings. Reconstruction and interpretation of these sculptural façades (B. Fash 1992) have provided important clues to the function of these structures for archaeologists working at other sites where elite architecture lacks explicit imagery.

Figure 9.14 The Copan epicenter (with ballcourt and hieroglyphic stairway)

Copan monuments and sculpted façades also show the changing political landscape in the face of intensifying inter-elite competition in the
eighth century. One of Copan's greatest kings was Wataklajuun Ub'aah
K'awiil (also known as "18 Rabbit" after elements in his name glyphs).
Copan's most beautiful full, round stelae (see Fig. 8.9) and many major
constructions were attributed to this great king. Yet in AD 738 he was
captured and probably sacrificed by the ruler of Copan's former vassal
state to the north, Quirigua. At the latter site the victorious Quirigua ruler
erected some of the tallest stelae in the Maya world (some over twelve
meters) with inscribed texts commemorating the defeat of his former
overlord (Fig. 9.15).

After this event the dynasty in the Copan Valley suffered a great loss
of prestige and managed to survive only by dividing up the previously
nucleated political and ideological power of the K'uhul Ajaw. This balka-
nization of authority was physically represented in a council chamber or
"mat house," identified by the woven mat symbol of governing authority. On its façade were toponyms believed to be associated with sublords
who now shared the ruling authority. The last two Copan rulers also
allowed even further distribution of power to nobles and bureaucrats,
whose carved thrones demonstrate their prestige and authority in Copan
valley politics (Fash 1991: 130–137, 160–183).

Figure 9.15 Stela E from Quirigua, Guatemala (from Maudslay 1889, Vol. II: Plate 26)

The Copan state may have been an example of the processes occurring throughout the Maya lowlands, including proliferation of elites, status rivalry, competitive display in architecture and ritual, warfare, and ulti- mately the weakening and division of the multifaceted power that had been nucleated in the hands of the K'uhul Ajaw. All aspects of this process, memorialized in stone in the Copan Valley, foreshadowed the ninth-century collapse of many of the Classic Maya kingdoms of the southern lowlands.

To the north in Belize, the Mopan Valley of the Petén, and the Maya Mountains (Fig. 9.10) were extremely variable patterns of small and large kingdoms with economies and political structure differing to reflect local ecosystems and specialized resources. In the Mopan region of the southeastern Petén, battling small kingdoms fought in shifting alliances (Laporte 1996). The giant center of Caracol with its complex, regional economy had begun to recover its political prestige and growth near the end of the eighth century (Martin and Grube 2000: 95–98). Along the Caribbean, small sites successfully specialized in a mixed maritime and farming adaptation as well as trade and exchange of salt and coastal products.

Meticulous studies of the smaller polities of coastal and northern Belize have revealed the presence of community specialization as well as smaller-scale religious and political patterns that formed the fabric of Maya society below the level of the great centers and their holy lords (e.g. McAnany 1989, 1991, 1993, 1995; McKillop and Healy 1989; Guderjan and Garber 1995). In central Belize, small kingdoms such as Cahal Pech show evidence of seasonal movement of royal courts and palace workshops which produced fine polychromes for inter-elite exchange (Ball 1993; Ball and Taschek 1991, 2001). At Colha in northern Belize, the presence of large deposits of extremely fine chert led to community specialization and production of chert cores, macroblades, and tools (e.g. Hester and Shafer 1984; Shafer and Hester 1983). Colha fine chert tools were exchanged between centers and appeared throughout the Maya lowlands in the Classic period.

*Regional polities of the northern lowlands*

The regional variability of the Classic Maya kingdoms is most strikingly evident in the northern Yucatan peninsula, where drier conditions and an absence of surface water in most areas influenced all aspects of culture. In Campeche in the Río Bec region (see Fig. 9.10), extensive systems of artificial terraces captured moisture and retained thin soils (Eaton 1975; Thomas 1994). This economic base supported central Yucatan sites such as Becan, Xpuhil, and Río Bec. In this area material culture combined northern Yucatan and southern Petén styles. Ceramics, for example, included both the hard fine monochrome "slate" wares and "trickle" decorative technique of the far north and the Petén-style polychromes and utilitarian vessels (Ball 1977b). Architecture at some sites included narrow spire-like "fake towers," actually miniature imitations of the tall temples of their southern neighbors at sites like Tikal and Calakmul. Yet other façades of the central Petén Chenes style included elaborate stone mosaics over concrete cores similar to the sites of the far north (Potter 1977).

On the eastern side of the Yucatan peninsula (Fig. 9.10), sites show closer ties in temple architecture, ceramics, and monuments to the standard southern lowland Classic-period corpus of traits. These southern affiliations may reflect the environmental unity of the Petén and eastern Yucatan which, as in the south, has greater rainfall, higher forest, lakes, and *bajos*. The largest of the centers of eastern Yucatan, Coba, was a truly gargantuan site in the Late Classic period. It had numerous towering temples, over thirty stelae monuments, and a network of paved *sacbe* causeways linking it to smaller vassal centers (Folan *et al.* 1983, 1995). The largest of these causeways was over a hundred kilometers long to the site of Yaxuna, probably defining a western defended frontier of the Coba regional state (Freidel *et al.* 1990; Suhler and Freidel 1998; Suhler *et al.* 2004).

Perhaps the most distinctive variant of lowland Classic Maya civilization began to flourish in the seventh and eighth centuries in the Puuc hill zone of the northwestern Yucatan peninsula (Fig. 9.10). By the eighth century many sites in this region, such as Oxkintok, Uxmal, Sayil, and Edzna, had the distinctive northern ceramic styles, including fine monochrome slatewares and ceramics decorated with "trickle" designs. Puuc architecture was constructed of fine thin stone veneers over strong rubble and cement cores. Roofs had well-made corbeled vault arches and sometimes lattice-like roof combs. Some sites had freestanding large arches (Fig. 9.16), and many sites had tall stepped multistorey palaces. Most characteristic of the Puuc style were the upper façades of buildings (Fig. 9.17), which were decorated in stone mosaics formed into elaborate geometric designs such as step-frets, lattices, and angular representations of houses, serpent deities, and long-nosed gods. Numerous new elements in Puuc architectural decoration indicate Mexican influence, including the use of round columns and design elements which appear also in sites in Veracruz and Oaxaca. These influences probably reflect Gulf Coast trade and exchange networks.

Another factor in the formation of the Puuc version of Late Classic culture may have been the need for collective community-level responses to the lack of surface water. Sites in western Campeche and Yucatan often relied heavily on bell-shaped chultun wells cut into the bedrock and used to store run-off from the rainy season (Dunning 1992; McAnany 1990). At Edzna in Campeche, much larger water storage and control

Figure 9.16 Puuc style arch at Labna, Mexico

Figure 9.17 Puuc stone mosaic decoration on the façade of the House of the Governor at Uxmal, Yucatan

systems included large canals and reservoirs (Matheny *et al.* 1983; Matheny 1987). In all of these Puuc sites the coordinated water control systems may have led to a somewhat different basis of power with more authority at the community level and perhaps more power shared by the rulers with councils and subordinates.

Perhaps such differing influences and bases for power were factors in the Terminal Classic florescence of the Puuc cities in the ninth century. While Classic Maya civilization was in decline in many areas of the southern lowlands from AD 800 to 900, the cities of the Puuc experienced a population increase and a cultural florescence. As we shall see (Chapter 10), however, this prosperity was short lived as intensified status rivalry, competition, and warfare between northern states led to decline, as had occurred earlier in many zones of the Petén.

## Overview

The highly variable nature of Classic Maya economies, political forms, and material culture overlay common features – and shared stresses. All of these forms of the Maya state were still heavily reliant upon the K'uhul Ajaw as central figure of both political and religious authority. This centralized, yet ideologically dependent, form of authority was a successful political system in the lowlands for over a millennium. Yet the status rivalry and costs of this system, together with ecological and economic challenges, had begun to show signs of great stress in many regions by the eighth century, if not earlier. In the Terminal Classic period that followed, many Maya kingdoms would collapse while others would undergo transformation to different forms of state.

We should note that the Classic Maya theater-states were never able to form a panregional centralized state, as arose in other world regions. For example, in Mesopotamia, the Early Dynastic period of unstable warring city-states led to the later, more unified hegemonies or macro-states of Agade, Babylonia, Assyria, and Persia. In central Mexico, Teotihuacan came to dominate the smaller centers of the region and to form a more centralized and unitary urban state. In Egypt, the beginning of the third millennium BC witnessed the unification of the variable regional "nome" states of Egypt into a single pharaonic kingdom. Similar processes of unification of unstable, less centralized, archaic polities into larger, more unitary states have been observed throughout the ancient world.

The Maya lowlands, however, continued throughout the Classic period to be a landscape of fluctuating, expanding and contracting theater-states, galactic polities, and unstable alliances. Like the Southeast Asian Negara theater-state kingdoms, the Maya never achieved political unification.

Instead, in the ninth and tenth centuries, many of the Classic Maya kingdoms in the southern lowlands declined or collapsed. Others were transformed into a new kind of state system, one *without* the central organizing principle of the K'uhul Ajaw "holy lords". As we shall see in the next chapter, the reasons for this failure to unify and integrate, and the causes of the decline of the Classic political system, are as complex and fascinating as Maya civilization itself.

# 10    The end of Classic Maya civilization: collapse, transition, and transformation

Since the beginnings of exploration in the Maya lowlands, the "mystery of the collapse" of Classic-period civilization has been a driving force in Maya archaeology. The vision of vast cities with stone temples, palaces, and hieroglyphic monuments abandoned and overgrown by the jungle has come to dominate popular images of archaeology. On a more scholarly level, the issues surrounding the "collapse" of the Classic Maya cities have been the subject of serious study and debate throughout the twentieth century. Probably only the "fall" of the Roman Empire has been cited as often in social theory on the decline of civilizations.

There has been, however, little agreement as to the nature of the decline of Classic civilization or its causes. The lack of consensus has been due in part to the incomplete nature of the archaeological record in the critical period of the ninth and tenth centuries. Although much progress has been made in the past twenty years toward filling the gaps in the data, recent symposia and conferences still show little agreement (see bibliographic essay). The most confusing factor may be the great regional variability of Classic Maya civilization and the tendency of scholars to use the events in the subregion of their own studies as the universal model for the decline or the transformation of all of Classic Maya culture. Disagreement also results from differences in terminology and epistemology. For that reason, I begin here with a clarification of the terms and concepts involved in addressing this inscrutable, but important, issue in Maya archaeology.

## Concepts of causality in the decline of civilizations

The concept of causality is fraught with philosophical and epistemological problems. Much apparent disagreement in Maya archaeology is simply due to scholars talking about different "levels" of causality. Often, archaeologists posit "causes" from the data in their particular regions or sites that would have been local *proximate* causes of the specific kind of culture change observed in that area. Yet such local economic and ecological conditions and regional political events were combined with pan-lowland

240

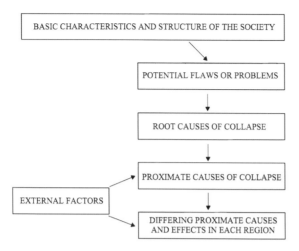

Figure 10.1 Levels of causality in the decline of civilization

problems or processes to generate the specific manifestation of the end of the Classic period political systems in any given area. Furthermore, external factors or events (e.g. foreign intrusion or influence, climatological factors, etc.) most often affect only a specific region, although some may have been of broader impact. As we shall see, the term "collapse," with its connotations of traumatic and rapid decline, may only apply to the western Petén kingdoms of the Classic Maya lowlands.

Underlying causes of widespread culture change, "ultimate" or "root causes," could be related to more general problems, flaws, or in Marxist terms, "contradictions" between aspects of the political, economic, or ecological institutions of the society. Such deeper problems relate to the basic characteristics of the society or political system in question and can only be considered "flaws" in the context of specific historical processes or external factors to which the political system fails to respond successfully (Fig. 10.1). In the case of the Maya, we can try to identify broad characteristics of Late Classic Maya society that led to problems and to counterproductive responses to challenges confronting southern lowland Classic Maya civilization as a whole in the eighth and ninth centuries. The differing (and to appearances, contradictory) manifestations of cultural change in specific areas of the lowlands at the end of the Classic period result from varied local responses to those common challenges as determined by regional conditions. As we shall see, the highly variable cultural histories of the lowland Maya kingdoms at the end of the Classic period can be broadly related to these common factors or "causes," but with very different local consequences.

A second terminological problem is scholars' varying definition of "collapse" or "decline." What is it that experiences collapse or decline? Maya kingdoms in many areas of eastern Mesoamerica were vigorous polities in the Postclassic period, and millions of Maya today are participating in a modern cultural and political resurgence (e.g. Fischer and Brown 1996). Whatever happened to many of the southern lowland cities, it was *not* a uniform, total collapse of these states, and it was in no way an end or even decline of the enduring Maya tradition. The fragmentation of the western Roman Empire after the fourth century AD was not an end of Western civilization. In the same way, the Maya tradition continued through the Postclassic, Colonial, and modern periods – long after the Classic Petén cities had been absorbed by the rain forest.

Recent analyses of the "collapse" of civilizations have shown that this term is best defined as a rapid decline in complexity in a particular political system (e.g. Tainter 1988; Yoffee and Cowgill 1988). In the lowland Maya case what actually collapsed, declined, or was transformed at the end of the Classic period was a particular political system and the features and institutions associated with it – namely, a political system of theater-states dominated by the K'uhul Ajaw, or the holy lords. The end of this system also led to the disappearance of its associated funerary cults (with their stelae, altars, and tomb-temples), "galactic" political hegemonies, and the state patronage networks of redistribution of fine ceramics and high-status exotic goods and ornaments. This system disappeared by the tenth century, and in some regions of the southern lowlands its passing was accompanied by the depopulation of major cities, drastic reduction of public architecture, and other dramatic changes. Such a true "collapse" seems to characterize events in the western Petén. In other areas, however, the end of the Classic period was one of more gradual change, in some cases even of florescence and transformation to a new political order. Still, in all cases the distinctive Classic Maya political order and many of its attendant institutions, features, and artifacts disappeared.

Viewed in this light, the enigma of the Classic Maya collapse becomes a more realistic and manageable problem. We can plot the various collapses, declines, florescences, or transformations of Classic Maya civilization across the highly variable kingdoms of the Maya lowlands and note the common underlying structural problems or changes, the varying proximate "causes" and external forces, and the resulting collapses, declines, or transformations in each region (e.g. Demarest, Rice, and Rice 2004a). The parallel features in the regional changes can help to identify common pressures and problems in Classic Maya society, while the differences in regional manifestations reflect the political and economic variability of the kingdoms of the Classic Maya lowlands.

**Characteristics of the Classic Period Maya**

| *Political and Ideological Structure* | *Infrastructure* |
|---|---|
| • Charismatic and Shamanistic Leadership (K'uhul Ajaw) | •Minimal Central Control by Elites |
| •Ajaw Leadership in Warfare and Ritual | •Regional and Local Economy not State Controlled |
| •Ideological Base for Power | •Agricultural System Well-Adapted to Tropical Rain Forest (Imitating its Dispersion and Diversity) |
| •Flexible System of Royal Succession | |
| •Control and Distribution of Status Reinforcing Goods | •Dispersed Urban and Rural Settlement Pattern |
| •Considerable Investment in Monumental Architecture, Art, Symbols of Status, and other Elements of Ritual and Propaganda | |
| •Elite Warfare for Limited Positions of Power | |

Figure 10.2 Some salient characteristics of most Classic Maya states

## Structural problems of the Classic Maya political order

The fundamental characteristics of Classic Maya civilization in the lowlands have been detailed in Chapters 5–8, and in Chapter 9 we glimpsed the volatile historical dynamics and the variable regional polities of the Classic period. Some salient characteristics of most Classic Maya kingdoms are summarized in Figure 10.2. These are, of course, broad generalizations, some of which apply only weakly to specific kingdoms. For example, some of the unusually large polities, such as Calakmul, Tikal, and Caracol, may have achieved a more integrated and centralized regional economic system. Other sites had a less dispersed population. Yet none achieved a population nucleation or an economic centralization comparable to Teotihuacan, Tiwanaku, or many other ancient civilizations.

The centralization of religious and political authority in the divine shamanistic kings of the Maya theater-states was a hallmark feature of Classic civilization. With their power based heavily on ritual performance and inter-center warfare, the K'uhul Ajaw wielded great power and authority, but with its basis more in ideology than economics. A flexible system of royal succession allowed a son (not necessarily the eldest), a brother, another male relative, or in some cases even a queen to take the throne upon the death of the ruler. Such a flexible system of succession has advantages in seeking a suitable heir with the requisite heritage and charisma to rule. Yet this flexible system of succession was also highly unstable, with frequent battles for the throne fought both physically through warfare and through other forms of status rivalry. The instability of the system was aggravated by the redundant, segmentary nature of the political order, with the subordinate minor centers or vassal kingdoms capable of most, if not all, of the same functions of the capitals. Change in the political order of all states was common through usurpation by rivals for the throne, defeat by other states, and revolt and overthrow by rulers of subordinate states or secondary centers. All of these blows to the dynastic order could result in rapid changes in the prestige of the center and the control of tribute labor – more so because power was based heavily on claims of supernatural power and personal authority.

In Chapter 9, we saw how the defeat or capture of prominent rulers could lead to a decline in construction activity and a retraction in the size of the "galaxy" of satellites paying tribute in labor or goods to the capital center. Even the greatest and most prestigious centers were subject to these fluctuations in power, as seen in the sixth-century defeat and "hiatus" at Tikal, the decline of Calakmul after its defeat in AD 695, and the fragmentation of dynastic power in the Copan kingdom after its defeat by a former vassal, Quirigua (Chapter 9). Conversely, the expansion of regional power could be brought about by success in alliance formation, war, and ritual by particularly charismatic kings, as seen at Tikal under the Early Classic foreign-affiliated kings, or at Caracol after its sixth-century victories. These unstable dynamics of expanding and contracting "galactic" hegemonies, such as those of Tikal and Calakmul, were merely the most spectacular versions of the ongoing status rivalry that was characteristic of the Maya theater-states (e.g. Webster 1999; cf. Tambiah 1977; Demarest 1992b). This status rivalry sometimes generated conflict and warfare but, more often, it stimulated the extraordinary Classic architecture, art, and monuments that were the settings for pageants, feasting, and rituals. These activities were the more common form of competition for the allegiance of subordinate centers and the support of the populace as a whole. Grand rituals, inter-elite visits and feasting, marriage alliances, and war were alternative paths to power for the K'uhul Ajaw.

All scholars have observed an intensification of these activities of status rivalry in the Late Classic period. Competitive investment in architecture and monuments for intensified ritual created the impressive Classic period epicenters, monuments, and artifacts. Alliance, warfare, and inter-site visits also increased. While these activities produced the beautiful corpus of Classic Maya art and ruins admired today, they had a high energetic cost for the supporting populations of the Classic period. Elite polygamy, a successful mode of extending power and forming alliances, would have exacerbated these pressures by increasing the size of the elite class and the number of rival princes competing for positions of power.

## Infrastructural stress and counterproductive responses

Most collapse theories have stressed problems of demography and ecological stress at the end of the Classic period (see Culbert ed. 1973 and bibliographic essay). Such analyses correctly point to the high population levels and densities in the Late Classic period as a major source of ecological stress on the productive, but fragile, rain forest agricultural system that sustained them. These models, however, implicitly accept a Malthusian logic that human populations outgrow the resources needed to support them. The last fifty years of comparative ethnography on human demography have demonstrated that societies regulate their growth through a wide variety of mechanisms, including postpartum taboos, celibate sectors of society, homosexual behavior, coitus interruptus, periodic abstinence, abortion, and infanticide (e.g. Beshers 1967; Devereux 1967; Mamdani 1974; Langer 1974; Polgar 1975; Coleman and Schofield 1986; Wrigley 1969). Archaeologists must, then, *explain* in cultural terms the posited episodes of demographic growth, especially if they led to stress on the society's infrastructure.

Other problems with demographic models for decline or collapse are more specific to the Maya case. As described below, political fragmentation, decline, and abandonment of centers occur first and most rapidly in the western Petén. Yet extensive ecological, osteological, and settlement studies in the Pasión region have found there complex agricultural regimes that were well adapted to population levels with no indications of increasing nutritional stress (e.g. Dunning *et al.* 1997; O'Mansky and Dunning 2004; Wright 1994, 1997; Emery 1997). It is difficult, then, to attribute political collapse in the west to demographic or ecological crises. In the central Petén, where population levels were much higher, political decline occurs more gradually and at least half a century later – followed by an Early Postclassic resurgence. In such areas, the high population levels may have been encouraged by elite ideology in order to generate the labor pools needed to support the intensifying construction projects, wars, and rituals of the competing rulers. Such Late Classic demographic and ecological stresses were more likely consequences, rather than causes, of Late Classic status rivalry and warfare. Aspects of Classic Maya political and ideological structure may have exacerbated many of the infrastructural and ecological problems observed in some regions, such as the central Petén and the Copan Valley (see Fig. 10.3 "a," "b," and "c").

Another basic question regarding the collapse, decline, or transformation of the lowland cities and kingdoms at the end of the Classic period is *why in many areas Maya leadership did not respond* with effective corrective measures for the stresses generated by internal, as well as external, factors. Cross-cultural studies of culture change show that "complex societies are problem-solving organizations, in which more parts, different kinds of parts, more social differentiation, more inequality, and more kinds of centralization and control emerge as circumstances require" (Tainter 1988:37). Yet the K'uhul Ajaw failed to respond with effective corrections of infrastructural problems. Their ineffectiveness was most likely due to the canons of Maya leadership and its limited range of action. The elites of most Classic Maya kingdoms, in general, did *not* manage subsistence systems or production or exchange of utilitarian goods. Most Maya polities, while held together by the rituals and authority of the center, were decentralized with local community or family-level management of most aspects of the economy. This decentralized system facilitated adaptation of farming systems to local microenvironments (e.g. Dunning *et al.* 1997; Dunning and Beach in press). Yet having their role defined in terms of ritual and inter-elite alliance and warfare, it is not surprising that the K'uhul Ajaw responded through these same mechanisms to problems such as demographic pressure or ecological deterioration. They naturally reacted by intensifying ritual activities, construction, or warfare – the activities within their purview. Such counterproductive responses would have only increased the stresses on Late Classic economies and led to internal fission, usurpations, fragmentation, and further conflicts – all processes observed to intensify in the eighth and ninth centuries (see Fig. 10.3 "d").

## The nature of the "Classic Maya collapse"

The stresses reviewed above may have left many of the Classic Maya states of the ninth century weakened and fragmented internally and unable to compete with other Mesoamerican states. Some of these neighbors had begun to evolve on the central Mexican pattern of multiple institutions of centralized power with elites more directly managing production and trade, as well as ritual and warfare. In the end, the K'uhul Ajaw system with its divine lords and theater-states may have been unable to respond to the very problems generated by the demands of its rituals, wars, and feasting, and the expensive stages, props, and costumes required for political and religious performances.

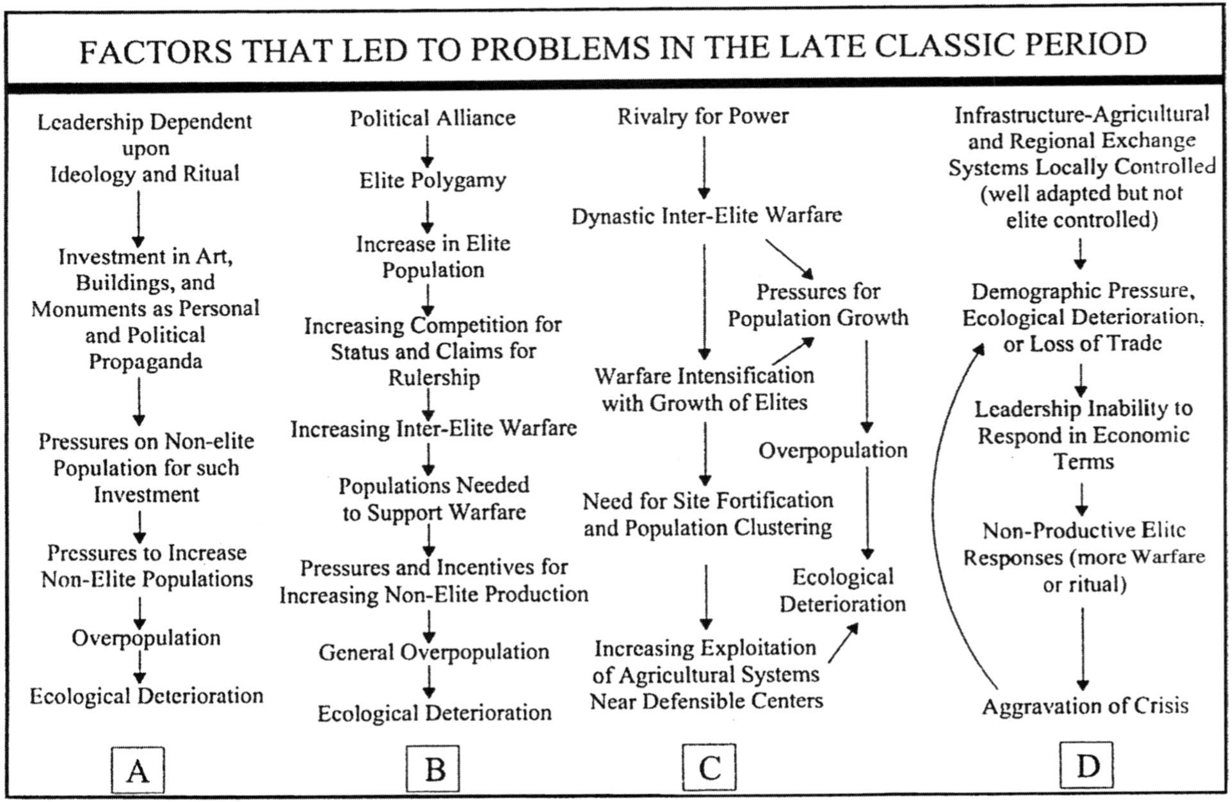

# FACTORS THAT LED TO PROBLEMS IN THE LATE CLASSIC PERIOD

**A**

Leadership Dependent upon Ideology and Ritual
↓
Investment in Art, Buildings, and Monuments as Personal and Political Propaganda
↓
Pressures on Non-elite Population for such Investment
↓
Pressures to Increase Non-Elite Populations
↓
Overpopulation
↓
Ecological Deterioration

**B**

Political Alliance
↓
Elite Polygamy
↓
Increase in Elite Population
↓
Increasing Competition for Status and Claims for Rulership
↓
Increasing Inter-Elite Warfare
↓
Populations Needed to Support Warfare
↓
Pressures and Incentives for Increasing Non-Elite Production
↓
General Overpopulation
↓
Ecological Deterioration

**C**

Rivalry for Power
↓
Dynastic Inter-Elite Warfare
→ Pressures for Population Growth
Warfare Intensification with Growth of Elites → Overpopulation
↓
Need for Site Fortification and Population Clustering → Ecological Deterioration
↓
Increasing Exploitation of Agricultural Systems Near Defensible Centers

**D**

Infrastructure-Agricultural and Regional Exchange Systems Locally Controlled (well adapted but not elite controlled)
↓
Demographic Pressure, Ecological Deterioration. or Loss of Trade
↓
Leadership Inability to Respond in Economic Terms
↓
Non-Productive Elite Responses (more Warfare or ritual)
↓
Aggravation of Crisis

Figure 10.3 Some structural problems of Classic Maya states

By the ninth and tenth centuries, in different specific ways in each region, the K'uhul Ajaw system was transformed or replaced in Yucatan, parts of Belize, and the Central Lakes area of the Petén. In its place arose states that gave more authority to multiple institutions of power – councils of lineage heads, the priestly class, elite merchant classes, warrior guilds, and so on. Some of these were the so-called *multepal* system states of the Postclassic, in which the heads of leading lineages shared power in uneasy alliances (e.g. Sabloff and Andrews 1986; Sharer 1994:402–406; Roys 1965a). In other areas of the lowlands (including much of the central Petén and the Mexican states of Campeche and Quintana Roo), Classic Maya kingdoms struggled and then declined in varying ways or underwent less traumatic changes. Yet in the western Petén and some other zones, many centers and cities were rapidly depopulated as the bulk of their population dispersed or moved off to other zones.

Thus, as reviewed in this chapter, each region experienced a different sequence of events and a distinctive configuration of proximate causes in their collapses, declines, or transformations. The specific culture histories in each region – with their different sequence of changes and endings – reflect the underlying variability in ecology, state forms, and historical influences in the Classic period. Yet in each case there were shared underlying factors in the structural problems and the political involution of the K'uhul Ajaw system. By the close of the tenth century, this system had disappeared from lowland Maya civilization. The notion of a uniform "fall" or "collapse" is now as obsolete for the Classic Maya as for the Roman Empire. Instead, as with Rome, a complex series of processes occurred over a period of over two centuries. For example, there was a political collapse in some regions (e.g. western Europe for Rome, the western Petén for the Maya), decline in other areas (e.g. North Africa for Rome, the central and southeastern Petén for the Maya), and florescence in yet other zones (e.g. Byzantium in the Roman case, and the northern lowlands for the Terminal Classic Maya). Scholars are now beginning to plot and to try to understand the complex nature of changes and continuity in each region, rather than arguing over the "cause" of a uniform "collapse" process.

Some of the "dynamic" models consider the changes at the end of the Classic period to be just another manifestation of the continuous volatility of Classic Maya politics and the pulsations of its expanding and contracting polities (e.g. Marcus 1993, 1998). This ninth-century transition, however, was fundamentally different because in some regions it was followed by depopulation and by the cessation of public architecture, and in other zones the political and economic order was irreversibly changed. Also with the passing of the Ajaw complex, its legitimating mechanisms (e.g. Freidel 1992) in art, architecture, and ritual also disappeared. Some of the Postclassic Maya states that flourished in the Guatemalan highlands and Yucatan were as populous and even more vigorous economically and politically than the Classic Maya theater-state, but they did not generate anything like the vast corpus of art and architecture of their Classic-period predecessors. They didn't need to. Their power was less dependent on the generation and the legitimization of authority through monumental display and ritual. In the Classic period, the most common smaller Maya state, like the Asian theater-state, "drew its force, which was real enough, from its imaginative energies, its semiotic capacity to make inequality enchant" (Geertz 1980: 123). It was this elegant but fragile system, as beautiful and seductive to modern scholars and readers as it was to the Maya populace, that came to an end in the ninth and tenth centuries – making way for a new, more flexible and adaptable political order.

### The beginning of the end: political devolution and warfare in the Petexbatun collapse

While the variable processes involved in the end of Classic lowland Maya civilization did not "begin" in any particular region, the earliest yet identified and studied "collapse" of Classic-period political systems occurred in the western Petén, and there perhaps the earliest in the Petexbatun region (Fig. 10.4). For over a decade, large multidisciplinary projects investigated ecology, history, ritual, economics and trade, settlement, subsistence systems, nutrition, and warfare, as well as undertaking intensive study of the many kilometers of cave systems below the sites of the Petexbatun region (Demarest 1997, in press b). The evidence from these independent investigations has been used to test alternative hypotheses on the rapid decline of the Classic Maya kingdoms there. The results revealed a clear and consistent, albeit complex, sequence of events in the Petexbatun.

In the early seventh century a new regime with Tikal affiliations was established as a military outpost of the Tikal alliance in the Petexbatun region with its seat at the site of Dos Pilas. Yet by the mid-seventh century, the young king of Dos Pilas was conquered by the ruler of Calakmul and drawn into that center's stratagems of regional alliance and war against Tikal and its allies (Fahsen et al. 2003; Demarest and Fahsen 2003). Then the rapidly constructed capital center at Dos Pilas was used as a base to wage war in collaboration with Calakmul against Tikal and to conquer their Pasión River Valley neighbors. Through Dos Pilas, Cancuen, and other vassal centers, the Calakmul alliance controlled the western river route until the end of the eighth century. Then, after Calakmul's AD 695 defeat by Tikal, Dos Pilas remained as the great military power of the Pasión region (Demarest and Fahsen 2003; Demarest 1993, 1997).

Figure 10.4 Petexbatun region and some major sites (drawn by Luis F. Luin)

By the mid-eighth century, Dos Pilas controlled through conquest or alliance most of the Pasión River Valley, the main route of transport and trade between the lowlands and the highlands to the south and, consequently, the source of jade, hard stone, quetzal feathers, and other status-reinforcing goods. Through marriage alliance the regime extended the dynasty's hegemony to include an alliance with the Cancuen kingdom, which controlled the head of navigation of the Pasión and the passes to the highlands (Fahsen and Jackson 2002).

This control and tribute from vassals were primary sources of economic support for Dos Pilas, probably even including food from nearby vassals (Dunning *et al.* 1997; Dunning and Beach in press). The wealth of this predatory kingdom filled tombs, caches, and the caves beneath the center

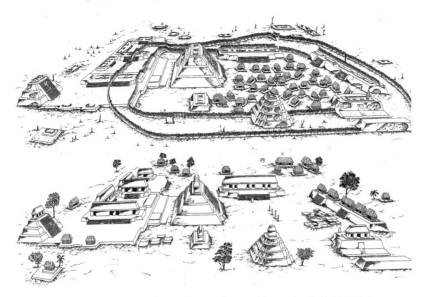

Figure 10.5 Dos Pilas Western Group (drawn by Luis F. Luin).
Bottom: group before AD 761. Top: group after AD 761 with
encircling palisades and stone base walls built by dismantling earlier
temples and palaces

with polychromes, eccentrics, and other artifacts (Demarest 1993, 1997;
Brady *et al.* 1991, 1997). The K'uhul Ajaw of Dos Pilas established a
second dynastic seat at the older defensible hilltop center of Aguateca
to facilitate control of their sprawling hegemony (e.g. Inomata 1997). At
Dos Pilas itself, temples, plazas, monuments, sacred caves, and multiple
palaces were connected by a cosmologically patterned circuit of procession paths (Demarest *et al.* 2003; see Chapter 8).

In AD 760–761, the galactic polity of Dos Pilas violently fragmented.
The proximate cause of this catastrophe was the siege, defeat, and
destruction of the capital at Dos Pilas. The war and defeat of the Petexbatun K'uhul Ajaw by their former vassal of Tamarindito was recorded in
monuments at that site and celebrated on the inscriptions on the funerary
temple of the victorious Tamarindito lord (Valdés 1997b). The archaeological excavations at Dos Pilas uncovered a hastily constructed series
of defensive walls around parts of the site epicenters. The West Plaza
Group was encircled by walls 1 to 1.5 meters high that were hastily
constructed from the blocks ripped from the sacred temples and palaces
there (Fig. 10.5). Topped by a wooden palisade, these walls (each over
500 meters long) encircled some of the temples and palace structures and

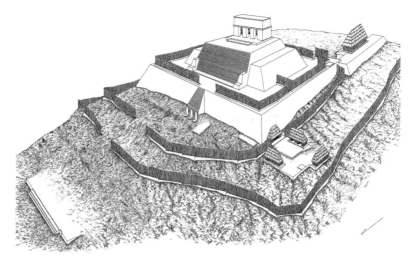

Figure 10.6  Eighth-century defensive systems around the El Duende
complex, Dos Pilas, Guatemala (drawn by Luis F. Luin)

the large west courtyard (Demarest *et al.* 1997). There, in the former
setting of the spectacular pageants of the theater-state, the besieged
remaining inhabitants of Dos Pilas constructed a densely packed siege
village.

A similar system of low walls bearing palisades surrounded the towering
El Duende complex a kilometer to the east. The three concentric walls
and palisades turned this huge sacred temple and the court behind it into
a formidable fortress (Fig. 10.6). Between the two complexes the central
Murcielagos palace of the last ruler (see Chapter 8) lay abandoned atop
its sacred hill. The inscribed monumental throne there was overturned
and broken into fragments with offerings before it (a typical Maya act of
ritual destruction, i.e. a "termination ritual") (Mock 1998). Population
at Dos Pilas declined within the next few years to five to ten percent
of previous levels. By the ninth century there were only a few scattered
households, whose inhabitants farmed and hunted amongst the ruins.
The many nobles of Dos Pilas fled during this period to the second royal
seat at Aguateca, and also perhaps farther south to join their in-laws at
Cancuen (Demarest and Barrientos 2002; Demarest 2003).

In the subsequent period from AD 761 to 830, the Petexbatun and
middle Pasión regions collapsed into a state of endemic warfare. Initially
it appears that major centers such as Aguateca, Tamarindito, Seibal, and
La Amelia battled to become the new royal seat of the Petexbatun region.
But the escalating warfare appears to have spiraled out of control, with
tremendous energetic expenditures on wall palisade systems in all areas

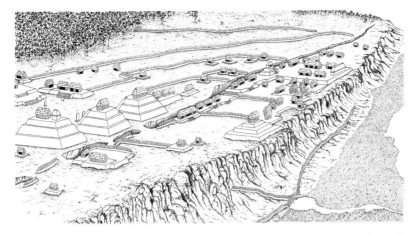

Figure 10.7 Portion of the fortification system at Aguateca (drawn by Luis F. Luin)

and a shift of populations to defensible enclaves (Demarest *et al.* 1991, 1997; O'Mansky and Dunning 2004; see bibliographic essay). Trade systems in polychromes and other outside goods were disrupted, and even local exchange was limited by the intensifying warfare (Foias 1996; Foias and Bishop 1997).

By the close of the eighth century, the Petexbatun region had become a "landscape of fear" with settlement patterns determined only by defensibility (Dunning and Beach in press; O'Mansky and Dunning 2004). Fortification systems have been found by excavation and survey throughout the region (Fig. 10.4). Wall and palisade systems varied greatly in scale and extent. Some were low stone walls merely to foot wooden palisades, others were impressive ramparts over four meters in height. At Aguateca, the remaining stronghold of the Dos Pilas elite, over five kilometers of wall systems were constructed to supplement that center's natural defenses of high cliffs to the west and a fifty- to seventy-meter deep gorge to the east (Fig. 10.7). Despite these awesome fortifications, not long after AD 800 Aguateca was overrun and burned by its enemies. Many artifacts were left *in situ* on the surface by its unfortunate defenders, while its royal palace was ritually destroyed (Inomata 1995, 1997, 2003, in press).

In some areas of the Petexbatun region even small hamlets were moved to defensible positions and fortified with low walls and palisades (Fig. 10.8). Some fortifications had ingenious features such as baffled gateways and "killing alleys" in which enemy assailants could be trapped between walls and pummeled with projectiles (Fig. 10.5). Areas near some of the defended zones may have been intensively farmed, as

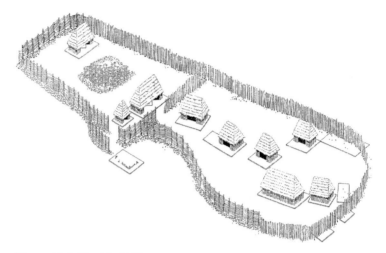

Figure 10.8 Fortified hilltop village in the Petexbatun (drawn by Luis F. Luin)

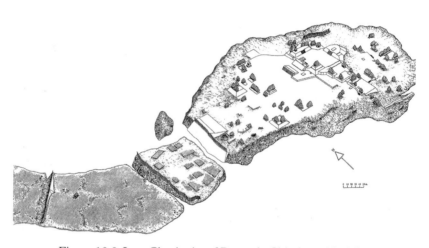

Figure 10.9 Late Classic site of Punta de Chimino with defensive moats and protected intensive garden zones (drawn by Luis F. Luin)

indicated by phosphate analyses and terrace features (Dunning *et al.* 1997; O'Mansky and Dunning 2004; see Fig. 6.4). For example, the fortification system of the center of Punta de Chimino included stone box gardens and areas of intensive agriculture and fertilization within the second and third outer moat and rampart systems (Figs. 10.9, 6.3).

This militarized landscape, with a reduced population concentrated in fortified enclaves, contradicted the norms of the Classic Maya settlement strategy. With field systems concentrated near defended enclaves, overuse of soils in these loci could have followed, contradicting the Classic Maya subsistence strategy of diversity and dispersion of different types of farming systems (cf. Chapter 6). More importantly, this militarized landscape, with its very reduced and defended zones of settlement, could no longer provide safe residence for the previous high population levels, probably leading to emigration. By AD 830 population in the region had been reduced to scattered small hamlets and lone households.

The only remaining major center after AD 830 was Punta de Chimino, situated on a naturally defensible peninsula in Lake Petexbatun (Demarest 1996a, 2004; Demarest, Escobedo, and O'Mansky 1997; Demarest and Escobedo 1997; Wolley and Wright 1991; Wolley 1993). Three moat and wall systems separated the center from the mainland and protected its areas of intensive agriculture. The largest moat was excavated over ten meters deep into the bedrock, allowing the waters of the lake to pass through it and making the site epicenter an artificial, virtually impregnable island fortress (Fig. 10.9). Only this center survived the maelstrom of endemic warfare in the Petexbatun and continued to erect public architecture into the late ninth century (Demarest 2004). But even this lake center and the few hamlets inland were gradually abandoned by the tenth century. Major centers never returned to the region but later, in the Postclassic years, settlers from the central Petén established scattered hamlets and fishing camps along Petexbatun rivers and lakes (Morgan and Demarest 1995; Johnston et al. 2001), while the ruins of the great Classic centers remained unoccupied.

Thus, in this Petexbatun zone of the Maya lowlands the end of the Classic civilization was truly a "collapse" – a rapid decline in sociopolitical complexity. In this case it was also accompanied by endemic warfare and great population reduction. It was a dramatic example of the regional disintegration of a civilization.

## Causality in the Petexbatun collapse: alternative hypotheses

As the most studied regional example of the collapse, the Petexbatun political disintegration serves to test alternative models of external factors and internal problems in the ending of the Classic Maya political order (see bibliographic essay). Obviously, endemic warfare spiraled out of control in this region, disrupting economic systems and forcing a settlement and subsistence strategy capable of supporting only a fraction of previous population levels. This well-documented series of changes provides only the *proximate* causes of the collapse. The next question is, what were the underlying causes of this warfare?

Previous studies and interpretations had suggested that foreign invasions might have been the source of the intensified warfare in the western Petén at sites like Seibal and Altar de Sacrificios in the late eighth and ninth century (e.g. R.E.W. Adams 1973; Sabloff and Willey 1967). The introduction of fine-paste ceramics and new elements in monumental iconography at those sites were attributed to an invasion of "Mexicanized" Maya peoples from Tabasco. More recent studies have shown that the fine wares were locally produced in the Pasión region (Bishop 1994; Foias and Bishop 1997) and the unusual styles of ninth-century monuments at Altar de Sacrificias and Seibal also had antecedents within the Maya lowlands (Stuart 1993). Many of the features once believed to represent foreign influences, including militaristic iconography and C-shaped house forms, appear to have developed in the Petexbatun region itself (Demarest 1997, 2004; Tourtellot and Gonzales 2004). While warfare was clearly one factor in the collapse in the western Petén, its causes and impact cannot be attributed to foreign invasion.

Another popular recurrent theory for the Maya collapse posits great climatic change as having directly brought about the collapse or having led to drought, famine, and war over dwindling resources (e.g. Gill 2000). Such theories have experienced a resurgence in popularity due to evidence from pollen cores in northern Yucatan and elsewhere, suggesting a possible drought there in the tenth century (e.g. Curtis et al. 1996; Hoddell et al. 1995; Lucero 2002; Robichaux 2002; Haug et al. 2003). In the Petexbatun, however, the endemic warfare begins over a century before the proposed drought. This earliest lowland "collapse" is nearly over before the alleged drought process begins (O'Mansky and Dunning 2004; Demarest 2004). Furthermore, the Petexbatun paleoecological researches show no evidence of Late or Terminal Classic drought, famine, or radical change of any kind in climate, ecology, or nutrition (e.g. Dunning et al. 1997; Dunning and Beach in press; Wright 1994, 1997, in press; Wright and White 1996).

The most popular theories to explain the political disruptions and decline at the end of the Classic period are those positing overpopulation and consequent overexploitation of the environment, followed by ecological deterioration and political problems (e.g. Culbert 1974, 1977, 1988; Santley et al. 1986). It does appear that such problems did arise in the central Petén, the Copan Valley, and other regions. Yet again, in the Petexbatun and western Petén, where centers and states first decline, there is no such evidence of rapid ecological deterioration. The extensive paleoecological and settlement studies conducted in the Petexbatun revealed a fairly stable Late Classic environment with a complex mix of subsistence adaptations designed to minimize environmental damage (Dunning et al.

1997; Dunning and Beach in press). There was no increase in malnutrition or disease evident in Late Classic human bones, and even deer bones indicate a stable diet and good nutrition in the eighth and ninth centuries (Wright 1997a, in press; Emery 1997, in press; Emery *et al.* 2000). Thus, for the Petexbatun, the hard evidence does not indicate ecological stress – be it caused by climate change or ecological exploitation – as the underlying cause of the region's early and violent collapse (Demarest 1997, 2004, in press b).

For the causes of the endemic warfare and disintegration of polities in the Petexbatun, we must look to the political and economic stresses created by the K'uhul Ajaw system itself. As described at the beginning of this chapter, the collapse in the Petexbatun can be regarded as an early and extreme manifestation of the general problems of the Classic Maya political system and its demands. The latter were exacerbated in the seventh and eighth centuries by increasing inter-elite status rivalry, the growing proportion of elites in the population, and the consequent increase in inter-elite competition for limited positions of royal power and for status-reinforcing exotic goods. This cycle of contradictory demands on the system increased inter-center warfare, rapidly devolving into more widespread conflict as the basic infrastructure of the region was disrupted. In turn, in the context of such competitive political relations, general demographic growth would be encouraged rather than controlled. Figure 10.10 provides a detailed but hypothetical model of potential underlying stresses, probable effects, and the consequent sequence of maladaptive responses and negative consequences that may have destroyed the political systems of the Petexbatun.

### Collapse in the western Petén

Within less than seventy years of the fall of Dos Pilas as a political capital, the fragmentation and warfare in the region had led to rapid depopulation of centers and the countryside. By AD 830, only one major center remained, the massively fortified site of Punta de Chimino. Population in the Terminal Classic period (AD 830 to 1000) in the rest of the Petexbatun region was reduced to scattered households and small hamlets near water sources (O'Mansky and Dunning 2004; Demarest 2004). Such a rapid depopulation would have involved emigration of tens of thousands to other areas where refugee populations would have further destabilized polities that were already under stress from the cycle of pressures on Classic political and economic systems generated by status rivalry, the demands of Maya elites, and varying regional difficulties. In the Petexbatun, the fall and abandonment of Dos Pilas was

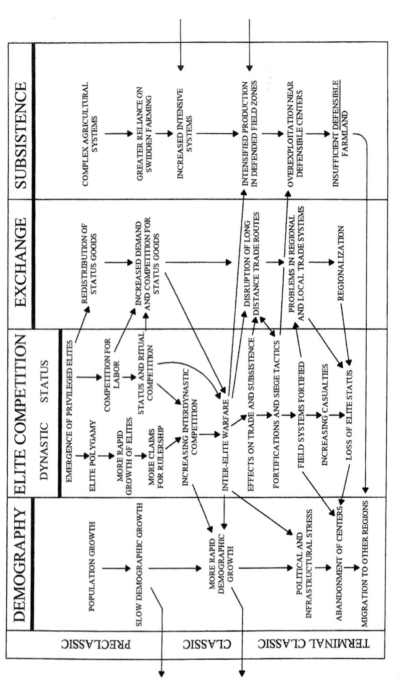

Figure 10.10 Schematic interpretation of causality in the collapse of the Late Classic Petexbatun kingdom

followed a few decades later by that of Tamarindito, Arroyo de Piedra, and Aguateca (Demarest and Valdés 1995). Families and larger groups may have moved to other areas, initially in adjacent zones and later to more distant regions (Demarest 2004). Elsewhere in the western Petén, parallel processes appear to have been under way.

In the Usumacinta region of the western Petén, sudden termination of construction was followed by rapid depopulation early in the ninth century. Notably, this region was characterized by warfare between centers in the eighth century, with a proliferation of minor centers with new 'holy lords' and the presence of many subordinate lords or sajals (Mathews 1988, Stuart 1995). Major rival centers such as Yaxchilan and Piedras Negras were in constant competition with prestige-enhancing construction projects, public rituals, inter-elite visits, feasts, and, most directly, wars (e.g. Schele and Mathews 1991; Schele 1991). They also had to compete with potential rivals at lesser centers in their realms.

Finally, major centers such as Piedras Negras fell into rapid decline after the defeat and capture of their rulers by holy lords of rival centers such as Yaxchilan, or even defeat by smaller, previously subordinate, centers, as in the case of the decline at Palenque (Schele 1991; Schele and Matthews 1991). The fragmentation of the segmentary or "galactic" polities of the Late Classic was clearly under way and the structural flaws of redundancy of function between capitals and subordinate centers were providing the fissures for this process. The loss of prestige and the undermining of sacred authority of the K'uhul Ajaw would follow, as worsening stresses on the society raised doubts about the ruler's power with ancestors and supernatural forces. The weakening of rulers' authority would have been worsened by events upriver, where endemic warfare in the Petexbatun and middle Pasión would have restricted the flow of status-reinforcing exotic goods from the highlands (Demarest and Fahsen 2003). With a growing elite, proliferating independent dynasties, and intensified ritual and warfare, the kings, their courts, and their subordinate centers would have badly needed such imported goods for the rituals, gift-giving, and tribute that were so critical to the formation and maintenance of alliance and patronage networks.

All of these pressures could have contributed to the cessation of construction and then the depopulation of the major western centers, first Palenque, then Piedras Negras, Yaxchilan, and other centers (Mathews 1988; Schele 1991; Holley 1983). Military defeats often provided the final blow to prestige, but the cycle of causality came from the building problems and contradictions of the Classic Maya theater-state system.

The subordinate populations, literally "disenchanted" with their sacred lords and frustrated by a multitude of problems, gradually drifted away to more distant centers or regions (Demarest and Valdés 1995; Demarest 2004; Demarest, Rice, and Rice 2004b; Holley 1983; Houston *et al.* 2001; Webster *et al.* 1999).

## Migration and enclave formation in the Pasión Valley and other regions

The impact of the collapse and depopulation of the Petexbatun and other regions of the western Petén would have been felt throughout the Maya lowlands. In the 1990s we have seen that the greatest cost of warfare is the displacement of populations. In Somalia, Yugoslavia, and Central Africa, the United Nations and other international agencies have struggled, with limited success, to deal with refugee migrations and the consequent famines, disease, and spread of conflict in the wake of wars (e.g. UNDHA 1994; Annan 1997). In each case, warfare between major states or larger opposition groups led to fragmentation within smaller units, finally disintegrating into a wholly militarized landscape from which large numbers of people were forced to flee, spreading chaos to adjacent zones (UNDHA 1994).

There are additional interesting parallels between recent events in Somalia and the western Petén collapse. In Somalia, migration from the troubled southern region of open warfare spread conflict and collapse to other areas (McKinley 1997). Yet in some zones, such as the town of Bassaso in the north, warring leaders established new mechanisms of government, drawing on ancient, traditional, clan-based ideology to create and legitimate a councilar form of leadership. By 1997 this and other northern enclaves had experienced a florescence amid the chaos of Somalia, as they incorporated thousands of refugees moving as families and even whole villages from the embattled surrounding regions. Recent political analyses have characterized these events as "an experiment in government that created a new form of power centralized in a council and not in individual chiefs or warlords" (McKinley 1997).

This process may be broadly analogous to what was occurring in the ninth century in the Pasión River Valley and some other regions. As the neighboring Petexbatun region lay in ruins, there was a florescence at Seibal and Altar de Sacrificios with a distinctive (but Classic Maya) sculptural style and technically sophisticated monochrome Fine Orange and Fine Gray ceramics (again new, but locally developed in the Pasión River Valley). These material changes also may have marked a shift in the ideology of power. Seibal fully participated in the warfare of the eighth and early ninth centuries in the Petexbatun. With its highly defensible location (Tourtellot 1988: 432–436), access to water, and probable agricultural terraces in defended areas (Dunning *et al.* 1997: 261; Dunning and Beach in press), Seibal was able to survive the eighth-century maelstrom, like its smaller neighbor to the south at Punta de Chimino. During the AD 760–830 epoch of endemic conflict, Group D at Seibal may have served as a defensive fortress with high parapets and a defensible position similar to that of the Aguateca fortress (Tourtellot 1988: 432–436; Tourtellot and Gonzales 2004; Demarest 2004). Unlike most of their unfortunate neighboring states, the lords of Seibal and Altar de Sacrificios presided over a florescence at their enclave centers. At the same time, the only remaining ninth-century enclave in the Petexbatun to the south, Punta de Chimino, survived with architecture, ceramics, and artifacts very similar to those of Seibal and Altar de Sacrificios (Demarest and Escobedo 1997; Demarest, Escobedo, and O'Mansky 1997).

The new architectural and sculptural forms at Seibal, Altar, and Punta de Chimino were not foreign, but rather were an amalgam of traditional Classic Maya forms combined into a distinctive new variant (Tourtellot and Gonzales 2004). The new K'uhul Ajaw of Seibal appear to have had close ties to the Central Lakes area to the east (Stuart 1993). On the other hand, the fine-ware monochrome ceramics of the period were local variants of technologies earlier introduced into the Petexbatun from the west (Foias and Bishop 1997). Many of the unusual features in the sculptures, strange costumes, long hair styles, and ubiquitous serpents (Fig. 10.11) may have been part of an experimentation with new legitimating ideologies (e.g. Ringle *et al.* 1998) that would help these surviving enclaves pull together a kingdom from the fragmented political systems and populations of the collapsed states of the Petexbatun and other adjacent zones.

Perhaps like the Bassaso leaders of modern Somalia, the rulers of the Altar and Seibal Pasión Valley enclaves were drawing on both ancient Maya symbols and new styles and concepts to legitimate these states and pull together their disparate populations. These adaptations allowed Seibal, Altar, and Punta de Chimino to survive for an additional century (AD 830 to 950/1000). In the end, though, these experiments in new concepts and ideologies were but a variant of the traditional Classic-period political order, and by the end of the tenth century these Lower Pasión centers were abandoned (Demarest 1997; Demarest and Escobedo 1997; Demarest *et al.* eds. 1997; Demarest 2004; Tourtellot and Gonzales 2004).

Figure 10.11 Monument 3 of Seibal showing unusual Terminal Classic iconography and garb

## Decline of the Classic tradition in the central Petén

In most areas of the southern Maya lowlands, the end of the Classic period was less dramatic. Fragmentation of political authority occurred, but it was accompanied by only slow decline in population and architectural activity. In the eighth century, Tikal experienced its greatest period of constructional activity. The great ruler Jasaw Chan K'awiil I and his eighth-century successors directed the vast Tikal architectural programs (see Chapter 9). This "revitalization" of Tikal may be regarded more as a symptom of stress than of strength (Ashmore and Sharer 1975; Dahlin 1976). As we have seen, such expensive, counterproductive responses to problems were a potential flaw of the K'uhul Ajaw competitive power structure (see Fig. 10.3, page 247).

The eighth century was a time of particularly intense status rivalry in the central Petén. This was sometimes expressed in terms of warfare between centers, but perhaps because of the dominance of Tikal, it was more often manifest in competitive architectural and ritual programs. Steep temples and twin-temple complexes, as well as palaces and ballcourts, were built at major centers throughout the region. Perhaps stimulated by leadership policy and ideology, estimated population levels rose to a peak by the beginning of the ninth century (Culbert *et al.* 1990; Rice and Rice 1990). Some recent population estimates for "greater" Tikal are as high as 280,000 for AD 800, and for the entire Tikal region over one-and-a-half million (Turner 1990: 321). Contrary to previous assertions, such population levels probably *could* be sustained by farming systems at Tikal, which we now know included extensive use of sunken swamp *bajo* areas surrounding the site zone (Culbert *et al.* 1996; Kunen *et al.* 2000). Still, such high levels – combined with the growing burden of elite consumption, construction, and ritual display – would certainly have strained local resources and left little margin for periodic subsistence or political difficulties (Culbert 1988).

By the ninth century these stresses were becoming apparent with a process of fragmentation of power like that observed earlier in the west and at Copan in the southeast. K'atun-ending monuments and ceremonial architecture were erected in the late ninth century at Uaxactun, Ixlu, Jimbal, Xultun, and other secondary centers, previously vassals of Tikal. Historical evidence indicates that this change may represent a shifting in the seats of major ceremonies corresponding to a sacred cycle of thirteen K'atuns (P. Rice in press; see Chapter 8). In this interpretation, the shifting of ceremonial seats at the end of the thirteen-K'atun cycle is responsible for much of the change in settlement and architecture after AD 830. It also seems probable, however, that the rulers of Tikal used this ritual mechanism as a power-sharing device to avoid further competition, just as one of the last Copan kings, Yax Pasaj, adopted the Council House power-sharing with local leaders in the Copan Valley (Chapter 9). Such ritual and political mechanisms for power-sharing may have effectively functioned for a short time to reduce conflict, but they also would have produced weaker individual polities with less prestigious leaders. In turn, the more limited authority of leaders meant less tribute labor for construction, again reducing further their prestige. This negative political feedback cycle, together with ecological stresses, led to a decline and then a cessation of public architecture at Tikal itself and a diminishing population throughout the region. Family-level decisions, affected by cultural malaise, may have helped to lower fertility rates and initiate emigration to other areas.

Figure 10.12 Tikal in ruins in the (Eznab) Terminal Classic period (drawn by Luis F. Luin)

By AD 830 to 850 some palaces at Tikal were abandoned or reoc-cupied by non-elite populations who inscribed their walls with graffiti crudely portraying scenes of warfare and sacrifice (Schele and Math-ews 1998; Valdés and Fahsen 2004). In the mid-ninth to tenth centuries this impoverished version of central Petén culture, the Eznab complex, is found at Tikal and the surrounding region. With little polychrome, the reduced population lived in the ruins of the site's earlier monumen-tal architecture (Fig. 10.12), much of which had ceased to host state rituals, feasts, or ceremonies (Culbert 1973; Valdés and Fahsen 2004). The last Tikal stone monument was erected in AD 869 to commemo-rate the K'atun ending at that time. The simplified ceramic assemblage of this period, together with some chronological markers of the Pasión region's fine-paste wares, was left in Tikal's palaces along with the house-hold debris of the new occupants (Harrison 1970; Culbert 1973). Other temples and palaces may have been the scene of formal termination ritu-als for architecture or monuments, with burning and the deposition of hundreds of broken vessels to desacralize previously holy places (Mock 1998; Freidel 1998, in press).

To the north, Calakmul had been in slow decline since its loss of pres-tige in military defeats at the beginning of the eighth century. By AD 900 Calakmul and the Río Bec centers and their hinterlands may have been reduced in population to 10 percent of apogee levels of the late seventh century (Turner 1990). In this zone of the far northern Petén and southern Quintana Roo and Campeche (see Fig. 9.10) climatic change and reduced rainfall may well have been a contributing factor in the regional decline of great centers and the lack of a vigorous recovery (Braswell *et al.* 2004; Demarest *et al.* in press; cf. Haug *et al.* 2003). There, in the Terminal Classic period, populations concentrated near former public architecture, as at Tikal. In the case of Calakmul, however, the remnants of leadership in the Terminal Classic used the combined temple-palace architecture form seen earlier at Caracol and characteristic of the contemporary Puuc centers of the north (Braswell *et al.* 2004). These temple-palace combined structures may indicate a greater degree of involvement in the economy, since some of them may also include workshops making lithic tools, textiles, and pottery (Braswell *et al.* 2004). It is equally likely, however, that these multiple functions reflect the reduction of population and consequent concentration of people and diverse activities on these high, defensible structures (Demarest, Rice, and Rice 2004b).

### Decline, transition, or transformation in the eastern Petén

To the east and southeast, changes in the Terminal Classic period were far more complex and are still poorly understood. To the southeast the frontier Maya kingdoms of Copan and Quirigua experienced political fragmentation in the eighth century followed by political collapse in the ninth. As we have seen (Chapter 9), the intense status rivalry manifest in ritual architecture, monuments, and (more directly) in warfare reached a critical point in the mid-eighth century, when Copan was defeated by its vassal Quirigua. The power-sharing experiments of the subsequent Copan ruler seem to have failed, being followed within sixty years by the collapse of the elite center and the cessation of public construction after AD 822 (Fash and Stuart 1991; Fash *et al.* 2004). A parallel political collapse occurred at their rival center of Quirigua, where the last monument was raised at AD 810, although some constructional activity continued in the center for a few years (Sharer 1991).

Controversy and debate surround what exactly happened to the general population outside of the regional centers after the political collapse of the Copan and Quirigua city-states. Bear in mind that the neighboring population surrounding both Copan and Quirigua may have been only marginally involved in the Classic Maya tradition. After the political collapse of both centers, the populations of their regions returned to local traditions of ceramics and artifacts in societies with a much lower level of political complexity (Manahan 2000, 2003; Fash *et al.* 2004).

There is disagreement on how long this non-elite population contin-ued, how rapidly populations declined, and how quickly artifact patterns changed from Classic to Postclassic styles. Some evidence from ceramic chronology and excavations has been interpreted as indicating a rapid collapse and decline of population after the end of the dynastic centers (Braswell 1992; Manahan 2000, 2003; Fash *et al.* 2004), while chronol-ogy based on the obsidian hydration dating techniques argues for a slower decline in the Copan Valley, with large populations only gradually dimin-ishing over two to three centuries (Freter 1988, 1994; Webster and Freter 1990; Webster *et al.* 2003). This type of disagreement over regional details in archaeology is common. In this case, resolution of the debate has fewer implications for the nature of the end of the Classic Maya political order than for broader interpretations of the degree of dependence of local populations on the economic or ideological leadership of the K'uhul Ajaw (see Chapter 7).

Meanwhile, in the southeastern Petén and Belize, events and processes in the period from AD 750 to 950 were highly variable. In the southeast-ern Petén region of the Mopan Valley and the Maya Mountains, there was decline of some centers in population and public construction, but expan-sion of other centers as the capitals of small conquest states (Laporte 1996, 2004). Centers such as Ixtonton, Ucanal, Sacul, and others flour-ished at the expense of their neighbors, and some of these conquest states were able to survive for over two centuries. These centers also reflect influ-ences from northern Yucatan in architectural façades, monument style, and ceramics (Laporte 2004).

A similar variable mosaic of some Classic centers collapsing while others flourished with new eclectic assemblages was seen throughout Belize and the eastern side of the Yucatan peninsula. Between AD 750 and 950 some sites were dramatically and rapidly abandoned, including both epicenters and their surrounding countrysides (R.E.W. Adams *et al.* 2004), while others were stable or even grew in population and epicenter construction (A. Chase and D. Chase 2004). Yet other centers such as Lamanai and some coastal sites simply carried on, and changes in arti-fact styles and interregional contacts were gradually incorporated into local traditions (e.g. Pendergast 1986). Some areas in northern Belize and on coastal islands, peninsulas, and lagoons experienced an irregular but pronounced increase in population at the end of the Classic period and in the ninth- and tenth-century Terminal Classic era. This pattern may indicate movement into the region of refugee populations, perhaps from the collapsing polities to the west (Adams *et al.* 2004; Masson and Mock 2004), with some centers creating successful mercantile enclaves.

One of the more aggressive regional polities in the Terminal Classic-period is Belize. Despite shifts and changes, populations there continued to be high and monuments were erected until the very end of the ninth century (A. Chase and D. Chase 1987). There, and at other northern Belize sites such as Nohmul (D. Chase and A. Chase 1982), monuments, architecture, and some artifacts show influence from the Terminal Classic polities of northern Yucatan (A. Chase 1985b). Evidence of intensification of warfare has been found at some sites in Belize – in some cases associated with expanding conquest states such as Caracol, in others related to the introduction of northern traits. At some centers the Classic period occupations ended with grim episodes of warfare and the mass sacrifice of captives. At Colha one such massacre was that site's "skull pit," in which the skeletons of thirty sacrificed individuals were heaped in a mass grave (Steele *et al.* 1980).

The overall picture on the eastern margin of the Maya world was a complex mix of historical events and processes later and more variable than the central Petén decline – and unlike the dramatic collapse seen at western Petén centers. Conquest states at sites like Caracol were able (for a time) to take advantage of the chaos around them, while kingdoms such as Xunantunich were greatly depopulated or even abandoned (Ashmore *et al.* 2004). Polities continued, but with an influx of new economic and stylistic elements moving down the Caribbean coast of Yucatan from the north. It is still unclear whether these northern influences were transmitted by actual migrations, by the intrusion of smaller elite groups, merchants, or warriors, or by the adoption of new ideas by local elites. The historical processes may have involved a mix of such mechanisms, since some sites such as Colha and Nohmul register more dramatic changes, while others such as Lamanai appear to have added northern elements to a more continuous tradition.

It is interesting that some sites, like Caracol, which thrived in the Terminal Classic, experienced a rather dramatic decline by the eleventh century and the beginnings of the Postclassic era. This pattern of militaristic enclave formation and then a delayed decline parallels events far to the west at Seibal, Altar de Sacrificios, and Punta de Chimino. Indeed, studies of sculptural styles and concepts indicate considerable interaction between the elites of these conquest enclaves in the west and those in Belize, Yucatan, and near Lake Petén-Itza (A. Chase 1985b; Chase and Chase 1998; Ringle *et al.* 1998). In all cases, by the tenth to the eleventh century, the Classic-period political order had ended throughout the eastern Maya lowlands. Some kingdoms had either declined to a lower level of sociopolitical complexity or been abandoned. Others, however, had been transformed to a new economic and political order engaged in long-distance trade, and large-scale commodity production, with less investment in the architecture and artifacts of royal funerary cults.

### Florescence, conflict, and decline in the northern lowlands

The period from AD 750 to 1050, which had seen collapse or decline in various zones of the southern Maya lowlands, was arguably the period of greatest florescence in northern Yucatan. It is a complex period, still poorly understood, with many debates in progress on the relative and absolute chronology of the different developments there. The distinctive forms of architecture and iconography in northern Yucatan had previously been attributed to late Mexican invasions, and the Puuc cities and Chichen Itza long had been mistakenly dated to the Postclassic period after AD 1000. Chronology is still problematic in the north due to the lack of deep stratigraphy at most northern lowland sites and the scarcity of dated inscriptions. Still, a consensus is beginning to emerge among experts (e.g., Sabloff and Andrews 1986; Carmean *et al.* 2004; Cobos 2004) about the broad parameters of cultural history in the northern lowlands during the confusing, and at times violent, transition from the Classic to the Postclassic era.

Developments in the northern lowlands can be viewed as at least three distinctive regional developments: the innovative Puuc centers of western Yucatan; the more traditional Classic Maya kingdom of Coba and its satellites in the east; and the expanding conquest state of Chichen Itza in north central Yucatan (Robles and Andrews 1986).

#### The Puuc

As described in Chapter 9, the Puuc centers of western Yucatan (see Fig. 9.10) included sites such as Uxmal, Sayil, Labna, and Kabah with their unique stone mosaic architectural façades, free-standing arches, and multi-story palaces. As many southern kingdoms went into decline, the Puuc cities experienced major growth, perhaps absorbing elites and populations from the south (Carmean *et al.* 2004; Schele and Mathews 1998: 258–260). During the AD 770 to 900 period, Puuc centers grew, populations expanded into marginal areas, and Puuc elite culture drew upon an amalgam of ideas from the south, from Oaxaca, and from Gulf coast cultures to the west (Kowalski 1998; Carmean *et al.* 2004).

On a larger scale than Seibal and Caracol in the southern lowlands, the Puuc centers may have built a splendid florescence upon the very collapse of other Maya states. While initially a series of small independent kingdoms, status rivalry and warfare led to the growth of larger regional alliances in the Puuc area in the ninth century. Intense warfare is testified to by fortifications around the epicenters of Uxmal and other Puuc sites and by grisly scenes of battle in murals, graffiti, and artifacts (Kowalski 1998; Schele and Mathews 1998: 234–235). Rapid growth and immigration to this area, combined with status rivalry and its associated costs in labor and conflict, may have created a political environment in the late ninth and tenth centuries similar to that of the southern lowlands in the eighth century. Yet in the north, the need for centralization of authority through alliance or conquest might have been even greater given their reliance on careful cooperative husbandry of scarce water sources.

The Puuc leaders responded to these challenges with programs of conquest, but they also drew upon new religious ideologies (e.g. Ringle *et al.* 1998) and power-sharing arrangements involving councils of lineage heads (e.g. Carmean *et al.* 2004). In the Puuc centers, *popolna* "mat" or council houses were used to allow rulers to confer with lineage heads or local leaders (Kowalski 1987; Prem 1994; Kowalski and Dunning 1999). Such lineage council governments were more evident at some Puuc centers, such as Xcalumkin, and later would become characteristic of Postclassic states (Carmean *et al.* 2004; Grube 1994b). Perhaps such experiments were more successful in the Yucatan than at Copan because long-distance trade along the Gulf of Mexico, inland–coastal trade, and water storage systems had helped to evolve a more flexible set of institutions of leadership that was also more directly involved in the economic and subsistence aspects of society.

By the late ninth and early tenth centuries, competition, warfare, and alliance had ended in the unification of most of the western Puuc cities under the leadership of the alliance of the king of Uxmal, identified in texts and monuments as "Lord Chaak," and his associates (Grube 1994b: 323–324; Schele and Mathews 1998). This ruler, through sharing power with other leaders, revived much of the symbolism and monuments of the Classic-period K'uhul Ajaw system of divine rulership. The most spectacular of the structures at Uxmal (Fig. 10.13), with their elaborate mosaic motifs, were constructed during his reign (Kowalski 1987; Kowalski and Dunning 1999). By AD 900, Uxmal's urban area covered over twenty square kilometers and the site was linked by *sacbe* causeways to a number of subordinate centers (Dunning 1992; Carmean *et al.* 2004). These expansionistic efforts affected the Coba sphere of influence in eastern Yucatan, where fortifications were constructed around satellite centers in a futile effort to defend them from western Puuc conflicts (Robles and Andrews 1986; Suhler and Freidel 1998; Suhler *et al.* 2004).

Figure 10.13 The Nunnery Quadrangle at Uxmal

Termination rituals of architectural destruction at these sites and subsequent occupation with western "Cehpech-style" Puuc ceramics indicate that the conquest of these centers was one factor in the decline of Coba itself.

Ultimately, however, the Terminal Classic political formations of the Puuc cities also declined. The stresses of status rivalry, warfare, and population increase may have been exacerbated by drought (Hodell *et al.* 1995) and by conflict with the competing regional alliance of Chichen Itza (Robles and Andrews 1986; Andrews and Robles 1985; Cobos 2004). Shortly after the reign of "Lord Chac" all the monumental construction ceased, and by AD 950 the city of Uxmal was in decline. Other great Puuc cities such as Sayil followed a similar trajectory and most were abandoned by the eleventh century (Carmean *et al.* 2004; Tourtellot *et al.* 1990; Tourtellot and Sabloff 1994). Even with innovative characteristics in economics and ideology, this modified form of Classic Maya political organization came to an end. Here, however, in contrast to the western Petén, Postclassic lineage-based kingdoms and alliances quickly developed from the Puuc kingdoms.

*Coba and eastern Yucatan*

As described in Chapter 9, the great sprawling city of Coba in eastern Yucatan and related centers were culturally very close to the southern lowlands in architecture, monuments, and all aspects of material culture. This similarity was probably due to the settlement of eastern Yucatan and Quintana Roo by peoples from the south seeking its similar wet rain forest environment broken by lakes and *bajos*. It is not surprising, then, that the chronology of the decline of Coba and the eastern Yucatan centers correlates somewhat more closely with that of some of the Maya kingdoms of the southern lowlands.

During its apogee, Coba constructed a system of causeways to connect its epicenters with satellite kingdoms. By the ninth century, the Coba kingdom was experiencing significant pressure from the Puuc hegemony to the west and the rising power of Chichen Itza to the northeast. Coba may have sought to hold together its kingdom through defensive constructions and the use of its causeways to supply perimeter sites (Suhler and Freidel 1998). The largest causeway ran over one hundred kilometers, connecting Coba to a series of satellite centers to the west, and ending at Yaxuna, an important center which appears to have been the first line of defense against the expanding alliances to the west and later against the Chichen Itza expansion. By the late ninth century, Yaxuna was surrounded by concentric encircling defensive walls (Freidel 1986c; Suhler and Freidel 1998; Suhler *et al.* 2004). As the stresses and status rivalry of the Terminal Classic intensified, other centers in northern Yucatan were fortified by defensive wall systems. Ek Balam, Chaccob, Cuca, Dzonot Ake, and other centers had fortification systems of encircling walls (Webster 1978; Bey *et al.* 1997; Ringle *et al.* 2004; Suhler *et al.* 2004) that were remarkably similar to those in the Petexbatun over a century earlier (Fig. 10.14).

Battered by Terminal Classic competing hegemonies, cut off from its traditional southern trade in elite goods, and perhaps under added stress from the beginnings of a drought, the Coba hegemony of eastern Yucatan and Quintana Roo disintegrated. Coba itself had a greatly reduced population by the tenth century and its satellite centers were either abandoned or reoccupied by groups with a new ceramic tradition, most often the "Sotuta" style of ceramics of the north central Yucatan conquest state of Chichen Itza.

### Chichen Itza

The third major player in these final political struggles of the Terminal Classic period of Maya civilization was the complex and enigmatic city of Chichen Itza and its expanding regional state. Views on the dating and cultural affiliates of Chichen Itza have changed radically in recent years. It was long believed to be a fully Postclassic state established by conquering Toltec invaders from central Mexico (e.g. Morley 1946). This Mexican

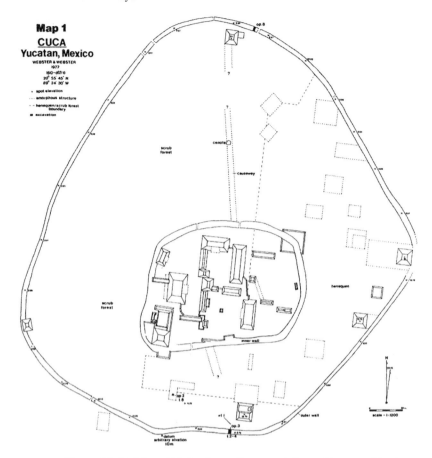

Figure 10.14 Map of defensive walls around Cuca, Yucatan, Mexico
(from Webster 1979: Map 1)

invasion hypothesis was based on many stylistic elements believed to be
traceable to highland Mexico, including atlantean columns, feathered
serpent imagery, colonnaded halls, *chacmool* sacrificial altars, *tzompantli*
carved stone skull racks, and warriors with Toltec-style armor, headdresses, shields, and weaponry. Many of these elements, and the layout
of some major structures at Chichen (Fig. 10.15), were closely parallel to structures and art at the Toltec capital center of Tula, Hidalgo in
Central Mexico. Furthermore, the sixteenth-century oral religious and
historical sources, including the Chilam B'alam K'atun prophecies (a
"circular" history/prophecy) associated Chichen with the Itza Maya and
characterized them as foreigners with new cults of human sacrifice and
idolatry.

Figure 10.15 Temple of the Warriors at Chichen Itza, Yucatan, Mexico

Despite these evidences, there were always problems with the Postclassic dating of Chichen Itza (e.g. Kubler 1961, 1962). In the last twenty years of excavations, detailed ceramic studies and reassessments of art and ethnohistory have revised the dating of Chichen Itza, placing it primarily, if not entirely, in the Terminal Classic period, from about AD 750/800 to 1050. This placement makes Chichen contemporary with the end of the Classic kingdom of Coba and its satellites in the east and coeval with the Puuc florescence to the west and south (e.g. Bey *et al.* 1997; Cobos 1998, 2004). Indeed, we now know that the rulers of Chichen Itza interacted with the Puuc kings, such as Lord Chaak, sometimes in alliance and sometimes at war (Prem 1994; Schele and Mathews 1998: 257–290; Carmean *et al.* 2004).

Many centers under the Coba realm were conquered and absorbed into these new hegemonies – first by the Puuc centers, led by Uxmal, and later by Chichen Itza (Andrews and Robles 1985; Suhler and Freidel 1998; Schele and Freidel 1990: 346–376). As the Coba regional kingdom rapidly declined in the east, the western Puuc and northern Chichen hegemonies came into conflict (Robles and Andrews 1986). The Puuc cities eventually lost this struggle – not only because of pressure and competition from Chichen, but also due to a delayed manifestation of the same stresses that had ended many of the Classic kingdoms to the south: the high costs of status rivalry, its stimulation of warfare and population increase, and the consequent ecological stresses. Increased aridity may have also contributed to the decline of the Puuc centers (Hoddell *et al.* 1995; Robichaux 2002).

By AD 1000 to 1050, Chichen Itza had become the dominant power in northern Yucatan. The short-lived success of the Chichen Itza hegemony was probably due to a number of factors. New concepts, some reworked ancient Maya ideas and some of Mexican origin, helped the rise of the power of Chichen as both a conquest state and a religious pilgrimage center (e.g. Ringle *et al.* 1998). The influence of Chichen Itza and its new styles and ideologies was felt at many of the remaining enclaves at the end of the Classic period, including Seibal in Guatemala and Nohmul in Belize (e.g. Tourtellot and Gonzales 2004; D. Chase and A. Chase 1982; A. Chase 1985b). Chichen Itza's Terminal Classic success can also be attributed to its greater involvement in interregional sea trade from its port at Isla Cerritos (Andrews *et al.* 1988, 1989; Andrews 1984). Chichen's long-distance trade in commodities such as salt, textiles, and cacao may have been on a greater scale than in the more regionally focused Classic Maya kingdoms (Freidel 1986b). Combined with its new cults and militarism, this mercantile activity may have helped Chichen to overcome its Classic Maya and Puuc rivals.

Chichen Itza's ascendancy was, however, a very short-lived one. Within a century, perhaps just a few decades, Chichen itself declined (Cobos 2004). The Itza polity may have been very predatory in its degree of reliance on conquest and tribute. With the decline of its vanquished Puuc and eastern Maya rivals, Chichen's flow of tribute resources and labor would have ended, precipitating its own decline – probably by about AD 1050 or 1100 (Robles and Andrews 1986).

In a sense, the battling alliances of Coba, Uxmal, and Chichen in the Terminal Classic marked the death throes of the Classic-period political order. With the decline of Chichen, successor states of the Postclassic reigned over Yucatan, albeit with less spectacular architecture and somewhat lower population levels. Important aspects of Classic civilization, such as the K'atun-centered rituals and histories, continued in the subsequent centuries. But the great charismatic cults of the K'uhul Ajaw and many other aspects of Classic-period high culture did not survive the interregional struggles of the Puuc cities and Chichen.

## Rethinking the "collapse" of ancient Maya civilization

The phrase "the collapse" or "the fall" of a civilization is a colorful, but misleading, term. Unlike poetic metaphors that guide our colloquial descriptions of the trajectory of cultural traditions, civilizations never "die." These anthropomorphic descriptions ignore the fact that a civilization is a complex configuration of institutions built upon a foundation of shared religious, political, and economic ideas and concepts. Even after major catastrophes, traumas, and declines, these elements can continue and be transformed into subsequent new configurations. Such was clearly the case with the "fall" of Rome or the "collapse" of Classical civilization as it is referred to in common parlance and even in some historical studies. The Roman Empire actually declined in the west through a slow and irregular process over several centuries, with episodes of revitalization and regional variations until the fifth century, when the western Roman Empire broke up into a series of Gothic kingdoms. Then, the eastern empire continued and flourished under Byzantium, and even the western Gothic states maintained many institutions from ancient Rome.

Underestimating the complexity of Classic Maya civilization itself, archaeologists initially expected a simpler process, a clear, unicausal "collapse," for the end of Classic Maya civilization. Yet, like the Roman Empire, an erratic and very complex – but definable – series of events and processes occurred, as we have seen, between AD 750 and 1050 in the Classic lowland Maya civilization. Beginning in the eighth century, caused by problems and stresses with even greater time depth, the western and southeastern Classic Maya kingdoms began to disintegrate into chaos (as with the Petexbatun), to fragment into smaller units (as with the Copan Valley), or to reinvent themselves as militaristic enclaves with modified forms of the K'uhul Ajaw system (as at Seibal and Altar). Refugees from these collapsing southern and western political systems moved to the east and north, causing population increase in parts of Belize and Yucatan. In the north, Gulf of Mexico coastal trade routes and the influx of southern populations may have initially provided preliminary advantages for aggressive innovative leadership, helping to stimulate the Puuc florescence and its more "Mexicanized" Chichen Itza version. Yet, as with the Terminal Classic Seibal enclave, attempts to revive the K'uhul Ajaw system, albeit buttressed by systems of lineage councils, ultimately failed. They still suffered from some of the same stresses and structural problems inherent in Classic Maya competitive divine kingship and status rivalry that had brought down the southern cities.

With the decline of the Puuc centers and Chichen, the Classic Maya political order had ended, and its theater-state kingdoms had been abandoned, or were replaced, or transformed into Postclassic polities with a different political and economic rationale. What had disappeared was the unique Classic-period combination of theater-state politics and divine kingship with a complex rain forest adaptation that had evolved for over two millennia in the southern lowlands. The end of Classic civilization took with it the magnificent (but costly) legitimating monuments, architecture, and art of these theater-states. Ultimately, the structural stresses inherent in this system of competing K'uhul Ajaws led to elite proliferation, massive labor costs, warfare, and nonelite demographic growth that together strained – and at times, completely contradicted – their brilliant ecological adaptation. In the face of such internal strains, as well as external competition, lowland Maya political systems collapsed or were replaced by new kinds of Maya states that were more closely tied into interregional Mesoamerican economies. The Classic-period "holy lords" had passed into history, but Maya civilization and the Maya tradition continued.

# 11 The legacy of the Classic Maya civilization: Postclassic, Colonial, and Modern traditions

While the focus of this text is on the Classic period of Maya civilization, it is important to take note of the enduring tradition that followed. The disappearance or reduction of the Classic hallmarks in architecture, monuments, and art had led Mayanist scholars to view the Postclassic as an epoch of decline and impoverishment. Indeed, one form of the traditional chronology labels the Late Postclassic in Yucatan as the "Decadent Period" (e.g. Thompson 1966). Such perspectives misperceive the nature of the Classic to Postclassic transition and the significance of elite architecture, artifacts, monuments, and even writing. All of these Classic-period hallmarks of "florescence," "greatness," or a "golden age" (in colloquial terms) were in fact specific instruments of elite ideological and political power. They helped generate power for the rulers in the particular type of political system of the Classic period by enhancing performance in theater-state rituals and by solidifying fealty or alliance through propagandistic monuments and history. These Classic-period hallmarks should be viewed as important elements of their political system that were not always particularly beneficial to the society as a whole (e.g. Sabloff and Rathje 1975). By the eighth century, if not sooner, the cost to the economic and ecological systems that supported these elite instruments of power had become onerous, contributing to the demise of this political system. Viewed in objective economic terms, many Postclassic states were larger and more successful than their flamboyant Classic-period antecedents.

## The Postclassic: what ended, what continued, and what changed

In Yucatan, the Postclassic states after the Puuc and Chichen declines were built on a more flexible set of political and economic institutions that were also more similar to those of polities elsewhere in Mesoamerica. The *multepal* system of governance by councils of lineage leaders focused far less political power and religious authority in a single individual. Lineages re-emerged as the political, as well as the social, unit of power, and councils of the lineage leaders participated in most major decisions (Tozzer 1941; Scholes and Roys 1948; Roys 1965a). Complex divisions present in the Classic period between elites in roles as merchants, priests, or warriors became even more pronounced and occupational class interests were better represented in state decisions (see bibliographic essay). In many areas local economies became somewhat less self-sufficient, with more overproduction of commodities such as cotton, textiles, salt, honey, chocolate, and ceramic styles, and with considerable long-distance exchange (Sabloff 1977; Sabloff and Rathje eds. 1975; Freidel 1986b). The latter was more often carried out via Gulf and Caribbean Sea trade rather than the Classic-period inland river and land routes.

Conquest and tribute, always important in the Maya world, became even more central to the support of the noble families that led each lineage. Similarly, warfare, tribute, and construction of political hegemonies continued but were less tied to the ruler and more to longstanding conflicts between lineages and self-defined larger groups. In the southern lowlands, fortified hilltop, island, or peninsular centers became more common in the Postclassic as the heritage of Late and Terminal Classic warfare became institutionalized in political structure and settlement strategy (D. Rice 1986; Rice et al. 1993; Jones et al. 1981, 1986).

Another great shift was the decline of the "managed mosaic" ecological adaptation in the southern Maya lowlands, although intensive systems and terraces continued in some lowland areas and in the highlands. The southern lowland area no longer had large but dispersed cities intermingled with the complex Classic mix of gardens, slash-and-burn fields, raised fields, and other subsistence systems. Local sensitivity to environmental variation was well suited to the Classic-period political system of minimal elite involvement in the economy and tribute to the K'uhul Ajaw in respect for his ideological and military authority. Most Postclassic centers, particularly in the highlands, were smaller, but many had more concentrated populations. Better-developed markets and exchange systems involved more regional overproduction and exchange, especially in commodities and manufactured goods (Freidel 1986b; Fox 1987; Carmack 1981).

All of these changes were shifts in degrees or emphases in patterns already present, to varying extents, in Classic-period societies. The degree of change versus continuity between Classic and Postclassic society is much debated by archaeologists (e.g. Chase and Rice 1985; Sabloff and Andrews 1986; P. Rice, Demarest, and D. Rice 2004). Many aspects of economy, ideology, and even political dynamics continued. The key role of calendric systems and rituals continued to be critical as seen in the shifting of ceremonial capitals at K'atun endings (approximately twenty-year intervals) and especially at the end of thirteen K'atun *May* cycles (P. Rice and D. Rice 2004, P. Rice in press). Other aspects of political structure and dynamics may also be continuous between Classic and Postclassic periods (e.g. Marcus 1993).

Nonetheless, there were still major changes after the ninth-century decline of the great cities of the southern lowlands and later of Coba, Uxmal, and the other Puuc centers in the north. Most visible to the archaeologists was the disappearance of the cults of the K'uhul Ajaw and the great display of public and ceremonial architecture and art that were elements of the theater-state system. Postclassic ceremonial centers were more modest in scale and extent of public architecture, even though many of these sites grew to have populations comparable to Classic centers. Ancestor worship also continued to be a central element of religion, but with emphasis on lineage and family shrines and idols. The latter were also common in the Classic period but were overshadowed by the spectacular cults of veneration of the divine ancestors of the royal dynasties.

### The lowland Postclassic

The Postclassic period in the lowlands has been studied as much through ethnohistorical and historical sources as through archaeology (see bibliographic essay). The Conquest-period and Colonial recording of oral history, K'atun prophecies, and regional concepts, together with descriptions of the world of the Maya at that time, are a foundation for all of our studies of Maya civilization but are, of course, most accurate and informative on the Postclassic society and politics.

Still, historiographic interpretation of sources is not a simple matter. The biases and conceptual misunderstandings of the priests, soldiers, and administrators who left these sources require careful evaluation, since indigenous ideas and history were often forced into European cultural form. In addition, more baffling problems were caused by the Maya cyclical view of time, in which history and prophecy were one and the same. For many passages in sacred oral texts, such as the *Chilam B'alam of Chumayel* and the *Chilam B'alam of Tizimin,* it is difficult to assign a chronological date in the Gregorian calendar, since dating relied primarily on K'atun ending dates and the Short Count, Calendar Round, and other purely cyclical systems (Roys 1967; Farriss 1987; Edmonson 1979, 1982). For many years the ethnohistorical sources have been almost as much an obstacle as an aid to understanding Postclassic events. Now, however, with the archaeological sequences and hieroglyphic texts better understood, the Conquest- and Colonial-period sources have become of great utility in refining our understanding of the Maya perspective on Late Classic to Conquest-period events (e.g. Jones 1998; Schele *et al.* 1995; D. Rice *et al.* 1993, 1995, 1996; P. Rice in press; Schele and Mathews 1998).

Archaeological and ethnohistorical evidence often indicates that Chichen Itza was destroyed and many of its major structures were ritually "terminated" (Mock 1998; Freidel 1998, in press). The leaders of the war against Chichen were identified by sources as members of other noble lineages of the Itza Maya. They also state that many of the Itza Maya of Chichen moved to the south at this time, eventually settling on the islands and peninsulas of the Central Petén lake that today bears their name, Lake Petén-Itza. Recent archaeological studies have confirmed the movements and interactions of the Central Petén and northern Yucatec Itza groups (Jones *et al.* 1981; D. Rice *et al.* 1993, 1995, 1996; Jones 1998).

To the north, after the decline of Chichen Itza, the Cocom lineage led the establishment of a new capital at the site of Mayapan (see Fig. 9.5). There, a *multepal* government council of lineage heads was formed to rule a federation of states in northern Yucatan. The capital center at Mayapan reflects the uneasy nature of this alliance and the conquest warfare characteristic of the Postclassic era. In contrast to the mosaic of dispersion and diversity in field systems and residences, even in epicenters, Mayapan had much of its population concentration within a dense urban area surrounded by a defensive wall (Fig. 11.1). The walls, protected gateways, and an interior *cenote* provided security against raids by enemies. They also facilitated the Cocom strategy of keeping the residences of all of the noble heads of lineages in the capital center, providing political consultation and alliance in a highly coercive context. The principal public buildings at Mayapan included small temples and palaces with frontal colonnaded porches. Low property walls separated tightly packed residential compounds in the walled center, which had over 3,000 houses and a population of over 15,000 persons (Bullard 1952; Pollock *et al.* 1962; Shook 1954; Smith 1954; Thompson 1954). The new ceramic styles showed continuity with earlier periods, but with even more emphasis on incensarios and other forms for household and lineage rites and ancestor worship, especially large figurine censers.

Ceramic styles and ethnohistorical accounts demonstrate great involvement by Mayapan and other Late Postclassic sites in Yucatec trade with Veracruz, Tabasco, and other areas to the west. The leaders of Mayapan apparently even contracted mercenaries from that region to help control its shaky federation and the conflictive ruling lineages. Together with tribute from groups throughout Yucatan, trade with the west and down

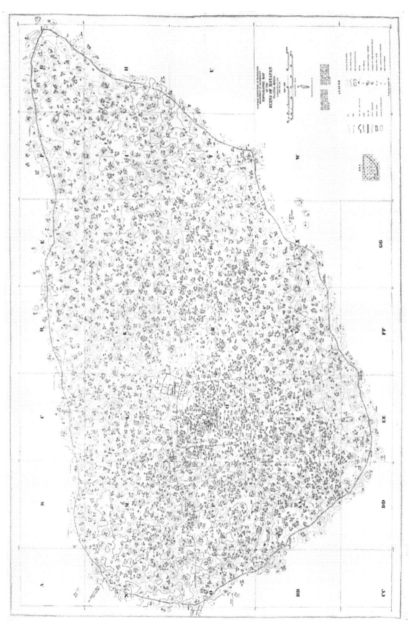

Figure 11.1  Map of the Postclassic capital of Mayapan (from Jones 1957)

Figure 11.2 Ruins of Postclassic temple complex at Tulum (drawn by Luis F. Luin)

the Caribbean coast was a mainstay of the Postclassic economies. Many of the Postclassic centers were located at strategic points in this coastal commercial network (e.g. A.P. Andrews 1990, 1993; Andrews IV and A.P. Andrews 1975; Andrews and Sabloff 1986; Robles and Andrews 1986). Sites such as Tulum, Cozumel island, and Santa Rita Corozal to the south were all important ports in this trading system, which ran from Veracruz along the Gulf coast of Mexico, down the Yucatan peninsula, and past Quintana Roo and Belize to ports as far south as Honduras, if not beyond (Sabloff 1977; Sabloff and Rathje 1975, eds. 1975).

Tulum was one of the sites on this trade network (Fig. 11.2). This small walled city which controlled safe portages through the reefs and cliffs of Yucatan's east coast was immortalized by the early explorers Stephens and Catherwood in popular travelogues and Catherwood's drawings (see Fig. 3.1). Offshore, the island of Cozumel also facilitated this Caribbean trade. With shrines, merchant residences, and storage facilities, the island was a major shipping point for the growing coastal trade in salt, other commodities, and manufactured goods (Freidel and Sabloff 1984). Farther down the coast, Santa Rita Corozal and Cays along the Belize coast were part of this booming coastal economy of the later Postclassic period (e.g. D. Chase 1985, 1986, 1990; Masson and Mock 2004). Murals at many of these sites, including Tulum, Tancah, and Santa Rita, feature coastal deities and imagery and Mexican elements of style that moved together with goods on this international trade network (e.g. Miller 1977, 1982, 1986; D. Chase 1991).

Farther inland, Early and Late Postclassic communities thrived in northern Belize and in the central Petén lake area (e.g. Chase and Rice 1985; Pendergast 1986; P. Rice 1986, 1987c; D. Rice 1986). At Tayasal and Topoxte on the Petén lakes and at sites in northern Belize, figurine censers, colonnaded elite residences, elements of iconography, and ceramic styles had strong similarities to those in northern Yucatan and along the coasts (A. Chase 1976, 1979, 1985a; Jones et al. 1981). Ethnohistoric sources also confirm ongoing relations and population movements between the Itza and other Maya groups in the Petén lake area and their relatives and rivals in the north at Mayapan and later Postclassic centers (Jones 1998; D. Rice et al. 1995, 1996; P. Rice 1986). Such long-distance relations, trade, and population movements continued through the Postclassic and into the sixteenth century. Battling hegemonies in the southern lowlands established towns, some of them fortified, around the lake area and were joined at times by affiliated groups from the north to aid in the struggles (Jones 1998). Meanwhile, in Belize similar kingdoms remained involved in coastal–inland trade as well as the interregional canoe traffic in manufactured goods and Belizean commodities such as shell, cacao, honey, cotton, and fine chert (e.g. D. Chase 1985, 1986; A. Chase 1985a; Chase and Chase 1980, 1982). Many of these centers continued to be occupied through the time of the Conquest and into the Colonial period (e.g. Pendergast 1986; D. Rice et al. 1996; Jones et al. 1986; Jones 1998). The flexible forms of lineage governance combined with full market economies and long-distance exchange systems sustained this Postclassic form of Maya civilization until the Spanish Conquest.

Meanwhile in the north, Mayapan fell to a revolt by rival lineages in the fifteenth century. It was sacked and burned according to the chronicles and as confirmed by archaeological evidence (Pollock et al. 1962; Shook 1954; Thompson 1954). Over eighteen small kingdoms then ruled in the north, continuing the ancient Maya pattern of episodes of hegemonic federation alternating with periods of petty kingdoms (e.g. Marcus 1993). These Late Postclassic kingdoms continued the institutional systems of the Postclassic with community production, trade, conquest, and tribute as the economic basis of the state and great involvement in long-distance trade. They also continued the K'atun-based rituals and periodic move-ments of ceremonial "capitals" of the *May* cycle (P. Rice in press). Large-scale population movements and constant warfare marked the instability of the period. Battles, massacres, and inter-lineage hostility weakened the north before the Spanish Conquest, as did plagues brought by the first contacts with Europeans in the early sixteenth century.

## Postclassic Conquest states of the southern highlands

To the south in the volcanic highlands of Chiapas and Guatemala, the Postclassic was a period of great cultural florescence, as measured in population sizes and territorial extent of polities. Postclassic highland ceremonial centers, while not on the scale of those of the lowland Classic-period city-states, were impressive concentrations of architecture. Temples, altars, ballcourts, and palaces served the leading families of the most important lineages. As with the lowland Postclassic polities, the highland states had a *multepal* system of governance with one lineage head, or more often two, being considered somewhat more powerful than the others.

Again our understanding of these highland Postclassic states is guided by a mixture of archaeology and ethnohistory. For the latter, scholars utilize a rich base of archival material from the sixteenth and seventeenth centuries, as well as from ethnographic observation of modern highland Maya groups whose beliefs and lifeways retain many ancient patterns that inform all of our archaeological interpretations. Such use of analogy must be applied with great care, since the many highland groups have been constantly adapting to changing circumstances and varying degrees of Western involvement and oppression. It is difficult to determine the origins of any particular trait, belief, or ritual given the great Mexican influence in the Postclassic period and the subsequent impact of conquest, disease and Spanish Colonial domination. Nonetheless, scholars have gained inestimable insights from the ethnohistoric and ethnographic record. The sacred oral histories of the K'iche" Maya, the *Popul Vuh*, and that of the Kaqchiquel Maya, the *Anales de los Kaqchikeles,* have been especially important to archaeological and historical interpretation of the Postclassic and even Classic-period evidence (e.g. D. Tedlock 1985; Edmonson 1971; Carmack 1973, 1981; Fox 1987, 1989; Farris 1984; Arnauld 1986; Schele and Mathews 1998: 291–317).

The elite nobles of the highlands traced their ancestry to "Toltec" Mexican origins in the west. In fact, many aspects of highland society do show the addition of new cults, architectural elements, and artifact forms and styles that may have originated in various parts of Mexico. Yet the core of their cultural forms evolved within the Maya world in response to militarism and population movements at the end of the Classic era. In addition to Western contacts and influences, population movements between the lowlands and highlands may have been critical in the formation of highland states (e.g. Fox 1987, 1989; Fox *et al.* 1992). Direct relations with Chichen Itza, the "Tollan of the west," were among these contacts. Major population movements from the western Petén Classic

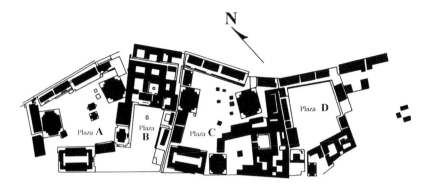

Figure 11.3 Map of the Postclassic highland Kaqchikel capital at
Iximche', showing architecturally redundant compounds of the
epicenter that housed the courts of four of the leaders in the *multepal*
political system of the sixteenth century (drawn by Luis F. Luin after
George Guillemin 1965)

Maya kingdoms after their ninth-century disintegration may also have
helped create the unstable, but dynamic, political environment of the
Guatemalan highlands in the Postclassic.

By the Late Postclassic some large highland hegemonies had emerged
from the wars and alliances of the Early Postclassic. The largest of these
was the K'iche' hegemony with a major capital at Q'umarkah (previously
known as Utatlan). This capital center manifests combined Classic, Postclassic, and Mexican features that define the structure and the details of
the highland states (Wallace 1977; Wallace and Carmack 1977). It was
built on a highly defensible hilltop location, as were its competing highland capitals, Iximche' of the Kaqchiquel Maya hegemony (Guillemin
1965, 1977; Schele and Mathews 1998), Zaculeu of the Mam Maya, and
Chitinamit, the fortified island capital of the Tzutuhil Maya. Defensive
considerations were also manifest in the dense concentration of population, often on terraces, around these fortress capitals (Wallace and
Carmack 1977; Guillemin 1977).

The internal architecture of these centers presents a diagram of the
political nature of these states. Separate site segments, each a kind of
mini-capital, were constructed (Fig. 11.3) to house the nobles of each
lineage, with redundant ballcourts, temples, altars, and palaces for each
lineage head (see especially Schele and Mathews 1998: 291–317). Altars
and temples to Tohil, a solar deity, reflect Mexican influence in cult
form and architectural details. The multiple-ruler, lineage-based organization of these states seems unwieldy to Western concepts of statehood
and contrasts sharply with the Classic-period focus on the K'uhul Ajaw.

Nonetheless, such a system has great flexibility, allowing internal shifts in power and avoiding the traumas that occurred in the Classic period states when the K'uhul Ajaw was killed or captured in war. In any case, the success of the Postclassic system was demonstrated by the rapid expansion of powerful hegemonies from these lineage capitals.

By the time of the Spanish Conquest, the hegemony of the K'iche' lineages from Q'umarkah and of the Kaqchiquel from Iximche' had become the largest in extent, each covering thousands of square kilometers in the highlands in a loose alliance of tributary states. As in Yucatan, the centuries of warfare between the highland states had created long-standing enmity between these groups by the sixteenth century. The Conquistadors were able to exploit these divisions in their subjugation of the highland Maya from 1524 to 1527 (Alvarado 1924).

## The Spanish Conquest of the highland and lowland Maya kingdoms

The European discovery and conquest of the Maya kingdoms was, of course, the greatest trauma for that civilization. There is much to be learned about the nature of Classic and Postclassic Maya society and about the greater Maya tradition in general from the impact of the Spanish contact and the resistance to conquest and colonial rule (see especially Jones 1989, 1998; Farriss 1984, 1987; Lovell 1992; Rice et al. 1993; Roys 1972). Yet all of our uses of the Contact-period and Colonial Maya societies for analogies with earlier periods must be tempered by an understanding of the radical impact of contact even before the scribes and administrators of the Spanish crown arrived.

In 1511, a Spanish vessel sank in the Caribbean and a lifeboat with eleven survivors washed up on the east coast of Yucatan a fortnight later. They were seized by the local Maya lord. Some were sacrificed in Postclassic ceremonies, others were killed, and two survived to serve Maya rulers – one as a scribe, the other as a warrior. Contrary to the ethnocentric perspective of fictional contact tales and speculations about transoceanic diffusion, these Westerners did not transform Postclassic Maya society, which was, arguably, far better adapted to its environment than the later European Colonial and modern regimes. They did, however, introduce new diseases, such as smallpox, to the Maya world that ravaged the highland and lowland kingdoms. By the time of the first European descriptions of Maya kingdoms, they had already been greatly reduced and politically destabilized by ten to twenty years of plague. This catastrophe probably also rendered the Maya easier to subjugate and convert by the waves of conquistadors and priests that would soon engulf them.

The second stage of the conquest of the Maya was the launching of expeditions from Cuba to subjugate the Yucatan. It is testimony to the organization and effectiveness of the Postclassic kingdoms that Spanish expeditions in 1517 and 1518 were met with stiff resistance and were forced eventually to return to Cuba without success and with large casualties. Despite being ravaged by disease and torn by warfare between ruling hegemonies (in both Yucatan and the highlands), the Maya repelled Spanish attempts at subjugation far more effectively than the Aztec empire had in central Mexico (e.g. Jones 1989). In 1519, Cortez himself marched through the Maya lowlands, but the target of this military expedition was a rebellious lieutenant in Honduras. The record of the endeavor is a fascinating description of the Maya lowland societies and the rigors of the rain forest environment (Cortes 1928; Diaz del Castillo 1963), but the Maya kingdoms remained independent.

The successful conquest of the Maya did not begin until Pedro de Alvarado's conquest of the K'iche' hegemony in the southern highlands from 1524 to 1527 (Alvarado 1924). Alvarado used treachery to pit one group against the other. The expanding K'iche' hegemony from their capital at Q'umarkah had conquered much of the highlands, making enemies of their neighbors. With the aide of the Kaqchikel alliance, Alvarado defeated the K'iche', massacred their leaders, and burned Q'umarkah. Then he led an army of Kaqchikels and indigenous mercenary allies from Central Mexico to destroy the Tzutuhil leaders and destroy their capital center, the Lake Atitlan island fortress of Chitinamit. By this time, he had established the first Spanish capital in Central America at Iximche', the Kaqchikel center (Fig. 11.4). Not surprisingly Alvarado found a pretense to turn on his Kaqchikel hosts, destroy their capital, and slay their leaders (Alvarado 1924; Lovell 1992).

Meanwhile in the north, conquistador Francisco de Montejo faced even more effective resistance from the Yucatec Maya. After a number of disastrous and unsuccessful attempts, the Spanish finally succeeded in conquering much of Yucatan between 1540 and 1546. Large areas of Quintana Roo remained unsubjugated, however, and revolts plagued the Spanish Colonial regime. Indeed, as late as the nineteenth century the Maya continued to mount successful revolts, rallying around ancient symbols and revitalization movements to periodically drive out their Spanish, and later Colonial Mexican, overlords (e.g. Jones 1989; Farriss 1984, 1987; Reed 1964; Restall 1997).

The final, fascinating episode in the Maya conquest occurred in 1696, long after most indigenous peoples had been conquered, if not assimilated, throughout the hemisphere. In the central Petén lakes area, populous Maya kingdoms had survived the plagues and multiple attempts

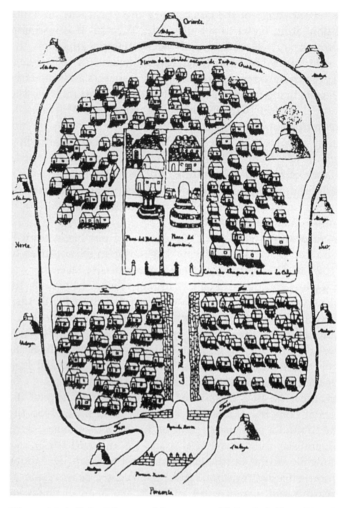

Figure 11.4 Colonial map of the center of Iximche' (from Maudslay 1889, Vol. II: Plate 73)

at Spanish domination. Recent discoveries of new archival texts include firsthand descriptions of the vigorous Itza Maya kingdom of Tayasal in the Lake Petén-Itza region (Jones 1992, 1998). With ceremonial centers, a flotilla of war canoes, hieroglyphic codices, and calendric and sacrificial rituals, the Itza kingdom ruled by the lord Kan Ek' was described as if it were one of the magnificent states of the Classic period. Only with great difficulty was the Spanish expedition finally able to subdue Kan

Ek' and his forces (Jones 1998). Ongoing ethnohistorical and archaeological studies of these Postclassic and Contact period kingdoms of Lake
Petén-Itza and Yaxha promise to revolutionize our understandings of the
characteristics of Maya polities and their adaptive responses in the face of
competition, warfare, migrations, plague, and finally, Spanish aggression
(Jones 1992, 1998; D. Rice *et al.* 1993, 1995, 1996).

## The continuing tradition and the impact of Conquest: the Colonial and modern Maya

Much of the interpretation and speculation in this and all other texts on
ancient Maya civilization has been based on analogy, presumed survival
of traits, and, most convincingly, on structural and conceptual elements
that have endured in the Maya tradition through the centuries. Hundreds
of ethnographic studies of the many ethnically and linguistically distinct
Maya groups have been carried out in the past century (see Bricker 1981;
Bricker and Gossen 1989; B. Tedlock 1993 for summaries of some recent
work and trends). Scholars have had to struggle to determine which
patterns and features can be used to help interpret the ancient record.
Research has proven that many Colonial and modern Maya institutions
and concepts once believed to be ancient "survivals" from Classic or Postclassic times are, in fact, part of the continuing adaptation and resistance
of Maya societies to European domination, acculturation, and aggression
(e.g. Bricker 1973, 1977, 1981; Farriss 1984, 1987; Hill 1992; Restall
1997; B. Tedlock 1992).

Indeed, modern scholarly work in archaeology may draw upon the
modern Maya as a more probable source of concepts and analogies, but
in the end these must be tested against the archaeological and epigraphic
record just as analogies from unrelated civilizations must be tested. This
text has used models and concepts for interpretation and speculation on
ancient possibilities drawn from the theater-states of Southeast Asia, the
segmentary polities of Africa, contemporary Somalia, and other societies.
While perhaps more likely to survive testing through correlation with the
archaeological record, contemporary and Colonial Maya traits and institutions must also be tested for applicability (see Marcus 1983a, 1993 for
an alternative perspective). Still, it is unlikely that the details of the writing
system, the calendar, and the complex Maya conceptions of time, space,
sacredness, and cosmology would ever have been penetrated without the
guiding assistance of our knowledge of the Colonial and contemporary
Maya.

In the Colonial period, the Maya communities, depopulated by disease
and conquest, were systematically reduced and concentrated by their

Spanish overlords into towns of European form. Grid patterns of streets, central plazas with public buildings and churches, and densely placed homes with little or no garden areas replaced the more ecologically appropriate dispersed form of living that was still practical in some areas. The demands of Spanish taxation and of tribute to local haciendas and public officials led to the abandonment of local self-sufficiency and to the over-production of corn and other storable, mobile, and taxable products. As the colonial European population grew, in many regions monocultural plantations growing cotton, indigo, chocolate, and later coffee and sugar cane replaced the more complex mosaic of subsistence crops and commodities of the pre-Columbian Maya.

Finally, the introduction of steel axes and saws encouraged forms of slash-and-burn (*roza*) agriculture that were far more ecologically destructive than the indigenous methods of pre-Columbian agriculture. This led to several centuries of deforestation, erosion, and environmental deterioration. Another result of these changes was the obscuring to modern study of pre-Columbian patterns of agriculture, settlement strategy, commodity production, and ecological adaptation.

Other radical changes under Spanish domination had an impact on Maya political and ideological systems. The political system had already been greatly modified by the Postclassic transitions and by the influence of Mexican and Gulf coast models of political, economic, and religious institutions of power. The Spanish Conquest virtually destroyed the political order, replacing all higher-level authorities with the European Hapsburg bureaucracy whose prime directive was tribute extraction. The latter system distorted many aspects of both subsistence and the economy, furthering the process of abandonment of ancient Maya settlement patterns that had been better adapted to their environment.

Political leadership of an indigenous nature was reduced to local shamans and committees of elders, the latter seldom organized in forms traditional to the Maya. Priests and sacred authority were suppressed by the Inquisition. Much of the detailed calendric and cosmological models fell from common usage. Political leaders and most elites were killed by either genocidal war or disease. Others were incorporated into Colonial tribute extraction systems, often destroying their moral and ideological authority with the indigenous population.

For these reasons we must utilize the ethnographic record with extreme caution. Many traits that seem exotic and perhaps ancient to Western eyes were generated by the Colonial Maya in an effort to survive, culturally and physically. These institutions and rituals interwove ancient structural elements and details with Catholic doctrine and European religious concepts (e.g. Bricker 1981; Bricker and Gossen 1989).

Figure 11.5 A modern Q'eqchi' Maya Wa'atesink ritual

## The enduring and resurgent Maya

Despite the brutal impact of conquest and domination on the indigenous population, it is amazing how the Maya tradition has continued to evolve and thrive. Maya groups modified ancient patterns and developed new institutions to cope with colonial and modern circumstances. In scattered instances, however, some elements of Maya cosmology and calendrics survived virtually intact into the seventeenth or eighteenth centuries and even to the present day (e.g. Jones 1998; Tedlock 1992). Such individual elements – and more often, broader cosmological principles – have been continually reincorporated into new systems of ethnic and economic survival as the Maya tradition continues to adapt and thrive (Fig. 11.5).

Recently, the indigenous Maya peoples of Mexico and Guatemala have begun to experience a new period of revitalization and cultural change. After the past half-century of civil war in Guatemala and Chiapas in Mexico, the Central American and world political communities have finally become engaged in the struggle for Maya survival. The Zapatista revolt in Mexico and the consequent ongoing negotiations, especially the 1996 Peace Accords in Guatemala, are ushering in a new chapter in the history of the Maya – a chapter yet to be written.

For the first time, the Maya communities themselves are beginning to play a major role in national politics and public policy. Gradually, no

Figure 11.6 Archaeologists participating in a Q'eqchi' Maya Hac
ritual at the archaeological site of Cancuen

doubt with great challenges to come, the Maya are being incorporated
into the democratic system and are struggling to use it to help protect
and preserve their own interests. Together with this political change has
come a cultural renaissance and activism with renewed interest in protect-
ing indigenous languages, institutions, and lifeways (e.g. Fischer and
Brown eds. 1996). Undoubtedly, this very movement will change Maya
culture and self-definition as much as, or more, than it will "preserve"
it. Nonetheless, it represents a continuation and evolution of the Maya
tradition.

Some scholars have criticized archaeology for its at times romantic,
simplistic, or "essentializing" views of ancient Maya civilization (e.g.
Montejo 1991; Wilks 1985; Hervik 1999). Yet modern archaeology has
helped greatly in the Maya peoples' political struggles for contemporary equality and justice by recovering and celebrating the magnificent
achievements of the Maya tradition, contradicting the prejudiced colonial
view of *indios tontos*, "simple-minded Indians" (Demarest and García
2003). Nationalism in Guatemala and Mexico has come to identify more
closely with the indigenous cultural patrimony of those nations. Archaeology is now beginning to more directly benefit the neighboring Maya
communities themselves, while we benefit from the insights of the ancient
Maya. Epigraphic projects have been organized to teach native Maya

shamans and leaders the ancient writing system of their Classic-period ancestors (Schele and Mathews 1998: Ch. 8). While helping bolster Maya pride and prestige with the culturally European *ladino* community, such efforts also have led to surprising insights from fluent speakers of languages much closer to those of the inscriptions. Archaeological projects (Fig. 11.6) have begun to attempt to collaborate closely with the villages neighboring major sites (Demarest and García 2003). Such collaborations now seek not only approval from their host villages, but active involvement of the community in the planning and design of long-term projects of archaeological site/sacred site excavation, restoration, education, tourism, and development (e.g. García 2001; García *et al.* 2002). The goal of such projects is to help contemporary Maya communities to become the custodians of their own ancient heritage. In this way modern scholarship can assist the thousands of Maya communities of Mexico and Central America in their construction of a new, more independent, manifestation of the continuing Maya tradition (Demarest and García 2003).

# 12 The lessons of Classic Maya history and prehistory

It should be obvious from the preceding chapters on the Classic Maya civilization that their cultural and ecological adaptations, and even their decline, have many lessons for contemporary society and social science. These lessons range from insights into details of farming strategies to philosophical challenges to our personal worldviews.

Obviously, there are many specific lessons of Maya history and prehistory. Above all, we have emphasized the true "secret" of the Classic Maya, their adaptation to the rain forest. Their system of mimicking the diversity and dispersion of the rain forest in subsistence strategy and settlement patterns allowed the southern lowland Maya to maintain populations in the millions in the Petén for over 1,500 years without destroying that rich, but fragile, environment. Indeed, it has been argued here that the eventual decline in some areas of this system and the southern lowland cities was *not* brought about by a sudden loss of Maya skills in ecological or demographic planning (after fifteen or more centuries of knowledge). Rather it appears that in some zones of the Petén the elite sector of society grew too large and burdensome. Elite status rivalry for power and prestige led to an overburdening of the economic system, misdirection in demographic growth, and eventual decline through direct endemic warfare, population movements, and politically induced ecological and demographic stress. The collapse in the west and transformations elsewhere of the Classic Maya political system was, in terms of root causes, a *political* phenomenon.

The ecological lessons of the Maya are beginning to benefit indigenous lowland Maya communities today. Drawing on the wealth of information about specific ancient Maya agricultural systems and farming techniques, paleoecologists already have been able to provide specific examples and models, drawn from the Classic period, to guide contemporary development projects (e.g. Dunning *et al.* 1992; Demarest and Dunning 1989). As the Q'eqchi' and other Maya peoples continue to repopulate the rain forest, Guatemalan and international agencies are seeking to provide them information on these ancient skills of their ancestors. We are hopeful

294

that, together with modern innovations, this knowledge might assist the hundreds of thousands of recent Maya migrants into the Petén to live symbiotically with the remaining rain forest, using more sustainable non-Western general models of agriculture and specific ancient Maya techniques.

There are broader nonecological lessons from Maya prehistory and history that challenge academic theories, as well as our colloquial thinking, on the "rise and fall of civilizations." We have seen that the success, the nature, and the problems of ancient Maya civilization cannot be understood strictly in terms of traditional cultural-materialist, economically oriented theory. The rise of the Maya and their ecological adaptations were inseparably linked to their worldview and their distinctive political formations. Contrary to some theoretical dogmas, a primary (but certainly not the sole) basis of royal power in many Classic Maya kingdoms seems to have been religious and ideological. The rituals, pageants, patronage networks, and even wars of the theater-state seem to have been a major source of power, not merely a "legitimation" or "phantasmic representation" of economic power and inequality. For the Classic Maya, literally the "play was the thing" in theater-state politics.

As we have seen, the Maya civilization was not unique in this degree of ideological dependence (e.g. Geertz 1980). We should therefore broaden our views in pre-Columbian archaeology about the complex basis of power and the nature of political authority. The economically disembedded nature of many Classic-period elites and leaders may have, in fact, been beneficial to the success of the lowland Classic Maya cities. In most cases, it allowed local, econiche-sensitive management of each subsistence area, yet it provided the general benefits of central authority for group identity, arbitration, and collective activities such as inter-center warfare and major constructions. Only in the later Classic period did elite mismanagement, rivalry, and short-term goals negatively affect subsistence systems.

The general lessons of the Terminal Classic conflicts and the decline of most cities, particularly in the southern lowlands, are again primarily political ones. Leadership that becomes (for whatever reason) shortsighted and self-focused will guide society into troubled times. Inter-elite rivalry in the Classic Maya case affected general ecology and demography by encouraging great energetic expenditures and population growth. Elite growth and competition in ritual, construction, warfare, feasting, and other forms of status rivalry may have strained economic systems with a higher burden of tribute. In the end, the Classic Maya system unraveled, with collapse and demographic decline in some regions and transformation to new, different systems in other zones. The lessons are clear for contemporary society concerning the need for long-term *sustainable* adaptations and leadership strategies.

Finally, we should note the broader philosophical and personal challenges presented by this narrative on the ancient Maya. Postprocessual and postmodern theorists in anthropology and archaeology have warned us of the essentially self-reflective, subjective, and introspective nature of analyses of other societies (e.g. Preucel ed. 1991; Hodder 1982; Shanks and Tilley 1987, 1988; Geertz 1973). An awareness of this fact may help us to strive more effectively to achieve a higher level of "objectivity" – albeit with a suspicion of the unattainable nature of that goal. But we can also, at times, simply embrace the essentially subjective and introspective nature of history and archaeology and seek from it personal, philosophical insights.

In this regard, the study of the ancient Maya is fascinating precisely because their civilization appears to be so different from our own. The structure of ecological adaptations, settlement patterns, and political and economic institutions could not be more unlike the Western, Mesopotamian, Judeo-Christian tradition of our own civilization. For at least 6000 years, the hallmarks of the Western tradition have been linear concepts of time, monocultural agricultural systems, overproduction and exchange of surplus in full market economies, technology-driven development, a long history of attempts to separate religious and political authority, and judgmental gods concerned with individual, personal moral conduct. As we learn from the Maya, none of these traits is universal, none of them was characteristic of Classic Maya civilization, and none of them is critical to the florescence of high civilization.

Too often scholars and the public view non-Western societies with an implicit, unconscious condescension. We tend to regard their political and economic systems as incomplete ("less evolved") versions of our own. Ideology and cosmology are viewed as detailed esoteric collections of ideas fascinating for scholarly study and for a curious public. We also tend to emphasize aspects of ancient religion that attempted control of nature, "primitive science" (in the Maya case, not so primitive at all!). In so doing, we ignore the personal and philosophical challenges of experiencing another worldview – an alternative perspective on existence and death. For example, Maya archaeology is filled with descriptions of burials, tombs, discussions of Xibalba (the Maya underworld), and consideration of rituals of veneration of deified royal ancestors. Only recently have archaeologists begun to describe more holistically the nature of Maya ancestor worship. The ancient Maya did not simply venerate their dead; rather, both elites and nonelites "lived" with their ancestors (McAnany 1995). Buried beneath the floors of their homes and in household shrines, they venerated them daily as intercessors with the gods and cosmic forces. These common ancestors defined their political and social institutions. Maya beliefs and attitudes toward death should be regarded as a fundamental aspect of their worldview and an approach to the basic questions of existence.

As argued at the beginning of this text (Chapter 2), many fundamental aspects of ancient and modern cultures address existential questions: Why death? What is my identity? What is the broader context of my existence? Our own society continues to confront these metaphysical and moral concerns with systems of belief and identity. From an openly philosophical, subjective, and postmodern perspective our society and its science are no wiser than the Maya priests and shamans in the face of these mysteries. For that reason we can study the ancient Maya, and other non-Western cultures, as sources of alternative views of reality and of contemplation of our own culturally ingrained worldviews. We can view the Classic Maya not as a "less developed" society trying only to control the forces of nature and to survive economically. Instead they can be regarded as fellow travelers – who simply chose a different path – through the darkness.

# Bibliographical essay

CHAPTER 2

Excellent summaries of the geography of Mesoamerica and the concept of Mesoamerica as a culture area are provided by West (1964), Helms (1975), and Porter-Weaver (1993), building on Kirchoff's important essay (1943). Discussion of subregions and highland-versus-lowland distinctions is found in West (1964), Sanders (1973), and Sanders and Price (1968). The "isthmian zone" concept is elaborated by Parsons (1978) and Lowe (1978). Debates over alternative chronological schemes can be found in Wolf (1976), Sabloff (1990), Sanders, Parsons, and Santley (1979), and D. Rice (1993a). Broader processual and postprocessual trends in anthropological and archaeological interpretation and theory have been discussed in numerous recent texts and collected essays, including those of Miller and Tilley (1984), Demarest and Conrad (1992), Preucel (1991), Shanks and Tilley (1987), Tilley (1990), and Hodder (1982, 1985), among others. Recent developments in postmodern, poststructuralist, and postprocessual theory can be found in the primary works of Derrida, Foucault, Bourdieu, etc., and summaries of the nature and relevance of such theory for anthropology have been provided by Knauft (1996) and for archaeology by Tilley (1990).

CHAPTER 3

Excellent histories of Maya archaeology and changing interpretive approaches are given by Brunhouse (1973), Hammond (1983), Bernal (1977), Willey and Sabloff (1974), and especially Sabloff (1990). Fascinating excerpts from the works of the original explorers have been collected by Wauchope (1965) and Deuel (1967). A clever and amusing discussion of the diffusionist and "crackpot" theories on the origin of the Mesoamerican peoples is given by Wauchope (1962), and a more recent review can be found in Feder (1990). Changing trends in Maya settlement studies have been reviewed by Fash (1994). A concise popular review of the history of the decipherment of Maya writing is found in Michael Coe's 1992 text, *Breaking the Maya Code*.

CHAPTER 4

Evidence on the peopling of the New World is reviewed and discussed in Lynch (1991), Taylor and Meighan (1978), and Dillehay and Meltzer (1991), and recent syntheses of the Archaic period and the development of early village life and

298

agriculture are given by Lowe (1978), Stark (1981), and in many chapters in Blake (1999). Alternative interpretations and debate of the Formative and Olmec problem in eastern Mesoamerica can be found in Sharer and Grove (1989), Fowler (1991), and Benson (1981). Most recent discoveries and interpretations that are discussed here on the archaeology of the Middle and Late Preclassic periods in the Maya highland, including those at Kaminaljuyu and Abaj Takalik, have been published only in Spanish in the annual *Simposio de Arqueologia de Guatemala* volumes and in monographs and theses of the Guatemalan universities of San Carlos and del Valle. Hatch's synthesis (1997) is especially important for our revised understanding of the urban nature of Late Preclassic Kaminaljuyu. The data and debates on the development of complex society in the Maya lowlands were summarized in a 1977 edited volume (Adams 1977) but, as discussed in the chapter, these perspectives now require radical revision in light of subsequent discoveries at Nakbe (Hansen 1991, 1992, 1997); El Mirador (Dahlin 1984; Matheny 1986, 1987; Clark *et al.* n.d.); Cerros (Freidel and Schele 1998); Santa Leticia (Demarest 1986); Kaminaljuyu (Hatch 1997; Braswell 2003b); and many other sites.

## CHAPTER 5

General discussions of the nature of Classic Maya centers and settlement, as well as diagnostics of the Classic period, can be found in recent syntheses, e.g. Sharer (1994), Henderson (1997), Culbert (1998, 1994), Coe (1993), Hammond (1990), Marcus (1983b), and Sabloff (1990). More technical consideration of settlement pattern interpretation and problems has been synthesized by Ashmore (1981), Chase, Chase, and White (2001), Montmollin (1989), and more recently by Fash (1994). The most recent interpretations of the role of Teotihuacan in Maya history are found in Braswell (2003c). Perspectives here also rely heavily on conceptions of Maya political ideology presented in more detail by Demarest (1992b), Freidel (1992), McAnany (1995), and Webster (1999).

## CHAPTER 6

Considerations of Maya household group size and clusterings are discussed in Ashmore (1981). The most recent systematic review of evidence on regional Classic period populations in the Maya lowlands is given in Culbert and Rice (1990). That volume also includes consideration of the daunting problems of demographic estimation and interpretation. Perspectives on the nature of ancient lowland Maya subsistence adaptations have continued to be a subject of debate, disagreement, and new discoveries. A good sample of these varied and changing views is given by sequential collections of articles by paleoecologists and archaeologists edited by Turner and Harrison (1978), Flannery (1982), Pohl (1985), and more recently Fedick (1996). In turn, the demographic implications of subsistence interpretations are debated in the volume edited by Culbert and D. Rice (1990). Overviews of hydraulic systems in the lowlands by Scarborough (1996, 1998) provide the most recent data and a somewhat different position from this text. A good synthesis of the Late Classic environmental landscape is provided by

D. Rice (1993b). The most current summaries of evidence on Petén environment, agricultural systems, faunal assemblages, and paleodiet are given in the introductory chapters of respective monographs of the Vanderbilt Petexbatun Regional Archaeological Project on paleoecology and agricultural systems (Dunning and Beach in press), paleofauna (Emery in press), and paleodiet (Wright in press).

## CHAPTER 7

Unlike this chapter, Maya economics – in terms of studies of production, exchange, and consumption of goods – is usually not treated discretely from subsistence and settlement in general considerations of the Classic Maya. Nonetheless, excellent syntheses are available on the economics of individual commodities, such as salt (Andrews 1983); obsidian and chert (e.g. Aoyama 1999, 2001; Hester and Shafer 1984; Hester et al. 1983; P. Rice et al. 1985; McAnany 1989; Shafer and Hester 1994); and ceramic production and exchange (e.g. Bishop 1980, 1994; Fry 1979, 1980; P. Rice 1981, 1987b). Michael and Sophie Coe (1996) have written an excellent popular study of chocolate, including its Pre-Columbian production and uses. A recent volume edited by Masson and Freidel (2002) deals with a number of issues discussed in this chapter from various theoretical and methodological perspectives. More general treatments of issues in Maya economics and energetics have been provided by Abrams (1987), McAnany (1993), P. Rice (1987a), and Sanders and Santley (1983).

## CHAPTER 8

Maya religion has received more emphasis than any other aspect of ancient Maya culture. Detailed treatment is provided in most major general texts (see for example Sharer 1994; Freidel et al. 1993; Coe 1978; Miller 1986; Schele and Miller 1986). More detailed studies of the deities and rituals are given by Schellhas (1904), Thompson (1970), Leon-Portilla (1973), and more recently by Taube (1992). Classic Maya sacrifice is discussed in detail by Schele (1984), Joralemon (1974), and Stuart (1984), and more broadly in Schele and Miller (1986). Classic period ancestor worship and its prevalence at all levels of Maya society have been considered in detail by McAnany (1995) and Freidel et al. (1993). Shamanism has been explored by Schele and Freidel (1990), Freidel et al. (1993), Stuart (1995), and many others, all drawing heavily on ethnography and ethnohistory (e.g. Gossen 1974; Laughlin 1977; Nash 1970; D. Tedlock 1985; Thompson 1970; B. Tedlock 1992; Vogt 1976; Tozzer 1941; Edmonson 1982, 1986). Detailed consideration of Maya calendrics and astronomy is given in Bishop Landa's original work (Tozzer 1941) and many summary treatments by archaeologists and ethnohistorians (e.g. Thompson 1942, 1971; Morley 1915; Kelley 1976; Sharer 1994). Considerations of the role of cosmology and sacred geography in architecture and site and structure have recently been published by Ashmore (1991), Aveni (1980, 1992), Aveni and Hartung (1986), Benson (1981b), Brady (1997), Brady et al. (1997), Coggins (1979), and Demarest et al. (2003). The general theoretical perspective on the role of ideology in Maya politics and site structure given here is detailed further in Demarest (1989, 1992a,

1992b), McAnany (1995), Benson (1981b), Schele and Freidel (1990), Freidel (1992), and Freidel and Schele (1988a, 1988b), which in turn draw heavily on the concepts of Eliade (1954, 1961), Geertz (1980), and Tambiah (1976, 1977).

## CHAPTER 9

Classic Maya political history has been well summarized in recent texts. The epigraphic terms and issues have been summarized by Stuart (1995) and have been applied and debated in the important volume edited by Culbert (1991). The most complete summary of dynastic history, together with discussion of terms and some alternative interpretations, can be found in Martin and Grube (2000). Debate and discussion of aspects of Late Classic politics are also given in the volume edited by Sabloff and Henderson (1993). Speculative reconstructions of Classic Maya history have also been provided by a series of lively volumes by Schele, Freidel, and Mathews (Schele and Freidel 1990; Freidel *et al.* 1993; Schele and Mathews 1998). Interpretations of Classic Maya political dynamics here rely on interpretations by Demarest (1992b), Freidel (1992), Marcus (1993), Tambiah (1976, 1977, 1984), and especially Geertz (1980). Also see Sharer (1994: 491–512) for a good summary of some of the various alternative theories on Maya political organization. The debate on Maya politics published in *Current Anthropology* (1996, vol. 37, no. 5) also highlights the controversies on these issues and the variability in Classic Maya political formations. A new interpretation of lowland Maya political systems and political ideology is in P. Rice (in press), while a speculative synthesis on Classic Maya warfare and alliance is being completed by Freidel (in press).

The Early Classic interaction with Mexico has been most completely described and debated in the recent volume of essays edited by Braswell (2003c). The period of interregional alliances in the sixth and seventh centuries has been most completely described by Martin and Grube (1995, 1996, and 2000). Excellent alternative interpretations of Late Classic regionalism and political history are given in the volumes edited by Culbert (1991) and Sabloff and Henderson (1993) and in the works by Martin and Grube (2000), Schele and Mathews (1998), and Sharer (1999). Interpretations here of the political history of the ninth and tenth centuries in this and the following chapter draw upon the recent edited volume on the Terminal Classic (Demarest, P. Rice, and D. Rice 2004), which includes summaries of evidence, interpretation, and debates by fifty-five scholars representing dozens of projects across the lowlands.

## CHAPTER 10

Issues of causality in the decline of civilizations are most completely analyzed by Tainter (1988) and in the various chapters in the collection edited by Yoffee and Cowgill (1988). Eighth-century conditions precipitating the collapse are described by various archaeologists in the volume edited by Sabloff and Henderson (1993) and the publications of the Vanderbilt Petexbatun Archaeological Project (Demarest 1997, in press; Foias and Bishop 1997; Foias in press; Dunning, Beach, and Rue 1997; Dunning and Beach in press; Inomata 1997, in press; Escobedo 1997; Valdes 1997; Wright 1997, in press; Emery 1997, in press). Specific data reconstructions for the various eighth to tenth century regional transitions, transformations, or declines of Classic period civilization rely heavily on the most recent syntheses of regional and subregional Terminal Classic culture history in the volume edited by Demarest, P. Rice, and D. Rice (2004). The latter volume builds upon and updates earlier synthetic collections (Culbert 1973; Sabloff and Andrews 1986; Sabloff and Henderson 1993) yet many of the fifty-five authors in the more recent compendium contest the very concept of a uniform and profound "collapse" of Classic Maya civilization, a view reflected in my text.

## CHAPTER 11

As this volume is focused on the Classic period of Maya civilization, the Postclassic and Colonial periods are given only a cursory summary. Many excellent edited volumes present the variable regional evidence on the Postclassic, particularly the collections edited by Chase and Rice (1985) and Sabloff and Andrews (1986). The contentious issue of continuity versus discontinuity between Classic and Postclassic culture is debated by different authors from contrasting perspectives in the volume edited by Demarest, P. Rice, and D. Rice (2004). Ethnohistorical and archaeological evidence on lowland and highland Postclassic states is synthesized in the volumes by Carmack (1973, 1981), Fox (1987), Freidel and Sabloff (1984), Hill (1992), Jones (1998), and P. Rice (1987c). Recent interpretations of the ethnohistorical record can be found in Restall (1997), Famiss (1984, 1987), and G. Jones (1989, 1998). Recent Maya activism is described by Fischer and Brown (1996), Nelson (1999), and Fischer (2001), and the role of archaeology in collaborating with contemporary Maya communities and the Maya movement has been described by García and Demarest (García 2001; García et al. 2002; Demarest and García 2003).

# References

Abrams, Elliot M. 1987. Economic Specialization and Construction Personnel in Classic Period Copan, Honduras. *American Antiquity* 52: 485–499.

Abrams, Elliot M., and David G. Rue. 1988. The Causes and Consequences of Deforestation Among the Prehistoric Maya. *Human Ecology* 16: 377–395.

Adams, Richard E.W. 1969. Maya Archaeology 1958–1968: A Review. *Latin American Research Review* 4(2): 3–45.

1973. Maya Collapse: Transformation and Termination in the Ceramic Sequence at Altar de Sacrificios. In *The Classic Maya Collapse*, ed. T.P. Culbert, pp. 133–163. Albuquerque: University of New Mexico Press.

ed. 1975. Preliminary Reports on Archaeological Investigations in the Río Bec Area, Campeche, Mexico. In *Archaeological Investigations on the Yucatan Peninsula*. Middle American Research Institute Publication 31. pp. 103–146. New Orleans: Tulane University.

Adams, Richard E.W., ed. 1977. *The Origins of Maya Civilization*. Albuquerque: University of New Mexico Press.

1980. Swamps, Canals, and the Locations of Ancient Maya Cities. *Antiquity* 54: 206–214.

1981. Settlement Patterns of the Central Yucatan and Southern Campeche Regions. In *Lowland Maya Settlement Patterns*, ed. W.A. Ashmore, pp. 211–257. Albuquerque: University of New Mexico Press.

1983. Ancient Land Use and Culture History in the Pasión River Region. In *Prehistoric Settlement Patterns: Essays in Honor of Gordon R. Willey*, ed. E.Z. Vogt and R.M. Leventhal, pp. 319–335. Albuquerque: University of New Mexico Press.

1990. Archaeological Research at the Lowland Maya City of Rio Azul. *Latin American Antiquity* 1: 23–41.

Adams, Richard E.W., E. Wyllys Andrews IV and E. Wyllys Andrews V. 1980. *Excavations at Dzibilchaltun, Yucatan, Mexico*. Middle American Research Institute Publication 48. New Orleans: Tulane University.

Adams, Richard E.W., Walter E. Brown, Jr., and T. Patrick Culbert. 1981. Radar Mapping, Archaeology, and Ancient Maya Land Use. *Science* 213: 1457–463.

Adams, Richard E.W., and Norman D.C. Hammond. 1981. Maya Archaeology, 1976–1980: A Review of Major Publications. *Journal of Field Archaeology* 9: 487–512.

Adams, Richard E.W., and Richard C. Jones. 1981. Spatial Patterns and Regional Growth among Maya Sites. *American Antiquity* 46: 301–322.

Adams, Richard E.W., H. R. Robichaux, Fred Valdez, Jr., Brett A. Houk, and Ruth Mathews. 2004. Transformations, Periodicity, and Urban Development in the Three Rivers Region. In *The Terminal Classic in the Maya Lowlands: Collapse, Transition, and Transformation*, ed. A.A. Demarest, P.M. Rice, and D. Rice. Boulder: University Press of Colorado.

Adams, Robert McC. 1965. *Land Behind Baghdad*. Chicago: University of Chicago Press.

1969. The Study of Ancient Mesopotamian Settlement Patterns and the Problem of Urban Origins. *Sumer* 25: 111–124.

1981. *The Heartland of Cities*. Chicago: University of Chicago Press.

1984. Mesopotamian Social Evolution: Old Outlooks, New Goals. In *On the Evolution of Complex Societies: Essays in Honor of Harry Holjer*, ed. T. Earle, pp. 79–129. Malibu, CA: Undena Press.

Agurcia, Ricardo and William L. Fash. 1991. Maya Artistry Unearthed. *National Geographic* September 1991: 94–101.

Aldenderfer, Mark. 1991. Functional Evidence for Lapidary and Carpentry Craft Specialties in the Late Classic of the Central Peten Lakes Region. *Ancient Mesoamerica* 2: 205–214.

Aldenderfer, Mark, Larry Kimball, and April Sievert. 1989. Microwear Analysis in the Maya Lowlands: The Use of Functional Data in a Complex Society Setting. *Journal of Field Archaeology* 16: 47–60.

Alvarado, Pedro de. 1924. *An Account of the Conquest of Guatemala in 1524*, trans. S.J. Mackie. New York: The Cortes Society.

Anawalt, Patricia R. 1981. *Indian Clothing before Cortés: Mesoamerican Costumes from the Codices*. Norman: University of Oklahoma Press.

Andrews, Anthony P. 1980a. The Salt Trade of the Ancient Maya. *Archaeology* 33(4): 24–33.

1980b. Salt and the Maya: Major Prehispanic Trading Spheres. *Atlatl* 1: 1–17.

1983. *Maya Salt Production and Trade*. Tucson: University of Arizona Press.

1984. Long-Distance Exchange Among the Maya: A Comment to Marcus. *American Antiquity* 49: 826–828.

1990. The Role of Trading Ports in Maya Civilization. In *Vision and Revision in Maya Studies*, ed. F.S. Clancy and P.D. Harrison, pp. 159–168. Albuquerque: University of New Mexico Press.

1993. Late Postclassic Lowland Maya Archaeology. *Journal of World Prehistory* 7: 35–69.

Andrews, Anthony P., Tomas Gallareta N., J. Fernando Robles, Rafael Cobos P., and Pura Cervera R. 1988. Isla Cerritos, an Itza Trading Port on the North Coast of Yucatan, Mexico. *National Geographic Research* 4(2): 196–207.

Andrews, Anthony P., Helen V. Michel, Fred H. Stross, and Pura Cervera R. 1989. The Obsidian Trade at Isla Cerritos, Yucatan, Mexico. *Journal of Field Archaeology* 16: 355–363.

Andrews, Anthony P., and Shirley B. Mock. 2002. New Perspectives on the Prehispanic Maya Salt Trade. In *Ancient Maya Political Economies*, eds.

M.A. Masson and D.A. Freidel, pp. 307–334. Walnut Creek, CA: AltaMira Press.

Andrews, Anthony P., and J. Fernando Robles. 1985. Chichen Itza and Coba: An Itza-Maya Standoff in Early Postclassic Yucatan. In *The Lowland Maya Postclassic*, ed. A.F. Chase and P.M. Rice, pp. 62–72. Austin: University of Texas Press.

Andrews IV, E. Wyllys. 1965. Archaeology and Prehistory in the Northern Maya Lowlands: An Introduction. In *Handbook of Middle American Indians*, vol. 2: *Archaeology of Southern Mesoamerica, Part 1*, ed. G.R. Willey, pp. 288–330. Austin: University of Texas Press.

Andrews IV, E. Wyllys, and Anthony P. Andrews. 1975. *A Preliminary Study of the Ruins of Xcaret, Quintana Roo, Mexico, with Notes on Other Archaeological Remains on the Central East Coast of the Yucatan Peninsula.* Middle American Research Institute Publication 40. New Orleans: Tulane University.

Andrews IV, E. Wyllys, and E. Wyllys Andrews V. 1980. *Excavations at Dzibilchaltun, Yucatan, Mexico.* Middle American Research Institute Publication 48. New Orleans: Tulane University.

Andrews V, E. Wyllys. 1981. *Handbook of Middle American Indians, Supplement 1: Archaeology*, ed. J.A. Sabloff, pp. 313–344. Austin: University of Texas Press.

1986. Olmec Jades from Chacsinkin, Yucatan, and Maya Ceramics from La Venta, Tabasco. In *Research and Reflections in Archaeology and History: Essays in Honor of Doris Stone*, ed. E.W. Andrews V, pp. 11–49. Middle American Research Institute Publication 57. New Orleans: Tulane University.

Andrews V, E. Wyllys, and Norman D.C. Hammond. 1990. Redefinition of the Swasey Phase at Cuello, Belize. *American Antiquity* 54: 570–584.

Andrews V, E. Wyllys, William Ringle III, Philip J. Barnes, Alfredo Barrera R., and Tomas Gallareta N. 1984. Komchen: An Early Maya Community in Northwest Yucatan. *XVII Mesa Redonda, Sociedad Mexicana de Antropología: San Cristóbal de las Casas, Chiapas*, Vol. 1, pp. 73–92. Mexico, D.F.

Andrews V, E. Wyllys, and Jeremy A. Sabloff. 1986. Classic to Postclassic: A Summary Discussion. In *Late Lowland Maya Civilization: Classic to Postclassic*, ed. J.A. Sabloff and E.W. Andrews V, pp. 433–456. Albuquerque: University of New Mexico Press.

Annan, Kofi. 1997. Report of the Secretary-General on the Situation in Somalia. Report to the United Nations Security Council, New York.

Aoyama, Kazuo. 1994. Microwear Analysis in the Southeast Maya Lowlands: Two Case Studies at Copan, Honduras. *Latin American Antiquity* 6: 129–144.

1995. Socioeconomic Implications of Chipped Stone from the La Entrada Region, Western Honduras. *Journal of Field Archaeology* 21: 133–145.

1996. Exchange, Craft Specialization, and Ancient Maya State Formation: A Study of Chipped Stone Artifacts from the Southeast Maya Lowlands. Ph.D. dissertation, University of Pittsburgh, Pittsburgh, PA.

1999. *Ancient Maya State, Urbanism, Exchange, and Craft Specialization: Chipped Stone Evidence of the Copan Valley and the La Entrada Region, Honduras.* University of Pittsburgh Memoirs of Latin American Archaeology No. 12. Pittsburgh: University of Pittsburgh.

2001. Classic Maya State, Urbanism, and Exchange: Chipped Stone Evidence of the Copan Valley and its Hinterland. *American Anthropologist* 103: 346–361.

Arnauld, M. Charlotte 1986. *Archéologie de l'Habitat en Alta Verapaz, Guatemala.* Collection Etudes Mesoamericaines 10. Mexico, D.F.: Centre D'Etudes Mexicaines et Centramericaines.

Arnold, Dean E. 1978. Ceramic Variability, Environment, and Culture History among the Pokom in the Valley of Guatemala. In *The Spatial Organization of Culture*, ed. I. Hodder, pp. 39–59. London: Duckworth.

1985. *Ceramic Theory and Cultural Process.* New York: Cambridge University Press.

Arroyo, Bárbara. 2001. La Regionalización en la Costa del Pacífico: Sus Primeras Pobladores. In *XIV Simposio de Investigaciones Arqueologicas en Guatemala*, eds. J.P. Laporte, A.C. de Suasnávar, and B. Arroyo, pp. 3–9. Guatemala: Museo de Antropología y Etnología de Guatemala, Instituto Antropología e Historia, and Asociación Tikal.

Ashmore, Wendy A., ed. 1980. Discovering Early Classic Quirigua: A Unique Opportunity to Examine an Important Sector of the Early Center. *Expedition* 23(1): 35–44.

ed. 1981. *Lowland Maya Settlement Patterns.* Albuquerque: University of New Mexico Press.

1991. Site-Planning Principles and Concepts of Directionality Among the Ancient Maya. *Latin American Antiquity* 2: 199–226.

Ashmore, Wendy A., and Robert J. Sharer. 1975. *A Revitalization Movement at Late Classic Tikal.* Paper presented at the Area Seminar in Ongoing Research, Westchester State College. Philadelphia, PA: University Museum.

Ashmore, Wendy, Jason Yaeger, and Cynthia Robin. 2004. Commoner Sense: Late and Terminal Classic Social Strategies in the Xunantunich Area. In *The Terminal Classic in the Maya Lowlands: Collapse, Transition, and Transformation*, ed. A. A. Demarest, P. M. Rice, and D. Rice. Boulder: University Press of Colorado.

Aveni, Anthony F. 1979. Venus and the Maya. *American Scientist* 6: 274–285.

1980. *Skywatchers of Ancient Mexico.* Austin: University of Texas Press.

1992. *The Sky in Maya Literature.* New York: Oxford University Press.

Aveni, Anthony F., and Horst Hartung. 1986. *Maya City Planning and the Calendar.* Transactions of the American Philosophical Society, Vol. 76, Pt. 7. Philadelphia: American Philosophical Society.

Ball, Joseph W. 1977a. The Rise of the Northern Maya Chiefdoms: A Sociopro-cessual Analysis. In *The Origins of Maya Civilization*, ed. R.E.W. Adams, pp. 101–132. Albuquerque: University of New Mexico Press.

1977b. *The Archaeological Ceramics of Becan, Campeche, Mexico.* Middle American Research Institute Publication 43. New Orleans: Tulane University.

1983. Teotihuacan, the Maya, and Ceramic Interchange: A Contextual Perspective. In *Highland–Lowland Interaction in Mesoamerica: Interdisciplinary Approaches*, ed. A.G. Miller, pp. 125–146. Washington, DC: Dumbarton Oaks, Trustees for Harvard University.

1993. Pottery, Potters, Palaces, and Politics: Some Socioeconomic and Political Implications of Late Classic Maya Ceramic Industries. In *Lowland Maya Civilization in the Eighth Century A.D.* eds. J.A. Sabloff and J. Henderson, pp. 243–272. Washington DC: Dumbarton Oaks, Trustees for Harvard University.

Ball, Joseph W., and Jennifer T. Taschek. 1991. Late Classic Lowland Maya Political Organization and Central-Place Analysis: New Insights from the Upper Belize Valley. *Ancient Mesoamerica* 2: 149–165.

2001. The Buena Vista-Cahal Pech Royal Court: Multi-Palace Court Mobility and Usage in a Petty Lowland Maya Kingdom. In *Royal Courts of the Ancient Maya*, vol. 2, eds. T. Inomata and S. Houston, pp. 165–200. Boulder, CO: Westview Press.

Barrientos Q., Tomás. 1997a. *Desarrollo Evolutivo del Sistema de Canales Hidráulicos en Kaminaljuyu*. Unpublished licenciatura thesis, Departamento de Arqueología, Universidad del Valle de Guatemala, Guatemala.

1997b. Evolución Tecnologica del Sistema de Canales Hidraulicos en Kaminaljuyú y sus Implicaciones Sociopoliticas. In *X Simposio de Investigaciones Arqueológicas en Guatemala, 1996*, pp. 61–70. Guatemala: Ministerio de Cultura y Deportes, Instituto de Antropología e Historia, Asociación Tikal.

Barrientos Q., Tomás, Brigitte Kovacevich, Michael Callaghan, and Arthur A. Demarest, eds. 2003. *Proyecto Arqueologico Cancuen, Informe Preliminar No. 5, Temporada 2003*. Guatemala and Nashville, TN: Instituto de Antropología e Historia and Department of Anthropology, Vanderbilt University.

Beach, Timothy. 1996. Estudios de Catenas, Fertilidad, y Fosfatos de Suelos. In *Proyecto Arqueológico Punta de Chimino 1996, Informe Preliminar*, ed. A.A. Demarest, H. Escobedo, and M. O'Mansky, pp. 86–94. Guatemala and Nashville, TN: Instituto de Antropología e Historia and Department of Anthropology, Vanderbilt University.

Beach, Timothy, and Nicholas P. Dunning. 1995. Ancient Maya Terracing and Modern Conservation in the Petén Rainforest of Guatemala. *Journal of Soil and Water Conservation* 50: 138–145.

Becker, Marshall J. 1973a. Archaeological Evidence for Occupational Specialization among the Classic Period Maya at Tikal, Guatemala. *American Antiquity* 38: 396–406.

1973b. The Evidence for Complex Exchange Systems Among the Ancient Maya. *American Antiquity* 38: 222–223.

Bell, James A. 1987. Review of *Reading the Past*, by Ian Hodder. *Archaeological Review from Cambridge* 6: 74–86.

1991. Anarchy and Archaeology. In *Processual and Postprocessual Archaeologies: Multiple Ways of Knowing the Past*, ed. R.W. Preucel, pp. 71–80. Carbondale: Center for Archaeological Investigations, Southern Illinois University.

Benco, Nancy. 1988. Morphological Standardization: An Approach to the Study of Craft Specialization. In *A Pot for All Reasons: Ceramic Ecology Revisited*, ed. C.C. Kolb and L.M. Lackey, pp. 57–72. Philadelphia, PA: Temple University, Laboratory of Anthropology.

Benson, Elizabeth P. 1997. *Birds and Beasts of Ancient Latin America*. Gainesville: University Press of Florida.

Benson, Elizabeth P., ed. 1981a. *The Olmec and Their Neighbors: Essays in Memory of Matthew W. Stirling*. Washington, DC: Dumbarton Oaks, Trustees for Harvard University.

Benson, Elizabeth P. 1981b. *Mesoamerican Sites and World-Views: A Conference at Dumbarton Oaks, October 16th and 17th, 1976*. Washington, DC: Dumbarton Oaks, Trustees for Harvard University.

Bentley, G. Carter. 1986. Indigenous States of Southeast Asia. *Annual Review of Anthropology* 15: 275–305.

Berdan, Francis F. 1975. Trade, Tribute, and Markets in the Aztec Empire. Ph.D. dissertation, Department of Anthropology, University of Texas, Austin.

   1986. Enterprise and Empire in Aztec and Early Colonial Mexico. In *Research in Economic Anthropology*, Supplement 2, ed. B.L. Isaac, pp. 281–302. Greenwich: JAI Press.

   1993. Trade and Tribute in the Aztec Empire. In *Current Topics in Aztec Studies: Essays in Honor of Dr H. B. Nicholson*, pp. 71–84. San Diego Museum Papers, vol. 30.

Berlin, Heinrich. 1958. El glifo 'emblema' en las inscripciones mayas. *Journal de la Société des Américanistes de Paris, N.S.* 47: 111–119.

   1959. Glifos nominales en el sarcofago de Palenque. *Humanidades* 2(10): 1–8.

Bernal, Ignacio. 1977. Maya Antiquaries. In *Social Process in Maya Prehistory: Studies in Honour of Sir Eric Thompson*, ed. N.D.C. Hammond, pp. 10–44. New York: Academic Press.

Bernasconi, Antonio, and José Antonio Calderon. 1946. *Informe sobre la Cuidad Arruinada en la Provincia de Chiapas a tres Leguas del Pueblo de Palenque*. Mexico: National Institute of Anthropology and History.

Beshers, James M. 1967. *Population Processes in Social Systems*. New York: Free Press.

Bettelheim, Bruno. 1962. *Symbolic Wounds: Puberty Rites and the Envious Male*. New York: Collier Books.

Bey III, George J., Craig A. Hanson, and William M. Ringle. 1997. Classic to Postclassic at Ek Balam, Yucatán: Architectural and Ceramic Evidence for Redefining the Transition. *Latin American Antiquity* 8: 237–254.

Binford, Lewis. 1962. Archaeology as Anthropology. *American Antiquity* 28: 217–225.

   1965. Archaeological Systematics and the Study of Culture Process. *American Antiquity* 31: 203–210.

Bishop, Ronald L. 1980. Aspects of Ceramic Compositional Modeling. In *Models and Methods in Regional Exchange*, ed. R. Fry, pp. 47–65. SAA Papers No.1. Washington, DC: Society for American Archaeology.

   1994. Pre-Columbian Pottery: Research in the Maya Region. In *Archaeometry of Pre-Columbian Sites and Artifacts*, ed. D.A. Scott and P. Meyers, pp. 15–65. Los Angeles: The Getty Conservation Institute.

Bishop, Ronald L., Marilyn P. Beaudry, Richard M. Leventhal, and Robert J. Sharer. 1986. Compositional Analysis of Copador and Related Pottery in the Southeast Maya Area. In *The Southeast Maya Periphery*, ed. P.A. Urban and E.M. Schortman, pp. 143–167. Austin: University of Texas Press.

Bishop, Ronald L., Arthur A. Demarest, and Robert J. Sharer. 1989. Chemical Analysis and the Interpretation of Late Preclassic Intersite Ceramic Patterns in the Southeast Highlands of Mesoamerica. In *Archaeology of the Pacific Coast and Highlands of Mesoamerica*, eds. F.J. Bove and L. Heller, pp. 135–146. Tempe: Arizona State University Press.

Bishop, Ronald L., Edward V. Sayre, and Joan Mishara. 1989. *Compositional and Structural Characterization of Mayan and Costa Rican Jadeites*. Washington, DC: Conservation Analytical Laboratory, Smithsonian Institute.

Blake, Michael. 1991. An Emerging Early Formative Chiefdom at Paso de la Amada, Chiapas, Mexico. In *The Formation of Complex Society in Southeastern Mesoamerica*, ed. W.R. Fowler, Jr., pp. 27–46. Boca Raton, FL: CRC Press.

Blake, Michael, ed. 1999. *The Evolution of Archaic and Formative Cultures along the Pacific Coast of Latin America*. Pullman, WA: Washington State University Press.

Blake, Michael, and John E. Clark. 1999. The Emergence of Hereditary Inequality: The Case of Pacific Coastal Chiapas, Mexico. In *Pacific Latin America in Prehistory: The Evolution of Archaic and Formative Cultures*, ed. M. Blake, pp. 55–73. Pullman, WA: Washington University Press.

Blake, Michael, John E. Clark, Barbara Voorhies, George Michaels, Michael W. Love, Mary E. Pye, Arthur A. Demarest, and Bárbara Arroyo. 1995. Radiocarbon Chronology for the Late Archaic and Formative Periods on the Pacific Coast of Southeastern Mesoamerica. *Ancient Mesoamerica* 6: 161–183.

Blanton, Richard E. 1976. The Role of Symbiosis in Adaptation and Sociocultural Change in the Valley of Mexico. In *The Valley of Mexico*, ed. E.R. Wolf, pp. 181–202. Albuquerque: University of New Mexico Press.

1980. Cultural Ecology Reconsidered. *American Antiquity* 45: 145–151.

Blanton, Richard E., and Gary M. Feinman. 1984. The Mesoamerican World System. *American Anthropologist* 86: 673–682.

Blanton, Richard E., Gary M. Feinman, Stephen A. Kowaleski, Linda Nicholas, and Gary Feinman. 1999. *Ancient Oaxaca: The Monte Albán State*. Cambridge: Cambridge University Press.

Boggs, Stanley H. 1950. "Olmec" Pictographs in the Las Victorias Group, Chalchuapa Archaeological Zone, El Salvador. *Notes on Middle American Archaeology and Ethnology* 4(99): 85–92. Washington, DC: Carnegie Institution of Washington.

Boone, Elizabeth Hill, and Gordon R. Willey, eds. 1988. *The Southeast Classic Maya Zone*. Washington, DC: Dumbarton Oaks, Trustees for Harvard University.

Bourdieu, Pierre. 1977. *Outline of a Theory of Practice*. Cambridge Studies in Social Anthropology 16. Cambridge: Cambridge University Press.

1984. *Distinction: A Social Critique of the Judgment of Taste*. Translated by R. Nice. Cambridge, MA: Harvard University Press.

Bove, Frederick J., 1991. The Teotihuacan–Kaminaljuyu–Tikal Connection: A View from the South Coast of Guatemala. In *Sixth Palenque Round Table, 1986*, ed. V.M. Fields, pp. 135–142. Norman: University of Oklahoma Press.

Bove, Frederick J., ed. 1989. *New Frontiers in the Archaeology of the Pacific Coast of Southern Mesoamerica*. Anthropological Research Papers 39. Tempe: Arizona State University Press.

Bove, Frederick J., Sonia Medrano B., Brenda Lou P., and Bárbara Arroyo L., eds. 1993. *The Balberta Project: The Terminal Formative–Early Classic Transition on the Pacific Coast of Guatemala*. University of Pittsburgh Memoirs in Latin American Archaeology No. 6.

Bowditch, Charles P. 1910. *The Numeration, Calendar Systems, and Astronomical Knowledge of the Mayas*. Cambridge: Cambridge University Press.

Brady, James E. 1990. Investigaciones en la Cueva de "El Duende." In *Proyecto Arqueologico Regional Petexbatún, Informe Preliminar No. 2: Segunda Temporada*, eds. A.A. Demarest and S. Houston, pp. 334–352. Guatemala and Nashville, TN: Instituto de Antropología e Historia and Department of Anthropology, Vanderbilt University.

1991. Caves and Cosmovision at Utatlan. *California Anthropologist* 18: 1–10.

1994. El Impacto del Ritual en la Economía Maya. In *VII Simposio de Arqueología Guatemalteca*, eds. J.P. Laporte and H.L. Escobedo, pp. 87–91. Guatemala: Museo de Antropología y Etnología de Guatemala.

1997. Settlement, Architecture, and Cosmology: The Role of Caves in Determining the Placement of Architecture at Dos Pilas. *American Anthropologist* 99: 602–681.

Brady, James E., Joseph W. Ball, Ronald L. Bishop, Duncan C. Pring, Norman Hammond, and Rupert A. Housley. 1998. The Lowland Maya "Protoclassic": A Reconsideration of its Nature and Significance. *Ancient Mesoamerica* 9: 17–38.

Brady, James E., L. Fernando Luin, Carol Foncea, Lori E. Wright, and Sandra Villagrán de Brady. 1990. Investigaciones en la Cueva de Sangre y Otras Cuevas de la Región de Petexbatún. In *Proyecto Arqueologico Regional Petexbatún, Informe Preliminar No. 2: Segunda Temporada*, eds. A.A. Demarest and S. Houston, pp. 438–567. Guatemala and Nashville, TN: Instituto de Antropología e Historia and Department of Anthropology, Vanderbilt University.

Brady, James, and Irma Rodas. 1992. Hallazgos recientes y nuevas interpretaciones de la cueva de El Duende. In *V Simposio de Arqueología Guatemalteca, 1991*, eds. J.P. Laporte, H.L. Escobedo, and S. Villagrán de Brady, pp. 185–194. Guatemala: Ministerio de Cultura y Deportes, Instituto de Antropología e Historia, Asociación Tikal.

Brady, James E., Irma Rodas, Lori E. Wright, Katherine F. Emery, Nora Lopéz, Laura Stiver, and Robert Chatham. 1991. Proyecto Arqueológico Regional Petexbatun. In *Proyecto Arqueologico Regional Petexbatún, Informe Preliminar No. 3: Tercera Temporada*, eds. A.A. Demarest, T. Inomata, H.L. Escobedo, and J.W. Palka, pp. 652–748. Guatemala and Nashville, TN: Instituto de Antropología e Historia and Department of Anthropology, Vanderbilt University.

Brady, James E., Ann Scott, Allen Cobb, Irma Rodas, John Fogarty, and Monica Urquizú Sanchez. 1997. Glimpses of the Dark Side of the Petexbatún

Project: The Petexbatún Regional Cave Survey. *Ancient Mesoamerica* 8: 353–364.

Brasseur de Bourbourg, Charles Etienne. 1866. *Palenque et Autres Ruines de L'Ancienne Civilisation du Mexique*. Paris: Bertrand.

Braswell, Geoffrey. 1992. Obsidian Hydration Dating, the Coner Phase, and Revisionist Chronology at Copán, Honduras. *Latin American Antiquity* 3: 130–147.

2002. Praise the Gods and Pass the Obsidian?: The Organization of Ancient Economy in San Martín Jilotepeque, Guatemala. In *Ancient Maya Political Economies*, eds. M.A. Masson and D.A. Freidel, pp. 285–306. Walnut Creek, CA: AltaMira Press.

2003a. Introduction. In *The Maya and Teotihuacan: Reinterpreting Early Classic Interaction*, ed. G.E. Braswell, pp. 1–44. Austin: University of Texas Press.

2003b. Understanding Early Classic Interaction between Kaminaljuyu and Central Mexico. In *The Maya and Teotihuacan: Reinterpreting Early Classic Interaction*, ed. G.E. Braswell, pp. 105–142. Austin: University of Texas Press.

Braswell, Geoffrey. ed. 2003c. *The Maya and Teotihuacan: Reinterpreting Early Classic Interaction*. Austin: University of Texas Press.

Braswell, Geoffrey E., Joel D. Gunn, María del Rosario Domínguez C., William J. Folan, Laraine A. Fletcher, Abel Morales L., and Michael D. Glascock. 2004. Defining the Terminal Classic at Calakmul, Campeche. In *The Terminal Classic in the Maya Lowlands: Collapse, Transition, and Transformation*, ed. A.A. Demarest, P.M. Rice, and D. Rice. Boulder: University Press of Colorado.

Bricker, Victoria R. 1973. Algunas consecuencias religiosa y sociales del nativismo maya del siglo XIX. *America Indigena* 33: 327–348.

1977. The Caste War of Yucatan: The History of a Myth and the Myth of History. In *Anthropology and History in Yucatan*, ed. G.D. Jones, pp. 251–258. Austin: University of Texas Press.

1981. *The Indian Christ, the Indian King: The Historical Substrate of Maya Myth and Ritual*. Austin: University of Texas Press.

1986. *A Grammar of Mayan Hieroglyphs*. Middle American Research Institute Publication 56. New Orleans, Tulane University.

Bricker, Victoria R., and Gary H. Gossen, eds. 1989. *Ethnographic Encounters in Southern Mesoamerica: Essays in Honor of Evon Zartman Vogt, Jr.*, Studies on Culture and Society, No. 3. Albany: State University of New York.

Brothwell, Don, and Eric Higgs, eds. 1970. *Science in Archaeology: A Survey of Progress and Research*. New York: Praeger.

Brumfiel, Elizabeth. 1987. Consumption and Politics at Aztex Huexotla. *American Anthropologist*, 89: 676–686.

1998. The Multiple Identities of Aztec Craft Specialists. In *Craft and Social Identity*, ed. C.L. Costin and R. Wright. Archaeological Papers of the American Anthropological Association No. 8. Washington, DC: American Anthropological Association.

Brumfiel, Elizabeth M., and Timothy K. Earle, eds. 1987. *Specialization, Exchange, and Complex Societies*. Cambridge: Cambridge University Press.

Brunhouse, Robert L. 1971. *Sylvanus G. Morley and the World of the Ancient Mayas*. Norman: University of Oklahoma Press.

1973. *In Search of the Maya: The First Archaeologists*. Albuquerque: University of New Mexico Press.

Bullard, Jr., William R. 1952. Residential Property Walls at Mayapan. *Carnegie Institution of Washington Current Reports* 1(3): 36–44.

1960. Maya Settlement Patterns in Northeastern Petén, Guatemala. *American Antiquity* 25: 355–372.

Butzer, Karl W. 1976. *Early Hydraulic Civilization in Egypt: A Study in Cultural Ecology*. Chicago: University of Chicago Press.

1982. *Archaeology as Human Ecology: Method and Theory for a Contextual Approach*. Cambridge: Cambridge University Press.

Campbell, Lyle R. 1976. The Linguistic Prehistory of the Southern Mesoamerican Periphery. *XIV Mesa Redonda, Sociedad Mexicana de Antropología: Las Fronteras de Mesoamerica*, Vol. 1, pp. 157–183. Tegucigalpa, Honduras.

Campbell, Lyle R., and Terrence S. Kaufman. 1976. A Linguistic Look at the Olmecs. *American Antiquity* 41: 80–89.

Carlson, John B. 1981. A Geomantic Model for the Interpretation of Mesoamerican Sites: An Essay in Cross-Cultural Comparison. In *Mesoamerican Sites and World Views*, ed. E.P. Benson, pp. 143–215. Washington, DC: Dumbarton Oaks, Trustees for Harvard University.

Carmack, Robert M. 1973. *Quichean Civilization: The Ethnohistoric, Ethnographic, and Archaeological Sources*. Berkeley: University of California Press.

1981. *The Quiche Mayas of Utatlan: The Evolution of a Highland Guatemala Kingdom*. Norman: University of Oklahoma Press.

Carmean, Kelli, Nicholas Dunning, and Jeff Karl Kowalski. 2004. High Times in the Hill Country: A Perspective from the Terminal Classic Puuc Region. In *The Terminal Classic in the Maya Lowlands: Collapse, Transition, and Transformation*, ed. A.A. Demarest, P.M. Rice, and D. Rice. Boulder: University Press of Colorado.

Carneiro, Robert L. 1970. A Theory of the Origin of the State. *Science* 169: 733–738.

Castañeda, Quetzil E. 1996. *In the Museum of Maya Culture: Touring Chichén Itzá*. Minneapolis: University of Minnesota Press.

Castillo, Donaldo. 1991. La Ceramica de Abaj Takalik: Un Estudio Preliminar. In *II Simposio de Investigaciones Arqueológicas en Guatemala*. Guatemala: Ministerio de Cultura y Deportes, Instituto de Antropología e Historia, Asociación Tikal.

Charnay, Désiré. 1887. *The Ancient Cities of the New World*, trans. J. Gonino and H.S. Conant. New York: Harper and Brothers.

Chase, Arlen F. 1976. Topoxte and Tayasal: Ethnohistory in Archaeology. *American Antiquity* 41: 154–167.

1979. Regional Development in the Tayasal-Paxcaman Zone, El Petén Guatemala: A Preliminary Statement. *Ceramica de Cultura Maya* 11: 86–119.

1985a. Postclassic Petén Interaction Spheres: The View From Tayasal. In *The Lowland Maya Postclassic*, ed. A.F. Chase and P.M. Rice, pp. 184–205. Austin: University of Texas Press.

1985b. Troubled Times: Archaeology and Iconography of the Terminal Classic Southern Lowland Maya. In *Fifth Palenque Roundtable*, ed. V.M. Fields, pp. 103–114. San Francisco: Pre-Columbian Art Research Institute.

1991. Cycles of Time: Caracol in the Maya Realm. In *Sixth Palenque Round Table, 1986*, vol. 7, ed. V.M. Fields, pp. 32–42. Norman, OK: University of Oklahoma Press.

1992. Elites and the Organization of Classic Maya Society. In *Mesoamerican Elites: An Archaeological Perspective*, ed. D.Z. Chase and A.F. Chase, pp. 30–49. Norman: University of Oklahoma Press.

Chase, Arlen F., and Diane Z. Chase. 1987. *Investigations at the Classic Maya City of Caracol, Belize: 1985–1987*. San Francisco: Pre-Columbian Art Research Institute.

1996a. A Mighty Maya Nation: How Caracol Built an Empire by Cultivating its "Middle Class." *Archaeology* 49(5): 66–72.

1996b. More than Kin and King: Centralized Political Organization among the Late Classic Maya. *Current Anthropology* 37: 803–10.

1998. Late Classic Maya Political Structure, Polity Size and Warfare Arenas. In *Anatomía de una Civilización: Aproximaciones Interdisciplinarias a la Cultura Maya*, ed. A. Ciudad Ruiz, *et al.*, pp. 11–29. Madrid: Sociedad Española de Estudios Mayas.

2001. The Royal Court of Caracol, Belize: Its Palaces and People. In *Royal Courts of the Ancient Maya*, vol. 2: *Data and Case Studies*, ed. T. Inomata and S.D. Houston, pp. 102–137. Boulder, CO: Westview Press.

2004. Terminal Classic Status-Linked Ceramics and the Maya "Collapse": De Facto Refuse at Caracol, Belize. In *The Terminal Classic in the Maya Lowlands: Collapse, Transition, and Transformation*, eds. A.A. Demarest, P.M. Rice, and D. Rice. Boulder: University Press of Colorado.

Chase, Arlen F., and Diane Z. Chase, eds. 1992. *Mesoamerican Elites: An Archaeological Assessment*. Norman: University of Oklahoma Press.

Chase, Arlen F., Nikolai K. Grube, and Diane Z. Chase. 1991. *Three Terminal Classic Monuments from Caracol, Belize*. Research Reports on Ancient Maya Writing 36. Washington, DC: Center for Maya Research.

Chase, Arlen F., Diane Z. Chase, and Christine D. White. 2001. El paisaje urbnao Maya: La integración de los espacios construidos y la estructura social en Caracol, Belize. In *La Ciudad Antigua: Espacios, Conjuntos e Integración Sociocultural en la Civilización Maya*, eds. A. Ciudad, M.J. Iglesias, and C. Martines, Madrid: Sociedad Espanola de Estudios Mayas.

Chase, Arlen F., and Prudence M. Rice, eds. 1985. *The Lowland Maya Postclassic*. Austin: University of Texas Press.

Chase, Diane Z. 1985. Ganned But Not Forgotten: Late Postclassic Archaeology and Ritual at Santa Rita Corozal, Belize. In *The Lowland Maya Postclassic*, ed. A.F. Chase and P.M. Rice, pp. 104–125. Austin: University of Texas Press.

1986. Social and Political Organization in the Land of Cacao and Honey: Correlating the Archaeology and Ethnohistory of the Postclassic Lowland

Maya. In *Late Lowland Maya Civilization: Classic to Postclassic*, ed. J.A. Sabloff and E.W. Andrews V, pp. 347–377. Albuquerque: University of New Mexico Press.

1990. The Invisible Maya: Population History and Archaeology at Santa Rita Corozal. In *Prehistoric Population History in the Maya Lowlands*, ed. T.P. Culbert and D.S. Rice, pp. 199–214. Albuquerque: University of New Mexico Press.

1991. Lifeline to the Maya Gods: Ritual Bloodletting at Santa Rita Corozal. In *Sixth Palenque Round Table, 1986*, ed. V.M. Fields, pp. 89–96. Norman: University of Oklahoma Press.

1997. Southern Lowland Maya Archaeology and Human Skeletal Remains: Interpretations from Caracol, Belize, Santa Rita Corozal, Belize, and Tayasal, Guatemala. In *Bones of the Maya: Studies of Ancient Skeletons*, ed. S.L. Whittington and D.M. Reed, pp. 15–27. Washington, DC: Smithsonian Institution.

Chase, Diane Z., and Arlen F. Chase. 1980. New Finds at Santa Rita Show Corozal Site to be Thriving Maya Center. *Brukdown: The Magazine of Belize* IV(8): 18–21.

1982. Yucatec Influence in Terminal Classic Northern Belize. *American Antiquity* 47: 596–614.

2004. Hermeneutics, Transitions, and Transformations in Classic to Postclassic Maya Society. In *The Terminal Classic in the Maya Lowlands: Collapse, Transition, and Transformation*, ed. A.A. Demarest, P.M. Rice, and D.S. Rice. Boulder, CO: University Press of Colorado.

Chase, Diane Z., Arlen F. Chase, and William A. Haviland. 1990. The Classic Maya City: Reconsidering the "Mesoamerican Urban Tradition." *American Anthropologist* 92: 499–506.

Chase, Diane Z., Arlen F. Chase, Christine D. White, and Wendy Giddens. 1998. Human Skeletal Remains in Archaeological Context: Status, Diet, and Household at Caracol, Belize. Paper presented at the Fourteenth International Congress of Anthropological and Ethnological Sciences, Williamsburg, VA.

Christie, Jessica J., ed. 2003. *Maya Palaces and Elite Residences: An Interdisciplinary Approach*. Linda Schele Series in Maya and Pre-Columbian Studies. Austin: University of Texas Press.

Christie, Jessica J. and Patricia Sarro, eds. In press. *Palaces and Power in Ancient America: From Peru to the Northwest Coast*. Austin: University of Texas Press.

Churchward, James. 1932. *The Lost Continent of Mu*. New York: Ives Washburn.

Ciudad Real, Antonio de. 1872. *Relación de las cosas que sucedieron al R. P. Comisario General Fray Alonso Ponce . . . (1588)*. Madrid: Imprenta de la Viuda de Calero.

Clark, John E. 1986. From Mountains to Molehills: A Critical Review of Teotihuacan's Obsidian Industry. In *Research in Economic Anthropology*, Supplement 2, ed. B.L. Isaac, pp. 23–74. Greenwich: JAI Press.

1994. *The Development of Early Formative Rank Societies in Soconusco, Chiapas, Mexico*. Unpublished Ph.D. dissertation, Department of Anthropology, University of Michigan, Ann Arbor.

1997a. The Arts of Government in Early Mesoamerica. In *Annual Review of Anthropology* 26: 211–234.

1997b. Prismatic Blademaking, Craftsmanship, and Production: An Analysis of Obsidian Refuse From Ojo de Agua, Chiapas, Mexico. *Ancient Mesoamerica* 8: 137–159.

Clark, John E., and Michael Blake. 1989. El origen de la civilizacion en Mesoamerica: Los Olmecas y Mokaya del Socunusco de Chiapas, Mexico. In *El Preclásico o Formative: Advances y Perspecitvas*, ed. M. Carmona, pp. 385–403. Instituto Nacional de Antropología, Mexico: Museo Nacional de Antropología.

1994. The Power of Prestige: Competitive Generosity and the Emergence of Rank Societies in Lowland Mesoamerica. In *Factional Competition and Political Development in the New World*, ed. E. Brumfiel and J. Fox, pp. 17–30. Cambridge: Cambridge University Press.

Clark, John E., and Douglas Bryant. 1997. Technological Typology of Obsidian Blades and Debitage from Ojo de Agua, Chiapas, Mexico. *Ancient Mesoamerica* 8: 111–136.

Clark, John E., Richard D. Hansen, and Tomas Perez. n.d. *Maya Genesis: Towards an Origin Narrative of Maya Civilization*. Manuscript.

2000. La zona maya en el preclásico. In *Historia Antigua de Mexico*, 2nd edition, eds. L. Manzanilla and L. Lopez Luján, pp. 437–510. Mexico, D.F.: Universidad Nacional Autónoma de México.

Clark, John E., and Thomas A. Lee, Jr. 1984. Formative Obsidian Exchange and the Emergence of Public Economies in Chiapas, Mexico. In *Trade and Exchange in Early Mesoamerica*, ed. K.G. Hirth, pp. 235–274. Albuquerque: University of New Mexico Press.

Cobos, Rafael. 1998. Chichén Itzá y el Clásico Terminal en las Tierras Bajas Mayas. In *XI Simposio de Investigaciones Arqueologicas en Guatemala*, eds. J.P. Laporte and H.L. Escobedo, pp. 791–799. Guatemala: Ministerio de Cultura y Deportes, Instituto de Antropología e Historia, Asociación Tikal.

2004. Chichén Itzá: Settlement and Hegemony during the Terminal Classic Period. In *The Terminal Classic in the Maya Lowlands: Collapse, Transition, and Transformation*, ed. A.A. Demarest, P.M. Rice, and D. Rice. Boulder: University Press of Colorado.

Coe, Michael D. 1960. A Fluted Point from Highland Guatemala. *American Antiquity* 25: 412–413.

1965. Archaeological Synthesis of Southern Veracruz and Tabasco. In *Handbook of Middle American Indians*, vol. 3: *Archaeology of Southern Mesoamerica, Part 2*, ed. G.R. Willey, pp. 679–714. Austin: University of Texas Press.

1966. *The Maya*. New York: Praeger.

1968. *America's First Civilization*. New York: American Heritage.

1973. *The Maya Scribe and His World*. New York: Grolier Club.

1977. Supernatural Patrons of Maya Scribes and Artists. In *Social Process in Maya Prehistory: Studies in Honour of Sir Eric Thompson*, ed. N.D.C. Hammond, pp. 327–347. New York: Academic Press.

1978. *Lords of the Underworld: Masterpieces of Classic Maya Ceramics*. Princeton, NJ: Princeton University Press.

1981. Religion and the Rise of the Mesoamerican State. In *The Transition to Statehood in the New World*, ed. G.D. Jones and R.R. Kautz, pp. 157–171. Cambridge: Cambridge University Press.

1982. *Old Gods and Young Heroes: The Pearlman Collection of Maya Ceramics.* Jerusalem: Maremont Pavilion of Ethnic Arts, Israel Museum.

1988. Ideology of the Maya Tomb. In *Maya Iconography*, ed. E.P. Benson and G.G. Griffin, pp. 222–235. Princeton, NJ: Princeton University Press.

1992. *Breaking the Maya Code.* New York: Thames and Hudson.

1993. *The Maya.* 5th ed. New York: Thames and Hudson.

1994. *Mexico: From the Olmecs to the Aztecs*, 4th ed. New York: Thames and Hudson.

Coe, Michael D., and Kent V. Flannery. 1967. *Early Cultures and Human Ecology in South Coastal Guatemala.* Contributions to Anthropology 3. Washington, DC: Smithsonian Institution Press.

Coe, Michael D., and Sophie Coe. 1996. *A True History of Chocolate.* New York: Thames and Hudson.

Coe, William R. 1962. A Summary of Excavation and Research at Tikal, Guatemala: 1956–1961. *American Antiquity* 27: 479–507.

1965a. Tikal, Guatemala, and Emergent Maya Civilization. *Science* 147: 1401–1419.

1965b. Tikal: Ten Years of Study of a Maya Ruin in the Lowlands of Guatemala. *Expedition* 8(1): 5–56.

1968. Tikal: In Search of the Mayan Past. In *The World Book Yearbook*, pp. 160–190. Chicago: Field Educational Enterprises.

Coggins, Clemency C. 1975. Painting and Drawing Styles at Tikal: An Historical and Iconographic Reconstruction. Ph.D. dissertation, Department of Fine Arts, Harvard University.

1979. A New Order and the Role of the Calendar: Some Characteristics of the Middle Classic Period at Tikal. In *Maya Archaeology and Ethnohistory*, ed. N.D.C. Hammond and G.R. Willey, pp. 38–50. Austin: University of Texas Press.

Coggins, Clemency C., and Orrin C. Shane III. 1984. *Cenote of Sacrifice: Maya Treasures from the Sacred Well at Chichen Itza.* Austin: University of Texas Press.

Coleman, David, and Roger Schofield, eds. 1986. *The State of Population Theory: Forward from Malthus.* London: Basil Blackwell.

Conrad, Geoffrey W., and Arthur A. Demarest. 1984. *Religion and Empire: The Dynamics of Aztec and Inca Expansionism.* Cambridge: Cambridge University Press.

Cook, Orator F. 1921. *Milpa* Agriculture, A Primitive Tropical System. *Annual Report of the Smithsonian Institution, 1919*, pp. 307–326. Washington, DC: Smithsonian Institution.

Cortes, Hernan. 1928. *Five Letters of Cortes to the Emperor (1519–1526).* Trans. J.B. Morris. New York: Norton.

Costin, Cathy L. 1991. Craft Specialization: Issues in Defining, Documenting, and Explaining the Organization of Production. In *Archaeological Method and Theory,* vol. 3, ed. M. Schiffer, pp. 1–56. Tucson: University of Arizona Press.

Covarrubias, Miguel A. 1957. *Indian Art of Mexico and Central America.* New York: Alfred A. Knopf.

Cowgill, George L. 1979. Teotihuacan, Internal Militaristic Competition, and the Fall of the Classic Maya. In *Maya Archaeology and Ethnohistory,* ed. N.D.C. Hammond and G.R. Willey, pp. 51–62. Austin: University of Texas Press.

Cowgill, Ursula M. 1961. Soil Fertility and the Ancient Maya. *Connecticut Academy of Arts and Sciences, Transactions* 42: 1–56.

Culbert, T. Patrick. 1973a. The Maya Downfall at Tikal. In *The Classic Maya Collapse,* ed. T.P. Culbert, pp. 63–92. Albuquerque: University of New Mexico Press.

1974. *The Lost Civilization: The Story of the Classic Maya.* New York: Harper and Row.

1977. Maya Development and Collapse: An Economic Perspective. In *Social Process in Maya Prehistory,* ed. N.D.C. Hammond, pp. 510–530. New York: Academic Press.

1988. The Collapse of Classic Maya Civilization. In *The Collapse of Ancient States and Civilizations,* ed. N. Yoffee and G.L. Cowgill, pp. 69–101. Tucson: University of Arizona Press.

1994. *Maya Civilization.* Washington DC: Smithsonian Books.

1998. The New Maya. *Archaeology* 51(5): 48–52.

Culbert, T. Patrick, ed. 1973b. *The Classic Maya Collapse.* Albuquerque: University of New Mexico Press.

ed. 1991. *Classic Maya Political History: Hieroglyphic and Archaeological Evidence.* Cambridge: Cambridge University Press.

Culbert, T. Patrick, Laura J. Kosakowsky, Robert E. Fry, and William A. Haviland. 1990. The Population of Tikal, Guatemala. In *Precolumbian Population History in the Maya Lowlands,* ed. T.P. Culbert and D.S. Rice, pp. 103–122. Albuquerque: University of New Mexico Press.

Culbert, T. Patrick, Laura Levi, Brian McKee, and Julie Kunen. 1996. Investigaciones Arqueologicas en el *Bajo* La Justa, entre Yaxha y Nakum. In *IX Simposio de Investigaciones Arqueológicas en Guatemala,* eds. J.P. Laporte and H.L. Escobedo, pp. 367–372. Guatemala Ministerio de Cultura y Deportes, Instituto de Antropología e Historia, Asociación Tikal.

Culbert, T. Patrick, and Don S. Rice, eds. 1990. *Precolumbian Population History in the Maya Lowlands.* Albuquerque: University of New Mexico Press.

Curtis, Jason H., David A. Hoddell, and Mark Brenner. 1996. Climate Variability on the Yucatan Peninsula (Mexico) during the Past 3500 Years, and the Implications for Maya Cultural Evolution. *Quaternary Research* 46: 37–47.

Dahlin, Bruce H. 1976. An Anthropologist Looks at the Pyramids: A Late Classic Revitalization Movement at Tikal, Guatemala. Ph.D. dissertation, Temple University, Philadelphia.

1979. Cropping Cash in the Protoclassic: A Cultural Impact Statement. In *Maya Archaeology and Ethnohistory,* ed. N.D.C. Hammond and G.R. Willey, pp. 21–37. Austin: University of Texas Press.

1984. A Colossus in Guatemala: The Preclassic Maya City of El Mirador. *Archaeology* 37(5): 18–25.

Dahlin, Bruce H., and William J. Litzinger. 1986. Old Bottle, New Wine: The Function of Chultuns in the Maya Lowlands. *American Antiquity* 51: 721–736.

del Rio, Antonio. 1822. *Description of the Ruins of an Ancient City Discovered Near Palenque, in the Kingdom of Guatemala, in Spanish America*. London: Berthoud and Suttaby, Evance and Fox.

Demarest, Arthur A. 1976. A Re-Evaluation of the Archaeological Sequences of Preclassic Chiapas. In *Studies in Middle American Archaeology*, pp. 75–107. Middle American Research Institute Publication 22. New Orleans: Tulane University.

1981. *Viracocha: The Nature and Antiquity of the Andean High God*. Peabody Museum Monograph No. 6. Cambridge, MA: Harvard University Press.

1984a. Mesoamerican Human Sacrifice in Evolutionary Perspective. In *Ritual Human Sacrifice in Mesoamerica*, ed. E.H. Boone, pp. 227–247. Washington, DC: Dumbarton Oaks.

1984b. Conclusiones y Especulaciones acerca de El Mirador. *Mesoamerica* 7: 138–150.

1986. *The Archaeology of Santa Leticia and the Rise of Maya Civilization*. Middle American Research Institute Publication 52. New Orleans: Tulane University.

1987a. Archaeology and Religion. In *The Encyclopedia of Religion*, ed. M. Eliade, pp. 373–379. New York: MacMillan Publishing Company.

1987b. Recent Research on the Preclassic Ceramics of the Southeastern Highlands and Pacific Coast of Guatemala. In *Maya Ceramics: Papers from the 1985 Maya Ceramic Conference*, ed. P.M. Rice and R.J. Sharer, pp. 329–339. British Archaeological Reports 345. Oxford: BAR International Series.

1989a. Ideology and Evolutionism in American Archaeology: Looking Beyond the Economic Base. In *Archaeological Thought in America*, ed. C.C. Lamberg-Karlovsky, pp. 89–102. Cambridge: Cambridge University Press.

1989b. The Olmec and the Rise of Civilization in Eastern Mesoamerica. In *The Olmec and the Development of Formative Mesoamerican Civilization*, eds. R.J. Sharer and D.C. Grove, pp. 303–344. Cambridge: Cambridge University Press.

1992a. Archaeology, Ideology, and Precolumbian Cultural Evolution: The Search for an Approach. In *Ideology and Pre-Columbian Civilizations*, ed. A.A. Demarest and G.W. Conrad, pp. 1–13. Santa Fe, NM: School of American Research Press.

1992b. Ideology in Ancient Maya Cultural Evolution: The Dynamics of Galactic Polities. In *Ideology and Pre-Columbian Civilizations*, ed. A.A. Demarest and G. Conrad, pp. 135–157. Santa Fe, NM: School of American Research Press.

1993. The Violent Saga of a Maya Kingdom. *National Geographic* 183(2): 94–111.

1996a. Economía y Subsistencia Durante el Clásico Terminal: Interpretaciones de las Nuevas Evidencias en Punta de Chimino. In *Proyecto Arqueológico*

*Punta de Chimino 1996, Informe Preliminar*, ed. A.A. Demarest, H.L. Escobedo, and M. O'Mansky, pp. 95–106. Guatemala and Nashville, TN: Instituto de Antropología e Historia and Department of Anthropology, Vanderbilt University.

1996b. Concluding Comment on the Maya State: Centralized or Segmentary? *Current Anthropology* 37: 821–824.

1997. The Vanderbilt Petexbatún Regional Archaeological Project, 1989–1994: Overview, History, and Major Results of a Multidisciplinary Study of the Classic Maya Collapse. *Ancient Mesoamerica* 8: 209–227.

2001. Nuevas evidencias y problemas teoricos en las investigaciones e interpretaciones sobre los origines de las sociedades complejas en Guatemala. In *XIV Simposio de Investigaciones Arqueologicas en Guatemala*, eds. J.P. Laporte, A.C. de Sausnávar, and B. Arroyo. Guatemala: Ministerio de Cultura y Deportes, Instituto de Antropología e Historia, Asociación Tikal.

2002. Theoretical Speculations on the Rise of Complex Society on the South Coast of Guatemala. In *Incidents of Archaeology in Central America and Yucatán: Essays in Honor of Edwin M. Shook*, eds. M.W. Love, M.P. Hatch, and H.L. Escobedo, pp. 11–34. Lanham, MD: University Press of America.

2004. After the Maelstrom: Collapse of the Classic Maya Kingdoms and the Terminal Classic in the Western Petén. In *The Terminal Classic in the Maya Lowlands: Collapse, Transition, and Transformation*, ed. A.A. Demarest, P.M. Rice, and D. Rice, pp. 102–124. Boulder: University Press of Colorado.

In press-a. Sacred and Profane Mountains at Cancuen and Dos Pilas: Architecture as State Strategy. In *Palaces and Power in Ancient America: From Peru to the Northwest Coast*, eds. J. Christie and P. Sarro. Austin: University of Texas Press.

In press-b. *The Petexbatún Regional Archaeological Project: A Multidisciplinary Study of the Classic Maya Collapse*. Monographs of the Vanderbilt Institute of Mesoamerican Archaeology. Nashville, TN: Vanderbilt University Press.

Demarest, Arthur A., and Tomás Barrientos Q. 2002. *Proyecto Arqueológico Cancuen, Informe Preliminar No. 4: Temporada 2002*. Guatemala and Nashville, TN: Instituto de Antropología e Historia and Department of Anthropology, Vanderbilt University.

Demarest, Arthur A., and Geoffrey W. Conrad. 1983. Ideological Adaptation in the Rise of the Aztec and Inca Empires. In *Civilization in the Ancient Americas*, ed. R. Leventhal and A. Kolata, pp. 373–400. Albuquerque: University of New Mexico Press.

Demarest, Arthur A., and Geoffrey W. Conrad, eds. 1992. *Ideology and Pre-Columbian Civilizations*. Santa Fe, NM: School of American Research Press.

Demarest, Arthur A., and Héctor L. Escobedo. 1997. El proyecto arqueológico Punta de Chimino: objectivos, descubrimientos e interpretaciones preliminares de la temporada de campo de 1996. In *X Simposio de Investigaciones Arqueologicas en Guatemala*, ed. J.P. Laporte and H.L. Escobedo, pp. 381–384. Guatemala: Ministerio de Cultura y Deportes, Instituto de Antropología e Historia, Asociación Tikal.

Demarest, Arthur, Héctor Escobedo, Juan Antonio Valdés, Stephen Houston, and Kitty Emery. 1991. Operación DP6A: Excavaciones en la Estructura L5-1 y la Tumba del Gobernante 2 de Dos Pilas. In *Proyecto Arqueológico Regional Petexbatun: Informe Preliminar #3, Tercera Temporada 1991,* eds. A.A. Demarest, T. Inomata, H. Escobedo, and J. Palka, pp. 37–68. Instituto de Antropología e Historia, Guatemala, and Department of Anthropology, Vanderbilt University, Nashville.

Demarest, Arthur A., and Federico Fahsen. 2003. Nuevos Datos e Interpretaciones de los Reinos Occidentales. In *XVI Simposio de Investigaciones Arqueologicas en Guatemala,* eds. J.P. Laporte, H. Escobedo, A.C. de Suasnávar, and B. Arroyo, pp. 159–174. Guatemala: Museo de Antropología y Etnología de Guatemala.

Demarest, Arthur A., and Antonia E. Foias. 1993. Mesoamerican Horizons and the Cultural Transformations of Maya Civilization. In *Latin American Horizons,* ed. D. Rice, pp. 147–191. Washington, DC: Dumbarton Oaks, Trustees for Harvard University.

Demarest, Arthur A., and David García. 2003. Perspectivas Postmodernas acerca de Arqueología, Derechos Indigenas, y Desarollo Humano: Hacia Una Nuevo Modelo del Patrimonio Cultural en Guatemala. In *XVI Simposio de Investigaciones Arqueologicas en Guatemala,* eds. J.P. Laporte, H. Escobedo, A.C. de Suasnávar, and B. Arroyo, pp. 17–26. Guatemala: Museo de Antropología y Etnología de Guatemala.

Demarest, Arthur, Nora María López, Robert Chatham, Katherine F. Emery, Joel W. Palka, Kim Morgan, and Héctor L. Escobedo, 1991. Operación DP28: excavaciones en las murallas defensivas de Dos Pilas. In *Proyecto Arqueológico Regional Petexbatún, Informe Preliminar #3: Tercera Temporada 1991,* ed. A.A. Demarest, T. Inomata, H.L. Escobedo, and J.W. Palka, pp. 208–241. Guatemala and Nashville, TN: Instituto de Antropología e Historia and Department of Anthropology, Vanderbilt University.

Demarest, Arthur A., Kim Morgan, Claudia Wolley, and Hector L. Escobedo. 2003. The Political Acquisition of Sacred Geography: The Murciélagos Complex at Dos Pilas. In *Maya Palaces and Elite Residences,* ed. J. Christie, pp. 120–153. Austin: University of Texas Press.

Demarest, Arthur A., Matt O'Mansky, Claudia Wolley, Dirk Van Tuerenhout, Takeshi Inomata, Joel W. Palka, and Héctor L. Escobedo. 1997. Classic Maya Defensive Systems and Warfare in the Petexbatún Region: Archaeological Evidence and Interpretations. *Ancient Mesoamerica* 8: 229–253.

Demarest, Arthur A., Matt O'Mansky, Nicholas Dunning, and Timothy Beach. In press. Catastrofismo, Procesos Ecológicos, ó Crisis Política?: Hacia una Metodología Mejor para Interpretación del "Colapso" de la Civilización Clásica Maya. In *XVII Simposio de Investigaciones Arqueologicas en Guatemala,* eds. J.P. Laporte, H. Escobedo, and B. Arroyo. Guatemala: Museo de Antropología y Etnología de Guatemala.

Demarest, Arthur A., Mary E. Pye, J.T. Myers, and R. Mendez. 1988. *El Proyecto Mar Azul/El Mesak, Informe Preliminar.* Guatemala and Nashville, TN: Instituto de Antropología e Historia and Department of Anthropology, Vanderbilt University.

Demarest, Arthur A., Prudence M. Rice, and Don S. Rice, eds. 2004a. *The Terminal Classic in the Maya Lowlands: Collapse, Transition, and Transformation*. Boulder: University Press of Colorado.

Demarest, Arthur A., Prudence M. Rice, and Don S. Rice. 2004b. The Terminal Classic in the Maya Lowlands: Assessing Collapses, Terminations, and Transformations. In *The Terminal Classic in the Maya Lowlands: Collapse, Transition, and Transformation*, eds. A.A. Demarest, P.M. Rice, and D.S. Rice, pp. 545–572. Boulder: University Press of Colorado.

Demarest, Arthur A., Irma Rodas, and Kim Morgan. 1995. Investigación de Estructura N4-6, una Estructura Oratorio en el Grupo Murcielagos: suboperación DP39F. In *Proyecto Arqueológico Regional Petexbatún: Informe Preliminar No. 6, Tercera Temporada 1994*, ed. A.A. Demarest, J.A. Valdés, and H.L. Escobedo, pp. 357–361. Guatemala and Nashville, TN: Instituto de Antropología e Historia and Department of Anthropology, Vanderbilt University.

Demarest, Arthur A., and Robert J. Sharer. 1986. Late Preclassic Ceramic Spheres, Culture Areas, and Cultural Evolution in the Southeastern Highlands of Mesoamerica. In *The Southeast Maya Periphery*, ed. P.A. Urban and E.M. Schortman, pp. 194–223. Austin: University of Texas Press.

Demarest, Arthur A., Robert J. Sharer, William R. Fowler, Jr., Eleanor King, and Joyce Fowler. 1984. Las Excavaciones del Proyecto El Mirador, 1982. *Mesoamerica* 7: 14–52.

Demarest, Arthur A., Roy Switsur, and Rainer Berger. 1982. The Dating and Cultural Associations of the "Potbellied" Sculptural Style: New Evidence from Western El Salvador. *American Antiquity* 47: 557–571.

Demarest, Arthur A., and Juan Antonio Valdés. 1995. Guerra, regresión política y el colapso de la civilización Maya Clásica en la región Petexbatún. In *VIII Simposio de Investigaciones Arqueológicas en Guatemala, 1994*, eds. J.P. Laporte and H.L. Escobedo, pp. 777–781. Guatemala: Ministerio de Cultura y Deportes, Instituto de Antropología e Historia, Asociación Tikal.

Demarest, Arthur A., Héctor L. Escobedo, and Matt O'Mansky, eds. 1997. *Proyecto Arquelógico Punta de Chimino, Informe Preliminar de la Primera Temporada*. Guatemala and Nashville, TN: Instituto de Antropología e Historia and Department of Anthropology, Vanderbilt University.

Demarest, Arthur, and Tomás Barrientos Q., eds. 1999. *Proyecto Arqueologico Cancuen, Informe Preliminar No. 1, Temporada 1999*. Guatemala and Nashville, TN: Instituto de Antropología e Historia, Department of Anthropology.

2000. *Proyecto Arqueologico Cancuen, Informe Preliminar No. 2, Temporada 2000*. Guatemala and Nashville, TN: Instituto de Antropología e Historia Department of Anthropology, Vanderbilt University.

2001. *Proyecto Arqueologico Cancuen, Informe Preliminar No. 3, Temporada 2001*. Guatemala and Nashville, TN: Instituto de Antropología e Historia and Department of Anthropology, Vanderbilt University.

Derrida, Jacques. 1976. *Of Grammatology*. Baltimore, MD: Johns Hopkins University Press.

1981. *Dissemination*. Chicago: University of Chicago Press.

Deuel, Leo. 1967. *Conquistadors without Swords: Archaeologists in the Americas.* New York: Schocken Books.

Devereux, George. 1967. A Typological Study of Abortion in 350 Primitive, Ancient, and Pre-Industrial Societies. In *Abortion in America: Legal, Anthropological, and Religious Considerations*, ed. H. Rosen, pp. 97–152. Boston: Beacon Press.

Diaz del Castillo, Bernal. 1963. *The Conquest of New Spain*, trans. J.M. Cohen. Baltimore, MD: Penguin.

Diehl, Richard A., and Janet C. Berlo, eds. 1989. *Mesoamerica after the Decline of Teotihuacan, A.D. 700–900.* Washington, DC: Dumbarton Oaks, Trustees for Harvard University.

Dillehay, Tom D., and David J. Meltzer, eds. 1991. *The First Americans: Search and Research.* Boca Raton, FL: CRC Press.

Dillon, Brian D. 1977. *Salinas de los Nueve Cerros, Guatemala: Preliminary Archaeological Investigations.* Ballena Press Studies in Mesoamerican Art, Archaeology and Ethnohistory 2. Socorro, NM: Ballena Press.

Dominguez Carrasco, Maria del Rosario, William J. Folan, and Joel D. Gunn. 1996. Calakmul, Campeche: sus áreas de actividades ceremonials, cívicas y domésticas, derivadas de sus materiales líticos y Cerámicos. In *Los Investigadores de la Cultura Maya*, no. 4, pp. 80–106. Campeche, Mexico: Universidad Autónoma de Campeche.

Drennan, Robert D. 1976. Religion and Social Evolution in Formative Mesoamerica. In *The Early Mesoamerican Village*, ed. K.V. Flannery, pp. 345–368. New York: Academic Press.

1984. Long-Distance Movement of Goods in Prehistoric Mesoamerica: Its Importance in the Complex Societies of the Formative and Classic. *American Antiquity* 49: 27–43.

Dunning, Nicholas P. 1992. *Lords of the Hills: Ancient Maya Settlement in the Puuc Region, Yucatán, Mexico.* Madison, WI: Prehistory Press.

1993 Análisis de fosfato de la tierra arqueológica y el patrón agrícola en la región de Petexbatún. In *Proyecto Arqueológico Regional Petexbatún, Informe Preliminar No. 5: Quinta Temporada, 1993*, ed. J.A. Valdés, A.E. Foias, T. Inomata, H.L. Escobedo, and A.A. Demarest, pp. 165–169. Guatemala and Nashville, TN: Instituto de Antropología e Historia and Department of Anthropology, Vanderbilt University.

1994. Ancient Maya Anthrosols: Soil Phosphate Testing and Land Use. In *Proceedings of the First International Conference on Pedo-Archaeology*, ed. J.E. Foss, M.E. Timpson, and M.W. Morris, pp. 203–210. Knoxville: University of Tennessee.

1996. An Examination of Regional Variability in the Prehispanic Maya Agricultural Landscape. In *The Managed Mosaic: Ancient Maya Agriculture and Resource Use*, ed. S.L. Fedick, pp. 53–68. Salt Lake City: University of Utah Press.

Dunning, Nicholas, and Timothy Beach. 1994. Soil Erosion, Slope Management, and Ancient Terracing in the Maya Lowlands. *Latin American Antiquity* 5: 51–69.

2000. Stability and Instability in Pre-Hispanic Maya Landscapes. In *An Imperfect Balace: Precolumbian New World Ecosystems*, ed. D. Lentz, pp. 179–202. New York: Columbia University Press.

In press. *Ecology and Agriculture of the Petexbatun Region: An Ancient Perspective on Rainforest Adaptation.* Monographs of the Vanderbilt Institute of Mesoamerican Archaeology. Nashville, TN: Vanderbilt University Press.

Dunning, Nicholas P., and Arthur A. Demarest. 1989. *Sustainable Agricultural Systems in the Petexbatún, Pasión, and Petén Regions of Guatemala: Perspectives from Contemporary Ecology and Ancient Settlement.* Report to United States Agency for International Development, Guatemala City and Washington, DC.

Dunning, Nicholas P., Timothy Beach, and David Rue. 1995. Investigaciones paleoecologicas y los antiguos sistemas agricolas de la región de Petexbatún. In *Proyecto Arqueológico Regional Petexbatún; Informe Preliminar no. 6: Sexta Temporada 1994*, ed. A.A. Demarest, J.A. Valdés, and H.L. Escobedo, pp. 505–521. Guatemala and Nashville, TN: Instituto de Antropología e Historia, and Department of Anthropology, Vanderbilt University.

Dunning, Nicholas P., Timothy Beach, and David Rue. 1997. The Paleoecology and Ancient Settlement of the Petexbatun Region, Guatemala. *Ancient Mesoamerica* 8: 255–266.

Dunning, Nicholas P., Estuardo Secarra, and Arthur A. Demarest. 1992. *The Petexbatún Region and the Petén: A Legacy of Human Impact.* Report to United States Agency for International Development, Guatemala City and Washington, DC.

Dunning, Nicholas P., Timothy Beach, Pat Farrell, and Sheryl Luzzadder-Beach. 1998. Prehispanic Agrosystems and Adaptive Regions in the Maya Lowlands. *Culture and Agriculture* 20: 87–101.

Eaton, Jack D. 1975. Ancient Agricultural Farmsteads in the Rio Bec Region of Yucatán. In *Archaeological Research Facility Contribution 27*, pp. 56–82. Berkeley: University of California.

Edmonson, Munro S. 1971. *The Book of Counsel: The Popol Vuh of the Quiche Maya of Guatemala.* Middle American Research Institute Publication 35. New Orleans, LA: Tulane University.

Edmonson, Munro S. 1979. Some Postclassic Questions about the Classic Maya. *Estudios de Cultura Maya* 12: 157–178.

1982. *The Ancient Future of the Itzá: The Book of Chilam Balam of Tizimin.* Austin: University of Texas Press.

1986. *Heaven Born Merida and Its Destiny: The Book of Chilam Balam of Chumayel.* Austin: University of Texas Press.

Eliade, Mircea. 1954. *The Myth of the Eternal Return*, trans. W.R. Trask. New York: Pantheon Books.

1961. *Images and Symbols: Studies in Religious Symbolism*, trans. P. Mairet. London: Harvill Press.

Emery, Katherine F. 1997. *The Maya Collapse: A Zooarchaeological Investigation.* Ph.D. dissertation, Cornell University, Ithaca, NY.

In press. *Ancient Fauna, Bone Industries, and Subsistence History of the Petexbatun Region*. Monographs of the Vanderbilt Institute of Mesoamerican Archaeology. Nashville, TN: Vanderbilt University Press.

Emery, Katherine F., Lori E. Wright, and Henry Schwarcz. 2000. Isotopic Analysis of Ancient Deer Bone: Biotic Stability in Collapse Period Maya Land-Use. *Journal of Archaeological Science* 27: 537–550.

Fagan, Brian M. 1987. *The Great Journey: The Peopling of Ancient America*. New York: Thames and Hudson.

Fahsen, Federico. 2001. From Chiefdom to Statehood in the Highlands of Guatemala. In *Maya: Divine Kings of the Rainforest*, ed. Nikolai Grube, pp. 86–95. Cologne, Germany: Könemann.

Fahsen, Federico, Jeannette Castellanos, Arthur A. Demarest, and Luis Fernando Luin. 2003. Nuevos descubrimientos en 2001 de textos historicos en el sitio Dos Pilas, Petén. In *XVI Simposio de Investigaciones Arqueológicas en Guatemala*. Guatemala: Ministerio de Cultura y Deportes, Instituto de Antropología e Historia, Asociación Tikal.

Fahsen, Federico, and Arthur A. Demarest. 2001. El Papel del reinado Cancuen en la historia de las ciudades clasicas en las tierras bajas Mayas: nuevos datos e interpretaciones epigraficas, in *XIV Simposio de Investigaciones Arqueológicas en Guatemala*, eds. J.P. Laporte, A.C. de Suasnávar, and B. Arroyo, pp. 999–1016. Guatemala: Ministerio de Cultura y Deportes, Instituto de Antropología e Historia, Asociación Tikal.

Fahsen, Federico, and Sarah Jackson. 2002. Nuevos Datos e Interpretaciones sobre la Dinistía de Cancuen en el Período Clásico. In *XV Simposio de Investigaciones Arqueológicas en Guatemala*, ed. J.P. Laporte, H.L. Escobedo, and B. Arroyo Guatemala: Ministerio de Cultura y Deportes, Instituto de Antropología e Historia, Asociación Tikal.

Farriss, Nancy M. 1984. *Maya Society Under Colonial Rule: The Collective Enterprise of Survival*. Princeton, NJ: Princeton University Press.

    1987. Remembering the Future, Anticipating the Past: History, Time, and Cosmology among the Maya of Yucatan. *Comparative Studies in Society and History* 29: 566–593.

Fash, Barbara W. 1992. Late Classic Architectural Sculpture Themes at Copan. *Ancient Mesoamerica* 3: 89–102.

    In press. Iconographic Evidence for Water Management and Social Organization at Copan. In *Copan: The Rise and Fall of a Classic Maya Kingdom*, eds. E.W. Andrews IV and W.L. Fash, Jr. Santa Fe, NM: School of American Research Press.

Fash, Barbara W., William L. Fash, Jr., Sheree Lane, Rudy Larios, Linda Schele, Jeff Stomper, and David S. Stuart. 1992. Investigations of a Classic Maya Council House at Copán, Honduras. *Journal of Field Archaeology* 19: 419–442.

Fash, William L. 1991. *Scribes, Warriors, and Kings: The City of Copan and the Ancient Maya*. New York: Thames and Hudson.

    1994. Changing Perspectives on Maya Civilization. *Annual Review of Anthropology* 23: 181–208.

Fash, William L., and Barbara W. Fash. 2000. Teotihuacan and the Maya: A Classic Heritage. In *Mesoamerica's Classic Heritage from Teotihuacan to the Aztecs*, eds. D. Carrasco, L. Jones, and S. Sessions, pp. 433–463. Boulder: University Press of Colorado.

Fash, William L., E. Wyllys Andrews, and T. Kam Manahan. 2004. Political Decentralization, Dynastic Collapse, and the Early Post Classic in the Urban Center of Copan, Honduras. In *The Terminal Classic in the Maya Lowlands: Collapse, Transition, and Transformation*, ed. A.A. Demarest, P.M. Rice, and D. Rice. Boulder: University Press of Colorado.

Fash, William L., and David S. Stuart. 1991. Dynastic History and Cultural Evolution at Copán, Honduras. In *Classic Maya Political History: Hieroglyphic and Archaeological Evidence*, ed. T.P. Culbert, pp. 147–179. Cambridge: Cambridge University Press.

Feder, Kenneth L. 1990. *Frauds, Myths, and Mysteries: Science and Pseudoscience in Archaeology*. Mountain View, CA: Mayfield Publishing.

Fedick, Scott L. 1994. Ancient Maya Agricultural Terracing in the Upper Belize River Area. *Ancient Mesoamerica* 5: 107–127.

Fedick, Scott L., ed. 1996. *The Managed Mosaic: Ancient Maya Agriculture and Resource Use*. Salt Lake City: University of Utah Press.

Feyerabend, Paul K. 1988. *Farewell to Reason*. New York: Verso Press.

Fischer, Edward F. 2001. *Cultural Logics and Global Economics: Maya Identity in Thought and Practice*. Austin: University of Texas Press.

Fischer, Edward F., and R. McKenna Brown, eds. 1996. *Maya Cultural Activism in Guatemala*. Austin: University of Texas Press.

Flannery, Kent V. 1968. The Olmec and the Valley of Oaxaca: A Model for Interregional Interaction in Formative Times. In *Dumbarton Oaks Conference on the Olmec*, ed. E.P. Benson, pp. 79–117. Washington, DC: Dumbarton Oaks, Trustees for Harvard University.

1972. The Cultural Evolution of Civilizations. *Annual Review of Ecology and Systematics* 3: 399–426.

Flannery, Kent V., ed. 1976. *The Early Mesoamerican Village*. New York: Academic Press.

ed. 1982. *Maya Subsistence: Studies in Memory of Dennis Puleston*. New York: Academic Press.

Flannery, Kent V., and Joyce Marcus. 1976. Formative Oaxaca and the Zapotec Cosmos. *American Scientist* 64: 374–383.

Foias, Antonia E. 1996. Changing Ceramic Production and Exchange Systems and the Classic Maya Collapse in the Petexbatun Region, Department of the Peten, Guatemala. Ph.D. dissertation, Department of Anthropology, Vanderbilt University.

In press. *Ceramics, Trade, and Exchange Systems of the Petexbatun: The Economic Parameters of the Classic Maya Collapse*. Monographs of the Vanderbilt Institute of Mesoamerican Archaeology. Nashville, TN: Vanderbilt University Press.

Foias, Antonia E., and Ronald L. Bishop. 1997. Changing Ceramic Production and Exchange in the Petexbatun Region, Guatemala: Reconsidering the Classic Maya Collapse. *Ancient Mesoamerica* 8: 275–291.

Foias, Antonia E., James E. Brady, and Stephen D. Houston. 1996. La Producción e Intercambio de la ceramica impresa del Clasico en la region del Petexbatun, Petén. In *IX Simposio de Investigaciones Arqueológicas en Guatemala, 1995*, ed. J.P. Laporte and H.L. Escobedo, pp. 111–134. Guatemala: Minesterio de Cultura y Deportes, Instituto de Antropología e Historia, Associacion Tikal.

Folan, William J. 1988. Calakmul, Campeche: El Nacimiento de la Tradición Clásica en la gran Mesoamérica. *Información* 13: 122–190.

1992. Calakmul, Campeche: A Centralized Urban Administrative Center in the Northern Petén. *World Archaeology* 24: 158–168.

Folan, William J., Ellen R. Kintz, and Laraine A. Fletcher. 1983. *Coba: A Classic Maya Metropolis*. New York: Academic Press.

Folan, William J., Joyce Marcus, Sophia Pincemin, Maria del Rosario Dominguez-Carrasco, and Laraine Fletcher. 1995. Calakmul: New Data from an Ancient Maya Capital in Campeche, Mexico. *Latin American Antiquity* 6: 310–34.

Förstemann, Ernst W. 1904. Translation of Various Papers. *Bureau of American Ethnology Bulletin* 28: 393–590.

1906. *Commentary on the Maya Manuscript in the Royal Public Library of Dresden*. Peabody Museum of Archaeology and Ethnology Papers, vol. 4, no. 2. Cambridge, MA: Harvard University.

Foucault, Michel. 1965. *Madness and Civilization: A History of Insanity in the Age of Reason*. New York: Vintage Books.

1972. *The Archaeology of Knowledge*. New York: Harper & Row.

1973. *The Birth of the Clinic*. London: Tavistock.

Fowler, William R., ed. 1991. *Formation of Complex Society in Southeastern Mesoamerica*. Boca Raton: CRC Press.

1997. Introduction to Special Section: The Vanderbilt Petexbatun Regional Archaeological Project, 1989–1994. *Ancient Mesoamerica* 8: 207–208.

Fox, John W. 1987. *Maya Postclassic State Formation: Segmentary Lineage Migration in Advancing Frontiers*. Cambridge: Cambridge University Press.

1989. On the Rise and Fall of Tulan and Maya Segmentary States. *American Anthropologist* 91: 656–681.

Fox, John W., Garrett W. Cook, Arlen F. Chase, Diane Z. Chase. 1996. Questions of Political and Economic Integration: Segmentary Versus Centralized States among the Ancient Maya. *Current Anthropology* 37: 795–801.

Fox, John W., Dwight T. Wallace, and Kenneth L. Brown. 1992. The Emergence of the Quiche Elite: The Putun-Palenque Connection. In *Mesoamerican Elites: An Archaeological Assessment*, ed. D.Z. Chase and A.F. Chase, pp. 169–190. Norman: University of Oklahoma Press.

Freidel, David A. 1979. Cultural Areas and Interaction Spheres: Contrasting Approaches to the Emergence of Civilization in the Maya Lowlands. *American Antiquity* 44: 36–54.

1981. Civilization as a State of Mind: The Cultural Evolution of the Lowland Maya. In *The Transition to Statehood in the New World*, ed. G.D. Jones and R.R. Kautz, pp. 188–227. Cambridge: Cambridge University Press.

1986a. Maya Warfare: An Example of Peer Polity Interaction. In *Peer Polity Interaction and Socio-Political Change*, ed. C. Renfrew and J.F. Cherry, pp. 93–108. Cambridge: Cambridge University Press.

1986b. Terminal Classic Lowland Maya: Successes, Failures, and Aftermaths. In *Late Lowland Maya Civilization: Classic to Postclassic*, ed. J.A. Sabloff and E.W. Andrews V, pp. 409–430. Albuquerque: University of New Mexico Press.

1986c. *Yaxuna Archaeological Survey: A Report of the 1986 Field Season*. Report submitted to Committee for Research and Exploration, National Geographic Society, Washington, DC.

1992. The Trees of Life: *Ahau* as Idea and Artifact in Classic Lowland Maya Civilization. In *Ideology and Pre-Columbian Civilizations*, ed. A.A. Demarest and G.W. Conrad, pp. 115–133. Santa Fe, NM: School of American Research Press.

1998. Sacred Work: Dedication and Termination in Mesoamerica. In *The Sowing and the Dawning: Termination, Dedication, and Transformation in the Archaeological and Ethnographic Record of Mesoamerica*, ed. S.B. Mock, pp. 189–193. Albuquerque: University of New Mexico Press.

In press. *Flintshield: Maya War and the Classic Collapse*. Boulder, CO: Westview Press.

Freidel, David A., Kathryn Reese-Taylor, and David Mora-Marín. 2002. The Origins of Maya Civilization: The Old Shell Game, Commodity, Treasure, and Kingship. In *Ancient Maya Political Economies*, eds. M.A. Masson and D.A. Freidel, pp. 41–86. Walnut Creek, CA: AltaMira Press.

Freidel, David A., Robin A. Robertson, and Maynard B. Cliff. 1982. The Maya City of Cerros. *Archaeology* 35(4): 12–21.

Freidel, David A., and Jeremy A. Sabloff. 1984. *Cozumel: Late Maya Settlement Patterns*. New York: Academic Press.

Freidel, David A., and Linda Schele. 1988a. Kingship in the Late Preclassic Maya Lowlands: The Instruments and Places of Ritual Power. *American Anthropologist* 90: 547–567.

1988b. Symbol and Power: A History of the Lowland Maya Cosmogram. In *Maya Iconography*, ed. E.P. Benson and G.G. Griffin, pp. 44–93. Princeton, NJ: Princeton University Press.

Freidel, David A., Linda Schele, and Joy Parker. 1993. *Maya Cosmos: Three Thousand Years on the Shaman's Path*. New York: William Morrow and Company, Inc.

Freidel, David A., Charles Suhler, and Ruth J. Krochock. 1990. *Yaxuná Archaeological Survey: A Report of the 1989 Field Season and Final Report on Phase One*. Dallas, TX: Department of Anthropology, Southern Methodist University.

Freter, AnnCorrine. 1988. The Classic Maya Collapse at Copan, Honduras: A Regional Settlement Perspective. Ph.D. dissertation, Department of Anthropology, Pennsylvania State University, University Park.

Freter, AnnCorrine. 1994. The Classic Maya Collapse at Copan, Honduras: An Analysis of Maya Rural Settlement Trends. In *Village Communities and Complex Societies*, eds. G. Schwartz and S. Falconer, pp. 160–176. Washington DC: Smithsonian Institution Press.

Fried, Morton. 1967. *The Evolution of Political Society*. New York: Random House.

Friedman, Jonathan. 1974. Marxism, Structuralism, and Vulgar Materialism. *Man* 9: 444–469.

1975. Tribes, States, and Transformations. In *Marxist Analyses and Social Anthropology*, ed. M. Bloch, pp. 161–202. New York: John Wiley and Sons.

Fry, Robert E. 1979. The Economics of Pottery at Tikal, Guatemala: Models of Exchange for Serving Vessels. *American Antiquity* 44: 494–512.

1980. Models of Exchange for Major Shape Classes of Lowlands Maya Pottery. In *Models and Methods in Regional Exchange*, ed. R.E. Fry, pp. 3–18. Society for American Archaeology Papers 1. Washington, DC: Society for American Archaeology.

Fry, Robert E., and Scott C. Cox. 1974. The Structure of Ceramic Exchange at Tikal, Guatemala. *World Archaeology* 1: 209–225.

Furst, Peter T. 1976a. *Hallucinogens and Culture*. San Francisco: Chandler and Sharp.

1976b. Vision Quest and Auto-Sacrifice. In *The Art, Iconography, and Dynastic History of Palenque, Part III*, ed. M.G. Robertson, pp. 211–224. Pebble Beach, CA: Robert Louis Stevenson School.

Furst, Peter T., and Michael D. Coe. 1977. Ritual Enemas. *Natural History* 86(3): 88–91.

García, David. 2001. Resultados del Proyecto de Desarollo Comunitario en Cancuen. In *Proyecto Arqueológico Cancuen, Informe Preliminar No. 3: Temporada 2001*, eds. A.A. Demarest and T. Barrientos Q., pp. 345–364. Guatemala and Nashville, TN: Instituto de Antropología e Historia and Department of Anthropology, Vanderbilt University.

García, David, Arthur Demarest, and Tomás Barrientos. 2002. El Proyecto Arqueológico Cancuén: Un Plan Piloto para la Interacción entre Arqueología y Desarrollo Social. In *XV Simposio de Investigaciones Arqueologicas en Guatemala*, eds. J.P. Laporte, H.L. Escobedo, and B. Arroyo, pp. 401–411. Guatemala: Ministerio de Cultura y Deportes, Instituto de Antropología e Historia, Asociación Tikal.

Geertz, Clifford. 1973. *The Interpretation of Cultures: Selected Essays*. New York: Basic Books.

1980. *Negara: The Theatre State in Nineteenth-Century Bali*. Princeton, NJ: Princeton University Press.

Gesick, Loraine, ed. 1983. *Centers, Symbols, and Hierarchies: Essays on the Classical States of Southeast Asia*. Southeast Asia Studies Monograph Series, No. 26. New Haven, CT: Yale University Press.

Giddens, Anthony. 1979. *Central Problems in Social Theory: Action, Structure and Contradiction in Social Analysis*. London and Basingstoke: Macmillan Press.

Gifford, James C. 1976. *Prehistoric Pottery Analysis and the Ceramics of Barton Ramie in the Belize Valley*. Peabody Museum of Archaeology and Ethnology Memoirs 18. Cambridge, MA: Harvard University Press.

Gill, Richardson B. 2000. *The Great Maya Droughts: Water, Life, and Death.* Albuquerque: University of New Mexico Press.

Gilman, Antonio. 1981. The Development of Social Stratification in Bronze Age Europe. *Current Anthropology* 22: 1–7.

Godelier, Maurice. 1977. *Perspectives in Marxist Anthropology.* Cambridge: Cambridge University Press.

1978a. Economy and Religion: An Evolutionary Optical Illusion. In *The Evolution of Social Systems*, ed. J. Friedman and M. J. Rowlands, pp. 3–12. London: Duckworth.

1978b. Politics as "Infrastructure": An Anthropologist's Thoughts on the Example of Classical Greece and the Notions of Relations of Production and Economic Determinism. In *The Evolution of Social Systems*, ed. J. Friedman and M. J. Rowlands, pp. 13–28. London: Duckworth.

Goodman, Joseph T. 1897. The Archaic Maya Inscriptions (Appendix). In *Biología Centrali-Americana: Archaeology*, A.P. Maudslay. London: Murray.

Gordon, George B. 1896. *Prehistoric Ruins of Copán, Honduras.* Peabody Museum of Archaeology and Ethnology Papers, vol. 1, no. 1. Cambridge, MA: Harvard University.

Gordon, George B., and John A. Mason. 1925–1943. *Examples of Maya Pottery in the Museum and in Other Collections.* Philadelphia: University Museum, University of Pennsylvania.

Gossen, Gary H. 1974. *Chamula in the World of the Sun: Time and Space in a Maya Oral Tradition.* Cambridge, MA: Harvard University Press.

Graham, John A. 1973. Inscriptions and Sculptural Art of Seibal. In *The Classic Maya Collapse*, ed. T.P. Culbert, pp. 207–220. Santa Fe, NM: School of American Research.

1977. Discoveries at Abaj Takalik. *Archaeology* 30: 196–197.

1979. Maya, Olmecs, and Izapans at Abaj Takalik. *Actas* 8: 179–188.

Griscom, Ludlow. 1932. *The Distribution of Birdlife in Guatemala.* American Museum of Natural History Bulletin 64. New York: American Museum of Natural History.

Grove, David C. 1981. The Formative Period and the Evolution of Complex Culture. In *Handbook of Middle American Indians, Supplement 1: Archaeology*, ed. J.A. Sabloff, pp. 373–391. Austin: University of Texas Press.

1989. Chalcatzingo and its Olmec Connections. In *Regional Perspectives on the Olmec*, ed. R.J. Sharer and D.C. Grove, pp. 122–147. Cambridge: Cambridge University Press.

Grube, Nikolai. 1994a. Epigraphic Research at Caracol, Belize. In *Studies in the Archaeology of Caracol, Belize*, ed. A. Chase and D. Chase, pp. 83–122. San Francisco: Pre-Columbian Art Research Institute.

1994b. Hieroglyphic Sources for the History of Northwest Yucatan. In *Hidden Among the Hills: Maya Archaeology of the Northwest Yucatan Peninsula*, ed. H. Prem, pp. 71–92. Möckmühl, Germany: Verlag von Flemming.

Guderjan, Thomas H., and James F. Garber, eds. 1995. *Maya Maritime Trade, Settlement, and Populations on Ambergris Caye, Belize.* Lancaster, CA: Labyrinthos.

Guillemin, George F. 1965. *Iximché: Capital del Antiguo Reino Cakchiquel.* Guatemala: Instituto de Antropología e Historia.

1977. Urbanism and Hierarchy at Iximche. In *Social Process in Maya Prehistory: Studies in Honor of Sir Eric Thompson*, ed. N.D.C. Hammond, pp. 227–264. New York and London: Academic Press.

Haas, Jonathan. 1982. *The Evolution of the Prehistoric State.* New York: Columbia University Press.

Hammond, Norman D.C. 1972. Obsidian Trade Routes in the Mayan Area. *Science* 178: 1092–1093.

1973. Models for Maya Trade. In *The Explanation of Culture Change: Models in Prehistory*, ed. C. Renfrew, pp. 601–607. Pittsburgh: University of Pittsburgh Press.

1974. On the "Square" Model of Maya Territorial Organization. *Science* 193: 875–876.

1975. Maya Settlement Hierarchy in Northern Belize. In *Archaeological Research Facility Contribution 24*, ed. J.A. Graham, pp. 40–55. Berkeley: University of California Press.

1976. Maya Obsidian Trade in Southern Belize. In *Maya Lithic Studies: Papers from the 1976 Belize Field Symposium*, ed. T.R. Hester and N.D.C. Hammond, pp. 71–81. San Antonio: Center for Archaeological Research, University of Texas.

1977. The Earliest Maya. *Scientific American* 236(3): 116–133.

1978. The Myth of the Milpa: Agricultural Expansion in the Maya Lowlands. In *Prehispanic Maya Agriculture*, ed. P.D. Harrison and B.L. Turner II, pp. 23–43. Albuquerque: University of New Mexico Press.

1981. Settlement Patterns in Belize. In *Lowland Maya Settlement Patterns*, ed. W.A. Ashmore, pp. 157–186. Albuquerque: University of New Mexico Press.

1983. Lords of the Jungle: A Prospography of Maya Archaeology. In *Civilization in the Ancient Americas: Essays in Honor of Gordon R. Willey*, ed. R.M. Leventhal and A.L. Kolata, pp. 3–32. Albuquerque: University of New Mexico Press.

1990. *Ancient Maya Civilization.* New Brunswick, NJ: Rutgers University Press.

1991. Inside the Black Box: Defining Maya Polity. In *Classic Maya Political History: Hieroglyphic and Archaeological Evidence*, ed. T.P. Culbert, pp. 253–284. Cambridge: Cambridge University Press.

Hansen, Richard D. 1984. Excavations on Structure 34 and the Tigre Area, El Mirador, Peten, Guatemala: A New Look at the Preclassic Lowland Maya. M.S. thesis, Department of Anthropology, Brigham Young University.

1989. *Archaeological Investigations at Nakbe, Peten, Guatemala: 1989 Season.* Los Angeles: Institute of Archaeology, University of California.

1990. *Excavations in the Tigre Complex, El Mirador, Petén, Guatemala.* Papers of the New World Archaeological Foundation 62. Provo, UT: New World Archaeological Foundation.

1991a. *An Early Maya Text from El Mirador, Guatemala.* Washington, DC: Center for Maya Research.

1991b. The Maya Rediscovered: The Road to Nakbe. *Natural History* May: 8–14.

1992. The Archaeology of Ideology: A Study of Maya Preclassic Architectural Sculpture at Nakbe, Guatemala. Ph.D. dissertation, University of California, Los Angeles.

1994. Dinámicas Culturales y Ambientales de los Orígenes Mayas: Estudios Recientes del Sitio Arqueológico Nakbe. In *VII Simposio de Investigaciones Arqueológicas en Guatemala, 1993*, eds. J.P. Laporte and H.L. Escobedo, pp. 369–387. Guatemala: Ministerio de Cultura y Deportes, Instituto de Antropología e Historia, Asociación Tikal.

1996. El Clásico Tardío del Norte de Petén. *Utz'ib* 2: 1–15.

1997. Developmental Dynamics, Energetics, and Complex Interaction of the Early Maya of the Mirador Basin. Paper presented at the 62nd Annual Meeting of the Society for American Archaeology, Nashville, Tennessee.

1998. Ideología y arquitectura: poder y dinámicas culturales de los Mayas Preclásicos de las tierras bajas. In *Second Mesa Redonda de Palenque, 1997*, ed. S. Trejo. Mexico City: Instituto Nacional de Antropologia e Historia.

2001. The First Cities: The Beginnings of Urbanization and State Formation in the Maya Lowlands. In *Maya: Divine Kings of the Rainforest*, ed. N. Grube. Cologne, Germany: Könemann.

Harris, Marvin. 1964. *The Nature of Cultural Things*. New York: Random House.

1968. *The Rise of Anthropological Theory: A History of Theories of Culture*. New York: Crowell.

1979. *Cultural Materialism: The Struggle for a Science of Culture*. New York: Random House.

Harrison, Peter D. 1970. The Central Acropolis, Tikal, Guatemala: A Preliminary Study of the Functions of Its Structural Components During the Late Classic Period. Ph.D. dissertation, Department of Anthropology, University of Pennsylvania, Philadelphia.

1977. The Rise of the *Bajos* and the Fall of the Maya. In *Social Process in Maya Prehistory: Studies in Honour of Sir Eric Thompson*, ed. N.D.C. Hammond, pp. 470–508. New York and London: Academic Press.

1981. Some Aspects of Preconquest Settlement in Southern Quintana Roo, Mexico. In *Lowland Maya Settlement Patterns*, ed. W.A. Ashmore, pp. 259–286. Albuquerque: University of New Mexico Press.

1990. The Revolution in Ancient Maya Subsistence. In *Vision and Revision in Maya Studies*, ed. F.S. Clancy and P.D. Harrison, pp. 99–114. Albuquerque: University of New Mexico Press.

Harrison, Peter D., and B.L. Turner II, eds. 1978. *Pre-Hispanic Maya Agriculture*. Albuquerque: University of New Mexico Press.

Hassig, Ross. 1988. *Aztec Warfare: Imperial Expansion and Political Control*. Norman: University of Oklahoma Press.

Hatch, Marion Popenoe de. 1991. Comentarios sobre la cerámica de Abaj Takalik. In *II Simposio de Investigaciones Antropológicas en Guatemala*, pp. 10–11. Guatemala: Ministerio de Cultura y Deportes, Instituto de Antropología e Historia, Asociación Tikal.

1997. *Kaminaljuyú/San Jorge: Evidencia Arqueológica de la Actividad Económica en el Valle de Guatemala, 300 A.C. a 300 D.C.* Guatemala: Universidad del Valle de Guatemala.

Hatch, Marion Popence de, Christa Schieber de Lavarreda, Edgar Carpio R., Miguel Orrego C., José Héctor P., and Claudia Wolley. 2001. Observaciones sobre el desarollo cultural en Abaj Takalik, Departamento de Retalhuleu, Guatemala. In *XVI Simposio de Investigaciones Arqueológicas en Guatemala*. Guatemala: Ministerio de Cultura y Deportes, Instituto de Antropología e Historia, Asociación Tikal.

Haug, Gerald H., Detlef Günther, Larry C. Peterson, Daniel M. Sigmun, Konrad A. Hughen, and Beat Aeschlimann. 2003. Climate and the Collapse of Maya Civilization. *Science* 299: 1731–1735.

Haviland, William A. 1970. Tikal, Guatemala, and Mesoamerican Urbanism. *World Archaeology* 2: 186–197.

  1974. Occupational Specialization at Tikal. *American Anthropologist* 39: 494–496.

  1982. Where the Rich Folks Lived: Deranging Factors in the Statistical Analysis of Tikal Settlement. *American Antiquity* 47: 427–429.

  1992. Status and Power in Classic Maya Society: The View from Tikal. *American Anthropologist* 94: 937–40.

Haviland, William A., and Hattula Moholy-Nagy. 1992. Distinguishing the High and Mighty from the Hoi Polloi at Tikal, Guatemala. In *Mesoamerican Elites: An Archaeological Assessment*, ed. D.Z. Chase and A.F. Chase, pp. 50–60. Norman: University of Oklahoma Press.

Helms, Mary W. 1975. *Middle America: A Cultural History of Heartland and Frontiers*. Englewood Cliffs, NJ: Prentice-Hall.

  1979. *Ancient Panama: Chiefs in Search of Power*. Austin: University of Texas Press.

Helmuth, Nicholas M. 1977. Cholti-Lacandon (Chiapas) and Peten-Ytza Agriculture, Settlement Pattern and Population. In *Social Process in Maya Prehistory: Studies in Honour of Sir Eric Thompson*, ed. N.D.C. Hammond, pp. 421–448. New York and London: Academic Press.

Henderson, John S. 1997. *The World of the Ancient Maya*. Ithaca and London: Cornell University Press.

Hervik, Peter. 1999. The Mysterious Maya of National Geographic. *Journal of Latin American Anthropology* 4: 166–197.

Hester, Thomas R., ed. 1979. *The Colha Project, 1979: A Collection of Interim Papers*. San Antonio: Center for Archaeological Research, University of Texas.

Hester, Thomas R., Jack D. Eaton, and Harry J. Shafer, eds. 1980. *The Colha Project, Second Season, 1980 Interim Report*. San Antonio: Center for Archaeological Research, University of Texas.

Hester, Thomas R., and Norman D.C. Hammond, eds. 1976. *Maya Lithic Studies. Papers from the 1976 Belize Field Symposium*. San Antonio: Center for Archaeological Research, University of Texas.

Hester, Thomas R., and Harry J. Shafer. 1984. Exploitation of Chert Resources by the Ancient Maya of Northern Belize, Central America. *World Archaeology* 16: 157–173.

Hester, Thomas R., Harry J. Shafer, Jack D. Eaton, Giancarlo Ligabue. 1983. Colha's Stone Tool Industry. *Archaeology* 36: 46–52.

Hewett, Edgar L. 1912. The Excavations at Quirigua in 1912. *Archaeological Institute of America Bulletin* 3(3): 163–171.

    1916. Latest Work of the School of American Archaeology at Quirigua. In *Holmes Anniversary Volume Anthropological Essays*, ed. F.W. Hodge, pp. 157–162. Washington, DC: James William Bryan Press.

Hill, Robert M. 1992. *Colonial Cakchiquels: Highland Maya Adaptation to Spanish Rule, 1600–1700.* Fort Worth: Harcourt Brace Jovanovich.

Hirth, Kenneth G., ed. 1984. *Trade and Exchange in Early Mesoamerica.* Albuquerque: University of New Mexico Press.

Hoddell, David A., Jason H. Curtis, and Mark Brenner. 1995. Possible Role of Climate in the Collapse of Classic Maya Civilization. *Nature* 75: 391–394.

Hodder, Ian. 1982. *Symbols in Action.* Cambridge: Cambridge University Press.

    1985. Post-Processual Archaeology. In *Advances in Archaeological Method and Theory*, 8, ed. M.B. Schiffer, pp. 1–26. New York and London: Academic Press.

    1986. *Reading the Past: Current Approaches to Interpretation in Archaeology.* Cambridge: Cambridge University Press.

    1987. Comment on *Processual Archaeology and the Radical Critique*, by Timothy K. Earle and Robert W. Preucel. *Current Anthropology* 28: 516–517.

Hoffman, Michael A. 1979. *Egypt Before the Pharaohs: The Prehistoric Foundations of Egyptian Civilization.* New York: Dorset Press.

Holley, George R. 1983. Ceramic Change at Piedras Negras, Guatemala. Ph.D. dissertation, Department of Anthropology, Southern Illinois University.

Houston, Stephen D. 1992. Classic Maya Politics. In *New Theories on the Ancient Maya*, eds. E.C. Danien and R.J. Sharer, pp. 65–70. University Museum Monograph 77, University Museum Symposium Series, vol. 3. Philadelphia: University Museum, University of Pennsylvania.

    1994. Literacy among the Precolumbian Maya: A Comparative Perspective. In *Writing Without Words: Alternative Literacies in Mesoamerica and the Andes*, ed. E.H. Boone and W.D. Mignolo, pp. 27–49. Durham, NC: Duke University Press.

Houston, Stephen D., and Peter Mathews. 1985. *The Dynastic Sequence of Dos Pilas, Guatemala.* Monograph 1. San Francisco: The Pre-Columbian Art Research Institute.

Houston, Stephen D., and David S. Stuart. 1989. *The Way Glyph: Evidence for "Co-Essences" among the Classic Maya.* Research Reports on Ancient Maya Writing 30. Washington, DC: Center for Maya Research.

Houston, Stephen D., Héctor L. Escobedo, Mark Child, Charles Golden, and René Muñoz. 2003. Moral Community and Settlement Transformation among the Classic Maya: Evidence from Piedras Negras, Guatemala. In *Social Construction of Ancient Cities*, ed. M.L. Smith. Washington, DC: Smithsonian Institution.

Howell, Wayne K., and Denise R.E. Copeland. 1989. *Excavations at El Mirador, Petén, Guatemala: The Danta and Monos Complexes.* Papers of the New World Archaeological Foundation Nos. 60 and 61. Provo, UT: New World Archaeological Foundation.

Hunt, Eva M. 1977. *The Transformation of the Hummingbird: Cultural Roots of a Zinacantan Mythical Poem*. Ithaca, NY: Cornell University Press.

Inomata, Takeshi. 1995. Archaeological Investigations at the Fortified Center of Aguateca, El Peten, Guatemala: Implications for the Study of the Classic Maya Collapse. Ph.D. dissertation, Department of Anthropology, Vanderbilt University, Nashville, TN.

  1997. The Last Day of a Fortified Classic Maya Center: Archaeological Investigations at Aguateca, Guatemala. *Ancient Mesoamerica* 8: 337–351.

  2001. The Power and Ideology of Artistic Creation: Elite Craft Specialists in Classic Maya Society. *Current Anthropology* 42: 321–350.

  2003. War, Destruction, and Abandonment: The Fall of the Classic Maya Center of Aguateca, Guatemala. In *The Archaeology of Settlement Abandonment in Middle America*, eds. T. Inomata and R.W. Webb, pp. 43–60. Salt Lake City: University of Utah Press.

  In press. *Aguateca: Warfare and the Collapse of a Classic Maya Center*. Monographs of the Vanderbilt Institute of Mesoamerican Archaeology. Nashville, TN: Vanderbilt University Press.

Inomata, Takeshi, and Daniela Triadan. 2000. Craft Production by Classic Maya Elites in Domestic Settings: Data from Rapidly Abandoned Structures at Aguateca, Guatemala. *Mayab* 11: 2–39.

Inomata, Takeshi, and Ronald W. Webb, eds. 2003. *The Archaeology of Settlement Abandonment in Middle America*. Salt Lake City: University of Utah Press.

Jennings, Jesse D. 1978. Origins. In *Ancient Native Americans*, ed. J.D. Jennings, pp. 1–41. San Francisco: W.H. Freeman and Company.

Johnston, Kevin J. 1994. The "Invisible" Maya: Late Classic Minimally-Platformed Residential Settlement at Itzan, Petén, Guatemala. Ph.D. dissertation, Yale University, New Haven, CT.

Johnston, Kevin J., Andrew J. Breckenbridge, and Barbara C. Hansen. 2001. Paleoecological Evidence of an Early Postclassic Occupation in the Southwestern Maya Lowlands: Laguna Las Pozas, Guatemala. *Latin American Antiquity* 12: 149–166.

Johnston, Kevin J., Takeshi Inomata, Joel W. Palka, Antonia E. Foias, and Teresa Robles. 1989. Rescate y registro de restos arqueológicos en Dos Pilas. In *Proyecto Arqueológico Regional Petexbatún, Informe Preliminar No. 1: Segunda Temporada*, ed. A.A. Demarest and S.D. Houston, pp. 29–61. Guatemala and Nashville, TN: Instituto de Antropología e Historia and Department of Anthropology, Vanderbilt University.

Johnston, Kevin J., Fernando Moscoso Moller, and Stefan Schmitt. 1992. Casas No-Visibles de los Mayas Clásicos: Estructuras Residenciales sin Plataformas Basales en Itzán, Petén. In *V Simposio de Arqueología Guatemalteca, 1991*, eds. J.P. Laporte, H.L. Escobedo, and S. Villagrán de Brady pp. 147–162. Guatemala: Ministerio de Cultura y Deportes, Instituto de Antropología e Historia, Asociación Tikal.

Jones, Christopher. 1969. The Twin-Pyramid Group Pattern: A Classic Maya Architectural Assemblage at Tikal, Guatemala. Ph.D. dissertation, Department of Anthropology, University of Pennsylvania, Philadelphia.

1979. *Tikal as a Trading Center.* Paper presented at the 43rd International Congress of Americanists, Vancouver.

Jones, Grant D. 1989. *Maya Resistance to Spanish Rule: Time and History on a Colonial Frontier.* Albuquerque: University of New Mexico Press.

1992. The Last Maya Confederacy. *Natural History.*

1998. *The Conquest of the Last Maya Kingdom.* Stanford, CA: Stanford University Press.

Jones, Grant D., Don S. Rice, and Prudence M. Rice. 1981. The Location of Tayasal: A Reconsideration in Light of Petén Maya Ethnohistory and Archaeology. *American Antiquity* 46: 530–47.

Jones, Grant D., Robert R. Kautz, and Elizabeth A. Graham. 1986. Tipu: A Maya Town on the Spanish Colonial Frontier. *Archaeology* 39(1): 40–47.

Jones, Morris R. 1957. *Map of the Ruins of Mayapan, Yucatan, Mexico.* Carnegie Institution of Washington Current Reports, Vol. 2, 1954–1957. Washington, DC: Carnegie Institution of Washington.

Joralemon, Peter David. 1974. Ritual Blood-Sacrifice among the Ancient Maya: Part 1. In *First Palenque Round Table, 1973,* ed. M.G. Robertson, vol. 2, pp. 59–75. Pebble Beach, CA: Robert Louis Stevenson School.

Kaufman, Terrence S. 1973. Areal Linguistics in Middle America. In *Current Trends in Linguistics* 11, ed. T.A. Sebeok. The Hague: Mouton.

1976. Archaeological and Linguistic Correlations in Mayaland and Associated Areas of Mesoamerica. *World Archaeology* 8: 101–118.

Kelley, David H. 1962. Fonetismo en la Escritura Maya. *Estudios de Cultura Maya* 2: 227–317.

1976. *Deciphering the Maya Script.* Austin: University of Texas Press.

Kepecs, Susan, and Sylviane Boucher. 1996. Pre-Hispanic Cultivation of *Rejolladas* and Stone Lands: New Evidence from Northeast Yucatán. In *The Managed Mosaic: Ancient Maya Agriculture and Resource Use,* ed. S.J. Fedick, pp. 69–91. Salt Lake City: University of Utah Press.

Kerr, Barbara, and Justin Kerr. 1988. Some Observations on Maya Vase Painters. In *Maya Iconography,* ed. E.P. Benson and G.G. Griffin, pp. 236–259. Princeton, NJ: Princeton University Press.

Kerr, Justin. 1989. *The Maya Vase Book: A Corpus of Rollout Photographs of Maya Vases.* Vol. 1. New York: Kerr Associates.

1990. *The Maya Vase Book: A Corpus of Rollout Photographs of Maya Vases.* Vol. 2. New York: Kerr Associates.

1992. *The Maya Vase Book: A Corpus of Rollout Photographs of Maya Vases.* Vol. 3. New York: Kerr Associates.

Kidder II, Alfred V., Jesse D. Jennings, and Edwin M. Shook. 1946. *Excavations at Kaminaljuyú, Guatemala.* Carnegie Institution, publication 561. Washington, DC: Carnegie Institution of Washington.

Killion, Thomas W., ed. 1992. *Gardens of Prehistory: The Archaeology of Settlement Agriculture in Greater Mesoamerica.* Tuscaloosa: University of Alabama Press.

Killion, Thomas, Inez Verhagen, Dirk Van Tuerenhout, Daniela Triadan, Lisa Hamerlynck, Matthew McDermott, and José Genovés. 1991. Reporte de la Temporada 1991 del Recorrido Arqueológico Intersitio de Petexbatún. In *Proyecto Arqueológico Regional Petexbatún, Informe Preliminar No. 3:*

336     References

*Tercera Temporada, 1991*, ed. A.A. Demarest, T. Inomata, H.L. Escobedo, and J.W. Palka, pp. 588–645. Guatemala and Nashville, TN: Instituto de Antropología e Historia, and Department of Anthropology, Vanderbilt University.

Kingsborough, Edward King. 1831–1848. *Antiquities of Mexico*. London: Aglio.

Kirchhoff, Paul. 1943. Mesoamerica. *Acta Americana* 1: 92–107.

Knauft, Bruce M. 1996. *Genealogies for the Present in Cultural Anthropology*. New York: Routledge.

Knorosov, Yuri V. 1958. The Problem of the Study of the Maya Hieroglyphic Writing. *American Antiquity* 23: 284–291.

  1967. *The Writing of the Maya Indians*, trans. S. Coe. Russian Translation Series of the Peabody Museum of Archaeology and Ethnology, 4. Cambridge, MA: Harvard University.

Kosakowsky, Laura J., and Duncan C. Pring. 1998. The Ceramics of Cuello, Belize: A New Evaluation. *Ancient Mesoamerica* 9: 55–66.

Kovacevich, Brigitte, Tomás Barrientos Q., Arthur A. Demarest, Michael Callaghan, Cassandra Bill, Erin Sears, and Lucia Moran. 2001. Próduccion e intertercambio en el reinado de Cancuen. In XIV *Simposio de Investigaciónes Arqueológicas en Guatemala*, eds. J.P. Laporte, A.C. de Suasnávar, and B. Arroyo, pp. 589–612. Guatemala: Ministerio de Cultura y Deportes, Instituto de Antropología e Historia, Asociación Tikal.

Kovacevich, Brigitte, Tomás Barrientos Q., Michael Callaghan, and Karen Pereira. 2002. La economía en el reino clásico de Cancuén: evidencia de producción, especialización e intercambio.In *XV Simposio de Investigaciones Arqueológicas en Guatemala*, eds. J.P. Laporte, H.L. Escobedo, and B. Arroyo. Guatemala: Ministerio de Cultura y Deportes, Instituto de Antropología e Historia, Asociación Tikal.

Kowalski, Jeffrey K. 1987. *The House of the Governor: A Maya Palace at Uxmal, Yucatan, Mexico*. Norman: University of Oklahoma Press.

  1998. Uxmal and the Puuc Zone: Monumental Architecture, Sculptured Façades, and Political Power in the Terminal Classic Period. In *Maya*, ed. P. Schmidt, M. de la Garza, and E. Nalda, pp. 401–425. New York: Rizzoli International Publications.

Kowalski, Jeff K., and Nicholas P. Dunning. 1999. The Architecture of Uxmal: The Symbolics of Statemaking at a Puuc Maya Regional Capital. In *Mesoamerican Architecture as a Cultural Symbol*, ed. J.K. Kowalski, pp. 274–297. Oxford: Oxford University Press.

Kubler, George A. 1961. Chichén Itzá y Tula. *Estudios de Cultura Maya* 1: 47–80.

  1962. *The Art and Architecture of Ancient America: The Mexican, Mayan, and Andean Peoples*. Baltimore, MD: Pelican History of Art.

Kunen, Julie L., T. Patrick Culbert, Vilma Fialko, Brian R. McKee, Liwy Grazioso. 2000. Bajo Communities: A Case Study from the Central Petén. In *Culture and Agriculture* 22(3): 15–31. Tucson: University of Arizona Press.

Lamberg-Karlovsky, C.C. 1975. Third Millennium Modes of Exchange and Modes of Production. In *Ancient Civilization and Trade*, ed. J.A. Sabloff and C.C. Lamberg-Karlovsky, pp. 341–368. Albuquerque: University of New Mexico Press.

Lamberg-Karlovsky, C.C. ed. 1989. *Archaeological Thought in America.* Cambridge: Cambridge University Press.

Landa, Diego de. 1864. *Relation des Choses de Yucatan*, trans. C.E. Brasseur de Bourbourg. Paris: Arthus Bertrand.

Langer, William L. 1974. Infanticide: A Historical Survey. *History of Childhood Quarterly* 1: 353–366.

Lanning, L.P. 1970. Pleistocene Man in South America. *World Archaeology* 2: 90–111.

Laporte, Juan Pedro. 1996. Organización territorial y política prehispánica en el sureste de Petén. *In Atlas Arqueológico de Guatemala, No. 4.* Guatemala: Instituto de Antropología e Historia.

— 2004. Terminal Classic Settlement and Polity in the Mopán Valley, Petén, Guatemala. In *The Terminal Classic in the Maya Lowlands: Collapse, Transition, and Transformation*, ed. A.A. Demarest, P.M. Rice, and D.S. Rice. Boulder: University Press of Colorado.

Lathrap, Donald W. 1977. Our Father the Cayman, Our Mother the Gourd: Spinden Revisited, or a Unitary Model for the Emergence of Agriculture in the New World. In *Origins of Agriculture*, ed. C.A. Reed, pp. 713–752. The Hague: Mouton.

— 1982. Complex Iconographic Features by Olmec and Chavin and Some Speculations on Their Possible Significance. In *Primer Simposio de Correlaciones Antropológicas Andino-Mesoamericano*, eds. J. Marcos and P. Norton, pp. 301–327. Guayaquil, Ecuador: Escuela Politécnica del Litoral.

Laughlin, Robert M. 1977. *Of Cabbages and Kings: Tales From Zinacantan.* Smithsonian Contributions to Anthropology 23. Washington, DC: Smithsonian Institution.

Lee, Jr., Thomas A., and Carlos Navarrete, eds. 1978. *Mesoamerican Communication Routes and Cultural Contacts.* Papers of the New World Archaeological Foundation 40. Provo, UT: New World Archaeological Foundation.

León-Portilla, Miguel. 1963. *Aztec Thought and Culture: A Study of the Ancient Nahuatl Mind*, trans. J.E. Davis. Norman: University of Oklahoma Press.

— 1968. *Quetzalcóatl.* México, D.F.: Fondo de Cultura Económica.

— 1973. *Time and Reality in the Thought of the Maya.* Boston: Beacon Press.

Lesure, Richard G. 1997. Early Formative Platforms at Paso de la Amada, Chiapas, Mexico. *Latin American Antiquity* 8: 217–235.

— 1999. Platform Architecture and Activity Patterns in an Early Mesoamerican Village in Chiapas, Mexico. *Journal of Field Archaeology* 26: 391–406.

Lincoln, Charles E. 1985. Ceramics and Ceramic Chronology. In *A Consideration of the Early Classic Period in the Maya Lowlands*, ed. G.R. Willey and P. Mathews, pp. 55–94. Institute for Mesoamerican Studies Publication 10. Albany: State University of New York.

Longyear III, John M. 1952. *Copán Ceramics: A Study of Southeastern Maya Pottery.* Carnegie Institution of Washington, Publication 597. Washington, DC: Carnegie Institution.

Love, Michael W. 1991. Style and Social Complexity in Formative Mesoamerica. In *The Formation of Complex Society in Southeastern Mesoamerica*, ed. W.R. Fowler, Jr., pp. 47–76. Boca Raton, FL: CRC Press.

1998. Economía e ideología en El Ujuxte, Retalhuleu. In *XI Simposio de Investigaciones Arqueológicas en Guatemala*, eds. J.P. Laporte and H.L. Escobedo, pp. 309–318. Guatemala: Ministerio de Cultura y Deportes, Instituto de Antropología e Historia, Asociación Tikal.

1999a. Economic Patterns in the Development of Complex Society in Pacific Guatemala. In *Pacific Latin America in Prehistory: The Evolution of Archaic and Formative Cultures*, ed. M. Blake, pp. 89–100. Pullman: Washington State University Press.

1999b. La Cultura Olmeca en Guatemala. In *Historia General de Guatemala, Tomo: Epoca Precolombina*, vol. 1, ed. M. Popenoe de Hatch, pp. 191–200. Guatemala: Asociación de Amigos del Pais y Fundación para la Cultura y el Desarrollo.

Love, Michael W., and Donaldo Castillo. 1997. Excavaciones en zonas residenciales en El Ujuxte, Retalhuleu. In *X Simposio de Investigaciones Arqueológicas en Guatemala*, eds. J.P. Laporte and H.L. Escobedo, pp. 143–154. Guatemala: Ministerio de Cultura y Deportes, Instituto de Antropología e Historia, Asociación Tikal.

Lovell, W. George. 1992. *Conquest and Survival in Colonial Guatemala: A Historical Geography of the Cuchumatán Highlands, 1500–1821*, rev. ed. Montréal: McGill-Queen's University Press.

Lowe, Gareth W. 1975. *The Early Preclassic Barra Phase of Altamira, Chiapas: A Review with New Data*. Papers of the New World Archaeological Foundation 38. Provo, UT: New World Archaeological Foundation.

1977. The Mixe-Zoque as Competing Neighbors of the Early Lowland Maya. In *The Origins of Maya Civilization*, ed. R.E.W. Adams, pp. 197–248. Albuquerque: University of New Mexico Press.

1978. Eastern Mesoamerica. In *Chronologies in New World Archaeology*, ed. R.E. Taylor and C.W. Meighan, pp. 331–393. New York: Academic Press.

1983. Los Olmecas, Mayas y Mixe-Zoques. In *Antropología e Historia de los Mixe-Zoques y Mayas: Un Homenaje a Frans Blom*, eds. L. Ochoa and T.A. Lee, Jr., pp. 125–130. Mexico: Universidad Nacional Autónoma de México.

Lowe, Gareth W., Thomas A. Lee, Jr., and Eduardo Martínez E. 1982. *Izapa: An Introduction to the Ruins and Monuments*. Papers of the New World Archaeological Foundation 31. Provo, UT: New World Archaeological Foundation.

Lucero, Lisa J. 2002. The Collapse of the Ancient Maya: A Case for Water Control. *American Anthropologist* 104: 814–826.

2003. The Politics of Ritual: The Emergence of Classic Maya Rulers. *Current Anthropology* 44: 523–558.

Lundell, Cyrus L. 1933. The Agriculture of the Maya. *Southwest Review* 19: 65–77.

1938. Plants Probably Utilized by the Old Empire Maya of Peten and Adjacent Lowlands. *Papers of the Michigan Academy of Science, Arts, and Letters*, vol. 24, pp. 37–56. Ann Arbor: University of Michigan.

Lynch, Thomas F. 1978. The South American Paleo-Indians. In *Ancient Native Americans*, ed. J.D. Jennings, pp. 455–489. San Francisco: W.H. Freeman and Company.

1990. Glacial-Age Man in South America? A Critical Review. *American Antiquity* 55: 12–36.

1991. The Peopling of the Americas: A Discussion. In *The First Americans: Search and Research*, ed. T.D. Dillehay and D.J. Meltzer, pp. 267–274. Boca Raton, FL: CRC Press.

McAnany, Patricia A. 1989. Stone-Tool Production and Exchange in the Eastern Maya Lowlands: The Consumer Perspective from Pulltrouser Swamp, Belize. *American Antiquity* 54: 332–346.

1990. Water Storage in the Puuc Region of the Northern Maya Lowlands: A Key to Population Estimates and Architectural Variability. In *Precolumbian Population History in the Maya Lowlands*, ed. T.P. Culbert and D.S. Rice, pp. 263–284. Albuquerque: University of New Mexico Press.

1991. Ancestor Worship and Sanctification of Place: Excavations at K'axob, Belize. *Context* 9: 12–16. Boston: Boston University Center for Archaeological Studies.

1993. The Economics of Social Power and Wealth among Eighth-Century Maya Households. In *Lowland Maya Civilization in the Eighth Century A.D.*, ed. J.A. Sabloff and J.S. Henderson, pp. 65–90. Washington, DC: Dumbarton Oaks.

1995. *Living with the Ancestors: Kinship and Kingship in Ancient Maya Society*. Austin: University of Texas Press.

McAnany, Patricia A., and Barry L. Isaac, eds. 1989. *Prehistoric Maya Economies of Belize*. Research in Economic Anthropology supplement 4. Greenwich, CT: JAI Press.

McAnany, Patricia A., Ben S. Thomas, Steven Morandi, Polly A. Peterson, and Eleanor Harrison. 2002. Praise the Ajaw and Pass the Kakaw: Xibun Maya and the Political Economy of Cacao. In *Ancient Maya Political Economies*, eds. M.A. Masson and D.A. Freidel, pp. 123–139. Walnut Creek, CA: AltaMira Press.

McGuire, Randall. 1983. Breaking Down Cultural Complexity: Inequality and Heterogeneity. *Advances in Archaeological Method and Theory* 6: 91–117.

McKillop, Heather I., and Paul F. Healy, eds. 1989. *Coastal Maya Trade*. Peterborough, England: Trent University.

McKinley, James C. 1997. In One Somali Town, Clan Rule has Brought Peace. *New York Times*, 22 June 1997.

MacNeish, Richard S. 1964. Ancient Mesoamerican Civilization. *Scientific American* 211(5): 29–37.

MacNeish, Richard S., S. Jeffrey K. Wilkerson, and Antoinette Nelken-Terner. 1980. *First Annual Report of the Belize Archaic Archaeological Reconnaissance*. Andover: Robert F. Peabody Foundation for Archaeology, Phillips Academy.

Mahler, Joy. 1965. Garments and Textiles of the Maya Lowlands. In *Handbook of Middle American Indians*, Vol. 3: *Archaeology of Southern Mesoamerica, Part 2*, ed. G.R. Willey, pp. 581–593. Austin: University of Texas Press.

Maler, Teobert. 1901. *Researches in the Central Portion of the Usumatsintla Valley: Report of Explorations for the Museum, 1898–1900*. Peabody Museum of Archaeology and Ethnology Memoirs vol. 2, no. 1. Cambridge, MA: Harvard University.

1903. *Researches in the Central Portion of the Usumatsintla Valley: Report of Explorations for the Museum.* Peabody Museum of Archaeology and Ethnology Memoirs vol. 2, no. 2. Cambridge, MA: Harvard University Press.

1908. *Explorations in the Department of Peten, Guatemala, and Adjacent Region: Topoxte; Yaxha; Benque Viejo; Naranjo.* Peabody Museum of Archaeology and Ethnology Memoirs vol. 4, no. 2. Cambridge, MA: Harvard University Press.

1911. *Explorations in the Department of Peten, Guatemala: Tikal.* Peabody Museum of Archaeology and Ethnology Memoirs vol. 5, no. 1. Cambridge, MA: Harvard University Press.

Mallory III, Jack K. 1984. Late Classic Maya Economic Specialization: Evidence from the Copan Obsidian Assemblage. Ph.D. dissertation, Department of Anthropology, Pennsylvania State University, University Park.

Mamdani, Mahmood. 1974. The Myth of Population Control. *Development Digest* 12: 13–28.

Manahan, T. Kam. 2000. Reexaminando los Días Finales de Copán: Nuevos Datos de la Fase Ejar. In *XIII Simposio de Investigaciónes Arqueológicas en Guatemala,* ed. J.P. Laporte, H.L. Escobedo, A.C. de Suasnávar, and B. Arroyo, pp. 1149–1155. Guatemala: Ministerio de Cultura y Deportes, Instituto de Antropología e Historia, Asociación Tikal.

2003. The Collapse of Complex Society and its Aftermath: A Case Study from the Classic Maya Site of Copan, Honduras. Ph.D. dissertation, Department of Anthropology, Vanderbilt University, Nashville, TN.

Mann, Michael. 1986. *The Sources of Social Power.* Cambridge: Cambridge University Press.

Manzanilla, Linda, and Leonardo Lopez Luján, eds. 2000. *Historia Antigua de Mexico,* 2nd edition. Mexico, DF: Universidad Nacional Autónoma de México.

Marcus, Joyce. 1976. *Emblem and State in the Classic Maya Lowlands: An Epigraphic Approach to Territorial Organization.* Washington, DC: Dumbarton Oaks, Trustees for Harvard University.

1978. Archaeology and Religion: A Comparison of the Zapotec and Maya. *World Archaeology* 10: 172–191.

1983a. Lowland Maya Archaeology at the Crossroads. *American Antiquity* 48: 454–488.

1983b. On the Nature of the Mesoamerican City. In *Prehistoric Settlement Patterns: Essays in Honor of Gordon R. Willey,* eds. Evon Z. Vogt, Jr., and R.M. Leventhal, pp. 195–242. Albuquerque: University of New Mexico Press.

1984. Mesoamerican Territorial Boundaries: Reconstructions from Archaeology and Hieroglyphic Writing. *Archaeological Review from Cambridge* 2: 48–62.

1989. Zapotec Chiefdoms and the Nature of Formative Religions. In *Regional Perspectives on the Olmec,* ed. R.J. Sharer and D.C. Grove, pp. 148–197. Cambridge: Cambridge University Press.

1993. Ancient Maya Political Organization. In *Lowland Maya Civilization in the Eighth Century AD*, ed. J.A. Sabloff and J.S. Henderson, pp. 111–184. Washington, DC: Dumbarton Oaks, Trustees for Harvard University.

1995. Where is Lowland Maya Archaeology Headed? *Journal of Archaeological Research* 3: 3 – 57.

1998. The Peaks and Valleys of Archaic States. In *Archaic States*, ed. G.M. Feinman and J. Marcus, pp. 59–94. Santa Fe, NM: School of American Research Press.

2003. The Maya and Teotihuacan. In *The Maya and Teotihuacan: Reinterpreting Early Classic Interaction*, ed. G.E. Braswell, pp. 337–356. Austin: University of Texas Press.

Martin, Simon, and Nikolai Grube. 1994. *Evidence for Macro-Political Organization Amongst Classic Maya Lowland States*. Manuscript.

1995. Maya Superstates. *Archaeology* 48(6): 41–46.

1996. *Evidence for Macro-Political Organisation of Classic Maya States*. Manuscript on file. Washington, DC and Bonn, Germany: Dumbarton Oaks and University of Bonn.

2000. *Chronicle of the Maya Kings and Queens: Deciphering the Dynasties of the Ancient Maya*. London: Thames and Hudson.

Masson, Marilyn A., and David A. Freidel, ed. 2002. *Ancient Maya Political Economies*. Walnut Creek, CA: AltaMira Press.

Masson, Marilyn A., and Shirley B. Mock. 2004. Maya Cultural Adaptations from the Terminal Classic to Postclassic Period at Lagoon Sites in Northern Belize as Reflected in Changing Ceramic Industries. In *The Terminal Classic in the Maya Lowlands: Collapse, Transition, and Transformation*, ed. A.A. Demarest, P.M. Rice, and D.S. Rice. Boulder, University Press of Colorado.

Matheny, Raymond T., 1976. Maya Lowland Hydraulic Systems. *Science* 193: 639–646.

1980. *El Mirador, Peten, Guatemala: An Interim Report*. Provo, UT: Brigham Young University Press.

1986. Investigations at El Mirador, Peten, Guatemala. *National Geographic Research* 2: 322–353.

1987. Early States in the Maya Lowlands During the Late Preclassic Period: Edzna and El Mirador. In *City-States of the Maya: Art and Architecture*, ed. E.P. Benson, pp. 1–44. Denver, CO: Rocky Mountain Institute for Precolumbian Studies.

Matheny, Raymond T., Deanne L. Gurr, Donald W. Forsyth, and F. Richard Hauck. 1983. *Investigations at Edzna, Campeche, Mexico: The Hydraulic System*, Vol. 1, Part 1: New World Archaeological Foundation Paper 46. Provo, UT: New World Archaeological Foundation.

Mathews, Peter. 1985. Maya Early Classic Monuments and Inscriptions. In *A Consideration of the Early Classic Period in the Maya Lowlands*, ed. G.R. Willey and P. Mathews, pp. 5–54. Institute for Mesoamerican Studies Publication 10. Albany: State University of New York.

1988. The Sculptures of Yaxchilan. Ph.D. dissertation, Department of Anthropology, Yale University, New Haven, CT.

1991. Classic Maya Emblem Glyphs. In *Classic Maya Political History: Hieroglyphic and Archaeological Evidence*, ed. T.P. Culbert, pp. 19–29. Cambridge: Cambridge University Press.

Mathews, Peter and Gordon R. Willey. 1985. Early Classic Monuments and Inscriptions. In *A Consideration of the Early Classic Period in the Maya Lowlands*, ed. P. Mathews and G.R. Willey, pp. 5–55. Institute for Mesoamerican Studies Publication 10. Albany: State University of New York.

1991. Prehistoric Polities of the Pasión Region. In *Classic Maya Political History: Hieroglyphic and Archaeological Evidence*, ed. T.P. Culbert, pp. 30–71. Cambridge: Cambridge University Press.

Maudslay, Alfred P. 1889. *Biologia Centrali-Americana: Contributions to the Knowledge of Fauna and Flora of Mexico and Central America*, ed. F.D. Godman and O. Salvin. London: R.H. Porter and Dulau and Co.

Meggers, Betty J. 1954. Environmental Limitation on the Development of Culture. *American Anthropologist* 56: 801–824.

Merwin, Raymond E., and George C. Vaillant. 1932. *The Ruins of Holmul, Guatemala*. Peabody Museum of Archaeology and Ethnology Memoirs, vol. 3, no. 2. Cambridge, MA: Harvard University.

Michels, Joseph W. 1977. Political Organization at Kaminaljuyú: Its Implications for Interpreting Teotihuácan Influence. In *Teotihuácan and Kaminaljuyú: A Study in Prehistoric Culture Contact*, ed. W.T. Sanders and J.W. Michels, pp. 453–467. University Park: Pennsylvania State University Press.

1979. *The Kaminaljuyú Chiefdom*. University Park: Pennsylvania State University.

Milbrath, Susan. 1988. Astronomical Images and Orientations in the Architecture of Chichen Itza. In *New Directions in American Archaeoastronomy*, ed. A.F. Aveni. pp. 57–59. British Archaeological Reports 454. Oxford: BAR International Series.

Miller, Arthur G. 1977. The Maya and the Sea: Trade and Cult at Tancah and Tulum, Quintana Roo, Mexico. In *The Sea in the Precolumbian World*, ed. E.P. Benson, pp. 97–138. Washington, DC: Dumbarton Oaks, Trustees for Harvard University.

1982. *On the Edge of the Sea: Mural Painting at Tancah-Tulum, Quintana Roo, Mexico*. Washington, DC: Dumbarton Oaks.

1986. From the Maya Margins: Images of Postclassic Power Politics. In *Late Lowland Maya Civilization: Classic to Postclassic*, ed. J.A. Sabloff and E.W. Andrews V, pp. 199–222. Albuquerque: University of New Mexico Press.

Miller, Daniel. 1985. Ideology and the Harappan Civilization. *Journal of Anthropological Archaeology* 4: 34–71.

Miller, Daniel, and Christopher Tilley, eds. 1984. *Ideology, Power and Prehistory*. Cambridge: Cambridge University Press.

Miller, Mary E. 1986. *Art of Mesoamerica: From Olmec to Aztec*. New York: Thames and Hudson.

1991. Some Observations on the Relationship between Yaxchilan and Piedras Negras. Paper presented at the 7th Texas Symposium, Austin.

1993. On the Eve of the Collapse: Maya Art of the Eighth Century. In *Lowland Maya Civilization in the Eighth Century AD*, ed. J.A. Sabloff and J.S. Henderson, pp. 355–414. Washington, DC: Dumbarton Oaks, Trustees for Harvard University.

Millon, René. 1993. The Place Where Time Began: An Archaeologist's Interpretation of What Happened in Teotihuacan History. In *Teotihuacan: Art from the City of the Gods*, ed. K. Berrin and E. Pasztory, pp. 16–43. New York: Thames and Hudson.

Mock, Shirley B., ed. 1998. *The Sowing and the Dawning: Termination, Dedication, and Transformation in the Archaeological and Ethnographic Record of Mesoamerica*. Albuquerque: University of New Mexico Press.

Moholy-Nagy, Hattula. 1990. The Misidentification of Mesoamerican Lithic Workshops. *Latin American Antiquity* 1: 268–279.

1997. Middens, Construction Fill, and Offerings: Evidence for the Organization of Classic Period Craft Production at Tikal, Guatemala. *Journal of Field Archaeology* 24: 293–313.

Moholy-Nagy, Hattula, Frank Asaro, and Fred H. Stross. 1984. Tikal Obsidian: Sources and Typology. *American Antiquity* 49: 104–117.

Montejo, Victor. 1991. In the Name of the Pot, the Sun, the Broken Spear, the Rock, the Stick, the Idol, Ad Infinitum and Ad Nauseam: An Expose of Anglo Anthropologists' Obsessions with and Invention of Mayan Gods. Paper presented at the 1991 Annual Meeting of the American Anthropological Association, San Francisco.

1999. *Voices from Exile: Violence and Survival in Modern Maya History*. Norman: University of Oklahoma Press.

Montmollin, Oliver. 1989. *The Archaeology of Political Structure: Settlement Analysis in a Classic Maya Polity*. Cambridge: Cambridge University Press.

Morgan, Kim, and Arthur A. Demarest. 1995. Excavación de un Deposito Basural Post Clásico. In *Proyecto Arqueológico Regional Petexbatún, Informe Preliminar No. 6: Sexta Temporada*, eds. A.A. Demarest, J.A. Valdés, and H.L. Escobedo, pp. 321–327. Guatemala and Nashville, TN: Instituto de Antropología e Historia and Department of Anthropology, Vanderbilt University.

Morley, Sylvanus. 1915. *An Introduction to the Study of the Maya Hieroglyphs*. Bureau of American Ethnology Bulletin 57. Washington, DC: Smithsonian Institution Press.

1920. *The Inscriptions at Copán*. Carnegie Institution Publication, 219. Washington, DC: Carnegie Institution.

1937–38. *The Inscriptions of Petén*. Carnegie Institution Publication, 437. Washington, DC: Carnegie Institution.

1946. *The Ancient Maya*. Stanford, CA: Stanford University Press.

Morley, Sylvanus and George W. Brainerd. 1956. *The Ancient Maya*. 3rd edition. Stanford, CA: Stanford University Press.

Murie, Adolph. 1935. Mammals from Guatemala and British Honduras. In *Museum of Zoology, University of Michigan Miscellaneous Publications* 26: 7–30. Ann Arbor: University of Michigan Press.

Nash, June C. 1970. *In the Eyes of the Ancestors: Belief and Behavior in a Maya Community*. New Haven: Yale University Press.

Nations, James D., and Ronald B. Nigh. 1980. The Evolutionary Potential of Lancandon Maya Sustained-Yield Tropical Forest Agriculture. *Journal of Anthropological Research* 1: 1–30.

Neff, L.T., C. Robin, K. Schwartz, and M. Morrison. 1995. The Xunantunich Settlement Survey. In *Xunantunich Archaeological Project: 1995 Field Season*. Los Angeles and Belmopan: Xunantunich Archaeological Project.

Nelson, Diane. 1999. *A Finger in the Wound: Body Politics in Quincentennial Guatemala*. Berkeley: University of California Press.

Netting, Robert McC. 1977. Maya Subsistence: Mythologies, Analogies, Possibilities. In *The Origins of Maya Civilization*, ed. R.E.W. Adams, pp. 229–333. Albuquerque: University of New Mexico Press.

Nicholson, Henry B. 1971. Religion in Pre-Hispanic Central Mexico. In *Handbook of Middle American Indians*, Vol. 10: *Archaeology of Northern Mesoamerica, Part 1*, ed. G.F. Ekholm and I. Bernal, pp. 395–446. Austin: University of Texas Press.

Ohnstad, Arik, Walter Burgos M., and Claudia Arriaza C. 2003. A Lower Elite House Compound and Its Ritual Water System. In *Proyecto Arqueológico Cancuen, Informe Preliminar No. 5, Temporada 2003*, eds. T. Barrientos Q., B. Kovacevich, M. Callaghan, and A.A. Demarest. Guatemala and Nashville, TN: Instituto de Antropología e Historia and Department of Anthropology, Vanderbilt University.

O'Mansky, Matt, and Arthur A. Demarest. 1995. La Temporada de Reconocimiento de 1994 del Subproyecto del Patron de Asentamiento entre Sitios La Region de Petexbatún. In *Proyecto Arqueológico Regional Petexbatún, Informe Preliminar No. 6: Sexta Temporada*, Vol. 2, ed. A.A. Demarest, J.A. Valdés, and H.L. Escobedo, pp. 403–494. Guatemala and Nashville, TN: Instituto de Antropología e Historia, and Department of Anthropology, Vanderbilt University.

O'Mansky, Matt, and Nick Dunning. 2004. Settlement and Late Classic Political Disintegration in the Petexbatun Region, Guatemala. In *The Terminal Classic in the Maya Lowlands: Collapse, Transition, and Transformation*, ed. A. Demarest, P. Rice, and D.S. Rice. Boulder: University Press of Colorado.

O'Mansky, Matt, and Robert Wheat. 1997. Investigaciones del Transecto 2. In *Proyecto Arqueológico Punta de Chimino, Informe Preliminar de la Primera Temporada*, ed. A.A. Demarest, H.L. Escobedo, and M. O'Mansky. Guatemala and Nashville, TN: Instituto de Antropología e Historia, and Department of Anthropology, Vanderbilt University.

Orrego, Miguel. 1998. Problemática de la Multiplicidad de Estilos y Patrones Culturales en Abaj Takalik. In *Taller Arqueología de la Región de la Costa Sur de Guatemala*, ed. C. Schieber de Lavarreda, pp. 53–70. Guatemala: Ministerio de Cultura y Deportes.

Paine, Richard R., and AnnCorinne Freter. 1996. Environmental Degradation and the Classic Maya Collapse at Copan, Honduras, AD 600–1250: Evidence from Studies of Household Survival. *Ancient Mesoamerica* 7: 37–47.

Palka W., Joel. 1995. Classic Maya Social Inequality and the Collapse at Dos Pilas, Peten, Guatemala. Ph.D. dissertation, Department of Anthropology, Vanderbilt University, Nashville, TN.

1997. Reconstructing Classic Maya Socioeconomic Differentiation and the Collapse at Dos Pilas, Peten, Guatemala. *Ancient Mesoamerica* 8: 293–306.

Palerm, Ángel. 1973. *Obras Hidraulicas Prehispánicas en el Sistema Lacustre del Valle México*. Mexico: Instituto Nacional de Antropología e Historia.

Parsons, Jeffrey R. 1974. The Development of a Prehistoric Complex Society: A Regional Perspective from the Valley of Mexico. *Journal of Field Archaeology* 1: 81–108.

Parsons, Lee A. 1976. Excavations of Monte Alto, Escuintla, Guatemala. In *National Geographic Society Research Reports, 1968 Projects*, pp. 325–332. Washington, DC: The National Geographic Society.

1978. The Peripheral Coastal Lowlands and the Middle Classic Period. In *Middle Classic Mesoamerica: AD 400–700*, ed. E. Pasztory, pp. 25–34. New York: Columbia University Press.

1981. Post-Olmec Stone Sculpture: The Olmec-Izapan Transition on the Southern Pacific Coast and Highlands. In *The Olmec and Their Neighbors*, ed. E.P. Benson, pp. 257–288. Washington, DC: Dumbarton Oaks, Trustees for Harvard University.

1986. *The Origins of Maya Art: Monumental Stone Sculpture of Kaminaljuyu, Guatemala, and the Southern Pacific Coast*. Washington, DC: Dumbarton Oaks, Trustees for Harvard University.

1988. Proto-Maya Aspects of Miraflores-Arenal Monumental Stone Sculpture from Kaminaljuyu and the Southern Pacific Coast. In *Maya Iconography*, ed. E.P. Benson and G.G. Griffin, pp. 6–43. Princeton, NJ: Princeton University Press.

Pendergast, David M. 1986. Stability Through Change: Lamanai, Belize, from the Ninth to the Seventeenth Century. In *Late Lowland Maya Civilization: Classic to Postclassic*, ed. J.A. Sabloff and E.W. Andrews V, pp. 223–249. Albuquerque: University of New Mexico Press.

Pohl, Mary. 1985. *Prehistoric Lowland Maya Environment and Subsistence Economy*. Memoirs of the Peabody Museum of Archaeology and Ethnology 77. Cambridge, MA: Harvard University.

Polgar, Steven, ed. 1975. *Population, Ecology, and Social Evolution*. Ninth International Congress of Anthropological and Ethnological Sciences. The Hague: Mouton.

Pollock, Harry E.D., Ralph L. Roys, Tatiana Proskouriakoff, and A. Ledyard Smith. 1962. *Mayapan, Yucatán, Mexico*. Carnegie Institute of Washington Publication 619. Washington, DC: Carnegie Institution.

Pollock, Susan. 1999. *Ancient Mesopotamia: The Eden that Never Was*. Cambridge: Cambridge University Press.

Pope, Kevin O., and Bruce H. Dahlin. 1989. Ancient Maya Wetland Agriculture: New Insights from Ecological and Remote Sensing Research. *Journal of Field Archaeology* 16: 87–106.

Porter-Weaver, Muriel. 1993. *The Aztecs, Maya, and Their Predecessors: Archaeology of Mesoamerica*. 3rd ed. San Diego, CA: Academic Press.

Potter, David F. 1977. *Maya Architecture of the Central Yucatan Peninsula, Mexico.* Middle American Research Institute, publication 44. New Orleans: Tulane University Press.

Prem, Hanns, ed. 1994. *Hidden Among the Hills: Maya Archaeology of the Northwest Yucatan Peninsula.* Möckmühl, Germany: Verlag von Flemming.

Preucel, Robert W., ed. 1991. *Processual and Postprocessual Archaeologies: Multiple Ways of Knowing the Past.* Carbondale, IL: Center for Archaeological Investigations, Southern Illinois University.

Price, Barbara J. 1978. Secondary State Formation: An Explanatory Model. In *Origins of the State: The Anthropology of Political Evolution,* ed. R. Cohen and E.R. Service, pp. 161–186. Philadelphia, PA: Institute for the Study of Human Issues.

Pring, Duncan. 1977. The Preclassic Ceramics of Northern Belize. Ph.D. dissertation, University of London.

Proskouriakoff, Tatiana A. 1950. *Classic Maya Sculpture.* Carnegie Institution of Washington Publication 593. Washington, DC: Carnegie Institution.

1960. Historical Implications of a Pattern of Dates at Piedras Negras, Guatemala. *American Antiquity* 25: 454–475.

1961. The Lords of the Maya Realm. *Expedition* 4(1): 14–21.

1963. Historical Data in the Inscriptions of Yaxchilan, Part I. The Reign of Shield-Jaguar. *Estudios de Cultura Maya* 3: 149–167.

1964. Historical Data in the Inscriptions of Yaxchilan, Part II. *Estudios de Cultura Maya* 4: 177–201.

Puleston, Dennis E. 1974. Intersite Areas in the Vicinity of Tikal and Uaxactun. In *Mesoamerican Archaeology: New Approaches,* ed. N.D.C. Hammond, pp. 303–311. Austin: University of Texas Press.

1979. An Epistemological Pathology and the Collapse, or Why the Maya Kept the Short Count. In *Maya Archaeology and Ethnohistory,* ed. N.D.C. Hammond and G.R. Willey, pp. 63–74. Austin: University of Texas Press.

Pye, Mary E. 1995. Settlement, Specialization, and Adaptation in the Rio Jesus Drainage, Retalhuleu, Guatemala. Ph.D. dissertation, Department of Anthropology, Vanderbilt University, Nashville, TN.

Pye, Mary E., and Arthur A. Demarest. 1991. The Evolution of Complex Societies in Southeastern Mesoamerica: New Evidence from El Mesak, Guatemala. In *The Formation of Complex Society in Southeastern Mesoamerica,* ed. W.R. Fowler, Jr., pp. 77–100. W. Caldwell, NJ: Telford Press.

Pye, Mary E., Arthur A. Demarest, and Bárbara Arroyo. 1999. Early Formative Societies in Guatemala and El Salvador. In *Pacific Latin America in Prehistory: The Evolution of Archaic and Formative Cultures,* ed. M. Blake, pp. 75–88. Pullman: Washington State University Press.

Quezada, Heidy, Kim Morgan, Arthur A. Demarest, and Timothy Beach. 1996. Investigaciones en asentamientos residenciales, sistemas agrícolas y ecología de Punta de Chimino. In *X Simposio de Investigaciones Arqueologicas en Guatemala,* ed. J.P. Laporte, H.L. Escobedo, pp. 385–388. Guatemala: Ministerio de Cultura y Deportes, Instituto de Antropología e Historia, Asociación Tikal.

Quirarte, Jacinto. 1973. *Izapan-Style Art: A Study of Its Form and Meaning.* Studies in Pre-Columbian Art and Archaeology 10. Washington, DC: Dumbarton Oaks, Trustees for Harvard University.

1977. Early Art Styles of Mesoamerica and Early Classic Maya Art. In *The Origins of Maya Civilization,* ed. R.E.W. Adams, pp. 249–283. Albuquerque: University of New Mexico Press.

Rands, Robert L., and Ronald L. Bishop. 1980. Resource Procurement Zones and Patterns of Ceramic Exchange in the Palenque Region. In *Models and Methods in Regional Exchange,* ed. R.E. Fry, pp. 19–46. Society for American Archaeology Papers 1. Washington, DC: Society for American Archaeology.

Rathje, William L. 1971. The Origin and Development of Lowland Classic Maya Civilization. *American Antiquity* 36: 275–286.

1973. Trade Models and Archaeological Problems: The Classic Maya and Their E-Group Complex. In *Proceedings of the International Congress of Americanists,* vol. 4, pp. 223–235. Genova.

1975. *Changing Pre-Columbian Commercial Systems: The 1972–1973 Seasons at Cozumel, Mexico.* Peabody Museum of Archaeology and Ethnology Monograph 3. Cambridge, MA: Harvard University.

1977. The Tikal Connection. In *The Origins of Maya Civilization,* ed. R.E.W. Adams, pp. 373–382. Albuquerque: University of New Mexico Press.

Redfield, Robert, and Alfonso Villa Rojas. 1934. *Chan Kom: A Maya Village.* Carnegie Institution Publication 448. Washington, DC: Carnegie Institution.

Reed, Nelson A. 1964. *The Caste War of Yucatán.* Stanford: Stanford University Press.

Reents-Budet, Dorie. 1985. The Holmul Style Classic Maya Pottery. Ph.D. dissertation, University of Texas, Austin.

1987. The Discovery of a Ceramic Artist and Royal Patron Among the Classic Maya. *Mexicon* 9(6): 123–126.

1994. *Painting the Maya Universe: Royal Ceramics of the Classic Period.* Durham, NC: Duke University Press.

1998. Elite Maya Pottery and Artisans as Social Indicators. In *Craft and Social Identity,* ed. C.L. Costin and R. Wright. Archaeological Papers of the American Anthropological Association No. 8. Washington, DC: American Anthropological Association.

Reents-Budet, Dorie, and Ronald L. Bishop. 1985. History and Ritual Events on a Petexbatun Classic Maya Polychrome Vessel. In *Fifth Palenque Round Table, 1983,* ed. V.M. Fields, pp. 57–63. San Francisco: Pre-Columbian Art Research Institute.

1987. *The Late Classic Maya "Codex Style" Pottery.* Memorias del Primer Coloquio Internacional de Mayistas. Mexico, D.F.: Universidad Nacional Autonoma de Mexico.

Reents-Budet, Dorie, Ronald L. Bishop, and Barbara McLeod. 1994. Painting Styles, Workshop Locations, and Pottery Production. In *Painting the Maya Universe: Royal Ceramics of the Classic Period,* ed. D. Reents-Budet, pp. 164–233. Durham: Duke University Press.

Reina, Ruben E., and Robert M. Hill II. 1980. Lowland Maya Subsistence: Notes from Ethnohistory and Ethnography. *American Antiquity* 45: 74–79.

Renfrew, Colin, and John F. Cherry, eds. 1986. *Peer Polity Interaction and Socio-Political Change*. Cambridge: Cambridge University Press.

Restall, Matthew. 1997. *The Maya World: Yucatec Culture and Society 1550–1850*. Stanford: Stanford University Press.

Rice, Don S. 1981. Zacpeten: A Postclassic Center in the Central Peten, Guatemala. Paper presented at the 46th Annual Meeting of the Society for American Archaeology, San Diego.

    1986. The Peten Postclassic: A Settlement Perspective. In *Late Lowland Maya Civilization: Classic to Postclassic*, ed. J.A. Sabloff and E.W. Andrews V, pp. 301–344. Alburquerque: University of New Mexico Press.

    1993a. The Making of Latin American Horizons: An Introduction to the Volume. In *Latin American Horizons: A Symposium at Dumbarton Oaks, 11th and 12th October, 1986*, ed. D.S. Rice, pp. 1–13. Washington, DC: Dumbarton Oaks, Trustees for Harvard University.

    1993b. Eighth Century Physical Geography, Environment and Natural Resources in the Maya Lowlands. In *Lowland Maya Civilization in the Eighth Century A.D.*, ed. J.A. Sabloff and J.S. Henderson, pp. 11–63. Washington, DC: Dumbarton Oaks, Trustees for Harvard University.

Rice, Don S., and Prudence M. Rice. 1990. Population Size and Population Change in the Central Peten Lakes Region, Guatemala. In *Precolumbian Population History in the Maya Lowlands*, ed. T.P. Culbert and D.S. Rice, pp. 123–148. Albuquerque: University of New Mexico Press.

Rice, Don S., Prudence M. Rice, and Edward S. Deevey. 1985. Paradise Lost: Classic Maya Impact on a Lacustrine Environment. In *Prehistoric Lowland Maya Environment and Subsistence Economy*, ed. Mary Pohl, pp. 91–106. Papers of the Peabody Museum of Archaeology and Ethnology 77. Cambridge, MA: Harvard University.

Rice, Don S., Prudence M. Rice, and Grant D. Jones. 1993. Geografía política del Petén Central, Guatemala, en el Siglo XVII: La Arqueología de las Capitales Mayas. *Mesoamerica* 14(26): 281–318.

Rice, Don S., Prudence M. Rice, Romulo Sánchez P., and Grant D. Jones. 1995. *El Proyecto Geografía Política del Siglo XVII en el Centro del Petén, Guatemala: Informe al IDAEH de Guatemala sobre la Primera Temporada del Trabajo del Campo*. Unpublished report on file at Department of Anthropology, Southern Illinois University, Carbondale.

Rice, Don S., Prudence M. Rice, Romulo Sánchez Polo, and Grant D. Jones. 1996. *Proyecto Maya-Colonial, Geografía Política del Siglo XVII en el Centro del Petén, Guatemala: Informe al IDAEH de Guatemala sobre Investigaciones del Campo en los Años 1994 y 1995*. Unpublished report on file at Department of Anthropology, Southern Illinois University, Carbondale.

Rice, Prudence M. 1981. Evolution of Specialized Pottery Production: A Trial Model. *Current Anthropology* 22: 219–240.

    1984. Obsidian Procurement in the Central Petén Lakes Region, Guatemala. *Journal of Field Archaeology* 11: 181–194.

    1986. The Peten Postclassic: Perspectives from the Central Peten Lakes. In *Late Lowland Maya Civilization: Classic to Postclassic*, ed. J.A. Sabloff and E.W. Andrews V, pp. 251–300. Albuquerque: University of New Mexico Press.

1987a. Economic Change in the Lowland Maya Late Classic Period. In *Specialization, Exchange, and Complex Societies*, ed. E.M. Brumfiel and T.K. Earle, pp. 76–85. Cambridge: Cambridge University Press.

1987b. Lowland Maya Pottery Production in the Late Classic Period. In *Maya Ceramics: Papers from the 1985 Maya Ceramic Conference*, ed. P.M. Rice and R.J. Sharer, pp. 525–543. British Archaeological Reports 345. Oxford: BAR International Series.

1987c. *Macanché Island, El Petén, Guatemala: Excavations, Pottery, and Artifacts*. Gainesville: University of Florida Press.

1990. Ceramic Diversity, Production, and Use. In *Quantitative Diversity in Archaeology*, pp. 109–117. Cambridge: Cambridge University Press.

1991. Specialization, Standardization, and Diversity: A Retrospective. In *Ceramic Legacy of Anna O. Shepard*, eds. R. Bishop and F. Lange, pp. 257–259. Boulder: University Press of Colorado.

In press. *Maya Political Science: The Political Organization of the Lowland Maya*. Austin: University of Texas Press.

Rice, Prudence M., Arthur A. Demarest, and Don S. Rice. 2004. The Terminal Classic and the "Classic Maya Collapse" in Perspective. In *The Terminal Classic in the Maya Lowlands: Collapse, Transition, and Transformation*, eds. A.A. Demarest, P.M. Rice, and D.S. Rice, pp. 1–11. Boulder: University Press of Colorado.

Rice, Prudence M., Helen V. Michel, Frank Asaro, and Fred H. Stross. 1985. Provenience Analysis of Obsidians from the Central Petén Lakes Region, Guatemala. *American Antiquity* 50: 591–604.

Rice, Prudence M., and Don S. Rice. 2004. Late Classic to Postclassic Transformations in the Petén Lakes Region, Guatemala. In *The Terminal Classic in the Maya Lowlands: Collapse, Transition, and Transformation*, eds. A.A. Demarest, P.M. Rice, and D.S. Rice, pp. 125–139. Boulder: University Press of Colorado.

Ricketson, Jr., Oliver G., and Edith Bayles Ricketson. 1937. *Uaxactun, Guatemala, Group E, 1926–1931*. Carnegie Institution Publication 477. Washington, DC: Carnegie Institution.

Ringle III, William M., and E. Wyllys Andrews V. 1988. Formative Residence at Komchen, Yucatan, Mexico. In *Household and Community in the Mesoamerican Past*, ed. R.R. Wilk and W.A. Ashmore, pp. 171–199. Albuquerque: University of New Mexico Press.

Ringle III, William M., and E. Wyllys Andrews V. 1990. The Demography of Komchen, An Early Maya Town in Northern Yucatan. In *Precolumbian Population History in the Maya Lowlands*, ed. T.P. Culbert and D.S. Rice, pp. 215–244. Albuquerque: University of New Mexico Press.

Ringle, William M., George J. Bey III, Tara Bond Freeman, Craig A. Hanson, Charles W. Houck, and J. Gregory Smith. 2004. The Decline of the East: The Classic-to-Postclassic Transition at Ek Balam, Yucatán. In *The Terminal Classic in the Maya Lowlands: Collapse, Transition, and Transformation*, ed. A.A. Demarest, P.M. Rice, and D.S. Rice. Boulder: University Press of Colorado.

Ringle, William M., Tomas Gallareta N., and George J. Bey III. 1998. The Return of Quetzalcoatl: Evidence for the Spread of a World Religion during the Epiclassic Period. *Ancient Mesoamerica* 9: 183–232.

Robichaux, Hubert R. 2002. On the Compatibility of Epigraphic and Archaeological Data, with a Drought-Based Explanation for the Classic Maya Collapse. *Ancient Mesoamerica* 13: 341–345.

Robles, J. Fernando, and Anthony P. Andrews. 1986. A Review and Synthesis of Recent Postclassic Archaeology in Northern Yucatan. In *Late Lowland Maya Civilization: Classic to Postclassic*, ed. J.A. Sabloff and E.W. Andrews V, pp. 53–98. Albuquerque: University of New Mexico Press.

Rowe, John H. 1956. Cultural Unity and Diversification in Peruvian Archaeology. In *Men and Cultures: Selected Papers of the Fifth International Congress of Anthropological and Ethnological Sciences*, pp. 627–631. Philadelphia, PA.

Roys, Ralph L. 1962. Stages and Periods in Archaeological Interpretation. *Southwestern Journal of Anthropology* 18(1): 40–54.

1965a. Lowland Maya Native Society after the Spanish Contact. In *Archaeology of Southern Mesoamerica, Part 2*, ed. G.R. Willey, pp. 659–678. Handbook of Middle American Indians, Vol. 3. Austin: University of Texas Press.

1965b. *Ritual of the Bacabs: A Maya Book of Incantations*. Norman: University of Oklahoma Press.

1967. *The Book of Chilam Balam of Chumayel*. Norman: University of Oklahoma Press.

1972. *The Indian Background of Colonial Yucatan*. Norman: University of Oklahoma Press.

Roys, Ralph L, ed. 1949. The Prophecies for the Maya Tuns or Years in the Books of Chilam Balam of Tizimin and Mani. In *Contributions to American Anthropology and History* 51, pp. 153–186. Carnegie Institution of Washington Publication 585. Washington, DC: Carnegie Institution.

Ruppert, Karl J. 1931. The Temple of the Wall Panels, Chichén Itzá. In *Contributions to American Archaeology* 3, pp. 117–140. Carnegie Institution of Washington Publication 403. Washington, DC: Carnegie Institution.

1935. *The Caracol at Chichén Itzá, Yucatán, Mexico*. Carnegie Institution, Publication 454. Washington, DC: Carnegie Institution.

1943. The Mercado, Chichén Itzá, Yucatán, Mexico. In *Contributions to American Archaeology* 4, pp. 223–260. Carnegie Institution of Washington Publication 546. Washington, DC: Carnegie Institution.

Sabloff, Jeremy A. 1975. *Excavations at Seibal, Department of Peten, Guatemala: The Ceramics*. Memoirs of the Peabody Museum of Archaeology and Ethnology vol. 13, no. 2. Cambridge, MA: Harvard University.

1977. Old Myths, New Myths: The Role of Sea Traders in the Development of Ancient Maya Civilization. In *The Sea in the Pre-Columbian World*, ed. E. Benson, pp. 67–97. Washington, DC: Dumbarton Oaks, Trustees for Harvard University.

1985. Ancient Maya Civilization: An Overview. In *Maya: Treasures of an Ancient Civilization*, ed. C. Gallenkamp and R.E. Johnson, pp. 34–46. New York: Harry N. Abrams.

1986. Interaction among Classic Maya Polities: A Preliminary Examination. In *Peer Polity Interaction and Socio-Political Change*, ed. C. Renfrew and J.F. Cherry, pp. 109–116. Cambridge: Cambridge University Press.

1990. *The New Archaeology and the Ancient Maya*. New York: W. H. Freeman.

Sabloff, Jeremy A., and William L. Rathje. 1975. The Rise of a Maya Merchant Class. *Scientific American* 233(4):72–82.

Sabloff, Jeremy A., and Gordon R. Willey. 1967. The Collapse of Maya Civilization in the Southern Lowlands: A Consideration of History and Process. *Southwestern Journal of Anthropology* 23: 311–326.

Sabloff, Jeremy A., and E. Wyllys Andrews V, eds. 1986. *Late Lowland Maya Civilization: Classic to Postclassic*. Albuquerque: University of New Mexico Press.

Sabloff, Jeremy A., and John S. Henderson, eds. 1993. *Lowland Maya Civilization in the Eighth Century AD*. Washington, DC: Dumbarton Oaks, Trustees for Harvard University.

Sabloff, Jeremy A., and William L. Rathje. eds. 1975. *A Study of Changing Pre-Columbian Commercial Systems: The 1972–1973 Seasons at Cozumel, Mexico*. Monographs of the Peabody Museum No. 3. Cambridge, MA: Harvard University.

Sanders, William T. 1968. Hydraulic Agriculture, Economic Symbiosis, and the Evolution of States in Central Mexico. In *Anthropological Archaeology in the Americas*, ed. B.J. Meggars, pp. 88–107. Washington, DC: Anthropological Society of Washington.

1972. Population, Agricultural History, and Societal Evolution in Mesoamerica. In *Population Growth: Anthropological Implications*, ed. B. Spooner, pp. 101–153. Cambridge, MA: Massachusetts Institute of Technology Press.

1973. The Cultural Ecology of the Lowland Maya: A Reevaluation. In *The Classic Maya Collapse*, ed. T.P. Culbert, pp. 325–365. Albuquerque: University of New Mexico Press.

1977. Environmental Heterogeneity and the Evolution of Lowland Maya Civilization. In *The Origins of Maya Civilization*, ed. R.E.W. Adams, pp. 287–297. Albuquerque: University of New Mexico Press.

Sanders, William T., and Joseph W. Michels, eds. 1969. *The Pennsylvania State University Kaminaljuyu Project-1968 Season, Part 1. The Excavations*. University Park: Pennsylvania State University Press.

1977. *Teotihuacán and Kaminaljuyú: A Study in Prehistoric Culture Contact*. University Park: Pennsylvania State University Press.

Sanders, William T., Jeffrey R. Parsons, and Robert S. Santley. 1979. *The Basin of Mexico: Ecological Processes in the Evolution of a Civilization*. New York: Academic Press.

Sanders, William T., and Barbara J. Price. 1968. *Mesoamerica: The Evolution of a Civilization*. New York: Random House.

Sanders, William T., and Robert S. Santley. 1983. A Tale of Three Cities: Energetics and Urbanization in Pre-Hispanic Central Mexico. In *Prehistoric Settlement Patterns*, eds. E.Z. Vogt, Jr. and R.M. Leventhal, pp. 243–292. Albuquerque: University of New Mexico Press.

Sanders, William T., and David L. Webster. 1988. The Mesoamerican Urban Tradition. *American Anthropologist* 80: 521–546.

Santley, Robert S. 1983. Obsidian Trade and Teotihuacan Influence in Mesoamerica. In *Highland-Lowland Interaction in Mesoamerica: Interdisciplinary Approaches*, ed. A.G. Miller, pp. 69–124. Washington, DC: Dumbarton Oaks, Trustees for Harvard University.

1984. Obsidian Exchange, Economic Stratification, and Evolution of Complex Society in the Basin of Mexico. In *Trade and Exchange in Early Mesoamerica*, ed. K.G. Hirth, pp. 43–86. Albuquerque: University of New Mexico Press.

Santley, Robert S., Thomas W. Killion, Mark T. Lycett. 1986. On the Maya Collapse. *Journal of Anthropological Research* 42: 123–159.

Scarborough, Vernon L. 1996. Reservoirs and Watersheds in the Maya Lowlands. In *The Managed Mosaic: Ancient Maya Agriculture and Resource Use*, ed. S.L. Fedick, pp. 304–314. Salt Lake City: University of Utah Press.

Scarborough, Vernon L. 1998. Ecology and Ritual: Water Management and the Maya. *Latin American Antiquity* 9: 135–159.

Schele, Linda. 1981. Sacred Site and World-View at Palenque. In *Mesoamerican Sites and World Views*, ed. E.P. Benson, pp. 87–117. Washington, DC: Dumbarton Oaks, Trustees for Harvard University.

1982. *Maya Glyphs: The Verbs*. Austin: University of Texas Press.

1984. Human Sacrifice Among the Classic Maya. In *Ritual Human Sacrifice in Mesoamerica*, ed. E.H. Boone, pp. 7–48. Washington, DC: Dumbarton Oaks, Trustees for Harvard University.

1985. The Hauberg Stela: Bloodletting and the Myths of Classic Maya Rulership. In *Fifth Palenque Round Table, 1983*, vol. 7, ed. V.M. Fields, pp. 135–151. San Francisco: The Pre-Columbian Art Research Institute.

1986. *The Tlaloc Complex in the Classic Period: War and the Interaction Between the Lowland Maya and Teotihuacan*. Fort Worth, TX: Kimbell Art Museum.

1987. Reading Mayan Images. *Americas* 39(2): 38–43.

1991. An Epigraphic History of the Western Maya Region. In *Classic Maya Political History: Hieroglyphic and Archaeological Evidence*, ed. T.P. Culbert, pp. 72–101. Cambridge: Cambridge University Press.

1992. *Notebook for the 16th Maya Hieroglyphic Workshop at Texas, March 14–15, 1992*. Austin: University of Texas.

Schele, Linda, and David A. Freidel. 1990. *A Forest of Kings*. New York: W.M. Morrow and Co.

Schele, Linda, Nikolai Grube, and Erik Boot. 1995. *Some Suggestions on the K'atun Prophecies in the Books of Chilam Balam in Light of Classic-period History*. Texas Notes on Precolumbian Art, Writing, and Culture No. 72. Austin: University of Texas Press.

Schele, Linda, and Peter Mathews. 1974. Lords of Palenque: The Glyphic Evidence. In *Primera Mesa Redonda de Palenque, part 1*, ed. V.M. Fields, pp. 63–75. Pebble Beach, CA: Robert Louis Stevenson School.

1991. Royal Visits and Other Intersite Relationships Among the Classic Maya. In *Classic Maya Political History: Hieroglyphic and Archaeological Evidence*, ed. T.P. Culbert, pp. 226–252. Cambridge: Cambridge University Press.

1998. *The Code of Kings: The Language of Seven Sacred Maya Temples and Tombs*. New York: Scribner.

Schele, Linda, and Mary Ellen Miller. 1986. *The Blood of Kings: Dynasty and Ritual in Maya Art*. New York: George Braziller.

Schele, Linda, David S. Stuart, Nikolai K. Grube, and Floyd G. Lounsbury. 1989. *A New Inscription from Temple 22a at Copan*. Copan Note 57. Copan, Honduras: Copan Mosaics Project and the Instituto Hondureño de Antropología e Historia.

Schellhas, Paul. 1904. Comparative Studies in the Field of Maya Antiquities. In *Mexican and Central American Antiquities, Calendar Systems, and History*, ed. C.P. Bowditch, pp. 591–622. Bureau of American Ethnology Bulletin 28. Washington, DC: Government Printing Office.

Schieber de Lavarreda, Christa, ed. 1998. *Taller Arqueología de la Región de la Costa Sur de Guatemala*. Guatemala: Ministerio de Cultura y Deportes.

Schiffer, Michael B. 1976. *Behavioral Archeology*. New York: Academic Press.

Schmidt, Kristen P., and E. Wyllys Andrews IV. 1936. Notes on Snakes from Yucatan. *Field Museum of Natural History Zoological Series*, vol. 20, no. 18, 167–187. Chicago: Field Museum of Natural History.

Scholes, France V., and Ralph L. Roys. 1948. *The Maya Chontal Indians of Acalan-Tixchel: A Contribution to the History and Ethnography of the Yucatan Peninsula*. Carnegie Institution of Washington Publication 560. Washington, DC: Carnegie Institution.

Schortman, Edward M., and Patricia Urban. 1991. Patterns of Late Preclassic Interaction and the Formation of Complex Society in the Southwest Maya Periphery. In *The Formation of Complex Society in Southeastern Mesoamerica*, ed. W.R. Fowler, Jr., pp. 121–142. Boca Raton, FL: CRC Press.

Service, Elman. 1975. *The Origins of the State and Civilization: The Process of Cultural Evolution*. New York: Norton.

Shafer, Harry J. 1979. A Technological Study of Two Maya Lithic Workshops at Colha, Belize. In *The Colha Project, 1979: A Collection of Interim Papers*, ed. T.R. Hester, pp. 28–78. San Antonio: Center for Archaeological Research, University of Texas.

    1982. Maya Lithic Craft Specialization in Northern Belize. In *Archeology at Colha, Belize: The 1981 Interim Report*, ed. T.R. Hester, H.J. Shafer, and J.D. Eaton, pp. 31–38. San Antonio: Center for Archaeological Research, University of Texas.

    1983. The Lithic Artifacts of the Pulltrouser Area: Settlements and Fields. In *Pulltrouser Swamp: Ancient Maya Habitat, Agriculture and Settlement in Northern Belize*, ed. B.L. Turner II and P.D. Harrison, pp. 212–245. Austin: University of Texas Press.

Shafer, Harry J., and Thomas R. Hester. 1983. Ancient Maya Chert Workshops in Northern Belize, Central America. *American Antiquity* 48: 519–543.

    1986. Maya Stone-Tool Craft Specialization and Production at Colha, Belize: Reply to Mallory. *American Antiquity* 51: 148–166.

Shanks, Michael, and Christopher Tilley. 1987. *Re-Constructing Archaeology: Theory and Practice*. Cambridge: Cambridge University Press.

    1988. *Social Theory and Archaeology*. Albuquerque: University of New Mexico Press.

Sharer, Robert J. 1974. The Prehistory of the Southeastern Maya Periphery. *Current Anthropology* 15: 165–187.

    1989. The Olmec and the Southeast Periphery of Mesoamerica. In *Regional Perspectives on the Olmec*, ed. R.J. Sharer and D.C. Grove, pp. 247–271. Cambridge: Cambridge University Press.

    1991. Diversity and Continuity in Maya Civilization: Quirigua as a Case Study. In *Classic Maya Political History: Hieroglyphic and Archaeological Evidence*, ed. T.P. Culbert, pp. 180–198. Cambridge: Cambridge University Press.

1994. *The Ancient Maya*. 5th edition. Stanford, CA: Stanford University Press.

Sharer, Robert J., ed. 1978. *The Prehistory of Chalchuapa, El Salvador*. University Museum Monograph 36. Philadelphia: University of Pennsylvania Press.

Sharer, Robert J. 2003. Founding Events and Teotihuacán Influence at Copan, Honduras. In *The Maya and Teotihuacan: Reinterpreting Early Classic Interaction*, ed. G.E. Braswell, pp. 143–166. Austin: University of Texas Press.

Sharer, Robert J., and David C. Grove, eds. 1989. *Regional Perspectives on the Olmec*. Cambridge: Cambridge University Press.

Sharer, Robert J., Loa P. Traxler, David W. Sedat, Ellen E. Bell, and Marcello A. Canuto. 1999. Early Classic Architecture beneath the Copan Acropolis. *Ancient Mesoamerica* 10: 3–23.

Sheets, Payson D. 1975. A Reassessment of the Precolumbian Obsidian Industry of El Chayal, Guatemala. *American Antiquity* 40: 98–103.

1979. Environmental and Cultural Effects of the Ilopango Eruption in Central America. In *Volcanic Activity and Human Ecology*, ed. P.D. Sheets and D.K. Grayson, pp. 525–564. New York: Academic Press.

1992. *The Ceren Site: A Prehistoric Village Buried by Volcanic Ash in Central America*. Fort Worth, TX: Harcourt Brace Jovanovich.

1994. Tropical Time Capsule: An Ancient Village Preserved In Volcanic Ash Yields Evidence of Mesoamerican Peasant Life. *Archaeology* 47: 30–33.

2000. Provisioning the Ceren Household: The Verticle Economy, Village Economy, and Household Economy in the Southeastern Maya Periphery. *Ancient Mesoamerica* 11: 217–230.

Sheets, Payson D., Harriot F. Beaubien, Marilyn P. Beaudry, Andrea Gerstle, Brian McKee, C. Dan Miller, Harmut Spetzler, and David B. Tucker. 1990. Household Archaeology at Cerén, El Salvador. *Ancient Mesoamerica* 1: 81–90.

Sheets, Payson D., and Brian R. McKee, eds. 1989. *1989 Archaeological Investigations at the Cerén Site, El Salvador: A Preliminary Report*. Boulder: Department of Anthropology, University of Colorado.

Shook, Edwin M. 1954. Three Temples and Their Associated Structures at Mayapan. In *Carnegie Institution of Washington Department of Archaeology Current Reports* vol. 1, no. 14, pp. 254–291. Washington, DC: Carnegie Institution.

Shook, Edwin M., William R. Coe, Vivian L. Broman, and Linton S. Satterthwaite, Jr. 1958. Tikal Reports. University Museum Monograph 15, vols. 1–4. Philadelphia: University Museum, University of Pennsylvania.

Sidrys, Raymond V. 1976. Classic Maya Obsidian Trade. *American Antiquity* 41: 449–464.

1979. Supply and Demand among the Classic Maya. *Current Anthropology* 20: 594–597.

Sidrys, Raymond V., and Jerome Kimberlain. 1979. Use of Maya Obsidian Sources Through Time: Trace-Element Data from El Balsamo, Guatemala. *Journal of Field Archaeology* 6: 116–122.

Siemens, Alfred H. 1978. Karst and the Pre-Hispanic Maya in the Southern Lowlands. In *Pre-Hispanic Maya Agriculture*, ed. P. Harrison and B.L. Turner II, pp. 117–144. Albuquerque: University of New Mexico Press.

Smith, A. Ledyard. 1937. Uaxactun. *Carnegie Institution of Washington Yearbook* 36: 135–137.

1982. *Excavations at Seibal, Department of Peten, Guatemala: Major Architecture and Caches.* Memoirs of the Peabody Museum of Archaeology and Ethnology vol. 13, no. 2. Cambridge, MA: Harvard University.

Smith, Robert E. 1954. Exploration on the Outskirts of Mayapan. In *Carnegie Institution of Washington Department of Archaeology Current Reports*, vol. 1, no. 18, pp. 53–69.

Smith, Robert E., and James C. Gifford. 1965. Pottery of the Maya Lowlands. In *Archaeology of Southern Mesoamerica, Part 1*, ed. G.R. Willey, pp. 498–534. *Handbook of Middle American Indians*, vol. 2. Austin: University of Texas Press.

Spinden, Herbert J. 1913. *A Study of Maya Art: Its Subject Matter and Historical Development.* Peabody Museum of Archaeology and Ethnology Memoir 6. Cambridge, MA: Harvard University.

1924. *The Reduction of Mayan Dates.* Papers of the Peabody Museum of American Archaeology and Ethnology, 6(4). Cambridge, MA: Harvard University.

Spooner, Brian, ed. 1972. *Population Growth: Anthropological Implications.* Cambridge, MA: Massachusetts Institute of Technology.

Stark, Barbara L. 1981. The Rise of Sedentary Life. In *Handbook of Middle American Indians, Supplement I: Archaeology*, ed. V.R. Bricker and J.A. Sabloff, pp. 345–372. Austin: University of Texas Press.

Stark, Barbara L., and Barbara L. Voorhies, eds. 1978. *Prehistoric Coastal Adaptations: The Economy and Ecology of Maritime Middle America.* New York: Academic Press.

Steele, D.G., Jack D. Eaton, and A. J. Taylor. 1980. The Skulls from Operation 2011 at Colha: A Preliminary Examination. In *The Colha Project, Second Season 1980 Interim Report*, ed. T.R. Hester, J.D. Eaton, and H.J. Shafer, pp. 163–172. San Antonio: Center for Archaeological Research, University of Texas.

Stephens, John Lloyd. 1841. *Incidents of Travel in Central America, Chiapas, and Yucatan.* New York: Harper and Brothers.

1843. *Incidents of Travel in Yucatan.* New York: Dover Publications.

Steward, Julian. 1955. *Theory of Culture Change: The Methodology of Multilinear Evolution.* Urbana: University of Illinois Press.

Stromsvik, Gustav. 1942. Archaeology: Honduras. In *Carnegie Institution of Washington Yearbook* 41, pp. 249–250. Washington, DC: Carnegie Institution.

1952. The Ball Courts at Copan. In *Contributions to American Anthropology and History* 11, pp. 187–214. Washington, DC: Carnegie Institution.

Stuart, David S. 1984. Royal Auto-Sacrifice Among the Maya: A Study of Image and Meaning. *Res* 7/8: 6–20.

1987. Ten Phonetic Syllables. Research Reports on Ancient Maya Writing 14. Washington, DC: Center for Maya Research.

1988. Blood Symbolism in Maya Iconography. In *Maya Iconography*, ed. E.P. Benson and G.G. Griffin, pp. 175–221. Princeton, NJ: Princeton University Press.

1989. *The Maya Artist: An Epigraphic and Iconographic Study*. Unpublished B.A. thesis, Department of Art and Archaeology, Princeton University.

1993. Historical Inscriptions and the Maya Collapse. In *Lowland Maya Civilization in the Eighth Century A.D.*, eds. J.A. Sabloff and J.S. Henderson, pp. 321–354. Washington, DC: Dumbarton Oaks, Trustees for Harvard University.

1995. A Study of Maya Inscriptions. Ph.D. dissertation, Department of Anthropology, Vanderbilt University, Nashville.

2000. The Arrival of Strangers: Teotihuacan and Tollan in Classic Maya History. In *Meosamerica's Classic Heritage: From Teotihuacan to the Aztecs*, ed. D. Carrasco, L. Jones, and S. Sessions, pp. 465–513. Boulder: University Press of Colorado.

Stuart, David S., and Stephen D. Houston. 1994. *Classic Maya Place Names*. Studies in Pre-Columbian Art and Archaeology 33. Washington, DC: Dumbarton Oaks, Trustees for Harvard University.

Stuart, L.C. 1964. Fauna of Middle America. In *Natural Environment and Early Cultures*, ed. R.C. West, pp. 316–362. Handbook of Middle American Indians, Austin: University of Texas Press.

Sugiyama, Saburo. 1992. Rulership, Warfare, Human Sacrifice at the Ciudadela, Teotihuacan: An Iconographic Study of the Feathered Serpent Representations. In *Art, Ideology, and the City of Teotihuacan*, ed. J.C. Berlo, pp. 205–230. Washington, DC: Dumbarton Oaks, Trustees for Harvard University.

Sugiyama, Saburo, and Ruben Cabrera, eds. 2003. *Informe del Proyecto de Investigación en la Pirámide de la Luna, Teotihuacan*. Mexico, D.F.: Instituto Nacional de Antropología e Historia.

Suhler, Charles, and David Friedel. 1998. Life and Death in a Maya War Zone. *Archaeology* 51(3): 28–34.

Suhler, Charles, Traci Ardren, David Friedel, and Dave Johnstone. 2004. The Rise and Fall of Terminal Classic Yaxuna, Yucatan, Mexico. In *The Terminal Classic in the Maya Lowlands: Collapse, Transition, and Transformation*, ed. A.A. Demarest, P.M. Rice, and D.S. Rice. Boulder: University Press of Colorado.

Sullivan, Lauren. A. 2002. Dynamics of Regional Integration in Northwestern Belize. In *Ancient Maya Political Economies*, ed. M.A. Masson and D.A. Freidel, pp. 197–222. Walnut Creek, CA: AltaMira Press.

Symonds, Stacey, Bárbara Arroyo, and Stephen D. Houston. 1990. Operación DP11: Investigaciones en el Palacio de Dos Pilas. In *Proyecto Arqueológico Regional Petexbatún, Informe Preliminar No. 2: Segunda Temporada, 1990*, ed. A.A. Demarest and S.D. Houston, pp. 235–276. Guatemala and Nashville: Instituto de Antropología e Historia and Department of Anthropology, Vanderbilt University.

Tainter, Joseph A. 1988. *The Collapse of Complex Societies*. Cambridge: Cambridge University Press.

Tambiah, Stanley J. 1976. *World Conqueror and World Renouncer*. Cambridge: Cambridge University Press.

1977. The Galactic Polity: The Structure of Traditional Kingdoms in Southeast Asia. *Annals of the New York Academy of Sciences* 293: 69–97.

1982. Famous Buddha Images and the Legitimation of Kings. *Res: Anthropology and Aesthetics* 4: 5–20.

1984. *The Buddhist Saints of the Forest and the Cult of Amulets: A Study in Charisma, Hagiography, Sectarianism and Millennial Buddhism*. Cambridge: Cambridge University Press.

Tankersley, Kenneth B. 1998. Variation in the Early Paleoindian Economies of Late Pleistocene Eastern North America. *American Antiquity* 63: 7–20.

Tate, Carolyn E. 1992. *Yaxchilan: The Design of a Maya Ceremonial City*. Austin: University of Texas Press.

Taube, Karl A. 1992. *The Major Gods of Ancient Yucatan*. Studies in Pre-Columbian Art and Archaeology 32. Washington, DC: Dumbarton Oaks, Trustees for Harvard University.

2003. Tetitla and the Maya Presence at Teotihuacan. In *The Maya and Teotihuacan: Reinterpreting Early Classic Interaction*, ed. G.E. Braswell, pp. 273–314. Austin: University of Texas Press.

Taylor, R.E., and Clement W. Meighan, eds. 1978. *Chronologies in New World Archaeology*. New York: Academic Press.

Tedlock, Barbara. 1992. *Time and the Highland Maya*. 2nd ed. Albuquerque: University of New Mexico Press.

1993. Mayans and Mayan Studies from 2000 BC to A.D. 1992. *Latin American Research Review* 28: 153–173.

Tedlock, Dennis. 1985. *The Popol Vuh: The Mayan Book of Myth and History*. New York: Simon and Schuster.

Thompson, Edward H. 1932. *The People of the Serpent*. New York: Literary Classics.

Thompson, J. Eric S. 1950. *Maya Hieroglyphic Writing: Introduction*. Carnegie Institution of Washington Publication 589. Washington, DC: Carnegie Institution.

1954. A Presumed Residence of the Nobility at Mayapan. In *Carnegie Institution of Washington Department of Archaeology Current Reports*, vol. 2, no. 19, pp. 71–87. Washington, DC: Carnegie Institution.

1966. *The Rise and Fall of Maya Civilization*. 2nd ed. Norman: University of Oklahoma Press.

1970. *Maya History and Religion*. Norman: University of Oklahoma Press.

1971. Estimates of Maya Populations: Deranging Factors. *American Antiquity* 36: 214–216.

1974. "Canals" of the Rio Candelaria Basin, Campeche, Mexico. In *Mesoamerican Archaeology: New Approaches*, ed. N.D.C. Hammond. Austin: University of Texas Press.

Tilley, Christopher. ed. 1990. *Reading Material Culture: Structuralism, Hermeneutics, and Post-Structuralism*. Oxford: B. Blackwell.

Tolstoy, Paul. 1989. Western Mesoamerica and the Olmec. In *Regional Perspectives on the Olmec*, ed. R.J. Sharer and D.C. Grove, pp. 275–302. Cambridge: Cambridge University Press.

Tourtellot, Gair. 1988. *Excavations at Seibal, Department of Petén, Guatemala: Peripheral Survey and Excavations, Settlement and Community Patterns.* Memoirs of the Peabody Museum of Archaeology and Ethnology 16. Cambridge, MA: Harvard University.

Tourtellot, Gair, and Jason Gonzales. 2004. The Last Hurrah: Continuity and Transformation at Seibal. In *The Terminal Classic in the Maya Lowlands: Collapse, Transition, and Transformation,* ed. A.A. Demarest, P.M. Rice, and D.S. Rice. Boulder: University Press of Colorado.

Tourtellot, Gair, and Jeremy Sabloff. 1994. Community Structure at Sayil: A Case Study of Puuc Settlement. In *Hidden Among the Hills: Maya Archaeology of the Northwest Yucatan Peninsula,* ed. H. Prem, pp. 71–92. Möckmühl, Germany: Verlag von Flemming.

Tourtellot, Gair, Jeremy A. Sabloff, and Michael P. Smyth. 1990. Room Counts and Population Estimation for Terminal Classic Sayil in the Puuc Region, Yucatán, Mexico. In *Precolumbian Population History in the Maya Lowlands,* ed. T.P. Culbert and D.S. Rice, pp. 245–261. Albuquerque: University of New Mexico Press.

Tozzer, Alfred M. 1941. *Landa's Relacion de las Cosas de Yucatan: A Translation.* Peabody Museum of Archaeology and Ethnology Papers 28. Cambridge, MA: Harvard University Press.

Turner II, B.L. 1978. Ancient Agricultural Land Use in the Central Maya Lowlands. In *Prehispanic Maya Agriculture,* ed. P.D. Harrison and B.L. Turner II, pp. 163–183. Albuquerque: University of New Mexico Press.

1983. The Excavation of Raised and Channelized Fields at Pulltrouser Swamp. In *Pulltrouser Swamp: Ancient Maya Habitat, Agriculture, and Settlement in Northern Belize,* ed. B.L. Turner II and P.D. Harrison, pp. 30–51. Austin: University of Texas Press.

1985. Issues Related to Subsistence and Environment among the Ancient Maya. In *Prehistoric Lowland Maya Environment and Subsistence Economy,* ed. Mary D. Pohl, pp. 195–209. Papers of the Peabody Museum of Archaeology and Ethnology 77. Cambridge, MA: Harvard University Press.

1990. Population Reconstruction for the Central Maya Lowlands: 1000 BC to AD 1500. In *Precolumbian Population History in the Maya Lowlands,* ed. T.P. Culbert and D.S. Rice, pp. 301–324. Albuquerque: University of New Mexico Press.

Turner II, B.L., and Peter D. Harrison. 1978. Implications from Agriculture for Maya Prehistory. In *Prehispanic Maya Agriculture,* ed. P.D. Harrison and B.L. Turner II, pp. 337–373. Albuquerque: University of New Mexico Press.

Turner II, B.L., and Peter D. Harrison. eds. 1983. *Pulltrouser Swamp: Ancient Maya Habitat, Agriculture, and Settlement in Northern Belize.* Austin: University of Texas Press.

United Nations Department of Humanitarian Affairs. 1994. *Information Report, No. 14, 1994.* Geneva: United Nations Division for Humanitarian Relief and Rehabilitation.

Valdés, Juan Antonio. 1997a. El Proyecto Miraflores II Dentro del Marco Preclásico de Kaminaljuyú. In *X Simposio de Investigaciones Arqueológicas en Guatemala,* ed. J.P. Laporte and H.L. Escobedo, pp. 81–92. Guatemala:

Ministerio de Cultura y Deportes, Instituto de Antropología e Historia, Asociación Tikal.

1997b. Tamarindito: Archaeology and Regional Politics in the Petexbatun Region. *Ancient Mesoamerica* 8: 321–335.

Valdés, Juan Antonio, and Federico Fahsen. 2004. Disaster in Sight: The Terminal Classic at Tikal and Uaxactun. In *The Terminal Classic in the Maya Lowlands: Collapse, Transition, and Transformation*, ed. A.A. Demarest, P.M. Rice, and D.S. Rice. Boulder: University Press of Colorado.

Valdés, Juan Antonio, and Marion Popenoe de Hatch. 1996. Evidencias de Poder y Control Social en Kaminaljuyu. In *IX Simposio de Investigaciones Arqueológicas en Guatemala*, ed. J.P. Laporte and H.L. Escobedo, pp. 377–396. Guatemala: Ministerio de Cultura y Deportes, Instituto de Antropología e Historia, Asociación Tikal.

Varela Torrecilla, Carmen. 1998. *El Clásico Medio en el Noroccidente de Yucatan*. British Archaeological Reports 739. Oxford: BAR International Series.

Vogt, Jr., Evon Z. 1969. *Zinacantan: A Maya Community in the Highlands of Chiapas*. Cambridge, MA: Harvard University Press.

1976. *Tortillas for the Gods: A Symbolic Analysis of Zinacanteco Rituals*. Cambridge, MA: Harvard University Press.

1981. Some Aspects of the Sacred Geography of Highland Chiapas. In *Mesoamerican Sites and World Views*, ed. E.P. Benson, pp. 119–142. Washington, DC: Dumbarton Oaks, Trustees for Harvard University.

1983. Ancient and Contemporary Maya Settlement Patterns: A New Look From the Chiapas Highlands. In *Prehistoric Settlement Patterns: Essays in Honor of Gordon R. Willey*, eds. E.Z. Vogt, Jr., and R.M. Leventhal, pp. 89–114. Albuquerque: University of New Mexico Press.

Voorhies, Barbara L. 1976. *The Chantuto People: An Archaic Period Society of the Chiapas Littoral, Mexico*. Papers of the New World Archaeological Foundation 41. Provo, UT: New World Archaeological Foundation.

Voorhies, Barbara L. ed. 1989. *Ancient Trade and Tribute: Economies of the Soconusco Region of Mesoamerica*. Salt Lake City: University of Utah Press.

Waldeck, Frederick M. de. 1838. *Voyage Pittoresque et Archeologique Dans la Province d'Yucatan Pendant les Annees 1834 et 1836*. Paris.

Wallace, Dwight T. 1977. Ethnohistory of the Central Quiché. In *The Community of Utatlan: Archaeology and Ethnohistory of the Central Quiché*, ed. D.T. Wallace and R.M. Carmack, pp. 20–54. Institute for Mesoamerican Studies Publication 1. Albany: State University of New York.

Wallace, Dwight T., and Robert M. Carmack, eds. 1977. *The Community of Utatlan. Archaeology and Ethnohistory of the Central Quiché*. Institute for Mesoamerican Studies Publication 1. Albany: State University of New York.

Watson, Patty Jo, Steven A. LeBlanc, and Charles L. Redman. 1971. *Explanation in Archeology: An Explicitly Scientific Approach*. New York: Columbia University Press.

Wauchope, Robert. 1934. *House Mounds of Uaxactun, Guatemala*. Contributions to American Archaeology Publication 436. Washington, DC: Carnegie Institution.

1938. *Modern Maya Houses: A Study of Their Archaeological Significance.* Contributions to American Archaeology Publication 502. Washington, DC: Carnegie Institution.

1962. *Lost Tribes and Sunken Continents.* Chicago: University of Chicago Press.

1965. *They Found the Buried Cities: Exploration and Excavation in the American Tropics.* Chicago: University of Chicago Press.

Webb, Malcolm C. 1973. The Peten Maya Decline Viewed in the Perspective of State Formation. In *The Classic Maya Collapse,* ed. T.P. Culbert, pp. 367–404. Albuquerque: University of New Mexico Press.

1975. The Flag Follows Trade: An Essay on the Necessary Interaction of Military and Commercial Factors in State Formation. In *Ancient Civilization and Trade,* ed. J.A. Sabloff and C.C. Lamberg-Karlovsky, pp. 367–404. Albuquerque: University of New Mexico Press.

Webster, David L. 1976. *Defensive Earthworks at Becan, Campeche, Mexico.* Middle American Research Institute Publication 41. New Orleans: Tulane University.

1977. Warfare and the Evolution of Maya Civilization. In *The Origins of Maya Civilization,* ed. R.E.W. Adams, pp. 335–372. Albuquerque: University of New Mexico Press.

1979. *Cuca, Chacchob, Dzonot Ake: Three Walled Northern Maya Centers.* Occasional Papers in Anthropology. University Park: Department of Anthropology, Pennsylvania State University.

1978. Three Walled Sites of the Northern Maya Lowlands. *Journal of Field Archaeology* 5: 375–390.

1993. The Study of Maya Warfare: What It Tells Us about the Maya and What It Tells Us about Maya Archaeology. In *Lowland Maya Civilization in the Eighth Century A.D.,* eds. J.A. Sabloff and J.S. Henderson, pp. 415–444. Washington, DC: Dumbarton Oaks, Trustees for Harvard University.

1999. Warfare and Status Rivalry: Lowland Maya and Polynesian Comparisons. In *Archaic States,* ed. G. Feinman and J. Marcus, pp. 311–351. Santa Fe, NM: School of American Research.

Webster, David L., ed. 1989. *The House of the Bacabs, Copán, Honduras.* Studies in Pre-Columbian Art and Archaeology 29. Washington, DC: Dumbarton Oaks, Trustees for Harvard University.

Webster, David L., and Anncorrine Freter. 1990. The Demography of Late Classic Copan. In *Precolumbian Population History in the Maya Lowlands,* ed. T.P. Culbert and D.S. Rice, pp. 37–61. Albuquerque: University of New Mexico Press.

Webster, David L., Anncorrine Freter, and Rebecca Storey. 2004. Dating Copan Culture History: Implications for the Terminal Classic and the Collapse. In *The Terminal Classic in the Maya Lowlands: Collapse, Transition, and Transformation,* ed. A.A. Demarest, P.M. Rice, and D.S. Rice. Boulder: University Press of Colorado.

Webster, David L., Jennifer Kirker, Amy Kovak, and Timothy Murta. 1999. Investigaciones de Población y Ecología en Piedras Negras, Guatemala. In *XII Simposio de Investigaciónes Arqueológicas en Guatemala.* ed. J.P. Laporte, H.L. Escobedo, A.C. Monzón de Suasnávar, pp. 419–434. Guatemala:

Ministerio de Cultura y Deportes, Instituto de Antropología e Historia, Asociación Tikal.

West, Robert C. 1964. Surface Configuration and Associated Geology of Middle America. In *Natural Environment and Early Cultures*, ed. R.C. West, pp. 33–83. Handbook of Middle American Indians, vol. 1. Austin: University of Texas Press.

White, Christine D., and Henry P. Schwartz. 1989. Ancient Maya Diet: As Inferred from Isotopic and Chemical Analysis of Human Bone. *Journal of Archaeological Science* 16: 451–474.

White, Leslie A. 1959. *The Evolution of Culture: The Development of Civilization to the Fall of Rome*. New York: McGraw-Hill.

Whitley, David S., and Marilyn P. Beaudry, eds. 1989. *Investigaciones Arqueológicas en la Costa Sur de Guatemala*. Los Angeles: Institute of Archaeology, University of California.

Wilk, Richard R. 1985. The Ancient Maya and the Political Present. *Journal of Anthropological Research* 41: 307–326.

Willey, Gordon R. 1953. *Prehistoric Settlement Patterns in the Virú Valley, Perú*. Bureau of American Ethnology 155. Washington, DC: Smithsonian Institution Press.

1971. Commentary On "The Emergence of Civilization in the Maya Lowlands." In *Observations on the Emergence of Civilization in Mesoamerica*, ed. R.F. Heizer and J.A. Graham, pp. 97–111. Berkeley: University of California Press.

1973. *The Altar de Sacrificios Excavations: General Summary and Conclusions*. Peabody Museum of Archaeology and Ethnology Papers 64(3). Cambridge, MA: Harvard University.

1974. The Classic Maya Hiatus: A Rehearsal for the Collapse? In *Mesoamerican Archaeology: New Approaches*, ed. N.D.C. Hammond, pp. 417–430. London: Duckworth.

1976. Mesoamerican Civilization and the Idea of Transcendence. *Antiquity* 50: 205–215.

1977. The Rise of Maya Civilization: A Summary View. In *The Origins of Maya Civilization*, ed. R.E.W. Adams, pp. 383–423. Albuquerque: University of New Mexico Press.

1978. *Excavations at Seibal, Department of Peten, Guatemala: Artifacts*. Memoirs of the Peabody Museum of Archaeology and Ethnology 14(1–3). Cambridge, MA: Harvard University.

1981. Recent Researches and Perspectives in Mesoamerican Archaeology: An Introductory Commentary. In *Supplement to the Handbook of Middle American Indians, vol. 1: Archaeology*, ed. J.A. Sabloff, pp. 3–27. Austin: University of Texas Press.

1982. Maya Archaeology. *Science* 215: 260–267.

1987. Changing Conceptions of Lowland Maya Culture History. In *Essays in Maya Archaeology*, ed. G.R. Willey, pp. 189–207. Albuquerque: University of New Mexico Press.

Willey, Gordon R., ed. 1975. *Excavations at Seibal, Department of Peten, Guatemala*. Peabody Museum of Archaeology and Ethnology Memoirs, vol. 13, nos 1–2. Cambridge, MA: Harvard University.

Willey, Gordon R., and William R. Bullard, Jr. 1965. Prehistoric Settlement Patterns in the Maya Lowlands. In *Archaeology of Southern Mesoamerica, Part 1*, ed. G.R. Willey, pp. 360–377. Handbook of Middle American Indians, vol. 2: Austin. University of Texas Press.

Willey, Gordon R., William R. Bullard, Jr., John B. Glass, and James C. Gifford. 1965. *Prehistoric Maya Settlements in the Belize Valley*. Peabody Museum of Archaeology and Ethnology Papers 54. Cambridge, MA: Harvard University.

Willey, Gordon R., T. Patrick Culbert, and Richard E.W. Adams. 1967. Maya Lowland Ceramics: A Report from the 1965 Guatemala City Conference. *American Antiquity* 32: 289–315.

Willey, Gordon R., Richard M. Leventhal, Arthur A. Demarest, and William Fash. 1994. *The Ceramics and Artifacts from Excavations in the Copan Residential Zone*. Papers of the Peabody Museum of Archaeology and Ethnology 80. Cambridge, MA: Harvard University.

Willey, Gordon R., and Philip Phillips. 1958. *Method and Theory in American Archaeology*. Chicago: University of Chicago Press.

Willey, Gordon R., and Jeremy A. Sabloff. 1974. *A History of American Archaeology*. San Francisco: Freeman.

Williams, A.R. 2002. A New Chapter in Maya History: All Out War, Shifting Alliances, Bloody Sacrifices. *National Geographic* 202(4): 16–18.

Wittfogel, Karl A. 1957. *Oriental Despotism: A Comparative Study of Total Power*. New Haven: Yale University Press.

Wolf, Eric R., ed. 1976. *The Valley of Mexico: Studies in Pre-Hispanic Ecology and Society*. Albuquerque: University of New Mexico Press.

Wolley, Claudia. 1993. El Sistema Defensivo de Punta de Chimino, Petén. Licenciatura thesis, Universidad de San Carlos de Guatemala, Guatemala.

Wolley, Claudia, and Lori Wright. 1990. Punta de Chimino: Sondeos en el Sistema Defensivo. In *Proyecto Arqueológico Regional Petexbatún, Informe Preliminar No. 2: Segunda Temporada*, ed. A.A. Demarest and S. Houston, pp. 423–437. Guatemala and Nashville, TN: Instituto de Antropología e Historia and Department of Anthropology, Vanderbilt University.

1991. Sondeos en Punta de Chimino: Un Centro Fortificado del Clásico Tardio y Terminal. In *Proyecto Arqueológico Regional Petexbatún, Informe Preliminar No. 3: Tercera Temporada*, ed. A.A. Demarest, T. Inomata, H.L. Escobedo, and J.W. Palka, pp. 558–587. Guatemala and Nashville, TN: Instituto de Antropología e Historia and Department of Anthropology, Vanderbilt University.

Woodfill, Brent, Nicholas Miller, Margaret Tarpley, and Amalia Kenward. 2003. Investigaciones Subterráneo y de Superficie en Chisec, Alta Verapaz, y La Caoba, Sayaxche, Petén. In *Proyecto Arqueológico Cancuen, Informe Temporada 2002*, ed. A.A. Demarest and T. Barrientos, pp. 369–410. Guatemala and Nashville, TN: Instituto de Antropología e Historia and Department of Anthropology, Vanderbilt University.

Woodfill, Brent, Matt O'Mansky, and Jon Spenard. 2002. Asentamiento y sitios en la region de Cancuen. In *XV Simposio de Arqueologicas en Guatemala*, ed. J.P. Laporte, H.L. Escobedo, and B. Arroyo, pp. 909–922. Guatemala: Museo de Antropología y Etnología de Guatemala.

Woods, James, and Gene Titmus. 1996. Stone on Stone: Perspectives on Maya Civilization from Lithic Studies. In *Eighth Palenque Round Table, 1993*, ed. M. Marci and J. McHargue, pp. 479–489. San Francisco: Pre-Columbian Art Research Institute.

Wright, Henry T., and Gregory A. Johnson. 1975. Population Exchange and Early State Formation in Southwestern Iran. *American Anthropologist* 77: 267–289.

Wright, Lori E. 1994. The Sacrifice of the Earth: Diet, Health and Inequality in the Pasion Maya Lowlands. Ph.D. dissertation, University of Chicago.

Wright, Lori E. 1997. Biological Perspectives on the Collapse of the Pasión Maya. *Ancient Mesoamerica* 8: 267–273.

   In press. *Nutrition, Diet, and Health at the Time of the Maya Collapse: Osteological Evidence from the Petexbatun.* Monographs of the Vanderbilt Institute of Mesoamerican Archaeology. Nashville, TN: Vanderbilt University Press.

Wright, Lori, and Christine White. 1996. Human Biology in the Classic Maya Collapse: Evidence from Paleopathology and Paleodiet. In *Journal of World Prehistory* 10: 147–198.

Wrigley, Edward A. 1969. *Population and History.* New York: McGraw-Hill.

Yoffee, Norman, and George L. Cowgill, eds. 1988. *The Collapse of Ancient States and Civilizations.* Tucson: University of Arizona Press.

# Index